* FALL OF THE PEACOCK THRONE

THE STORY OF IRAN

William H. Forbis

McGraw-Hill Book Company

New York   St. Louis   San Fráncisco   Bogotá   Guatemala
Hamburg   Lisbon   Madrid   Mexico   Montreal   Panama   Paris
San Juan   São Paulo   Tokyo   Toronto

Reprinted by arrangement with Harper & Row, Publishers, Inc.

First McGraw-Hill Paperback edition, 1981

1234567890   FGFG   87654321

Designed by Sidney Feinberg

Maps by Bernhard W. Wagner

Library of Congress Cataloging in Publication Data

Forbis, William H
  Fall of the Peacock Throne.

  Bibliography: p.
  Includes index.
  1. Iran.   I. Title.
DS254.5.F6 1981   955   80-28092
  ISBN 0-07-021486-7 (pbk.)

Contents

Introduction *v*

PART ONE
A PERSIAN STORY

1. His Destined Hour 3
2. Cyrus, Darius, and Glory 10
3. "Defeat Makes Us Invincible" 26
4. The Pahlavi Dynasty 41
5. First Persian Singular 63

PART TWO
THE IRANIANS

6. "Drown Him, Even If I Drown Too" 87
7. The Veiled Society 117
8. The Case of the Hidden Imam 139
9. The Iranian Way of Life 165
10. The Great (Illiterate) Civilization 181
11. On Literature, Lutes, and the Chin of a Kitten 199

PART THREE
PETROLEUM POWER

12. King Oil 219
13. Industrialization—So Far 232

CONTENTS

14. Farming the Desert 251
15. Fire the Gun, But Not Loudly 268
16. The Iranian Revolution 283

Acknowledgments 291
Bibliography 293
Afterword 297
Index 301

MAPS   *Iran* viii
        Teheran 107

Introduction

Think, in this batter'd Caravanserai
Whose portals are alternate Night and Day,
  How Sultan after Sultan with his Pomp
Abode his destined Hour, and went his way.
         —*The Rubaiyat of Omar Khayyam*

Gone his way is Mohammed Reza Pahlavi, 446th and last of the Iranian shahs. Gone with him is the Pahlavi dynasty, founded fifty-six years ago by his father, the last of an uncountable number of dynasties. Gone with the dynasty is a monarchy which was at its demise the world's oldest, stretching back for twenty-five centuries. With this momentous event, Iran is cast into chaos—chaos that potentially contains the seeds of economic depression in the West from loss of Middle Eastern oil, and, worse yet, the seeds of war, should the disintegration of Iran or its strife with its neighbors lead the Soviet Union to make a grab for Iran's oil and its warm-water ports.

For fifteen years, Iran has throbbed and churned with transformation, with changes coming so fast that, as one observer in Teheran remarked to me, "only an impressionist can get them down." Decreed by a strong-willed Shah and fueled by billions of oil dollars, the changes wrenched society back and forth between the seductive goal of wealthy, materialistic modernization and the equally powerful impulse to preserve the sweet Persian traditions of mysticism, poetry, and devotion to a pure and moralistic Islam. Potent forces lashed the Iranians. Universities sprang up in large numbers, and the students—many of them children of illiterate farmers and city workers—learned to demand more change even as they suffered alienation from their families and the past. Industrialization worked its wry wonders, providing such combination boons and afflictions as mass car ownership, petrochemicals, and universal television. Villagers crowded into the cities, and mechanized agribusiness greened former deserts. Feudalism melted away in only fifteen years. The ancient and classical city of Isfahan became a center for the Iranian military-industrial complex, reflecting the fastest arms buildup in the world.

All these developments, capped by a revolution as authentic as the American, French, or (to cite a recent example) Cuban revolutions, were stunning and important events on the world stage. Iran has become a country crucial to everyone. It is the purpose of this book to get behind the headlines and explore more profoundly the country and its people.

FALL OF THE PEACOCK THRONE

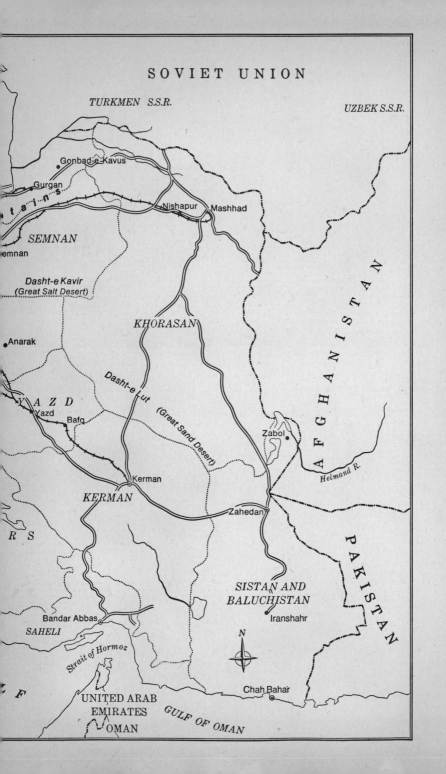

PART ONE

A PERSIAN STORY

1

His Destined Hour

❧

A few sheets of paper, covered with the squiggles of Persian script—this was what touched off the avalanche that, growing monthly, carried the Shah of Iran in one year from seemingly invincible absolute monarch to dethroned exile. The writer of the article was one Parviz Nik-Khah, a strange man who had once tried to assassinate Shah Mohammad Reza Pahlavi and had later become a loyal henchman to the king. Toward the end of 1977, the paper passed under the thoughtful eyes of the minister of court, Amir Abbas Hoveyda. He no doubt reflected on the consequences were the paper to be published. Certainly publication could bring trouble to Hoveyda's rival, Jamshid Amuzegar, the prime minister. Hoveyda sent the article to Dariush Homayun, head of the sinister Ministry of Information, which had power to compel newspapers to print whatever the ministry sent them. Once a foe of the Shah, Homayun had joined the ranks of the many bright people whom the Shah co-opted by the offer of high office. He passed the article to *Etelaat* *(Information)*, one of Teheran's two major dailies.

Published by *Etelaat* on January 7, 1978, the article was an attack on a man named Ruhollah Khomeini, the Shah's most dangerous political opponent. Khomeini is an *ayatollah,* the highest rank of the *mullahs*, the priest of the Shiite Moslem faith, which prevails in Iran. The article charged that fifteen years before Khomeini had incited deadly riots against reforms imposed by the Shah, notably land reform and votes for women, both anathema to Islam. The article added that Khomeini had done so at the behest of a strange combination of Communists and landlords. For other reasons, the Shah later deported Khomeini, and at the time the article was published, Khomeini was living in the holy city of Najef in Iraq, a vibrant and respected martyr to the Shah's persecution.

When copies of *Etelaat* reached Qom, Khomeini's former home and the theological center of Iran, five thousand devout Moslems gathered in a large mosque to protest the article. Emerging, the crowd ran into a hail of pistol and submachine-gun fire from policemen, which killed scores. Afterward, police prevented people from donating blood to the wounded, and more died in hospitals. Qom's Ayatollah Sayed Ghassem Shariatmadari called the shooting "un-Islamic and inhumane" and predicted that "Almighty God will in time punish those responsible."

In Islam, the fortieth day after a death is set aside for mourning. Mourning for the dead in Qom brought riots and new killings, and mourning for the latest victims forty days later brought another explosion, this time in Tabriz. Mobs stormed banks, stores, government offices, and movie houses that remained open in defiance of the clergy's call for a strike to commemorate the victims at Qom. The provincial government sent tanks into the streets, and killed about a hundred demonstrators. The Shah, for the first time sensing a need to make a concession, purged the governor general of the province and other officials blamed for ordering troops to fire at the mob. But forty days later, riots burst out again in fifty-five towns and cities, leading to another bloody explosion forty days after that.

The Shah, who had begun the year boasting, "Nobody can overthrow me; I have the support of 700,000 troops, all the workers, and most of the people," grew depressed and ineffective. In August came the insane and horrifying burning of the Rex Cinema in Abadan. Showing that night was *Reindeer,* an Iranian-made movie generally judged to be hostile to the regime because it told the story of a poor peasant struggling against corrupt officials. The fire killed almost the entire audience, for a total of 337 dead. They died because the theater's doors were locked and because firemen bungled efforts to quench the blaze. The government tried to blame anti-Shah Moslem zealots, on grounds that such fanatics had earlier burned empty movie theaters that violated Islamic precepts by showing pornographic films. But millions of Iranians, convinced that the doors had been locked by government troops, concluded that the burning of the theater was a provocation concocted by some mad general, an Iranian version of the Reichstag fire in Berlin.

The Shah tried further concessions, freeing newspapers and television for the first time in twenty-five years to print and show what they pleased. The press responded by publishing chilling accounts of the torture that SAVAK, the secret police, had inflicted on hundreds of oppositionists over many years. The Shah thereupon fired his longtime friend and confidant, the murderous General Nematollah Nassiri, head of SAVAK.

If it had been Hoveyda's intention to bring down Amuzegar, he succeeded. Not long after the Abadan fire, the prime minister quit. The Shah brought in Jafar Sharif-Emami, a veteran politician with some renown for his devotion to Islam. Sharif-Emami closed gambling casinos, nightclubs, and movie houses showing Western films. He consulted with Qom's Ayatollah Shariatmadari. He indicted Nassiri for torture and illegal imprisonment. For his part, the Shah passed out to his numerous corrupt brothers and sisters and nephews and nieces an extraordinary "code of conduct" aimed at preventing them from taking bribes to act as go-betweens in government contracts and from cutting themselves in on profitable businesses. He ditched Hoveyda and set his new court minister to enforcing the code. All of his relatives except his mother, wife, children, and his brother Hamid thereupon fled from Iran.

The concessions did not work. In early September new bloody riots exploded in Teheran and eleven other cities, and the Shah put Iran under martial law. Ayatollah Khomeini, whom Iraq had deported as an accommodation to the Shah, settled near Paris and by direct-dial telephone to other mullahs in Iran monotonously preached his message: "The Pahlavi dynasty must go. No compromise is possible." Tape-recorded and passed from mosque to mosque, his words spread through Iran almost as fast as though they had been televised. The Shah granted Khomeini amnesty; he refused it. On his fifty-ninth birthday, October 26, the Shah freed 1,126 political prisoners; crowds shouted, "Death to the Shah!"

A few days later, on Khomeini's call, a general strike began, a strike that with varying effectiveness would not end until after the Shah fell. Oil exports plummeted as production dropped to a fifth of the normal six million barrels a day, costing Iran $60 million daily in lost sales. On November 5, the biggest mobs yet rioted in Teheran, burning movie houses, airline offices, and the commercial building of the British Embassy. Troops fired; students fell dead. As smoke filled the sky, General Gholam Reza Azhari, the Shah's chief of staff, drove to the palace and demanded a military government. The next day Azhari went to work as prime minister and the Shah appeared on television to make an astoundingly contrite speech. "I renew my oath to be protector of the constitution and undertake that past mistakes shall not be repeated," the Shah said. "I hereby give assurance that government will do away with repression and corruption and that social justice will be restored."

Gradually, throughout the fall, the attention of Iran and the world had been drawn to a man named Karim Sanjabi, heir to the remnants of a political coalition called the National Front, which nearly deposed the Shah in 1953. He seemed a likely candidate for prime minister, to bring the opposition into the government and soothe the protest. Refusing the Shah's approaches, made through intermediaries, he went to France and sought Khomeini's backing. Khomeini, cool, merely said, "May God be with you." That was enough, though, for Azhari to arrest Sanjabi upon his return. So much, Iranians said, for the Shah's compromises.

On Armed Forces Day, November 17, the Shah, for the first time, chose not to show up to take the salute. The influential Association of Iranian Jurists and the Iranian Writers Association grew bold enough to condemn the military government and "commend all resistance." Meanwhile, instead of sticking by the Shah, thousands of Iranians rich from oil were fleeing to other countries, taking with them as much as $5 billion in capital. The Shah's wife, Empress Farah, journeyed to Najef, the Iraq shrine where Khomeini had lived for so many years, and by praying there demonstrated her attachment to Islam. This gimmicky gesture did not soothe the Shah's Moslem opponents.

In further concessions that must have pained him deeply, the Shah canceled many of the grand and showy projects that he had planned to make Iran an overnight Germany or Japan. The word from the people seemed to be that the money should go for the good of society—hospitals, schools, welfare, social security, agriculture—rather than for business and industry. Scrapped or deferred were a new airport for Teheran, sixteen nuclear power plants, $7 billion in arms purchases, a Brasília-like urbanization in northern Teheran, a subway for Teheran, a 470-mile highway along the Caspian Sea, a giant industrial park south of Isfahan, and electrification of the railroads.

In November 1978, the Shah and Azhari, handing out treasury-busting raises of as much as 100 percent, tried to get oil production up and the government ministries back in operation. But then they faced another crisis: the Islamic lunar calendar's month of Moharram, which in 1978 began on the solar calendar's December 2. Most worrisome: Ashura, the tenth of Moharram, a day of mourning and atonement for the death of a long-ago Shiite saint. During Moharram, the faithful more than ever show their attachment to the spiritual and contempt for the secular—now represented, respectively, by Khomeini and the Shah. The prospect of Ashura's traditional processions, with emotion-charged paraders wailing and flagellating themselves with chains, seemed like gunpowder to General Azhari; he banned the processions.

For his part, Khomeini called for "rivers of blood" to bring down the Shah. The French government warned Khomeini to lower his voice, but smugly convinced that France would need him when the Shah was overthrown, he refused. As Ashura approached, Iran burst with new violence. Protesters dressed in white shrouds to show their willingness to die were cut down by rifle and machine-gun fire. In an effort to placate them, the Shah released Sanjabi. The oil strike resumed; the cost had already reached $2 billion. In Isfahan, the administration building of Grumman Aerospace Corporation, which was training crews for F-14 fighter planes, was fire-bombed. Seven thousand Americans, mostly wives and children of employees of U.S. firms at work in Iran, split for the airports and jammed themselves aboard outbound commercial and U.S. Air Force planes, sometimes standing in the aisles.

The procession days approached with eerie tension. Each night, after the nine o'clock curfew, the Shah's opponents placed stereo speakers on windowsills and filled the air with taped chants of "There is no God but Allah" and "Death to the Shah," spaced out with tapes of machine-gun fire. At the palace, Ardeshir Zahedi, ambassador to the U.S. and former son-in-law of the Shah, who had been called in to give advice, argued that banning processions was inviting peril. He prevailed. The Shah may have had 700,000 men in the armed forces on his side, but it had already been proved that using them to shoot at protesters did not stop protest.

As it turned out, the paraders marched not only on Ashura but also on the day before. The processions were immense—probably nearly a million each day. Soldiers and policemen stayed far away; parade marshals with white armbands kept the marchers in perfect order. There was no flagellation; this day of religious observance had turned out to be a political event. After a year of violence, with thousands of deaths, the frail, aged, expatriate Khomeini proved that he owned the streets of Iran.

During the following month, the Shah grew increasingly fatalistic. Though he occasionally pondered the "iron-fist option" of "putting the Persians back in their cages," he more often felt that "God has already decided how everything is going to turn out." Would he be willing to become a constitutional rather than an absolute monarch? "It's O.K. with me," he replied limply. Could the United States help him in any way? "Search me," said the Shah.

Even the good news was bad news. Demonstrations supporting the Shah in Isfahan turned out to have been staged by soldiers and their families, or secret policemen, or peasants imported in military trucks. One Isfahan couple refused to shout "Long live the Shah" because soldiers the day before had shot a relative. For their refusal, soldiers

shot them. But other soldiers seemed to be under the influence of Khomeini. In a Teheran barracks, three of them burst into an officers'
mess and demanded shouts of praise for the Ayatollah. When the officers refused, the trio opened fire and killed twelve. For the Shah, these
shootings reemphasized the doubt that soldiers, particularly conscripts,
could be sent against their civilian "brothers." Compounding this doubt
was the arrogance of military officers, who live a life apart from their
men, pampered with high salaries, personal servants, and PXs.

The strikes went on, at heavy cost. Strikers erased National Iranian
Oil Company computer tapes, letting the company in for months of
reprogramming. Oil shortages caused by the loss of Iran's production
gave some members of the Organization of Petroleum Exporting Countries a reason to raise the price from $12.70 a barrel to $30 and more.
In the oil fields, gunmen killed two oil officials, one an American. As
December ended, oil production dropped first to 700,000 barrels a day,
less than Iran's own needs, and then to half of that. Fears that Iran's
oil shortfall could bring on even another price rise caused the U.S.
dollar to resume declining against other currencies. Strikes shut down
the Central Bank, oil refineries, the state airline, thousands of stores,
hundreds of bazaars.

Life became a day-to-day struggle. Troops and demonstrators
clashed incessantly; in the cemeteries women wailed at new graves.
The smells of the streets were tear gas and smoke from tire-fueled
bonfires. In the narrow moneychangers' shops on Teheran's Ferdowsi
Avenue, rich Iranians traded millions of rials to get marks, francs,
or dollars at premium prices—money to use for flight from Iran. The
exodus of foreigners accelerated as their embassies urged that wives
and children be sent home. The U.S.S.R. sent an airliner to evacuate
fifty Russian oil experts and their families from strike-bound Kharg
island, the big tanker terminal.

At last the Shah saw that his opponents could and would keep
the country in turmoil until he, too, fled from Iran. His choice became
not whether to go, but how to go without leaving Iran minus any kind
of government. To that end, he struck a deal with a courtly lawyer
named Shahpur Bakhtiar, whose lifelong opposition to the monarch
had several times landed him in prison. In this deal, Bakhtiar became
prime minister, the Shah agreed to take a "vacation" abroad, and the
two set up a regency council to represent the absent monarch. Khomeini implacably condemned the deal; Bakhtiar's party, the National
Front, rejected Bakhtiar and forced him to set up a cabinet of un-
knowns; the Shah dithered about departing. When he sent his mother
to the house of his sister Shams in Beverly Hills, Iranian students
stormed the place and tried to burn it, forcing the queen mother and

the princess to take refuge at the Palm Springs estate of former Ambassador to Great Britain Walter Annenberg. The Shah thus learned that his own exile would be perilous and constricted.

As he dawdled, pressures mounted. Clashes in one place or another brought daily killings. Cities began to look like battlefields. Shortages of gasoline infuriated drivers; shortages of kerosene left millions shivering through snowy nights. In the Persian Gulf, a hundred freighters waited to unload while customs agents struck. For the same reason, 750 trucks were backed up at the border crossing of the highway from Europe.

The jig was up. The Shah had sent his children to the United States, and on January 16 he and his wife were the last of the Pahlavi family (except for eccentric Prince Hamid) left in Iran. About 12:30 P.M., four helicopters took off from Niavaran Palace for Mehrabad airport (the Shah commonly used this ruse to prevent opponents from knowing which helicopter to shoot at). At the airport, the departure was a mournful scene. Eyes glistening, the Shah said: "I hope the government will be able to make amends for the past and also succeed in laying a foundation for the future." He bent and lifted a member of the Imperial Guard who tried to kiss the king's feet. Then, with a packet of Iranian soil in his pocket, the Shah took the controls of a silver-and-blue Boeing 707 and with his wife flew off to exile and eventual death.

2

Cyrus, Darius, and Glory

❀

The fall of Mohammed Reza Pahlavi was a decisive historical event for Iran and for the world. It ended the world's most ancient contemporary monarchy—a 2,500-year-old monarchy that rolled on nearly to the twenty-first century because its very antiquity seemed to make its continuation inevitable. With the Shah gone, no powerful king rules anywhere. Monarchy, that form of government so detestable to democracy but so prevalent through thirty centuries, is now done for. What the pharaohs began, Pahlavi ended. In Iran, the ancient king Cyrus, who built the world's first empire, and the Shah are linked together as founder and finisher of a history so grand that it chained Iran to its past; only with a tremendous, bloody, wrenching revolution could Iran shake free of it.

In a high, desolate desert in south-central Iran, there stands a lonely building as spare and bleak as its surroundings. Centuries of blowing sand have rounded the edges of the large building stones, and reamed out the cracks between them. But this structure is no ruin—far from it. The most awesome aspect of the tomb of Cyrus the Great, the world's first emperor, is that it is quite well enough preserved to let the viewer imagine the day when the king was buried there 2,508 years ago.

The tomb is not large: it looks like a one-car garage elevated on a stepped platform about fifteen feet high. Only the educated eye of the archaeologist may note the tomb's most extraordinary feature, which is its ordinary-looking gabled roof, slanted to shed heavy rains in a land where rain seldom falls. Such Nordic gables were the architectural style of lands far to the north; they had been brought to Iran by Cyrus's ancestors as part of their cultural baggage; and they thus symbolize the key event in Iranian history: the displacement of the aboriginal peoples by the Aryans from the north.

Within a couple of miles of Cyrus's tomb, in the confines of the mostly vanished ancient capital called Pasargadae, lie a few more of the works of this first king of kings. His private palace and his audience hall are there, though reduced to two white-stone floors like a pair of tennis courts, carrying square pedestals for many toppled columns and one that still stands (capped, when I was there, by the twiggy nest of a discriminating stork). Architecturally, this remnant city cannot compare with renowned Persepolis. Yet harsh, stark Pasargadae, silent but for the sighing wind, remains a compelling monument to history, stirring the visitor to connect himself, as a fellow human being, across the chasm of time to a towering king who liked to say, "Soft lands breed soft people."

One day in Teheran I met a remarkably accomplished scientist named Hind Sadek-Kouros, a paleological archaeologist who took her Ph.D. at Harvard. She had exciting news to tell, news of early man in Iran. Digging in Azerbaijan, she had found stone tools of the kind used by *Homo erectus,* the first man to walk upright. Her discovery pushed back the earliest date for the presence of man in Iran to a million years ago or more. Much remains to be discovered about man's origins everywhere, but Iran is certainly one of the sites where he has walked longest.

Evidence of Neanderthal Man, who lived 100,000 to 40,000 years ago, was found by American archaeologist Carlton Coon, and there are many signs of the Stone Age men of 15,000 years ago. At that time, an ice age in Europe and North America, Iran was a verdant, forested land of tumbling rivers whose waters emptied into inland seas that filled what are now the central deserts (shells and fossil fish are often found there). At length the rivers built fertile alluvial plains into the seas, and the hunters and berry-gatherers came down from the mountains to live on the meat of the animals that grazed in the new savannahs. After several millenniums, the women among these peoples learned not only to harvest wild emmer, the ancestor of wheat, but also to save seeds gathered in the fall and plant them in the spring. The arrival of agriculture heightened the need for storage; pottery, the archaeologists' main source of clues to prehistoric life, came into use. By the fifth millennium B.C., the villagers of what is now western Iran knew basketry (as basket designs on vases show), textile-making (as clay spindles show), and cosmetics (as pestles and mortars show). The artifacts found with this pottery, in such digs as Roman Ghirshman's excavation of the ancient village of Siyalk, 110 miles south of Teheran, included flint knives, polished axes, shell necklaces, bone tool handles carved like the head of a gazelle, and, as the Stone Age drew to an end, objects of hammered copper. Families buried their dead under the hearths of their rammed-earth houses, a mere foot below the floor.

In short, the peoples of what is now Iran were on the way toward emerging as one of mankind's first major cultures, ahead of every other part of the world except Egypt (which developed the plow, the sailboat, irrigation, writing, and the calendar about 4000 B.C.), Mesopotamia (where the wheel was invented and the Sumerian city-states were founded about 3500 B.C.), and India (which built an urban civilization in the Indus valley about 2700 B.C.). Slowly the aboriginal Iranians developed the plow, the brick, the potter's wheel, and the casting of copper. They domesticated the sheep. But the ever harsher drought, drying up rivers and the inland sea itself in the gradual process of reducing Iran to the desert land that it is today, kept the population sparse and scattered, preventing widespread urbanization, which always and everywhere is the key to cultural greatness. Excavations since 1970, led by Harvard archaeologist Carl Lamberg-Karlovsky, show that a sizable city, centered on a monumental building, existed at Tapeh Yahya, southeast of Kerman, perhaps as early as 4500 B.C.; and the future may bring other such discoveries among the innumerable mounds that in Iran bespeak once inhabited sites. But only when these people moved down from the Zagros Mountains to Iran's southwestern plain (now Khuzistan), which is a natural extension of Mesopotamia, did they build a major city, Susa, and the nation for which Susa was the capital, Elam. With that development, about 2500 B.C., this predecessor country of modern Iran initiated its two thousand years on the world stage as an advanced civilization, centuries ahead of Crete and Mycenae (2000 B.C.), Anatolia (1800 B.C.), China (1500 B.C.), Phoenicia (1300 B.C.), and the Hebrews (1200 B.C.).

One spring day in 1975, Professor Pinhas P. Delougaz, of the University of California at Los Angeles, unearthed in what was once Elam an exquisite vase in the shape of an ibex, not unique but still the sort of find that archaeologists spend their lives hoping for. Within an hour Delougaz was dead, from a heart attack evidently brought on by the thrill of the elegant discovery. This drama serves as a vivid measure of the excitement and depth of the Elamite culture. Susa was such a wondrous city that the French Archaeological Mission in Iran (headed for many years by Dr. Ghirshman) has not got to the bottom of the place in excavations that began way back in 1884. (In fact, this dig is an industry in itself, run from a vast crenellated headquarters building that looks like a chateau on the Loire.) The Elamite city that the French have so far exposed was an orderly place of long, broad thoroughfares, lined with the courtyard houses of rich merchants, and on high ground an acropolis for the royal palaces. The people who lived there at first used a pictographic writing, which scholars have not yet learned to read, but later they developed a cuneiform script suitable for their language, which is not related to any other known language.

Sharing the Mesopotamian plain, Elam absorbed Mesopotamian culture and warred with Mesopotamian states, notably Sumer and its successor, Babylonia, in the southern part of the area between the Tigris and the Euphrates, and Assyria in the north. In the eighteenth century B.C., the Elamites carried off the celebrated stele of Hammurabi, on which is engraved the legal code devised by the Babylonian king (the original is now in the Louvre, but the Teheran Archaeological Museum has a copy). Elam also carried its culture, presumably by war, into the Iranian plateau; at Siyalk Ghirshman found a thick layer of ash, indicating destruction of the village, followed by a switch in pottery style from the earlier painted kind to the monochrome red or gray used at Susa.

In many of the world's museums—including the Metropolitan in New York, the British Museum in London, and the Archaeological Museum in Teheran—you can spend an interesting hour or so looking at the little sculptures called Luristan Bronzes. They are mostly green-patinaed castings of horses, winged ibexes, dagger handles, urns, animal-head pins, bracelets, and plaques, as well as bits and headstalls intended for actual use on a horse, and chariot trappings. They were all dug up by peasants clandestinely and with no scientific control, from four or five hundred graves in the Iranian province of Luristan, during the course of about four years around 1930.

Luristan was part of Elam, and some of the bronzes are disk-headed pins depicting a woman giving birth: the mother goddess, it is thought, of the peoples of Elam and Mesopotamia. But "the collection as a whole bears a preponderant impress of foreign influence, both in form and subject," writes Ghirshman. In short, the bronzes from the period of greatest production, 1200 to 800 B.C., speak—particularly by their stress on horses and horsemanship—the message that the Aryans of the north had arrived among the original inhabitants of Iran.

The northerners burst out of the Eurasian plains of southern Russia in two migrations, one about 2000 B.C. and the other a thousand years later. The first migration did not penetrate what is now Iran so much as it did what are now Turkey and India. The evidence is not all in, but apparently the Hittite empire which ruled Asia Minor from 1900 to 1200 B.C. was founded by invaders who crossed the Balkans and the Bosporus. To the east, the Aryans traveled around the northern shore of the Caspian Sea, poured through the Khyber Pass, and quickly developed the strong civilization in the Indus valley that ultimately came to be India. But some of these first Aryans went south via the Caucasus, and got as far as the Zagros Mountains, while others parted from the Indus-bound migrants to enter Iran from east of the Caspian. These early arrivals melded with the original inhabitants and lost their Aryan identity, even though the crossbreeding produced some vigorous art, and a couple of energetic little kingdoms, as well as the stress on raising and training horses reflected in the Luristan Bronzes.

The cause of the second migration is, like that of the first, uncertain—overgrazing of the homeland, perhaps. The Aryans thrust out, some toward Europe, others once again through the Balkans to Asia Minor and this time on to Egypt (the wave included the Philistines, settlers of Palestine), and still others through the Caucasus. East of the Caspian these new invaders met firm resistance from their distant cousins in India, and were deflected westward to the Iranian plateau. This time the Aryans came with large numbers of horses, arms, flocks, and families, prepared not to blend into the existing population but to dominate it. "What occurred must have been somewhat analogous to the struggle of the Roman Empire against the barbarians," writes Ghirshman. But the Aryans were not barbarians. Besides the Nordic gable, they brought with them knowledge of brick and stone masonry, fortifications, urban life, and a prince-and-slave society.

Gradually distinct tribes formed among the Aryans, most memorably the Medes and the Persians. The distinctions between them were trifling—ethnically speaking, one man's Mede is another man's Persian. Yet forming significant kingdoms was among the Iranians a tardy process, compared to the rapid leap in Egypt or Sumer from hunter society to monarchy. Part of the reason is that the Iranian conquerors needed a lot of time to bring the indigenous inhabitants into submission. But at length among the Medes there came a couple of kings who unified the tribe as a nation, and by 584 B.C. made Media the first large Iranian power, stretching west to the Tigris and east to what is now Teheran, with a capital at Ecbatana, today's Hamadan.

The Persians, for their part, came to rest about 700 B.C. around Shushtar, in the foothills of the Zagros Mountains. This was part of Elam, but the declining Elamites could not prevent the Persians from moving in. The Persians built at least two imposing terraces of cyclopean stone, which may have been royal cities; one of them, Masjid-e-Sulaiman, was precisely on the spot where British petroleum engineers discovered Iran's first oil in 1908, and it was they who called the attention of archaeologists to the still existing terrace.

The first Persian king, who rose to power in the seventh century B.C., was Achaemenes, significant chiefly because from him comes the name of Iran's greatest dynasty, the Achaemenians. But from his descendants (including a now forgotten Cyrus I) emerged the king who became the foremost figure in Iranian history: Cyrus II, Cyrus the Great.

By the time Cyrus became king, Persia was already a large domain, probably including most of the modern province of Fars, centered on what was to become Persepolis and adjoining Media on the north. For openers, empire-builder Cyrus grabbed off the remnants of Elam and the sparsely populated Indian Ocean littoral eastward to what are roughly the modern borders of Iran. In a battle at Pasargadae in 550 B.C. he overcame Media, and with that began to aspire to nothing less than the conquest of the entire known world, beginning in the west.

In that direction, the once important nation of Urartu (present-day Armenia) had already been taken by the Medes, and Cappadocia and Cilicia (parts of modern central Turkey) proved to be pushovers. But between Cyrus and the Mediterranean Sea there yet lay Lydia, kingdom of the pecunious Croesus. Cyrus sent camels against Lydia's famed cavalry. King Croesus had learned from the Oracle at Delphi that he would "destroy a great empire," but he did not grasp that the empire would be his own. His terrified horses fell back in defeat, and Cyrus went on to capture, one by one, the rich Greek cities on the Ionian coast. The whole campaign took only two years.

Cyrus recognized that the "known world" he wished to conquer included Egypt, Carthage, Ethiopia, and Greek colonies on the Mediterranean coast as far as Gibraltar, but for the time being he thought he had better seize the known world to the east (except for distant, legendary China). In about a year he took lands as far away as what are now the Turkmen Soviet Socialist Republic, Afghanistan, and Pakistan. He rushed west again and fell upon Babylon by diverting the unfordable Gyndes River, a tributary of the Tigris which protected the city, into many shallow hand-dug channels. There he freed the forty thousand Jews held in the Babylonian captivity. A few years later, putting down a revolt in the east, Cyrus died in battle. His troops brought his body back to Pasargadae, and laid it to rest in the tomb with the Nordic roof.

Cyrus was not only the world's first great emperor; he was a humane man, who treated his victims benevolently, honored their gods, and set higher standards for the profession of kingship than most other monarchs down through the centuries. His son and successor, by contrast, was a brute who had earlier kicked his pregnant wife to death. He adored flattery, not blinking even when a courtier told him, "I do not think you are the equal of your father, because you do not have a son like the son he left behind." Nevertheless, before he mysteriously committed suicide, he managed to capture Egypt and pack the pharaoh back to Iran. Upon his death, according to Herodotus, the seven young nobles who formed the imperial council met and agreed to accept as king him among them whose horse should neigh first at dawn the next day. One groom made sure that his master would win by providing a delectable, neigh-worthy mare for the stallion. In this way the noble named Darius became king, although his own account of his ascent, which he left engraved on stone, differs in ways that do not make nearly as good a story.

Whatever the truth, Darius turned out to be second only to Cyrus as "Great King, King of Kings," and even more than Cyrus, the architect of the Persian Empire. Despite his chance choice, Darius had the royal blood of Achaemenes in his veins, for he descended from a collateral branch of the family. Darius ruled for thirty-five years, at first putting down rivals (he fought nineteen battles at the rate of nearly a battle a month, and defeated nine upstart kinglets), then giving the empire the institutions that Cyrus had been too busy to devise. He had to keep the subject populations contented enough not to revolt (for the conquered masses greatly outnumbered the ruling Persians), but disciplined enough to pay heavy taxes to support the court and the armies. Darius employed inspectors, called "the ears of the king," to spy on his own satraps, a function similar to the recent Shah's Imperial Inspectorate.

To bind his empire together, to use Iran on a large scale as a land bridge between east and west, Darius built the world's first highway network. The stone-paved Royal Road, 1,679 miles long, ran from the empire's winter capital at Susa to Ionian Ephesus on the Mediterranean, and Persian nobles drove along it in four-horse chariots. An eastern route ran via the Khyber Pass to the valley of the Indus, and another branch went to Babylon and Egypt. Royal couriers, changing horses at 111 relay stations, could carry mail from Susa to Ephesus in seven days; it was they who inspired Herodotus to the famous phrase that (as adapted for the inscription on the Main Post Office in New York City) reads: "Neither snow, nor rain, nor heat, nor gloom of night stays these couriers from the swift completion of their appointed rounds." Completing an Egyptian plan, Darius dug a canal between the Red Sea and the Nile, a forerunner of Suez.

With 360,000 soldiers—six army corps, each with six divisions of 10,000 men—Darius enlarged the empire until it measured 2 million square miles and contained 10 million people. Crossing the Bosporus, he pushed his borders to present-day Bulgaria (but could not take Greece); pressing eastward, he took what is now the Uzbek Soviet Socialist Republic, hard by the westernmost bulge of China. Where the Kabul River joins the Indus, in today's Pakistan, Darius built a fleet and sent it down the Indus, across the Arabian Sea, and up the Red

Sea to Egypt. He gave the empire "the law of the Medes and the Persians, which altereth not" (in reality it was derived from Hammurabi's Code); and when under it Darius's Babylonian friend the Biblical prophet Daniel was condemned to be thrown to the lions, the king let the law take its course. He made the economy work by establishing a common coinage based on the gold daric. Perceiving all these accomplishments to be excellent, Darius gathered sculptors and engravers at a stone cliff at Behistun (near modern Kermanshah), on the heavily traveled road from Babylon to Ecbatana, and set them to work on a monument to himself. Two hundred feet up on the jagged and jumbled face of the cliff, the artisans flattened an area about 50 feet high and 60 feet wide, like a gigantic billboard, and along the top carved a bas-relief of bearded Darius standing with one foot on a fallen foe as he faces a dozen captives with their hands manacled behind their backs. Beneath are cuneiform inscriptions enough to make a small book, written in Elamite, Babylonian, and Old Persian, boasting of Darius's conquests and achievements. This is the most important historical document of the time; unfortunately, it and a few others, mostly repetitious, are the only long texts by Persians about their empire. It is plain that they could write; whether they did write, and if so what happened to the writings, is unknown; and modern Persians, to their embarrassment, have to go to the Greeks, chiefly Herodotus, to learn their own history.

Darius created an empire where farmers raised wheat, barley, grapes, and olives; beekeepers produced honey; fishermen exploited the rivers and the Persian Gulf; workmen made shoes, tunics, and furniture; sea captains sailed beyond Gibraltar, or went to Ceylon for spices; caravans transported clothing, ores, balks of teak and cedar; and banks lent money, made investments, and accepted checks. Artisans flourished—witness such examples as the lovely lapis lazuli jug in the Archaeological Museum in Teheran, or the golden Oxus Treasure (so named for the dry riverbed where it was found in 1877) of Achaemenian art in the British Museum: snake bracelets, armlets, necklaces, and earrings.

In architecture, the Persians drew together styles and techniques from their own past and from their whole empire to create breathtaking splendor—especially at Persepolis.

Persepolis is Iran's entrant in the sweepstakes that measures the world's ancient architectural achievements against one another, its Roman Forum, Angkor Wat, or Machu Picchu.

As the emperor Darius designed it, Persepolis was neither quite a capital nor quite a city, but rather, in the words of author Jim Hicks, a "colossally immodest salute" to his own glory. When Darius was not out on his horse adding another province or two to his empire, he lived in lowland Susa in the winter and mountainous Ecbatana in the summer. He built Persepolis almost exclusively to stage the ceremonies of the Persian New Year, the spring equinox. When you put your foot on the threshold of the main entrance to Darius's palace, precisely where Darius put his foot so long ago, you notice that the stone is hardly worn. Persepolis was chock-full of royal palaces, treasuries, storehouses, and something that might have been a harem, but devoid of any place for ordinary mortals to live, except for the barracks of the imperial guards.

For Persepolis's site, Darius chose a short, rocky slope hard up against the westward-facing slope of the Mountain of Mercy. He probably started construction (according to recent research by Canada's scholarly former Ambassador to Iran James George) at the summer solstice almost exactly 2,500 years ago: the shadow of a stick held vertical just as the sun appears over the mountain on June 21 is precisely in line with the fronts and backs of all the main buildings. Why did Darius choose the solstice? His reasons appear to have stemmed from his Zoroastrian religious beliefs. "In the cosmic struggle between Light and Darkness, between Ahuramazda (or Ohrmazd) and his dark twin Angra Mainu (or Ahriman), June 21 was the most sacred day of the year—the day when there was the most light and the least darkness, when Ahriman's shadow was the least present," writes George.

Once Persepolis was lined up to the sun, Darius's masons, using stones as big as 24 feet by 7 feet on the face, built a front wall 50 feet high and side walls that ran back on a level until they melded into the mountain. Into the three-sided box thus formed workmen cast stone obtained from leveling the high side of the slope until they created a 32-acre platform measuring 1,400 feet from north to south, and 1,000 feet from front wall to mountainside (and—to throw in one more statistic—just 5,800 feet above sea level). At the north end of the front wall, masons cut twin staircases that rise, parallel to the wall on both right and left, for sixty-nine steps, to landings, and then reverse, for forty-two more steps, to reach the platform. The staircases served for horses as well as men, for with treads 15 inches deep and a rise of only 5½ inches per step, they climb at a gentle angle; and they are 22½ feet wide.

The sensation I got when I reached the top of the stairs was that I could spend two rapturous days exploring every corner of this sun-struck, walkable plateau, and I did. The first sight is the Gateway of All Nations, once a sort of palatial waiting room with lofty interior columns and a roof. Three of the four columns are standing, but the plan of the building is mainly suggested by the massive doorjambs of its east and west entrances. From the front of each of these jambs emerges a colossal winged bull, bearded and crowned (but defaced, literally, by latter-day Moslems heeding Islam's ban on the representation of visages). Through the gatehouse and to the left, you reach a parade ground, floored with the living rock as Darius's masons leveled it, or with gravel where it was filled. And 50 yards across this space lies Persepolis's largest, most sumptuous, and best preserved palace, Darius's great Hall of Audience, the Apadana. Christopher Marlowe's poem springs to mind:

> Is it not passing brave to be a King,
> And ride in triumph through Persepolis?

The Apadana sits on a square stone platform 8½ feet above terrace level, the east edge being part of the terrace's front wall. The north face of the platform generously gives you your first look at those bas-relief figures of the Medes and the Persians and the tribute-bearers of their empire that are the well-known trademark of Persepolis. On the platform stand thirteen columns, mostly at or near the full original height of 67 feet, and the bases of fifty-nine others. Also visible are the footings of the walls, and it is easy to make out the palace's plan: a 200-foot-square interior chamber containing six rows of six columns, surrounded by porticoes, each with two rows of six columns, on west, north, and east.

The walls are gone, because they were built of mud brick which dissolved in rain, but an abundance of evidence survives to show how the Apadana looked when it was completed by Darius's son Xerxes. The capitals of the columns were intricate and elongated carvings of volutes and sepal-like forms, capped by huge impost blocks depicting the forequarters of two bulls joined back to back like Dr. Dolittle's pushmi-pullyu, thus creating a saddle suitable for sustaining the ceiling beams. The walls, 17 feet thick, rose as high as the capitals, and a grid of cedar timbers, from Lebanon, laid on the walls and columns held up a roof made of lesser beams, straw mats, and mud, topped by as much as six feet of earth.

The only light filtered through gold lace hung in the doors, or came from torches, creating an intentionally dim interior and heightening the king's remoteness and mystery. Nevertheless, the chamber was gorgeously decorated, to judge from clues that come from Susa. At his capital there, Darius had earlier built a similar seventy-two column audience hall, and though now quite thoroughly ruined, it yielded to archaeologists fine specimens of glazed brick used for finishing mud walls. Since Darius moved many of the Susa craftsmen directly to Persepolis, they doubtless used similar brick, portraying lions, bulls, and plants. Where not brick-faced, the walls were apparently of pastel-painted plaster. The Book of Esther describes rich hangings of green, blue, and purple cloth in the Susa Apadana; probably Persepolis had the same sort of tapestry. In 1941 diggers found some fragments of hammered gold, incised with bull designs and punched for nails, which suggest that the wooden doors of the Apadana were sheathed from top to bottom in this gleaming metal.

Persepolis perfected must have been stately, brilliant, and the greatest gallery of sculpture extant. Luckily, a large proportion of the sculpture survives, the best of it being the bas-reliefs on the base of the Apadana. They show groups of bearers bringing New Year's tribute to the Persian throne at Persepolis from the whole vast distant empire, and constitute perhaps the most engrossing sociohistorical documentary ever put into stone.

Twenty-three delegations walk in the three registers of this hand-chiseled filmstrip of obeisance to the emperor. The Elamites bring a leashed lioness, who turns her head to snarl at two men carrying her cubs. A group from the northeast leads a stately two-humped Bactrian camel and bears vessels full of precious goods. The barefooted Egyptians tug at a bull; crinkly-haired Ethiopians (some of whom lived in Egypt) lead an okapi and carry an elephant tusk; the dhoti-clad Indians bring axes and a donkey. And if the carvings please the eye now, they must have stunned it in Persepolis's heyday, for they were painted in bright colors (carved figures inside the palaces also had real-gold crowns, bracelets, and necklaces, and beards of bronze and lapis lazuli). Thus did Darius leave posterity a panorama of the civilization of his time.

The end of Persepolis came when Alexander the Great attacked it in 330 B.C. and set it afire. Though the city was built of stone and brick, the tapestries and roof beams burned so hot that in Xerxes' audience hall the columns literally exploded. Over the centuries sand blown down from the Mountain of Mercy and mud from the dissolved bricks joined the ashes of Alexander's fire to cover the ruins of Persepolis as deep as twenty feet in places, marvelously preserving the sculpture. The explorer Pietro della Valle, visiting in 1621, found twenty-five of the Apadana's columns protruding from the rubble; another visitor, in 1627, found nineteen; another, in 1698, seventeen; another, in 1821, fifteen. From the height of the inscription above the ground, I would judge that the covering dirt must have been four or five feet deep when a reporter named McIlrath of the *Chicago Inter Ocean* chiseled his name into the Gate of All Nations in 1897.

Six miles from Persepolis, there stands a high cliff into which have been deeply cut four enormous Greek crosses. The vertical bars of each are 70 feet high and 35 feet wide, the horizontal bars 60 feet long and 25 feet high. The space where the bars cross is carved in bas-relief to simulate a portico with four columns and a frieze, and a small central door. Above the frieze, in the upper square of the vertical bar, bas-reliefs in two registers show many small human figures whose heads support the heroic sculpture above them, a king worshiping a flame, with a winged-disk symbol hovering overhead. These crosses are all tombs (though now empty), and one of them, the second from the right, is certainly the tomb of Darius, because the inscription above it says so. Archaeologists guess that the other tombs are those of Darius II, Artaxerxes I, and Xerxes. All the kings immortalized by these tombs, plus some others, ruled the Persian Empire after Darius, in what amounts to a long slide into decadence and utter defeat.

Only Xerxes, Darius's son, is memorable. Coveting conquests like those of his forebears, he took aim on Greece, which had turned back a thrust by Darius at Marathon in 490 B.C. The fifty-oared galleys of Xerxes' navy, lashed side by side, anchored fore and aft, and decked over, formed a bridge a mile and a quarter long over the Hellespont, and in 480 B.C. the Persian king marched probably 200,000 soldiers (Herodotus says 2,641,610) across it to take Thrace and Macedonia. Athens and Sparta put aside their differences to join in the defense of the lower peninsula at the narrow defile called Thermopylae. Leonidas and his three hundred stopped the Persians there, but a Greek traitor showed the invaders a route through the mountains. Xerxes took Athens, and moved his navy into the narrow channel between Athens and the island of Salamis. Having learned from a Greek spy that Greek sailors were scared sick of the Persians, he set up a throne on the seashore and prepared to watch the rout. But the spy had been a plant, a Greek trick; the valiant enemy rammed and sank scores of Persian ships and forced the rest to retreat. Squirming on his throne, Xerxes had to watch his fleet turned to wreckage while the bodies of his men washed up on the shore. Marathon, Thermopylae, Salamis—these historic battles put Persia on the skids.

In the year 336 B.C., two princes came to power, one in Persia and one in Greece, one a poltroon and one an innate hero. The Persian was Darius III, the temperamental opposite of his derring-do namesake. The Greek was twenty-year-old Alexander, son of Philip of Macedon. Most of Persia's battles during the history of the empire had been struggles with Greece, a formidable civilization unable to win wars because its city-states would not unite and fight together. To Alexander and most Greeks, Persia was the historic, dangerously powerful enemy. But Alexander went to war with four new assets: his own confidence and will power; a united Macedonia behind him; foot soldiers loyal directly to him; and an elite, devoted cavalry recruited from the nobility. Crossing the Hellespont in 334 B.C., Alexander first routed Persian troops at Issus (near modern Turkey's Alexandretta), where Darius fled, well before the battle was decided, leaving behind his mother, wife, and children. Alexander detoured to conquer Egypt and found Alexandria (he ultimately gave his own name to seventeen cities). He returned and backed the Persians up against the Zagros foothills of modern Iraq, where Darius again fled the field. The Greek then undertook a leisurely looting of Darius's capitals, Susa and Ecbatana, and of Persepolis. Since Alexander was not in the habit of destroying captured cities, scholars think he may have been out of his mind with drink when he burned Persepolis; in any case, the place must have been devastated after the Greeks seized treasure (including 5,500 tons of silver) that according to Plutarch required 20,000 mules and 5,000 camels to remove. Alexander finally caught up to Darius in 330 B.C. on the Iranian plateau about 150 miles east of modern Teheran; but the last Achaemenian had just been killed by his own men. Seven years later, Alexander, too, died, in bed, at Babylon, never having returned to his birthplace. But by then his empire, running from the Indus to Macedonia, was a bit larger than that of Cyrus and Darius I.

If Iranians have had to derive their factual ancient history from Greek historians and from modern French and American archaeologists, they have ingeniously and independently created a national mythology that endows the site of Persepolis with another kind of meaning. Only in the West is this ancient city known by its Greek nickname. The proud people of Persia have perennially referred to the site as Takht-e Jamshid, or Throne of Jamshid, an allusion to the beginnings of Iranian myth. In attempting to understand the revolution of 1978–1979, it helps, I think, to know something of the heritage of heroic mythology that may have been, subconsciously or not, on the minds of those rioters in the streets.

Like so many national cultures whose people immortalize their antiquity in literary forms, the Persians counted on their bards to tell of the heroics of olden times; and at length the most significant poet in Persian history collected these tales into an epic masterpiece. Just about 999 years ago, a landowner, later to be known simply by his literary title, Ferdowsi (Of Paradise), completed sixty thousand couplets of rhymed, metered verse based on a heritage of stories passed on by word of mouth up to that time. Entitled *Shahnama (Epic of the Kings)*, this saga of mythical and historical kings, queens, and warriors became the race memory of Persia's otherwise illiterate people. Poets then and poets now recite the heroic deeds and tragic failings of the fifty kings who traditionally inhabited the Iranian Empire until the Moslems arrived. It is still recited in Ferdowsi's purified Persian, which tried to avoid Arabic words adopted after the Moslem conquest. In the process Jamshid, most outstanding of the early mythical kings, melded with the Zoroastrian temple of Persepolis in the creative consciousness of the Persian people.

In the beginning the Zoroastrian god, like the Judeo-Christian counterpart, created matter out of nothing. Next he created man "to become the key to all those close-linked things," says Ferdowsi. From Kiyumars, the first mythical king, came civilization. But it took Jamshid, the fourth king, to improve and develop the Iranian civilization during his reign of seven hundred years. Having received the divinely ordained *Farr* or nimbus that would identify all future kings, Jamshid designed weapons of war and fabrics worn at feasts. He defined the crafts of artisans and identified the social classes. He discovered certain minerals and medicines to please his people. After two hundred years spent in these pursuits, the wise king boarded a ship that took him from one land to another. At the end of another fifty years he celebrated the grandeur of his kingdom in a spectacular fashion, according to Ferdowsi. "With the aid of the royal Farr, he fashioned a marvelous throne, which at his bidding was lifted by demons into the air. He sat upon that throne like the sun in the firmament. To celebrate, that day was called a new day—the festival of Now-Ruz—the first day of the new year."

But the epic of *Shahnama* is concerned not only with the virtuous rise but also with the iniquitous fall of its kings, and Jamshid is no exception. For the dualism of good and evil inherent in men's character is the essence of the religion that Zoroaster laid down in the sixth century B.C. Iran's mythology as retold by Ferdowsi diligently reflects this insight. So after three hundred years had passed, during which Jamshid guided the peace and pleasures of his people, he became consumed by pride, thereby losing the royal Farr, and "the world became full of discord."

As Jamshid's virtue declines, there comes upon the scene a Faustian desert warrior who submits his will to the devil and triumphs as emperor after he orders an ignominious death for Jamshid (he was sawed in two). This evil king's thousand years of iniquity end when an upright soldier named Faridun kills the evil monarch and inherits the royal Farr.

Good King Faridun gives the land of Iran to his youngest son, Iraj. But the jealous spirits of two other sons, Salm and Tur, unite in a plot to murder Iraj. A daughter is born to Iraj's widow and Faridun sadly but dutifully brings up the child. She marries a descendant of Jamshid and bears a son, Manuchehr. Faridun also raises him, determined to make him a single-minded warrior who will wreak vengeance for the death of his grandfather Iraj. Manuchehr overwhelms each of Iraj's wicked brothers in battles, and becomes king after the death of his great-grandfather Faridun. This theme of vengeance for the unjust death of an Iranian king or warrior is repeated over and over in the telling of Iran's heroic tales.

If vengeance is the mission of Iran's mythical heroes, for the warrior Rustam, greatest of them all, it is the consuming motive of three hundred years of service to Iran's monarchs. Born in the reign of Manuchehr, Rustam comes from distinguished parents. His father is a mighty warrior magically reared by an eagle-like bird known as Simorgh, and his mother is the beauteous daughter of an Arabian king. Rustam's size at birth is so great that his mother faints from labor pains and a feather from the omnipotent Simorgh provides for the safe delivery of the baby. His mother awakes and gives the child a name by crying: "I am now free [*rustam*] and my suffering has ended." It is no surprise that Rustam needs ten foster mothers to give him milk as a babe, and five men's meals to nourish him to adulthood. He grows to the height of eight men, "so that his stature was that of a noble cypress."

No other legend from the *Shahnama* has been so enthusiastically adapted for pictorial and theatric entertainment as the tale of the renowned and redoubtable Rustam. Compared to the lion or elephant in strength, Persia's Promethean hero exercises his vengeance with maces, swords, lassos, and lances, but most often with a taut bow whose arrows inevitably find their targets. His constant companion in adventure is the lion-hearted, elephant-sized horse Raksh.

But Rustam is a hero with a flaw. His single encounter with a woman produces a son named Sohrab. Years later Rustam is leading his army to victory over the nation called Turan, Iran's traditional enemy since Faridun created it for his infamous son Tur. Sohrab is manipulated by the Turan king to lead Turan's forces into a battle that can only end in the downfall of father or son. Rustam and Sohrab meet in single combat that lasts two days, such is the stamina of the two warriors. Only when Rustam succeeds in planting his dagger in Sohrab's chest do father and son recognize one another and their tragic destiny.

Rustam's flaw, as the American interpreter Reuben Levy has shown in his English translation of the *Shahnama,* is his monstrous pride. Pride has led him to kill his own son, and his pride will carry him to the final scene of his life. When a malevolent half-brother chal-

lenges his martial ardor, Rustam rushes impulsively to his fate, which
is to ride into a concealed pit bristling with up-pointed swords and
scimitars. Dying, Rustam aims his bow for the last time and the arrow
fatally wounds his assailant.

At Rustam's death the saga is only half told. Legendary exploits
of Darius and Alexander under Persian names follow. Alexander is
depicted as a wise and courageous leader whose troops visit Persepolis
and then overwhelm the fleeing troops of Darius III. The saga moves
majestically into the historical segment of Iran's national epic when
it narrates the reigns and romances of the Sassanian shahs.

This easy transition from mythical kings with human characteristics to historical kings with mythical adventures has a traditional Persian flavor. European archaeologists focus on the cliffside tombs of
Darius, Xerxes, Artaxerxes I, and Darius II, six miles from Persepolis,
but the Iranians still refer to this place as Naqsh-i-Rustam, or Picture
of Rustam, simply because they see no objection to confusing history
and mythology. Persian parents name their children Kiyumars and
Jamshid after the mythical kings as readily as Ardashir and Khosrow
after historical kings. Fact and fiction, for the Iranian imagination,
seem forms that fit familiarly into the same Persian miniature. This
characteristic has moved Sir Roger Stevens to write, in *The Land of
the Great Sophy:* "There can be no proper understanding of what un-
derlies modern Iran unless we recognize the significance of this triumph of legend over history, or art over reality, this preference for
embellishment as against unvarnished fact, for ancient folk beliefs
as against new-fangled creeds."

3

"Defeat Makes Us Invincible"

❊

In the days of Cyrus and Darius, nothing, it seemed, could stop the powerful and confident Persians. In most of the centuries since Alexander, the Iranians have had to accept military defeat and try to turn it into cultural victory, usually with remarkable success. A few years after Genghis Khan conquered and razed Iran, for example, his descendants had been converted into thoroughly Persian poets and calligraphers. "We were invaded by Greeks, Arabs, Mongols, and Turks, but we did not lose our originality," former Prime Minister Jamshid Amuzegar pointed out to me in a thoughtful discussion of Iran's past. "In Persia, the Bedouins found a richer culture than their own, and the Persians recognized that this more powerful enemy could not be annihilated. So we assimilated him." A wry Persian proverb says: "Defeat makes us invincible."

In this long sweep of history, dozens of dynasties, greater and lesser, reigned over an Iran that was sometimes a vast empire and sometimes an assortment of principalities. One must learn to distinguish Seleucids from Sassanians, Seljuks from Safavids. Reasonably independent and arguably native Iranian kings ruled for thirteen of the twenty-five centuries since Cyrus, in seven national dynasties: Achaemenian, Parthian, Sassanian, Safavid, Zand, Qajar, and Pahlavi. Foreign (or local) kings prevailed during the other twelve centuries. Yet in all those bad times, Iran, marvelous to say, never became anybody's colony. The Persians' sly technique of turning their conquerors into Persians saw to that.

Within thirty years after Alexander's death, his empire broke into three realms—Egypt, Macedonia, and Persia—each ruled by one of Alexander's generals. Seleucus, the Greek who inherited the reduced lands of the Achaemenians, imported thousands upon thousands of Greeks from their overpopulated homeland. They brought Greek gods and the Greek language, which replaced Aramaic as the country's lingua franca. Persia became part of the Hellenistic world. Archaeologists digging in sites that correspond to the Seleucid period find statues carved in classical Greek style from Greek marble, and the ruins of temples built on Western plans with poor imitations of Greek columns and capitals. But neither Seleucus nor the succeeding Seleucid kings could stop the empire from shrinking slowly to the westward. A century and a half later they were cornered into Syria, there to be snapped up by the newly puissant Romans.

Even as the Seleucids lost their grip on power, their subjects flourished in wealth, in liveliness of urban life, and in technological progress. The rise of China made the Iranian plateau into an indispensable land bridge for trade between east and west. The inns called caravanserais arose in the deserts, and camel caravans transported all the new, sophisticated luxury goods of the world: cameos, drugs, aromatics, purple dye. Iran itself exported precious stones, carpets, pedigreed dogs; and sent to upstart Rome such boons of civilization as cotton, the lemon, the melon, sesame seed, and the duck, causing a veritable agrarian revolution in Italy. But through it all, says Ghirshman, the Iranians refused to become Greeks, and in the end "this conquest of Iran was a defeat for Hellenism. By contrast it was a peaceful victory for Iran, which emerged materially richer and more advanced."

Concurrently with the contraction of Hellenistic Persia, the Aryans in the eastern plateau stirred and reasserted power, even minting coins that bore the names of Darius and Artaxerxes. At first centered in what the Greeks called Parthia (roughly, the modern province of Khorasan), they expanded until in 87 B.C. the Parthians held all land between India and Armenia.

For four centuries, until 224 A.D., the Parthians successfully held Iran together, defended it from its enemies, and built national pride and confidence. As the Parthian empire expanded westward, the Roman empire expanded eastward. They met at the Euphrates, and contested over this border for centuries. In what is now Azerbaijan, a Parthian king threw back a legion headed by Mark Antony; in Mesopotamia, the Parthians turned back a thrust led personally by the emperor Trajan. For their part, the Romans three times burned and looted the Parthian capital of Ctesiphon on the banks of the Tigris; and compelled one Parthian king to signify his vassalage by going to Rome to accept his crown from Nero. But it is misleading to view history as a mere succession of wars, and the more relevant truth is that Rome and Parthia managed between clashes to be ardent traders with one another, and with the rich nations farther east, India and China. Rome sent manufactured goods, wines, oils, and gold in return for ivory, perfume, spices, silk, and steel. The Parthians maintained good roads, which, together with the invention of the horseshoe, made it possible for a fast rider to go 350 miles in two days. After China sent an ambassador to the Parthian king, the Iranians improved Chinese cooking by sending saffron, the onion, and the cucumber, and in return got the apricot and the silkworm.

Parthia, in effect, stopped Rome from expansion to the east; but Rome, stretching westward to Spain and Scotland, remained by any measure the greater empire. It was left to the next dynasty, building upon the foundations that Parthia laid, to elevate Persia again to true world eminence. The Sassanian kings ruled for four centuries, and at the peak of their power and glory fell in a few years to an enemy they scarcely knew existed, the Arabs.

Persia—true Persia, the realm of the Persians but not of the Medes, the land adjacent to the Persian Gulf, the modern province of Fars— was only a subkingdom of Parthia in the first two centuries of the Christian era. Vassalage, the Persians felt, was bitter tea for the descendants of the Achaemenians. Finally one of them, Ardeshir (grandson of an obscure Persian kinglet named Sassan, and namesake of thousands of modern-day Iranians, including former Ambassador to Washington Ardeshir Zahedi) took arms and in 224 killed the Parthian king. Ardeshir appointed his son Shahpur (now also a popular namesake) co-king, and in no time Shahpur recaptured the eastern empire as far as Samarkand and the Indus River. Then he turned west against the attacking Roman emperor Valerian and had the marvelous luck to take Valerian "captive with my own hands." Shahpur exiled seventy thousand Roman legionaries to what is now Khuzistan, where they engineered and built bridges, dams, and roads, some of which still exist.

Militarily the Sassanians were strong and modern; they attacked with heavily armored cavalry backed up by lightly armored mounted archers in turn backed up by elephants (the tanks of the era), all followed by the infantry. Against fortresses they had siege engines the equal of the Romans'. As was the case in other dynasties, the history of the Sassanians reads like a litany of wars, as the succeeding kings defended the distant marches of the empire. Shahpur II, who reigned for seventy years beginning in 309, had to deal with the Romans close at hand after Constantine, converted to Christianity, moved his capital to Constantinople and inaugurated the Byzantine Empire. The Persian bloodily purged Christians within his own empire, and later bagged another Roman emperor, Julian "the Apostate," in battle just outside Ctesiphon.

The Metropolitan Museum in New York displays a haunting sculptured portrait of Shahpur II, as well as elegant Sassanian bowls engraved with wine-making scenes, and a dish depicting a king changing a buck to a doe by shooting off his horns and then back to a buck by adding arrows as horns. Between wars and behind the battlefronts, art and civilization under the Sassanians reached new heights of grace. What the world now thinks of as traditional Persian art took form: in mosaics and embossed silver, languorous women and madly dashing hunters; in textiles, lions and griffons; in architecture, arches and the vaulted and recessed portal called the *ivan*. The Avesta, the scripture of the Zoroastrian religion, was set down on paper, in the beginnings of a Persian written literature.

The members of the nobility reveled in harems, feasting, and the music of all-girl orchestras. They played chess and polo. The kings, to show their descent, sophistication, and power, had themselves depicted on the coinage facing right, like the Achaemenians, rather than left, like the crude Parthians. Persian motifs spread to Europe and the Far East. "In the sculptures and frescoes of the old French churches the artist reproduced, probably without understanding its significance, the gesture of the raised right hand with bent index finger, which was a sign of respect among the Sassanian nobles," says Ghirshman. Sassanian goblets and textiles found their way into the Shoso-in, that spooky storehouse of the treasures of Japanese emperors at Nara, near Kyoto, and remain there to this day. In fact, when the Sassanian dynasty fell, the imperial family fled to China with their court entertainers, who influenced Oriental actors and musicians with such astonishing upshots as the sculpting of long Persian noses on the masks used in the forerunner of the Japanese Noh theater.

Underneath the glitter, the society was going rotten. The mass of peasants, outright serfs or slaves, not only had to create the wealth from which the state drew brutally high taxes, but also had to give their services for the construction of royal palaces, for building roads, and for quartering the army. At length an event both strange and predictable took place. Late in the fifth century, the peasants rose in what most historians have seen fit to call a communistic revolt, long before Marx. Large-scale protests against oppression had taken place earlier in Egypt, Greece, and Rome, but the uprising in Iran, going beyond protest, had a well-worked-out ideology. It came from the teachings of Manes (A.D. 216?–276?), the Persian prophet who, drawing on Zoroaster, Buddha, and Christ, created the Manichean doctrine of conflict between light and dark, good and evil. To the peasantry, and to some nobles converted to their cause, this translated as equality in the distribution of worldly goods, in this case including women. The peasants struck bloodily, and again and again, looting the property of the nobility, expropriating land, setting the harem women free, fighting an authentic class war. The rebellions were put down, after half a century, by a strong king, Khosrow. But the monarchy was spent in the bitterness of the struggle, and soon toppled.

In all the empires formed in the Middle East from the earliest civilization until the seventh century after Christ, not one had ever bothered to try to conquer the cruel, sandy Arabian peninsula. But between the Bedouins of the desert and their civilized imperial neighbors there was a certain amount of trade and communication. One day in the year 610, a forty-year-old tribesman of Mecca named Mohammed, who had heard of Christ and the God of the Jews, received a revelation from a divinity whom he called Allah (meaning "*the* god"), and with it the body of law called the Koran. Islam, the faith that Mohammed founded, required submission to Allah alone, instead of to the pantheon of gods and goddesses hitherto worshiped in Arabia, and by this principle it deemed all men equal. No thought of separation of church and state intruded here: the prophet, the Koran, and Allah melded into a single theocracy.

In many battles, Mohammed unified Arabia. After he died, in 632, a member of his tribe named Abu Bakr ruled for two years. Then the holy warrior Omar succeeded to the role of caliph, military commander, and Allah's vicar on earth. His Bedouin itched for a war to conquer and convert Persia and Byzantium, a war that would bring booty if they lived and entry into paradise if they died. The Persians could not bring themselves to believe that the oafs from the desert were actually attacking. To one of their delegations, the last Sassanian king, Yazdegerd, sneered, "Aren't you the same people who eat lizards and bury your own children alive?" The Arabs plunged on, crying, "The Koran or the sword!" After he lost the last major battle between the Arabs and the Persians, Yazdegerd was murdered by his own men. By 652, when the Arabs reached the Oxus River, the present northern border of Afghanistan, the conquest of Persia was essentially over. Perhaps the major factor in the easy victory was the receptivity of the oppressed Persian peasants to the Islamic doctrine of the equality of men.

Thus, just about halfway through the long expanse of time between Cyrus the Great and the present, Iran took on a new God and that God's prophet and book, and with them came the nation's still problematic double identity. "Among the great Asiatic nations overthrown by the Arabs, Iran was the first and worst of sufferers, its day having been practically transformed into night," writes the Indian historian Firoze Davar, pointing out that "The symbol of the Zarathustrian faith is the sun; that of Islam is the crescent."

As they went on to conquer all of Asia Minor, North Africa, and even part of Spain, the Arabs put political power ahead of Mohammed's moralistic religion. In his inaugural speech, the first Arab satrap appointed to govern Iran thundered: "By Allah, I see heads before me that are ripe for cutting!" and he beheaded and tortured thousands. The Arabs forced the Persians to use Arabic for records and coinage. The Syrians, history's pawns for so many centuries, seemed proud to absorb Islam and make Damascus its capital. By contrast, the Persians resisted. Among other acts of opposition, they refused to speak Arabic in everyday life, although a scholar named Sibveyh, perceiving that the backward Arabs did not have an authoritative grammar of their own language, contemptuously wrote one, which the Arabs themselves had to use for generations.

At first the Arabs did not press the Persians to become Moslems; rather the Persians adopted Islam to escape the poll tax levied on infidels. But to make a distinction between themselves and the uncouth Arabs, the Persians gradually adopted the schismatic Shiah sect of Islam rather than the orthodox Sunni faith of the Arabs. In 750, the Sunnis, ruling from Damascus, split, and the Persians, by siding with the faction that successfully rebelled against the Damascus caliphate, were able to gain influence in the new court set up in Baghdad. This new caliphate began to let Persians serve as satraps over subdivided Iran, provided that they acknowledged Baghdad's supremacy.

Not for seven centuries did Iran again achieve a national government comparable to the Sassanian empire, but many tough and colorful lesser dynasties rose and ruled in principalities roughly corresponding to such modern provinces as Khorasan, Mazanderan, Sistan, and Isfahan. A ruler in what is now Gilan kept ninety-three wives in ninety-three palaces; one of these ladies was known as "She of the Heavy Earrings." It was an era of entertainment, of books and belly dancing and backgammon; and at the same time a period of cultural renaissance, in which kings patronized scientists and poets. The king who ruled in Bukhara (nowadays in the Uzbek Soviet Socialist Republic, but then included in what was generally recognized as Iran) drew to his court Razi, discoverer of medicinal alcohol and the kidney stone; Avicenna, Bukhara-born physician and philosopher; and Rudaki, the poet.

Pretty soon the kings of some of the principalities were getting so independent of the Arabs that they ordered the mullahs to omit the name of the caliph from the Friday prayers. Finally, toward the end of the tenth century, one of these principalities tumbled the Arab caliphate from power over Iran, and the Arab empire itself collapsed a little later.

But always, in Iran's history, there has been some covetous conqueror in the offing up to the north. The next invaders, about the year 1000, were the Turks, en route in a slow migration from Turkestan, their land of origin in central Asia, to their present realm in Turkey. They spoke, and speak, a language unrelated to the Aryan; theirs is an Altaic cousin of Mongolian, Korean, and Japanese. The newcomers were Sunni Moslems, having been converted by Arabs who had invaded Turkestan centuries before. The first conquering sultan, Mahmud, grabbed northeastern and central Iran, and by his sword converted adjacent India to Islam, which is why Pakistan today is a mostly Sunni Moslem country. Mahmud also gathered to his court cultivated men: the doctor Avicenna; Biruni, who made the first accurate calculations of latitude and longitude; and above all the towering Persian epic poet Ferdowsi, who wrote his masterly *Shahnama* under Mahmud's patronage.

The next wave of Turks, called Seljuks from the name of their tribal leader, descended about 1040, and after fifteen years spread to Baghdad, as unnecessarily zealous "protectors" of the caliph. The fiercest Seljuk king was Alp Arslan, whose mustaches were so long that they had to be tethered back while he was shooting, lest he entangle these handlebars in his bowstring and fire his entire upper lip at the enemy. He captured the emperor of Byzantium in battle near Lake Van, forcing that once potent empire back to Greece and opening to the Turks the country that now bears their name. For a hundred years what had been the Persian Empire was united under these rough and illiterate foreigners, and the Persians proceeded as ever to insinuate into the court and rule the rulers. The renowned vizier Nizam-al-Molk, a wise Machiavelli, laid down policy for Alp Arslan and his successor for thirty years, all the while building theological schools and mosques and an observatory for his friend Omar Khayyam, the mathematician, astronomer, and poet. The Seljuk court reigned first from Nishapur, which happens to be Khayyam's birthplace, then from Rey, now a suburb of Teheran, and finally from Isfahan, today Iran's most charming city. Under the Seljuks Isfahan grew to be a major trade center, with fifty caravanserais; and Nizam-al-Molk and others built there what historian Donald Wilber in *Iran Past and Present* calls "the most important monument of the Islamic centuries": the still-imposing Friday Mosque. The last of the Seljuk sultans constructed for himself a mausoleum whose splendor may be gauged by the fact that architectural historians regard it as the prototype of the Taj Mahal.

The Seljuks struggled through most of their reign against the breakaway Shiite sect of bloodthirsty drug addicts who gave the world the word "assassin," from *hashshashin,* "hashish-eaters." From mountain fortresses, chiefly Alamut (Eagle's Nest) in the Elburz Mountains, the secretive Assassins struck out to kill any political figure opposed to their faith. A charming story has it that the Assassins' original leader, whom Marco Polo called "The Old Man of the Mountains," lured recruits by drugging them with hashish and transporting them to the fortress. They awakened in a fragrant garden overrun with sensuous girls serving wine and fleshly favors. This, the Old Man assured them, was paradise, and they could return to it if killed on one of his missions of murder. One of the Assassins' victims was Nizam-al-Molk, whom they opposed because he enforced the orthodoxy of the Sunni Seljuks.

But it was not the hashish-eaters who broke the Seljuks. The next horrible blow from the north, the most destructive in Iran's history, came in 1220 from Genghis Khan, at the head of 700,000 Mongol tribesmen in the process of creating history's largest empire, which ran from the Pacific Ocean to Central Europe. Angered because some envoys whom he sent to Iran were put to death, Genghis annihilated five cities and looted, murdered, and raped throughout the rest of northern Iran. "Cities of a million were wiped out, and even the dogs and cats were killed," former Member of Parliament Mahmud Ziai, an amateur historian, told me, citing the Mongol invasion as a disaster that still shapes the Iranian mentality. Genghis Khan died in 1227, but his grandson Hulagu led a new invasion in 1251 that made Iran Mongol territory clear to the sea in the south, and from the Indus in the east to beyond the Euphrates in the west. While he was on the warpath, Hulagu considerately obliterated the Assassins.

If the Mongols brought the Iranians woe, they also brought some strange and ironic gifts. One was their own barbarism, another their indifference to religion, another their lack of ideology. Once again the Iranians rushed to aid, indoctrinate, educate, guide—and control—their vanquishers. Though they converted the conquerors to the Sunni faith, the Iranians more and more moved toward Shiah and in the process abandoned a good deal of religious orthodoxy. Iranian artists began to paint miniatures that depicted the human face and figure, a no-no to all Sunnis, and the Mongol courts, hungry for culture, encouraged the practice. Almost as fast as the Mongol disaster struck, it turned into a boon, the beginning of four centuries of Iranian brilliance and high civilization.

For their capital the Mongols chose Tabriz, and built mosques and schools there. The adored poet Saadi flourished under Hulagu, and the equally adored poet Hafez flourished in Shiraz until the Mongol dynasty faded away, through weaker and weaker rulers, after about a century.

In this long and exotic story of the formation of today's Iran, only two epochs remain to separate the last of the Mongols and the first of the Pahlavis. One was a period of religious intensity coupled with splendor and power that compelled respect from China to Europe. The second was a slide into decadence that left Iran with nowhere to go but up.

The splendor came with the Safavids, Turkish-descended tribesmen who dominated the parts of Iran that are now Azerbaijan and eastern Turkey. In 1490—just as far to the west Columbus prepared his ships for the voyage to America—control of the clan fell to a thirteen-year-old named Ismail. The boy proved to be a leader of men. Operating out of Tabriz, he captured and unified Iran to the Caucasus, the Euphrates, and the Oxus River in the northeast. Genealogists managed to prove that this new Turkish shah, who also had Arab and Greek blood, descended from the pure-Persian Sassanians, which together with his devout Shiism made him a divine-right king.

Now everyone in Iran converted to Shiah—on pain of death. The nation became the island of Shiah surrounded by Sunni domains that it is today. The establishment of Shiah polarized Iran in particular with Turkey, where the Ottoman tribe of Turks, having suppressed the last of the Seljuks, had founded the belligerent Ottoman Empire, which ultimately reached as far as Austria and lasted until 1918. Without winning any battles against the Ottomans, the Safavid shahs, relying on the strength of their faith and the religious unity that it conferred upon Iran, managed to avoid incorporation into the Ottoman Empire.

Because of the Ottoman threat, the Safavids moved their capital to Kazvin, just west of Teheran, for most of the sixteenth century, and finally, right around 1600, to Isfahan. There, roughly contemporary with Elizabeth I of England, Suleiman the Magnificent of Turkey, Emperor Akbar of India, and the shogun Ieyasu of Japan, reigned the most renowned of all Iranian kings, Shah Abbas the Great.

Militarily, Shah Abbas recovered parts of Azerbaijan and Mesopotamia lost to the Ottomans, and during Russia's "Time of Troubles" he advanced farther into Georgia than any Iranian before or since. In Mogul India, he penetrated to Kandahar, now a city of Afghanistan. But his own subjects, and the Europeans who now visited Iran in growing numbers, knew Shah Abbas as a charismatic reformer. He liked to walk unassumingly in the streets and bazaars, or to drop unannounced into teahouses and even private residences for a meal. He induced Iranian men to adopt the custom of shaving; at the same time he foresightedly urged them to give up the custom of smoking, introduced a little before by Portuguese traders in the Persian Gulf. He collected art; his blue-and-white Chinese porcelains, alive with dragons, birds, and lions, fill a splendid room at the Archaeological Museum in Teheran. But the preeminent bequest that Shah Abbas left to Iran and to the world was a work of art on a larger scale, a great creation in green and gold and turquoise: the quintessentially Persian city that bears the euphonious name Isfahan.

I first surveyed Isfahan from the top of a minaret, a privilege arranged by a small bribe to the custodian of the glorious seminary-mosque called Madresseh Madar-e Shah. A paraphrase from Coleridge ran through my head: In Isfahan did Shah Abbas a playful pleasure dome decree, where Zayandeh, the gentle river, ran. Isfahan's beauty is not the beauty of stateliness; it is the beauty of color and delight. The eye travels up the wooden column of an Isfahan palace not in awe at its perfect proportions (as in a Greek column) but in amusement at its absurd slenderness and its exaggerated capital. The celebrated bridges over the Zayandeh give pleasure in their harmony, their color, their Orientalism—and their fun. Mosques and minarets ravish the eye. And that's not all. In Isfahan's stores you can buy the tastiest nougats in the world.

A mosque is a contrary sort of building: it has an inside but not an outside. That is to say, mosque architects, rarely wasting time on exterior form or decoration, have traditionally been content to let the outside look like a plain high wall—a wall that is usually half hidden by the buildings of a bazaar or some habitation built smack against it. One does not properly reach a mosque until one goes through a gate in the wall, along a passage, and out into the rectangular courtyard, open to the sky and usually at least 150 feet in the longest dimension. In the original Arabic mosque, what one sees while standing in the courtyard is the four double-arcaded walls that form it, with a square spire and some minarets. One wall, with deeper arcades than the others, is oriented so that a person facing it faces Mecca.

The basic Iranian mosque (although almost all mosques vary from the basic in one way or another) is broadly like the Arabic except that it adds the Sassanian ivan. Essentially a portal in a large bay, an ivan looks like a vertical cross section of the interior of a pointed dome; that is, the side walls curve inward, and the ceiling is a hemi-hemisphere. In an Iranian mosque, ivans indent one, two, three, or all four of the walls, and lead to the mazes of vaulted space (prayer rooms, seminaries) that form the outer structure of the mosque. In the Mecca-facing wall, the ivan, which is the largest of the set and is often flanked by minarets, leads to a sanctuary roofed by the vast, high dome that is the trademark of Persian architecture. In the back wall of the sanctuary (as in the back walls of Arabic mosques) there is an altar and a pulpit.

The most prodigious of all the mosques in Iran—in the sense of combining antiquity, grandeur, classical plan, and the architectural styles of the Seljuk, Mongol, and Safavid dynasties (running from 1037 to 1729)—is Isfahan's Masjid-e Jomeh, Friday Mosque. One mosque or another has stood on this site from shortly after the Moslem conquest. Nizam-al-Molk, serving as vizier to the third Seljuk king, began the construction of what now stands. He built the Mecca-facing southwest sanctuary, long since bereft of interior tile and left with the naked brick structure showing—leading architecture critic Robert Byron to exclaim over the "Twelve massive tiers [that] engage in a Promethean struggle with the weight of the dome." Nizam's motive was to honor the shah, which led a rival court flatterer to build another domed sanctuary 190 feet to the northeast. In both cases the designers shaped the domes empirically, following models they knew would hold up; modern architects say that their form is within 2 percent of what a computer would prescribe. The accretions of later dynasties walled in the rest of the mosque in double arcades, with giant ivans leading to both sanctuaries and forming towering façades in the northwest and southwest walls as well. Back of the walls on all sides are ghostly chambers with low ceilings supported by alternately square and cylindrical columns.

Christian churches, to fit their stern theology, are often gray and stony; but Moslems seem to get their fill of sternness in the desert, and mosques are brilliantly colorful, especially in Iran. Glorious glazed tiles cover the ivans and courtyard arcades of the Friday Mosque, and since they are laid as a mosaic, each piece cut to the shape of the touch of color that it adds, they represent the finest technique. But the tiles have fallen from many surfaces in this old mosque; the place to find stupendous color is in the much newer Shah Mosque of Isfahan.

What a generous place the Shah Mosque is! Everyone who visits it is temporarily a billionaire in the color that he possesses through his eyes. The entrance ivan—designed to be magnificent because it leads to the mosque through the arcaded wall of Isfahan's grand main square—is a masterpiece all by itself. Two thirds as tall as the 108-foot minarets that flank it, this portal is an orchestration of brilliant color on every visible suface except the marble wainscot at the bottom. A triple rope molding of turquoise outlines the pointed arch of the ivan. At each side are ceramic tapestries in predominantly blue and white patterns that tantalize and baffle the eye: rosettes, peacocks, spirals, stylized leaves and flowers. The half-dome is a masonry marvel of small Gothic arches whose points angle toward the center of the vault, so that the peak of each arch forms a support for the common leg of two arches above it, in a continual narrowing of the vault's diameter. The effect is a little like stalactites in a cave. Tiles of ultramarine, rose, yellow, and white cover the spherical triangles formed by these arches in patterns of flowers, vase shapes, and arabesques.

Inside the courtyard of the enormous mosque—eighteen million bricks went into its making—"enchantment takes effect and critical faculties are dulled [as Roger Stevens puts it]. Only prejudice born of too much knowledge could fail to succumb to those encircling walls of dazzling blue, those soaring minarets, their reflections in the tank of the great court, or the deep shade of the ivans which reveal man's pigmy stature. . . . The hand may be the King's but the glory, there can be little doubt about it, is to God."

The Mecca-side ivan leads to the sanctuary, covered by an onion-shaped dome that rises to 170 feet from street level. Since the architects, with exemplary restraint, deemed that a mere 121 feet was sufficient height for the interior, they provided an inner dome as well as an outer one. (What ghosts live in that black space between the domes?) The inner dome is not pointed but parabolic, so that if you stand directly beneath the golden star in its center and clap your hands, the sound will return to you, a split second later, concentrated to the intensity of a rifle shot. The ceiling tilework is breathtaking, floral designs in gold on a ground of deep blue. Windows with grilles of arabesques perforate the drum beneath the dome, and when a bright sun creates arabesque shadows that fall against the arabesques of the tiles on the walls, the effect is deliriously beautiful. To be inside a fine Iranian mosque, to see the play of geometry as you move among its vaults and columns, to let the eye delight in the patterned color that over-whelms the banal architecture—to do these things is to remember that "paradise" is one of those words that Persian gave to English.

The Zayandeh is a puny river that originates in the Zagros Mountains 120 miles west of Isfahan and dies in a desert sink 75 miles east of the city. But it is the greatest river in the central Iranian plateau, and it has given human beings cause to live in the Isfahan area since the reign of the Babylonian king Nebuchadnezzar, who established a colony of Jews in the section of northeast Isfahan that now surrounds the Friday Mosque. (Jews still live there.) But it was the sophisticated Shah Abbas who shaped Isfahan to its outlines of today.

Shah Abbas first platted an enormous plaza, 1,674 feet long and 540 feet wide, which he conceived as a park, a place of assembly, and, not least, a polo ground. He chose this land because it had some pre-Islamic history as a public square, but its orientation created problems for the planners of the Shah Mosque at the south end; to make it face Mecca they had to create a 45-degree left turn in the passageway between the portal on the square and the courtyard of the mosque.

For his own palace in the western wall of the plaza, Shah Abbas put up a building so ridiculous that it greatly adds to Isfahan's delights; even the name sounds playful: Ali Qapu (Grand Gate). The front looks like a Medici palace surmounted by a quaint grandstand; the back is a precocious high-rise in New Mexican cliff-dweller style. Both parts have flat roofs, not domes, which together with the elongated capitals of the columns show that the building was derived from Persepolis rather than from any Sassanian or Islamic source. The king actually used the high porch in the front to watch races and polo games; now it is a rickety veranda with eighteen thin, worm-eaten wooden columns that bend and lean. The back of the palace is a romantic warren of small domed chambers, passageways, stairs that twist and turn, doors five feet high, unexpected balconies, and, way up on the sixth floor, little banquet rooms; one can easily imagine the hanky-panky that went on there. Artistically, Ali Qapu's attraction is its frescoes, though many are peeling or flaking; the European style of the paintings in the throne room, behind the porch, reflects the fact that Shah Abbas often entertained European visitors in this "brick boot-box," as Byron dubbed it. One caller was the Englishman Sir Anthony Sherley, who departed deeply impressed by Abbas: "His furniture of mind [is] infinitely royal, wise, valiant, liberall, temperate, merciful, and [he is] an exceeding lover of Justice, embracing royally other virtues, as farre from pride and vanitie, as from all other unprincely signs or acts."

The gifts of Shah Abbas to Isfahan include one more setting for pleasure: the boulevard called Chahar Bagh (Four Gardens), Isfahan's main thoroughfare—a street of cinemas and banks, heavily damaged in 1978. The young men of Isfahan, who do not seem to have much to do in the evening but stroll and eat nougats, like to promenade under the plane trees of this avenue. Going south, Chahar Bagh crosses the Zayandeh River on one of those Isfahan bridges that for architectural fantasy outclass the bridges over the Arno in Florence. This one, Shah Abbas's Bridge of the Thirty-Three Arches, is 660 feet long, but it crosses only a little running water, the rest being grassy marsh. The thirty-three arches support not only the roadway but also, on each side of it, running arcades of one hundred arches. Walls separate these arcades from the automobile traffic, which puts vehicular traffic into a sort of open-roofed tunnel, but leaves charming outer walkways for pedestrians.

After the glory of Isfahan, after Shah Abbas, writes historian Richard N. Frye in *Persia,* "All that was necessary to be said had been said in an incomparable fashion; all that was to be created had already been made with consummate skill." The culture seemed to have no choice but to decline. The great shah himself, revealing the obverse of his character, had one of his sons murdered and two others blinded, and kept five hundred executioners busy. As the dynasty weakened, the new rulers in Afghanistan built that country's one and only empire, and one day in 1722 the Afghan emperor Mahmud appeared in Isfahan to receive the abdication of the last Safavid.

What followed was not only bloody but also bloody confusing. Some of the shahs raised money by letting princes purchase fleas gathered from the monarch's garments: to kill a flea that had threatened the royal person was a prized privilege. Famines followed wars that followed invasions. A general named Nadir emerged from the power struggle to throw out the Afghanis. Roaring on eastward, he raided the Mogul court in Delhi and returned to Iran with the celebrated Peacock Throne. This hard-bitten conqueror was surprisingly interested in matters of the soul, though apparently he was neither a Moslem nor a Christian (which was a possibility: he had the Bible translated into Persian). "I'd invent a new religion, if I only had the time," he once said. Nadir Shah was murdered in 1747. After twelve years of warfare among claimants to the throne, a surprisingly kindly ruler named Karim Khan Zand imposed twenty-one years of peace before his death in 1779.

The testicles of a young tribal leader named Agha Mohammed had a lot to do with the next phase of Iran's history, because they were cut off by his enemies, making him ultimately the bitterest and cruelest monarch of all. He was a member of the Turkish-descended Qajar tribe, which centered in Mazanderan. "His rise to power," writes historian Peter Avery in *Modern Iran,* "was marked by pyramids of skulls, holocausts, mass blindings"—he put out the eyes of twenty thousand citizens of Kerman who would not bow to him. But just before he was assassinated in 1797, he succeeded in reforming and uniting Iran sufficiently to found the Qajar dynasty, move the capital to Teheran, and assure the throne to his successor (in this case perforce not a son, but a nephew), Fath Ali Shah. Overcompensating for his uncle, Fath Ali fathered two thousand princes and princesses during his thirty-seven-year reign, and had no time left over to face what became Iran's main nineteenth-century problem: the expansionist Russians and the sticky-fingered British. In 1835 he died—in bed, one presumes. The shah who reigned for most of the rest of the century—he was assassinated in 1896—was Nasir al-Din, whose passion was to go to Europe and take in world's fairs: Vienna 1873, Paris 1878 and 1889.

For centuries Europeans had thought Persia, as they called it, to be a great power, but the Qajars quickly set them straight. Czarist Russia got back Georgia in 1801, and by 1882, taking Tashkent, Samarkand, and Bukhara, had pushed Iran back to its present border east of the Caspian. The Ottoman Empire regained Mesopotamia and parts of modern Turkey. The British, now rulers of India, pushed the Iranians out of the buffer state Afghanistan during a brief war in 1856.

Worse than losing territory, the Qajars lost sovereignty within Iran. The second half of the nineteenth century was the unabashed heyday of economic imperialism, and Britain, guarding the sea routes of the empire, and Russia, looking for an Indian Ocean port, moved in on Iran. Both demanded and got extraterritoriality (the right to apply their own laws to their own citizens within Iran). British entrepreneurs obtained a concession to found the Imperial Bank of Persia. For their part, the Russians also founded a bank, dominated the commerce of Azerbaijan, and induced Nasir al-Din to officer his army with Russians, creating the famous Persian Cossacks. Nasir al-Din needed some kind of force, for he was losing control of some of his own subjects, namely the tribes—the Qashqais, the Bakhtiaris, the Kurds, the Turkomans— whose kings increased their power as fast as the Qajar throne relinquished it.

As the tiles fell and smashed in Isfahan's neglected mosques, the Qajars took Iran to ruin. Muzaffar as-Din, Nasir al-Din's son and successor, sold out Iran's most vital interests merely to get money to travel in Europe. At length came the inevitable revolution. Muzaffar Shah gave in after nothing so serious as a war, but merely a *bast*, a protest expressed by taking refuge, in this case in the spacious grounds of the British Embassy. The resulting constitution of 1906, modeled on the Belgian charter, established a parliament to rule Iran with the king as figurehead. (This gesture of reform and independence did not impress the Russians and the British, who blithely signed a convention that formalized their hegemony over Iran: the north to Russia, the center a neutral zone, the south to Britain—which discovered oil there the next year.) Finally a shah named Ahmad succeeded to the throne to preside over the end of "that last medievalism," as E. A. Bayne puts it. The Qajars were decadent to the finish line: Ahmad was known as the Grocery Boy Shah, because he bought up the whole grain crop during a famine and sold it to the starving at holdup prices. Iranians felt no regrets when the recent Shah's father sent Ahmad packing in 1925.

4

The Pahlavi Dynasty

❊

His Imperial Majesty Mohammed Reza Pahlavi, erstwhile King of
Kings and late Light of the Aryans, was born a commoner, and his
father, who started his working life as a soldier at the age of fifteen,
was an even commoner commoner. He got the throne by seizing it.
Foreigners made fun of this fact; Iranians, knowing that in the long
reaches of their history many an upstart had toppled many a king,
were resigned to accepting the coup. By the same token, anyone want-
ing to overthrow the Shah seemed to have the authorization of history.
And in 1979 that's just what happened, except that with the institution
of monarchy dead, no one proposed to start a new dynasty.

The Pahlavis themselves never made any attempt to hide their
background. "Our father was of very low origins," said Princess Ashraf,
the Shah's twin sister. Added the Shah suavely: "In Iran, as in America,
it has always been possible for exceptional people to rise from the
bottom to the top. My father provided an example of just that."

Indeed. The Shah's father was one of the thirty-two children born
to the seven wives of Colonel Abbas Ali Khan, an officer of the regular
Iranian army, stationed at the village of Alasht in the mountains northeast of Teheran. There, in a thatch-roofed house, still partly standing,
Reza Khan was born on March 16, 1878. The colonel died eight months
later, and in the spring of 1879 the baby's mother took him on a snowy,
terrifying journey through the mountains to Teheran.

There they lived with one of her brothers, who eventually managed
to place the child in the home of a local general. Tutors came to this
house and taught the general's children, as well as Reza Khan, how
to read and write; the much-repeated allegation that he was illiterate
is wrong. When Reza Khan reached man size at fifteen, his uncle enlisted him in the Persian Cossacks, then a force of eleven thousand
men commanded by Russians loaned by the czar. One of his first assign-

ments was as orderly at the German Embassy, which still preserves some yellowing passes with his spidery signature. At eighteen, a six-footer in Cossack mustache and caracul hat, he went out on horse against the nomad tribesmen who perennially challenged the sybaritic rule of Nasir al-Din Shah. In one battle, surrounded by Lur tribesmen on all sides and poltroons within the lines, he kicked aside his gunners, took over their Maxim machine guns, and fired so murderously that he broke the encirclement and won the sobriquet Reza Khan Maxim. By 1920 he was a general and one of the most distinguished officers in Iran. He had also begun to suspect that his true enemy was his foolish king, rather than the lowly tribesmen he was sent to fight.

Reza kept these doubts mostly to himself through the worsening national disintegration under the last of the Qajars. By 1914, the recent Shah once pointed out, the breakdown was so bad that "to travel from Teheran to Mashhad in northeastern Persia you had to go by way of Russia, to avoid the decrepit and bandit-infested roads. To go from Teheran to the southwestern province of Khuzistan, you had to pass through Turkey and Iraq." During World War I, foreigners—Turks, Russians, Germans, Britons, and Afghans—marched through Iran, and Reza had no power to stop them; in frustration he drank strong liquor and once got into a dagger fight that left him with a scar on his nose. His first wife, a humble woman whom he married in 1903, had given birth only to a daughter. Yearning for a son, in 1915 he took a second wife, the sixteen-year-old daughter of an army officer from a prominent family. Four years later he had the pleasure of dropping in on some fellow officers to say, "Last night twins were born, and one was a boy"—the boy who was to become the greatest shah on earth.

By then the Turks, defeated along with the Germans, had pulled back out of Iran, and the October Revolution had temporarily distracted the Russians from masterminding Iran through the Cossacks who still commanded Reza's regiment. Thus the British came out of the war dominant in the Persia that they had always coveted as one of a "chain of vassal states reaching from the Mediterranean to the Pamirs" (in Lord Curzon's words). British greed was all the greater because this particular vassal-elect contained the Anglo-Persian Oil Company's reserves of petroleum, discovered in 1908 and vital for the British navy. Inconveniently, Iran did not care to fall in with Britain's plans, specifically resisting an agreement proposed in 1919 for Britain to supply Iran with loans and military aid in return for virtual domination of the country. Just at this point the perennial Russian threat to Iran took another color: Red.

By threatening to withdraw their troops from Iran, the British in early 1921 tried to use the new Communist danger to induce Iran to accept the 1919 proposal. The thought of thus being left exposed to the Russians caused the Qajar shah Ahmad to announce that he wanted to move south. Ostensibly to provide the shah with an escort, a brilliant young journalist and politician named Seyyid al-Din Zia Tabatabaie, pro-British and anti-Communist, took measures to reorganize the Persian Cossacks, left in shambles by the departure of their czarist officers. For these troops Tabatabaie got British boots, British ammunition, British money, and a British liaison officer. To lead them he chose the smoldering Iranian nationalist Reza Khan. On February 21, 1921, the force, two thousand strong, marched on Teheran—not to escort the shah south but rather to depose his prime minister and install an anti-Communist, pro-British government. That afternoon Ahmad Shah named the young journalist prime minister, and on April 30 he made Reza Khan minister of war and commander in chief of the armed forces.

Now it turned out that Reza Khan might have had his fingers crossed when dealing with Tabatabaie and the British. After three months he deposed and deported Tabatabaie. Warming to his work, he ran in a series of straw-man prime ministers and made them take the rap for a number of decisions displeasing to the British. Yearning for purely Persian forces comparable to the Cossacks or to Britain's South Persian Rifles, Reza detached those outfits from foreign command and began to build up, with French advice, an army that finally numbered five divisions. He built small-arms factories. He attacked the tribesmen who had long collaborated with the British, reducing the power of their chiefs. The British withdrew their troops southward to the oil fields.

Reza came right out and made himself prime minister on October 28, 1923, and at once told Shah Ahmad to go off to France and have a good time. Reza deeply admired Kemal Atatürk—who by happenstance became president of Turkey the day after Reza became prime minister of Iran—and in imitation broached the idea of making Iran a republic. The Iranian clergy pronounced republicanism to be a major sin against the Koran. *Enshallah,* said Reza, God wills it, and on December 13, 1925, at the age of forty-eight, the rough-edged general forced the Iranian Parliament to make him the new shah of Iran. Ahmad, thus deposed, tossed rubies at the chorus girls of Deauville and Biarritz for a few more years, and died of some fantastically expensive illness in the American Hospital in Paris.

Until then, most Iranians went by their given names alone; one of Reza's first decrees commanded everyone to take a family name, and for his own dynasty he chose the name Pahlavi. This is the word used to denote the ancient form of the Persian language, and Reza's use of it linked him with pre-Islamic Persian glory—but he had his doubts about his choice. Once, at Persepolis, he drew aside archaeologist Ernst Herzfeld and asked him candidly, "What does the word Pahlavi *really* mean?" Reza also assumed the royal titles Shahanshah, Shadow of the Almighty, Vice-Regent of God, and Center of the Universe—rather grand for a monarch who had to borrow money from the merchants in the bazaar to give a dinner for a visiting foreign dignitary. But Reza had in mind some profound reforms, and swiftly set out to make them.

His most astonishing early success was loosening the hold of foreigners on Iran. He banned extraterritoriality. With the help of an American financial adviser, he ended the power of foreigners to collect Iranian customs and to issue the nation's banknotes. Though ardently opposed to the "Bolsheviks," and the promulgator of a tough anti-Communist law in 1931, he kept on good terms with Lenin, who pulled Russian troops out of Iran and gave Iran valuable commercial rights in the Caspian Sea.

The name Reza derives from a revered Shiite Moslem saint, and Reza Shah made it the middle name of all his seven sons as a token of his devotion to the faith. But as king, Reza Shah found Moslem tradition to be a stubborn barrier in the way of modernizing Iran, and he fought the mullahs right and left. He suppressed their bloody passion plays, banished dervishes from the cities, required licenses of those wearing religious garb. Against Koranic laws he banned the clothes of old Persia—flowing pantaloons, long vests, and turbans or tarbooshes for men; pantaloons, chemises, and veils for women. Within six months of his decree, men were wearing Western dress and the "Pahlavi cap," a paramilitary headpiece that broke religious regulations against praying in any kind of hat with a brim that prevents the head from touching the ground. (Later, men switched to derbies and straw boaters.) Also in defiance of the mullahs, Reza Shah raised the marriage age for women from nine to fifteen, forced men to tell prospective brides how many wives they already had, started coeducational schools, and made it possible for foreigners to visit some historic mosques. Against Koranic bans on necropsy, he authorized courses in anatomy in medical schools, and once forced his cabinet ministers to accompany him in viewing two cadavers in vats. Islam's resentments against the Pahlavis, which burst into flame in 1978, go back a long way.

Reza Shah also decreed Iran to be the official designation of the country, that being the proper name in the Persian language, and ordered the post office to send back mail addressed to Persia. He replaced the Moslem calendar with a modernized form of the ancient Zoroastrian calendar. He founded the University of Teheran, Iran's first, and encouraged the importation of Western music, architecture, and cinema. He introduced metric measure, the recording of deeds for land, and the keeping of vital statistics.

Brutally, with veritable massacres, Reza Shah brought under central control the sheiks who led the hitherto autonomous nomadic tribes, then composing one third of Iran's population. To stop brigandage, he set up such a rigid gendarmerie that for a few years travelers had to go through police checks upon both entering and leaving every village. The shah's spies kept an eye on every mailbox. The Parliament ceased to have power. To one deputy who had asked a fortuneteller if he would be reelected, Reza Shah said: "You should have come and asked me. You will not be reelected."

But even as he brutalized, he built. The government put up cement, sugar, and textile mills, constructed roads and ports, established an Iranian national bank to supplant the foreign banks. Above all, using not foreign loans but rather crushing taxes on tea and sugar, Reza Shah built the wondrous Trans-Iranian Railway from the Persian Gulf to the Caspian Sea. This line crosses both of Iran's grand mountain ranges, requiring 4,000 bridges and 224 tunnels, some of them spirals inside mountains. Not only that, the old shah, unlike Mussolini, really made the trains run on time.

"Reza Shah started the transformation of Iran—and starting is very important," one Iranian oil executive remarked to me. The old shah's own summary of his achievements went like this: "I have made the Iranians realize that when they get up in the morning they must go to work and work hard all day long." He worked hard, too, and rewarded himself. Ultimately he seized a quarter of Iran's arable land as his own, becoming probably the biggest landholder in Asia at the time. Apart from a little French wine and a pipe of opium, however, he lived a spare life and rejected comforts. His office contained a desk, a chair, a sofa, a rug, and a map on the wall. He slept on a mattress on the floor. He dressed in a simple Cossack uniform, with down-at-the-heel boots. Tall, bald, hatchet-faced, he carried on the affairs of state while pacing back and forth, his fingers endlessly flipping the beads of the Moslem rosary that he always held in one hand. He imposed his will by calculated furies, expressed through eyes that "could make a strong man shrivel up inside," as his son once put it. One day he arrived at the Ministry of Finance at opening hour, ordered all the doors locked, and fired everyone who arrived late, including the minister. Another offending minister suffered defenestration; the powerful, broad-shouldered shah simply picked the man up and bum's-rushed him through the office window. He stomped into a barracks once, and with his cane smashed all the windowpanes. "They were filthy," he told the officer in command. "Have them replaced by tomorrow morning." When an unknown Turkoman tribesman had the effrontery to outride a Persian officer at the races, Reza Shah summoned the winner, and in full view of the diplomatic corps, "delivered a short lecture and proceeded to kick the tribesman in the stomach," as the *Times* of London described it. "My father relied more on punishment than he did on reward," said his son.

Not surprisingly, he also said: "My father influenced me more by far than has anyone else." Reza Shah believed that a king needed some harsh and unsavory qualities: suspicion of everyone, distrust of clemency, willingness to hit first. The old man adored his son and heir— and at the same time doubted that the tearful little daydreamer was material for a king. For one thing, the boy was sickly. Just after he became crown prince at the same Golestan Palace ceremony in which Reza placed the crown of Iran on his own head, Mohammed, aged six and a half, nearly died of typhoid, and in the next few years he came close to death from diphtheria and malaria. The Shah remembered many pleasant hours in his boyhood—snowball fights, bicycle polo, constructing things with his Meccano set, playing cops and robbers in the palace's spooky underground passages—but his father made him take the rank of colonel at seven and turned him early toward the military life. Mohammed was given a household separate from his mother, and put under a governess. He went to a military elementary school created for him, with olive drab uniforms, much stress on drill, and a student body of twenty drawn from among sons of high officers and government officials. Mohammed was to be treated more harshly than the other boys, the old shah said, but at the same time Reza saw to it that his son should be treated with the deference due a future king. One can imagine the light taps the prince got from his boxing instructor, a man who did not deem it necessary to remove his pince-nez during the bouts. With hourly sessions beginning just after Mohammed became crown prince, and with long lunchtime lessons after the boy was nine, the old shah drove home his concepts of royal omnipotence. "Give the impression that you control everything," he told his son. "Trust nobody." From the age of eight, Mohammed attended meetings of the shah's high council, and took the salute at parades and inspections. But sometimes, when they were completely alone, his father would "play light-heartedly" and "sing me little songs."

Reza Shah's reluctant admiration of the West dictated that his son should go to prep school in Europe, and in 1932, Mohammed, conveyed in a canary-yellow Hispano-Suiza, drew up in front of Le Rosey Institute in the town of Rolle on Lake Geneva. He at once indicated to the other students that they must stand at attention in the royal presence, whereupon an American kid beat the daylights out of the princeling. Rising from the pavement, the future shah pushed back his hair, straightened his shirt, smiled broadly, and shook his conqueror's hand.

In that ivy-covered chateau the prince made himself popular, grew physically strong at soccer, tennis, and track sports, got his only taste of democratic life, and learned history, geography, natural science, and mathematics. His room was often full of friends, but he was sometimes lonely, too, when his physician-bodyguard made him stay at the school while the other boys went off to holiday dances. The prince's closest friend was not a fellow student but a youth ten years older than he, Ernest Perron, son of the school's handyman. Mohammed befriended this humble boy, butt of the other students' jokes, and in return Ernest revealed a talent that intrigued Mohammed: he was a capable poet.

Meeting a poet was just the kind of disaster that Reza Shah feared would happen to his son in an unmilitary Western boarding school. When the prince returned to Iran in the spring of 1936, Reza Shah rushed him back into uniform at the Iranian army's Military College, organized by French advisers. With thirty other cadets, Mohammed underwent commando training, made forced marches, studied strategy and tactics. Lunchtimes, the old shah resumed his counseling on the art and practice of kingship. Two years in the academy was Mohammed's last formal schooling. About this time he learned English, from an Iranian English literature professor at the University of Teheran. He graduated as a second lieutenant and took up duty as an inspector in the army. His father pursued the kingship course by taking his son all over Iran. They toured in a venerable Rolls-Royce along roads cleared of other traffic by orders sent out the day before. If they stayed overnight in a village, the townspeople took care to kill all dogs—Reza Shah was a light sleeper. Constantly, the king posed actual problems of statecraft to his son, for practice in decision-making. Sample question: Should that trouble-making plotter Mohammed Mossadegh be released from prison? Sorry for the shah's sick and aging opponent, the prince said yes—which is how Mossadegh got his freedom to try to overthrow his pardoner fifteen years later.

Amid such trials, the prince also frolicked. "I was a popular crown prince," he told me. At nineteen, he began to build what became a respectable international legend for liking fast cars, fast horses, and fast women. Time for the lad to marry, the old shah decided, his chief concern being that his heir must also have an heir. Iran's embassies made inquiries around the Moslem world, and soon singled out a lovely bride of royal blood, Fawzia, daughter of Egypt's King Fuad and sister of his successor, the late fat King Faruk. Without a word to his son, and with a bluntness "perhaps better adapted to engineering projects than to affairs of the heart" (as the prospective groom put it later), Reza Shah proposed to Fuad that their children should marry. The Egyptian decided that all things considered, such as Reza Shah's oil and his military power, the two royal families should be united by marriage. Each monarch sent a photograph of his offspring to be shown to the other's child, so that the bride and groom could recognize one another at the wedding. "The first thing I knew, I was betrothed," recalled the Shah. He married Fawzia twice, first, pro forma, in Cairo, and second, for real, in Teheran. Greeting Fawzia, Reza Shah waved a hand toward his dowdy capital and intoned, "My child, your country and your people!"

After that, it was first the good news and then the bad news. The good news, early in 1940, was that Fawzia was pregnant. Reza Shah exulted. The bad news, in October, was that the baby was a girl. Reza Shah picked up his cane and cholerically battered the top of his desk. In all the Qajar families, the birth of a princess had preceded the birth of the vital male heir—and all the Qajar crown princes had come to disastrous ends as kings. The lesson, as Reza Shah deduced it, was that "it is a bad sign when a girl is born in a court before a boy."

"For reasons still obscure to medical science, Queen Fawzia bore only one child; thus unfortunately no male heir issued from our marriage," wrote the Shah in his autobiography. To this shortcoming Fawzia added another: snobbishness toward the Pahlavis. Once, when Taj-ol-Moluk, the queen mother, became confused while seating guests at a formal dinner, Fawzia was distinctly heard to titter. This new empress of Iran never learned to speak Persian properly. Soon Taj-ol-Moluk and the princesses Shams and Ashraf contrived a soiree at which they induced Mohammed to dance with a series of beautiful courtesans, leaving Fawzia a wallflower. That night the young queen moved to separate quarters in the palace, and in 1947 she went to Cairo, where she got a divorce the next year.

Reza Shah proclaimed neutrality upon the outbreak of World War II, but geography and history were against him, and before the war was well under way it shattered his life's work and forced him into exile, a strong man broken by the fates.

When Germany invaded the Soviet Union in June 1941, Iran at once turned into the most strategic bridgehead in the world. How were Britain and the United States going to send arms and supplies to the eastern front? The Germans controlled the Black Sea; ice blocked Murmansk on the Arctic Ocean for much of the year; Germany's ally Japan ruled the Sea of Japan and therefore Vladivostok. But in Iran—what irony!—the Allies found just the route they needed: Reza Shah's brand-new railroad, which he had cunningly built from north to south, avoiding all big cities, so that foreigners could never exploit it. (His concern had been that the West could force Iran to be part of a rail link between Europe and India, or even Singapore.)

Not for this reason alone did Iran find itself so uncomfortably in the strategic spotlight. Hitler aspired not only to bring Russia to its knees; he wanted Iran, too. The German offensive through the Caucasus Mountains in the Soviet Union was aimed at ultimately seizing the Iranian oil fields and Abadan refinery, as well as at getting within striking distance of India. More irony: the old shah had thought of the Germans as his friends. In the late 1930s, still obsessed by fear of the British and the Russians, he had invited the Germans to strengthen themselves in Iran as a counterforce. A joke went around that he had insisted on calling the country Iran, which means Aryan, because Hitler was threatening annihilation to non-Aryans. Actually, Nazi propagandists made much of the "common Aryanism" of the Germans and the Iranians. The links between the two countries were many. German engineers, supplying expertise for Iran's railroad, chemical, machinery, and airline industries, lived all over the country. Iranian students went in droves to German universities. The army's training was French, but its equipment German. Iran's number-one trading partner was Germany, and the largest foreign colony in Teheran, 470 families, was German.

Tactlessly, the Allies demanded, rather than suggested, the expulsion of these Germans. The king might have been open to the argument that the Allies needed Iran as a route for reinforcing the Red Army in order to save Iran itself—indeed, it turned out that only the war goods shipped into the U.S.S.R. via Iran prevented German conquest. As it was, Reza Shah got his back up, fearing that the Shadow of the Almighty and the Center of the Universe might have to take orders from "some little British or Russian captain." He deluded himself into hoping that if Hitler conquered the Caucasus, the Führer would return to Iran lands there and in Turkmenistan that had been Persian in the nineteenth century. Reza Shah disregarded the sensible advice of his son, which was to throw in with the Allies. Thus it was that what Reza Shah feared most came about. On August 25, 1941, the British navy sailed into Khorramshahr and sank Iran's four-warship navy, and the Red Army took over the northern province of Azerbaijan so swiftly that the Iranian army did not even have time to retreat, much less fight. Reza Shah found himself just where he had been at the beginning of his career, his country occupied by Britons and Russians, and his fighting forces a shambles. And it turned out that the Germans he had admitted to Iran were fully prepared to sabotage his railroad and his ports: two German freighters pretending to be trapped in the Persian Gulf proved to be floating bombs that were blown up by their crews (but failed to block any important channel).

The awful realization of his deception and failure broke the old man's spirit. He wrote out a letter of abdication and showed it to his prime minister, Mohammed Ali Forughi. It is too vengeful? he asked in effect. Yes, said Forughi; you must have the courage to avoid irritating the British and the Russians if you wish your son to succeed to the throne. Forughi devised a softer note. Reza signed it, and set out by Rolls-Royce for the port of Bandar Abbas. British warships took him to the Indian Ocean island of Mauritius. After a couple of years he moved to Johannesburg, where he died in 1944.

At three-fifteen in the afternoon of September 16, 1941, the day that his father abdicated, the new Shah, twenty-one years old, presented himself before deputies gathered in the Parliament chamber, and swore "to reign accordingly and in conformity with established laws."

This freshly minted monarch had almost no power, and what power he had mattered little either to Iran or to the world. "I found myself plunged into a sea of trouble," he later recalled. In the next dozen years, the Soviet Union tried twice to gain control of Iran, and a wispy septuagenarian named Mohammed Mossadegh came to be a far more famous Iranian than Mohammed Reza Pahlavi.

The young king's seemingly impossible task was to regain some authority in his own country while two foreign powers roamed it like a couple of thrashing diplodocuses. But the Shah had two sound human assets. One, his fiery sister Ashraf, pumped courage into him. The other, Prime Minister Forughi, devised a clever damage-control plan: a tripartite alliance with the British and the Russians which seemed to give them everything they wanted—that is, control of railroads, ports, rivers, landing fields, telephones and telegraphs, and pipelines—but despite these concessions established Iran as a partner in the war effort with some rights of its own.

This disguised boon was soon followed by another: the United States added its presence in Iran to those of Britain and the Soviet Union. Looking far beyond the panicky effort to stop Hitler in the Caucasus, Franklin D. Roosevelt perceived that his good allies might well turn against one another after the war and convert Iran into British and Soviet satellites faced off along an armed and explosive frontier. As Korea and Vietnam later proved, this was a real possibility. That is, it was until Roosevelt created the Persian Gulf Command and sent in thirty thousand Americans—forebears of the U.S.-Iranian military relationship that ended so traumatically with the American flight in 1979. The Americans raised the British-Soviet transport capacity across Iran tenfold, while reducing British-Soviet chances of postwar occupation of the country by about the same amount. The arrival of the Americans gave the Shah one more foreign power to be humble to—and he was, gladly and intelligently, appreciating the subtlety that three occupiers were better than two.

Thus, while the Allies collaborated to transport across Iran the supplies that defeated Hitler, they covertly struggled with one another over the future of Iran. The British stirred up the Qashqai tribesmen of central Iran to make trouble for the Shah; the Russians organized Tudeh, the Communist party, which fought the Shah for the next twenty years; the Americans brought in experts who virtually took over such government functions as finance, public health, provincial administration, municipal policing, farm support, and irrigation. One of the experts was Colonel Norman Schwartzkopf, the New Jersey policeman who handled the Lindbergh kidnaping case in 1932; his job in Iran was to stop the spread of Tudeh.

In 1943 all three Allied leaders met in Teheran, which was as far as Stalin would agree to go beyond the borders of the Soviet Union. For security, the meetings took place within the compounds of the British and Soviet embassies. An enclosed passageway was built across the street that separates the two. Stalin induced Roosevelt to stay in the Russian compound rather than risk getting shot by some Nazi while going back and forth to the U.S. Embassy, three quarters of a mile away.

Nevertheless, Stalin did not hesitate to leave the compound to call on the Shah, flattering the king by this protocolary nicety. Grandly, Stalin offered Iran tanks and warplanes, but the Shah suspected that the offer was a ruse for infiltrating Iran with Soviet "training" officers, and said no, thanks. Roosevelt did not call on the Shah, compelling the Shah to swallow his monarchical dignity and call on Roosevelt. Surprisingly, the American President gabbled on and on about reforesting Iran, a real problem but not one the Shah thought Roosevelt would be so concerned about. But Roosevelt was, as part of his growing concept that Iran could be a showcase of American development aid after the war, a dream that came partly true.

The fall of Hitler actuated a clause in the Tripartite Alliance pact which required the British and the Russians to get out of Iran by six months after the end of the war in Europe—that is, by March 2, 1946. The British departed. The Americans departed. The Russians stayed, audaciously proposing to take over part of Iran.

It seemed as though northern Iran had come to feel like home to them. Azerbaijan had been the sector where the Red Army took possession of war goods moved north by highway from the Persian Gulf; here was where the Tudeh party was strongest. The party seized government buildings in Tabriz; then the Communists cut communications with Teheran. On November 19, 1945, the Russian army turned back Iranian troops sent to regain the province. On December 12, a new, Tudeh-controlled legislature in Tabriz set up the Autonomous Republic of Azerbaijan, with Jafar Pishevari, an Iranian Communist who had been groomed for many years in the Soviet Union, as prime minister. Using Soviet arms and troops, he forced all Iranian troops in the north to surrender. A couple of months later the Soviet Union announced that before it withdrew its forces, Iran would have to recognize the Republic of Azerbaijan, "coordinate" Iran's foreign policy with that of the U.S.S.R., give the Soviets oil concessions in northern Iran (to this day no oil has ever been found there), and permit the U.S.S.R. to station troops in Azerbaijan. In sum, Stalin told the Shah to become a Russian puppet.

On March 3, 1946, the day after the deadline for leaving Iran, Soviet troops moved out of Tabriz not northward but southward, toward Teheran. Iranian soldiers dispatched to stop the Russians understandably panicked. The Shah perceived with dismay that his prime minister, sent to Moscow to try to contain the Russians, was failing. Desperately, he played his last card. Earlier, his ambassador to Washington, Hossein Ala, had placed Iran's plight before the United Nations Security Council, the first complaint ever lodged in that newly fledged body. President Harry Truman, who had already become alarmed by reports that the Red Army was pouring tanks and men across the border into Azerbaijan, was jarred into action. He sent what he later called "a blunt message" to Stalin: Get your troops out of Iran in six weeks, or the United States Navy will sail into the Persian Gulf and land American forces. A few days later, Andrei Gromyko, the Soviet delegate to the Security Council, rose to announce that Russian troops would be out of Iran in five weeks—and so they were.

This test of strength between the U.S. and the U.S.S.R. was the opening battle of the cold war, but within Iran the struggle was soon over. The Shah sent troops under General Ali Razmara to do bloody battle against Pishevari's forces, and on December 15, 1946, the king himself entered Tabriz, where mobs butchered camels for meat for the triumphal festivities. "Except in France in 1944 I have never seen such violent and spontaneous enthusiasm," wrote the British correspondent Christopher Sykes.

One snowy day in February 1949, the Shah of Iran—only twenty-nine years old and in the eyes of the world a playboy who danced in the nightclubs of London and had affairs with such actresses as Martine Carol, Yvonne De Carlo, Silvana Mangano, and Gene Tierney—went to the University of Teheran for the annual ceremony commemorating its founding. As he started up the stairs of the Faculty of Law building, an assassin pretending to be a news photographer took a Belgian six-shooter out of his fake camera and fired four times from behind the king.

Three of the shots went through the Shah's military cap without even grazing the scalp. He turned, and a fourth bullet entered his right cheek and came out under his nose. On all sides, bemedaled generals, policemen, and young officers, forgetting the king, scrambled over one another to get out of the murderer's range. The Shah was left alone, six feet from the killer. He recalled a "lucidity that astonishes me even today": while making a mental note to demote an officer whom he saw crawling beneath a car, he quickly calculated that the assassin's gun had only two shots left. He dodged and weaved. The fifth shot grazed his shoulder. The assassin squeezed the trigger again. Click. The gun had jammed.

Now the military men closed in and shot and clubbed the gunman. His death made certain that his motives would forever be a mystery. In the light of later events, most historians now believe that the assassin was inspired by religious fanaticism, but the villain that the Shah chose to blame was the Tudeh party. Two days later the minister of the interior dissolved it, and to be a Communist has been illegal in Iran ever since.

The Shah's close escape stirred a wave of sympathy, prayers, and pledges of allegiance. He himself reasoned that he had been spared by fate or heaven for some destiny, although, he said, "I know that some supposedly sophisticated people would be irritated by such a notion." In four ways he began to gather power to make this destiny come true. He put over a law to control the press. He created a senate (provided for in the 1906 constitution but never realized), and by virtue of his legal right to appoint half of its sixty members made it a pro-monarchy counterweight empowered to veto bills enacted by the more democratic lower house. He gained power to dissolve both houses, provided that he gave a reason and called a new election. And he won the right to appoint prime ministers, until then named by the Parliament itself.

The Shah sent his bloodstained uniform to be put on display in a glass case at the Officers Club in Teheran. The way that he had outmaneuvered a determined killer proved his coolness and nerve, but the

American Embassy had already learned about those qualities. "I am disturbed by fact that shah has recently become enthusiastic aviator," Ambassador George Allen had cabled the State Department in 1946. "He has had only twenty hours in air but considers himself good pilot. Shah had bump last week on landing and cut his forehead rather badly" (the Shah had felt compelled to tell people that he had walked into a door). When the Shah invited Allen to fly with him to a meadow up on the Elburz Mountains, the ambassador threw protocol out the window, and shudderingly refused. The Shah later acquired an old Flying Fortress bomber and hired a World War II pilot to teach him how to fly it, and in the years since then he has piled up five thousand hours of flying time.

Next in the Shah's life came another queen—a queen he madly loved and regretfully divorced.

Green-eyed Soraya was Iranian born and European bred. Her family name was Esfandiari, signifying a subtribe of the formidable Bakhtiaris, who center around Isfahan. The word "tribe" in Iran has the connotation of what Americans mean when they say "Indian tribe," and also the connotation of what they mean when they say "Kennedy tribe." The rank-and-file tribesmen are nomads or poor rustics, but the leaders are among the aristocrats of the country, with wealth, education, and Teheran town houses. Soraya's grandfather was conspicuously among the leaders: he dominated the area of southwest Iran where oil was first found. Two of her uncles were so powerful and rebellious that Rèza Shah, the father of the man Soraya was to marry, had them executed. Her own father was a university student in Berlin when he met a Russian-born German girl and married her in a Moslem ceremony. Soraya was born to them in 1932, after they had settled in Isfahan.

Soraya grew up in Berlin, Isfahan, Zurich, Lausanne, and London, learning German, Persian, and French along the way. This foreign background led some to question her devotion to Iran—to which she rebutted that she always wrote her shopping lists in Persian. She was perfecting her English in London at the age of eighteen when she first heard the electrifying suggestion that she might become queen. The Shah's divorce from Fawzia two years before had set in motion a good deal of matchmaking, and one of the matchmakers was a cousin of Soraya's with close links to the court. Soraya was summoned to the rooms of visiting Princess Shams, the Shah's elder sister, at Claridge's. Immediate approval. The Shah scrutinized pictures, and before long Soraya was produced before him. After just one evening of the parlor games that used to pass for entertainment at the palace, he proposed through an intermediary, and she accepted.

The Shah adored his bride and smiled at her extravagances. For a long time, she kept a pet seal in the fountain of the reception room of the Marble Palace, throwing him fresh fish and laughing when he climbed out of the pool and slithered on wet fins across the Persian rugs. Later these diversions palled. Soraya did not like Iran, and grew moody.

Early on the evening of October 26, 1954, the king and queen dressed for a pleasant occasion, his thirty-fifth birthday, to be celebrated by the family with a dinner party in the palace. Only Prince Ali Reza, the Shah's next-younger brother and presumable successor, had not yet arrived. Four days before, the prince had flown to the Caspian, promising to return for the celebration.

To Ali Reza's disappointment, however, a storm had come up, and he and his pilot had decided that they had better not try to fly over the high Elburz Mountains to Teheran in their three-seater plane. Ali Reza was walking away to telephone the palace, when some peasants approached carrying a man on a stretcher. He was dying of pneumonia. They had heard that the prince might be able to take him in the plane to a Teheran hospital. Changing his mind about the risks, the prince decided to attempt the flight. Not until a week later did searchers in the mountains find the wreck of the plane, and the bodies of the pilot, the peasant, and the prince.

Ali Reza's death left the Pahlavi dynasty without a successor. Three years after their marriage, Soraya had not become pregnant. And four years after that, she had still not produced a child. "Increasingly I realized that the high interests of the nation required an heir," the Shah has written. Finally, "for reasons of state, I found it necessary to divorce Queen Soraya." The marriage ended in March 1958. Since then, to Iranians, Soraya has been a European peripatetic—and a street in the capital.

Mohammed Mossadegh—"Old Mossy." Sick and thin, yellow of skin, weeping and fainting, dressed in pajamas and governing from bed, living off tea, milk, cakes, and power. A terror, a delight, a brain, an imp—and the only authentically popular politician in Iran's history. For two years in the early 1950s, he turned the spotlight of world politics to his hitherto generally ignorable country, shouting a thunderous, unequivocal "No!" to the economic colonialism of the West. The editors of *Time* magazine, rejecting John Foster Dulles and Dwight Eisenhower, chose Mohammed Mossadegh Man of the Year for 1951: "In a few months he had the whole world hanging on his words and deeds, his jokes, his tears, his tantrums."

Mossadegh was about seventy when he came to power; he would never reveal his birth date, but he was born about the same time as Reza Shah. Mossadegh grew up in the royal court at Teheran; his mother was a Qajar princess and his father served for thirty years as finance minister to Qajar shahs. He was apprenticed to the Finance Ministry at fifteen, and served ten years in eastern Khorasan province. In gratitude for good service, the shah of the era granted him the title Mossadegh, meaning "tested and true," whereupon Tested and True joined a revolt against the shah, and failing, went into exile in Paris. There Mossadegh studied finance and political science during several moody and ulcerous years spent in a small room on the Left Bank. Later, in Switzerland, he took a law degree. What stirred him to run for Parliament, after he returned to Iran, was the egregious treaty by which Britain in 1919 proposed to make Iran a protectorate. He helped Iran fight off the treaty, and ever after hated the British. When British-backed Reza Shah dethroned the Qajars and put the crown on his own head in 1925, Mossadegh, from his seat in Parliament, distinguished himself by crying, "I am against it! It is contrary to law!" By house arrest and actual imprisonment, including a period in a basement cell where he was so mistreated that he emerged temporarily unable to walk, Mossadegh was sidetracked during Reza Shah's reign. Back in Parliament after Reza Shah's abdication, he made himself an expert on the injustices of the contract between Iran and the Anglo-Iranian Oil Company. In speeches that sometimes lasted two days, he preached to Parliament, and by 1950 he made his proposal for nationalizing Anglo-Iranian into the touchstone issue of Iranian freedom from foreign control.

To gain support, he patched together a National Front of nearly everyone who hated outside influence: University of Teheran professors and students, small parties from both right and left, and above all, the merchants in the bazaars and their Moslem spiritual confidants, the mullahs. Among the mullahs, one stood out: the ruthless, colorful Ayatollah Abolqasem Kashani, a holy warrior whose father had been killed by the British.

The young Shah Mohammed Reza Pahlavi agreed, in a gingerly way, that Iran should have more control over its oil; he, too, resented the fact that other countries, such as Venezuela, got more from the oil companies than Iran did; but he had neither the nerve nor any strategy for taking on the British government, the majority owner of Anglo-Iranian. Late in 1949, he had gone to Washington and appealed to Harry Truman for financial aid, but Truman refused because Iran's government was so notoriously corrupt. To clean house, the Shah gave the prime ministry to Ali Razmara, that cruel general, all muscle and nerve, who was favored by the American Embassy because he had been so effective in wiping out the Communist rebels in Azerbaijan in 1946. But Razmara, who opposed taking over the oil industry, was in the eyes of the National Front exactly the wrong man to lead Iran toward the new nationalism. On March 7, 1951, it fell to Razmara, as a traditional duty of the prime minister, to attend a fervent religious ceremony at the Shah Mosque in the Teheran bazaar—right in the heart of the enemy. In a foreshadowing of the Shah's later downfall, a fanatic member of something called the Crusade of Islam shot and killed the general.

The Shah knew then that he would have to attempt to ride and control the new nationalism. Public opinion, expressed by rioters shouting "The oil is ours!" (and by the murder of three Britons), held that only Mossadegh had the nerve to seize the oil fields. Finally, Mohammed Reza Pahlavi named Mohammed Mossadegh prime minister.

Now came Mossadegh's chance to deliver on the "$1 million a day" that he promised to wring for Iran from the oil company. OLD MOSSY SEIZES BRITISH OIL—NAVY TO RESCUE, blared a confident headline in London's *Daily Express*. Old Mossy laughed, and at American urging, the British government restrained its navy from entering the Persian Gulf. Closing down the wells and the Abadan refinery, the British appealed to the United Nations Security Council. In the fall of 1951 Mossadegh flew to New York, to fall sick at once and run his fight from a bed in New York Hospital. The Security Council decision favored Iran.

"In London clubs, the dashed fellow was regarded as a confounded maniac," wrote *New York Times* reporter Albion Ross. "The world marched through Mossadegh's bedroom and left shaking its head. Iranians loved it. To them the show was worth the price." This confounded maniac understood very well two facts of Iranian life. First, he comprehended that his emotional confrontation of the big powers—his very craziness—in some mystical way made it plausible that kicked-around Iran could get away with nationalizing its oil. Second, he knew that his weakness was his strength, just as did the frail, aged, and unarmed Ayatollah Khomeini. The specific weakness was a clause in Iran's 1921 treaty with the U.S.S.R. that permitted the Russians to invade Iran if foreign forces menaced it. Neither the British nor Mossadegh talked out loud about that clause, but both sides were always aware of it, and for two years it remained Mossadegh's secret strength.

On the other hand, Mossadegh had weaknesses that were weaknesses. He thought that the world would come begging for Iranian oil, but the oil companies opened the valves of their wells in Arab countries and quickly made up the Iranian loss. Apart from misjudging the oil market, Mossadegh, as the Shah put it, "spent his entire tenure in office fighting the company in an amateur fashion and regardless of the effects upon his country." The American political scientist Richard Cottam writes in *Nationalism in Iran* that "Nowhere in the world is British cleverness so wildly exaggerated as in Iran, and nowhere are the British more hated for it." Mossadegh embodied this blindness, and when the World Bank made a proposal, advantageous to Iran, for a rational way of nationalizing the oil industry, he angrily turned it down because, as one of his supporters explained, the bank was an "agent for British imperialism."

As what Albion Ross called "a symbol for the yearning for decency, sovereignty and the better life," Mossadegh managed to stay popular for many months, even though loss of oil revenue wrecked Iran's development plans. At length, inaction began to stir discontent. Mossadegh, sensing loss of control, responded by crackdown: he dissolved Parliament, muzzled the press, and finally allied himself with the Tudeh party. The National Front broke in two as Ayatollah Kashani pulled his religious contingent out in protest to Mossadegh's link with the Communists. From his iron bed Mossadegh in May 1953 sent a letter to Dwight Eisenhower, referring to the "present dangerous situation in Iran." Translation: Help me or I'll turn the country over to the Russians. Eisenhower's reaction was to call in Allen Dulles, director of the six-year-old Central Intelligence Agency.

The CIA concluded that Mossadegh had spent his good will, that between Mossadegh and the Shah, the Iranian people would choose the Shah if given a choice. The task was to create a chance for a choice. Presently there appeared on the Iran-Iraq border a thirty-seven-year-old man wearing horn-rimmed glasses and a pleasant grin. He was Kermit Roosevelt, grandson of Theodore Roosevelt, and the CIA's Middle East operations chief (salary: $12,000 a year). By early July he was in a "safe house" in Teheran, and deep in consultation with General Fazlollah Zahedi. This army officer was a favorite of the Pahlavis; Reza Shah had commissioned Zahedi a brigadier general at twenty-five after he lost four ribs fighting the Russians in Azerbaijan in 1921. Landowner, hunter, poker player, Zahedi had shared Reza Shah's sympathy for the Nazis, and the British had imprisoned him in Palestine during World War II. When he returned to Iran, he became Norman Schwartzkopf's assistant. He was the father of Ardeshir Zahedi, Iran's ambassador to Washington until the revolution sent him packing, and young Ardeshir was present as Kim Roosevelt conspired with his father. Like Roosevelt, General Zahedi was lying low: he had killed Mossadegh's chief of Teheran police a few weeks before.

Their plot was simple: they would organize, by the cell system, so much secretly committed support for the Shah that when he fired

Mossadegh and appointed Zahedi prime minister, the king would have a visibly commanding segment of public opinion behind him. Among the bazaar merchants and the mullahs—the Kashani people—the recruiting was easy, ironical as that may seem now. They also found support among rank-and-file Iranians who for good historical reasons distrusted the Russians. Curiously enough, the armed forces were not so susceptible to joining, having been seduced in large numbers by Mossadegh and even by Tudeh, but Zahedi finally organized a nucleus of about fifty colonels and generals loyal to the king.

Then came an unexpected problem: recruiting the king himself. The Shah, depressed and fearing betrayal, perhaps even from the Americans, if things went wrong, refused to discharge Mossadegh. The Shah's apprehensions were realistic, as the American waffling in 1979 proved. Moreover, some army officers, among them Gamal Abdel Nasser, had just dethroned King Faruk in Egypt. But when assured that the whole Iranian air force was in his corner, he finally agreed to act.

To mislead Mossadegh, the Shah went on August 11 to "relax" at a royal villa on the Caspian. On August 15, he secretly summoned Colonel Nematollah Nassiri, commander of the Imperial Guard, and dispatched him to the capital to deliver, that night, a decree ordering Mossadegh to leave office and Zahedi to replace him. But there had been a leak. Mossadegh arrested Nassiri and most of the other military officers who were to have rallied around the Shah.

Hearing by radio the next morning of Mossadegh's countercoup, the Shah flew with Soraya to Baghdad. During the next two days mobs toppled statues of the Shah and his father in Teheran, and Tudeh newspapers screamed THE POWER IS OURS. The name of a prominent avenue in Teheran was changed from Pahlavi to People. But these events, as Kim Roosevelt perceived, were open to another interpretation. The Communists, sucked in by appearances, were exposing themselves too ardently as partisans of Mossadegh. Someone profaned the tomb of Reza Shah—a dismaying example of excess zeal. In Gilan, the Communists tipped their hand by seizing the provincial government. By the end of August 18, the Moslem element and other anti-Communists were frightened, and Mossadegh saw that he had snatched defeat from the jaws of victory. He turned his troops and policemen out to club and dispel the stupidly overexultant members of Tudeh.

After Nassiri's arrest, Eisenhower's advisers in Washington had urged the abandonment of Roosevelt's mission, but Kim ignored them, convinced that he had a new chance to win. Among other measures, he hired the services of a famous mobster named Shaban ("Brainless") Jafari, leader of a sort of Mafia sports club in south Teheran. On the morning of August 19, Brainless's men danced northward to Parliament Square, a bizarre athletic troupe twirling iron bars, turning handsprings, and showing off their wrestlers' biceps. "Long live the Shah!" they shouted. Elsewhere, other young men passed out hundred-rial ($1.50) bills—American bribes for anyone who would raise the same shout. The shouts encouraged the Shah's real partisans, Moslems and merchants disillusioned by Mossadegh, and traditionalists who had always favored the monarchy. As the day wore on, the throngs of Teheran had a chance to make a choice that Roosevelt proposed. Only a day after tearing down his statues, they opted for the Shah. Without opposition from civilians, Zahedi's troops attacked Mossadegh's house. After several hours of gunfire, Mossadegh got out of bed, threw a coat on top of his pajamas, and nimbly climbed over his garden wall.

When the Shah returned to Teheran on August 23, his ministers kissed his knees, and the crowds cheered him to the echo. It was Colonel Nassiri who had the satisfaction of finding and arresting Mossadegh. The old man was condemned to death, but the Shah commuted the sentence to three years in jail. Mossadegh then returned to his estate fifty miles west of Teheran. At once a mob gathered and threatened him with death. The motivations of this mob may be gauged by the fact that its leader was the mercenary Brainless. Resignedly, Mossadegh telephoned the police, perhaps foreseeing that their "protection" would never be withdrawn. He died a prisoner in his own house in 1967, somewhere around eighty-six years old.

Mossadegh's time of power in Iran coincided with Senator Joe McCarthy's time of anti-Communist hysteria in the United States, which led many Americans to write Mossadegh off as a Communist. That was a strange niche for Mossadegh, who as Iran's number-three or number-four landowner held property worth perhaps $100 million, and his real defects were quite different from his imagined ones.

He called his philosophy "negative nationalism," meaning that Iran must mainly strive to free itself of foreign control. To a nation paranoiacally ashamed of foreign domination all down through the centuries, negativism was—initially, at least—enough. To this attitude Mossadegh added his own unique style. As Reza Shah had demonstrated when the British swept him away, important-looking authority figures could not necessarily impress the foreigners. Mossadegh was the antithesis, "the figure of tragedy, the man of sorrow who took upon himself burdens and obligations to be resolved by self-sacrifice," as historian Donald Wilber expresses it. Iranians could unconsciously have seen in Mossadegh the image of the martyred saint Husain, son of Ali, who was the son-in-law of Mohammed. In any case, "during the two years of Mossadegh's regime, the Persians were cooperative, their officials were less corrupt, and they took more interest in the affairs of the nation because they believed a new day had dawned," writes Yahya Armajani, Iranian-born professor of history at Macalester College, in *Iran*. Even the Shah confessed that "in a strange way Mossadegh filled a temporary need." Historian Cottam calls Mossadegh's rule a period of "much verve but little order," and the Shah's subsequent reign a period of "much order but little verve."

Mossadegh failed because significant elements of the population at length decided that negativism was not enough, giving the CIA the opportunity to bring him down. Though it's hard to knock success, the American intervention was probably a bad mistake. The old man was not too crazy to have led Iran, under happier circumstances, to what he sometimes proposed, a republic governed by its parliament, under a king who reigned but did not rule. Instead he proved to Iranians, by his fall, that they had to accept what followed, the form of government that Cottam called "royal dictatorship."

The Shah claimed that his flight was the consequence of contingency planning, to "force Mossadegh and his henchmen to show their real allegiances" and "help crystallize Persian public opinion." (He may have had this delusion in mind when he fled in 1979.) When he reached Baghdad, he told Iraq's authorities: "I ask exile in your country only for a few days. I have not abdicated." But when he and Soraya heard in Rome, where they went after a day in Baghdad, that mobs were tearing down his portraits in Teheran, he faltered in his hopes. Soraya says in her memoirs that she asked him, "Where would you like to go?" and he replied, "Probably America," and suggested that he would like to buy a farm there. When an Associated Press correspondent next day brought a wire report of the Shah's sudden rehabilitation by the people of Iran, the king "went so pale I feared he might faint," Soraya says, and he confessed: "I have not played a great role in the fight." According to Soraya, the Shah later had to reward General Zahedi with $600,000 for ousting Mossadegh. Even then, the Shah "harbored a suspicion that Zahedi had his eye on the throne itself," and eventually exiled him to Switzerland. But that's shah business. "The experiences of August 1953 made the Shah resolve that he, rather than the fickle parliament, would lead the country," writes Professor Frye. The Shah told me: "It was through sweat and tears that I came to this position. The war years were bad, and the postwar years, with Mossadegh, worse."

In effect, the Shah concluded that, to his own surprise, he was no longer a purely hereditary king, but rather an "elected" one—elected by the cheers of the throngs of August 19, which he made an Iranian national holiday. During the war, the British ambassador had pronounced the boy king to be weak, and stubborn as a result of this weakness. Perhaps because until then his father had made all the decisions, the young Shah was deemed singularly indecisive. The American ambassador privately judged him to be "not effectively interested in reform." Both nations viewed the Iranian prime ministry as more consequential than the throne.

"Election" changed all that. The ever more confident Shah set about the tasks—land reform, political control, economic development, military build-up, diplomacy of independence—that largely formed the Iran of today. Weak he may have been once, but he proceeded by shrewdness and intelligence to make himself the master of his difficulties, and of Iran. "Once you win power, you must exercise it to retain it," he concluded.

His rise did not at all points seem irresistible. In 1965, he came close again to being drilled by an assassin's bullet. A soldier of the Imperial Guard sprayed fire from his tommy gun around the entrance to the old Marble Palace as the Shah alighted from his car. The Shah managed to get inside an office, but the assassin, by then fatally wounded, put his last bullet through the door, and it missed the king by inches. To prove that he could not be frightened out of making public appearances, the Shah on the next day drove, alone and unescorted, in an open convertible along Teheran's busy Istanbul Street, to the cheers of pedestrians. Later, Parviz Nik-Khah, a student sentenced to death as an accomplice of the gunman, demanded an audience with the Shah—his legal right. The Shah, curious, received him alone, but the encounter was undramatic. The student pleaded for pardon; the Shah commuted his sentence to life, and four years later freed him. A little later this one-time plotter got a good job in Iran's government-run television network. In 1978 Nik-Khah wrote the article that touched off the Khomeini revolution (see page 3), and in 1979 the Khomeini government executed him.

On his birthday in 1967, the Shah acknowledged his own success by carrying out a long-delayed ceremony: he crowned himself, setting upon his own head his father's heavy emerald-and-diamond-studded crown. Then, at the same ritual in the throne room of the Qajars' old Golestan Palace, he placed another thickly jeweled crown, this one fresh from Pierre Arpels' Paris workshops, on the head of the Queen Farah. The coronation in effect announced to the nation and the world that Mohammed Reza Pahlavi now considered himself to be a fully certified king, qualified for the practice of all branches of the profession of monarchy.

5

First Persian Singular

✿

The Shah stood in the center of his unostentatious office, a man of five feet eight, dressed in a quiet blue suit, squarely built but springy and muscular, his back as straight as a yardstick. By sparing me the embarrassment of a long, silent walk up to his desk, he showed a courteous concern for putting me at ease. After shaking my hand, he led me to chairs around a low table, and a servant, in black tail coat, brought tea. Then we were alone. When he was riding high, several years ago, His Imperial Majesty Mohammed Reza Pahlavi did not need advisers at his elbow to prompt him with statistics or guard him from misstatements, no matter whom he addressed or what the subject.

Pahlavi was at that time like no other mortal on earth, a living king in the potent ancient sense, *the* Shah, leading a nation that could (and did) vitally change the course of the world. By driving up the price of petroleum, he had made the whole globe remodel its economy, and had given Iran influence out of all proportion to its size and population. On energy questions, he could tell entire populations to pull up their socks and shape up. "We decided to give you a break," he said, condescendingly, to the American public in 1977, upon promising not to raise the price of oil for a while. His military strength gave him control of the Persian Gulf, vital supplier of petroleum to the United States, Europe, and Japan. With his oil, his arms, and his dictatorial control of his 33 million subjects, he had for many years had power greater than that of all but perhaps half a dozen other men on earth.

Though the Shah let pride and arrogance bring him down, he had undeniable qualifications for leadership. He was subtle and intelligent; he had cunning, rigor, something close to total recall, and accomplished eloquence in Persian, English, and French. He was skilled, versatile, observant, and attentive to duty. He was fatalistically imperturbable, having twice survived assassins' bullets fired at close range. And by virtue of becoming king at twenty-one in 1941, he had at fifty-nine stretched his reign to thirty-seven years and stored up unmatchable experience in statecraft. He had dealt, at length and substantively, with every American president from Roosevelt to Carter, with every Soviet leader from Stalin to Brezhnev, with every British prime minister from Churchill to Callaghan, with every German chancellor from Adenauer to Schmidt, with every French president from de Gaulle to Giscard; with Chiang Kai-shek and Hua Guofeng; with Tito; with Franco; with George VI and Elizabeth II; with Emperor Hirohito and most of the prime ministers of Japan; with most of the leaders of India, Pakistan, and the Arab nations; and with scores of other current rulers, down to and including Gabon's President Bongo.

Early in his reign, the Shah took the role of divine-right king, accepting the support of the mullahs, the priests of Islam. Seen in retrospect, this appears to have been a ruse to gain power when the Shah was young and under constant attack. By 1960, he had established his authority, and emerged as the nonreligious, even antireligious, managing director of the empire of Iran, orchestrating the country's modernization in day-to-day charge. This confidence in his own skill at the profession of kingship—to which was added the humane influence of his third wife, Farah, whom he married that year—made him into a sort of monarchical revolutionary, driving Iran from its only-yesterday feudalism toward today's largely state-run industrial economy.

His style of rule was rigid. "An Iranian cannot be allowed to insult the king," he told me; and to others he said, "No Iranian shall be permitted to betray his country in any way." The all-inclusive manner in which these rules were construed in practice made Iran a subjugated place, and Iranians a cautious race. The secret police were everywhere, and to educated Iranians this was a sound cause for reticence or downright fear (as well as a perpetual embarrassment). On first meeting, I frequently noticed, Iranians much preferred not to pick up on my references to the king, and if they did mention him, they took care to call him reverently, "His Imperial Majesty" or "the Shahanshah." I imagined that if I could gain the confidence of such people they would denounce the king in bitter and anonymously quotable language. Eventually some did. The surprise was that so many Iranians, when I got to know them, pronounced generally favorable verdicts on him. Then they offhandedly called him "the Shah," and made such comments as: "Well, he listens to people," or "He's realistic," or "An expert can always make the Shah change his mind by presenting the facts." There was a feeling that the king recognized limits to his power. One professor who had returned to teach at the University of Teheran after some years of self-exile and opposition told me vehemently: "The Shah cannot put himself up against me because he has a son who will be the king and he does not want my son to be against his son."

This up-to-date king admired science, counted on technology, knew the uses of the computer. He preferred colleagues of modern minds, Western educations, technical ability. He was intrigued beyond reason by the newest in weaponry (and spent billions buying it). But living in the same body was another Shah, whose spirit came from twenty-five centuries of the Persian past. In his modern mode, the king wore business suits and worked twelve hours a day, making decisions that might typically call into play his exhaustive knowledge of the petroleum business; in his traditional role, he put on uniforms laden with medals and braid and commanded his ministers to kiss his hand. "The Iranian's sense of history, his need to feel that his national leader is lifted above mundane life, can be satisfied only with a monarch," wrote the American scholar E. A. Bayne, who worked closely with the Shah as an economic consultant. The Shah could never see any reason to dispute that theory: "If this country had the choice, it would choose the same," he told Bayne. One of the king's loyalists told me: "For you Americans monarchy means the tyranny of George III, but for us Iranians it is the essence of the country."

With his brushed-back, gray-steaked hair, heavy black eyebrows, strong chin, and fine Persian nose, the Shah was a handsome man, and I found him, face to face, to be suave, worldly, and yet more casual than I had thought he might be. At the end of my audience, as he escorted me to the door, my eye caught a glass-encased ship model in a corner. "It's a nineteenth-century German warship," the Shah explained. I was gauche enough to venture a personal remark: "An excellent job. I used to build ship models." "It must be an interesting hobby, if you have the time," said the Shah, with a rueful smile. In such ordinary human contacts, he did not put on airs. Sitting and talking, he hooked his thumbs under his vest, or laced his fingers together, looking like the grandfather he is. Many foreigners who dealt with the Shah during his visits to developmental projects around Iran found him impatient with protocol and quite ready to talk facts man to man.

Nevertheless, the Shah's private informality did not conceal his worried concern for conserving the Iranian monarchy, for vigilance in protecting his own position. When one looks at a painting of such a Qajar-dynasty king as Fath Ali Shah, one sees a total, if fatuous, confidence in the institution of monarchy. When one looked at his modern-day successor, one saw more anxiety and edginess than might be expected from a man of such achievements and power. There was about him a noticeable touch of defensiveness and harassment. The

Shah's outward easy confidence was undercut to some unknown extent by insecurity, excessive sensitivity, vulnerability.

These are traits that sometimes lead men to overprove themselves—typically, in the case of national leaders, by military conquest. Was the Shah a "nut," as Secretary of the Treasury William Simon said in 1974? Was he a menace to his neighbors, as General George Brown, chairman of the Joint Chiefs of Staff, suggested in 1976? One scenario worked up by the Central Intelligence Agency speculated that the Shah could be the victim of the kind of insecurity that leads to megalomania—insecurity that comes, according to this psychohistorical analysis, from domination by his father, humiliation over his ineffectiveness during the first years of his reign, and embarrassment over his inability for many years to father a male heir to succeed him. Some American Embassy people to whom I talked in Teheran pronounced this diagnosis to be "just about right."

As with any other man, emotion and reason were at war within him. When he was at the height of his power, the emotions that showed most frequently in public statements were anger, arrogance, and touchiness, which go with megalomania. How thin-skinned he could be! Criticized for effrontery in proposing in 1974 to buy part of Pan American Airways, he shot back that he refused to be treated "as if we were a microbe invading some beautiful, immaculate thing." He canceled a similar negotiation with Occidental Petroleum because "it was as if they wanted to deal with jungle Africans in the heyday of the British Empire." His sense of humor was minimal and primitive: in the darkened royal movie theater he used to drop rubber spiders and frogs on the laps of women guests as a joke. Ingratitude led him to bitterness: "I don't give bribes to anyone to claim patriotism and attachment to the monarchy. We are determined to lead this nation to the Great Civilization by force, if necessary." He seemed to suffer jabs of guilt at restricting democracy in Iran, and compensated with elaborate scorn for the democratic nations, picturing them as abominations. "What, really, is the meaning of democracy? For some people, democracy means waylaying people, especially women, in broad daylight in the center of major cities and capitals and robbing them before stabbing them to death, with the thief-murderer then walking away in front of passive onlookers." Haughtily, he said to Westerners: "I have had and been able to put into force a number of ideas which you yourselves have been unable to apply in your so-called democracies."

But his pragmatism overrode emotion in the working out of events. He claimed to be a man of peace "because the alternative is immeasurable calamity and suicide," and his acts proved it. In 1969 he relinquished Iran's ancient claim to Bahrain, after the British pulled out

of it, and let that island become an independent nation. In 1975, he
ended a sputtering war with Iraq that could have been converted into
an Iranian conquest if the Shah were a belligerent maniac. One look
at the long hair and beards of Iranian men, so much in contrast to
the mandated short trims of Ferdinand Marcos' Philippines or Lee Kuan
Yew's Singapore, told you that the Shah did not suffer from petty
conformity hang-ups. The Shah proposed that a king should be "kind
in principle, tough against evil things like corruption and enemies
of his country, understanding towards all, forgiving them when it is
possible." He tried to practice what Iranians call *farmandehi,*
leadership command. This concept placed him often in the role of
father-lecturer to the country, pressing for "hard work, self-sacrifice,
and greater effort." To a farmer who complained that the government
had failed to build his village a bathhouse, the Shah replied with a
sermon on self-reliance which ended: "Who clips your nails for you?"
He had paternal opinions about everything, right down to what to do
about rich children so well fed at home that they only "toy with" their
free school meals (let them toy).

The Iranian monarchy was a court, a cult, and a grand conceit—
the conceit being that it ruled an empire. The words, in French, on
the cover of the Iranian passport said so: *Empire d'Iran.* Actually, Iran
has not been a true empire, a nation ruling other nations, since it
lost Turkmenistan and Afghanistan in the nineteenth century, and
the term was an anachronism. But the tradition provided a basis for
the Shah to insist upon being addressed as His Imperial Majesty, and
for Farah to be called Empress. Mohammed Reza Pahlavi was also
known formally as the Shahanshah (King of Kings, like Cyrus, who
reigned 559–530 B.C.) Aryamehr (Light of the Aryans, a flourish the
Shah adopted a couple of decades ago). Informally, he was the Shah,
the king, the emperor, the monarch, the sovereign, and—among Westerners who wished to be irreverent or to frustrate eavesdroppers—Himself, Ralph, or George (from which it followed that Farah was Martha).
In decrees the king styled himself "We Pahlavi Shahanshah of Iran."

By the terms of the 1906–1907 charter, as revised, Iran became a
constitutional monarchy "vested by the people through the Constituent
Assembly in the person of His Imperial Majesty Reza Shah Pahlavi
and his male descendants in succession." This constitution provided
the king with much real power. Under it, he hired and fired the cabinet
ministers, the top military officers, and the public prosecutors; he declared war, made peace, and commanded the armed forces; he negotiated treaties; he convened and at his own pleasure dissolved the Parliament, appointed half the senators, and could reject money bills unless

overridden by a three-fourths majority. The constitution supposedly protected people from arbitrary royal action through a bill of rights, but all these rights carried the loophole "except in cases specified by law," and royal decrees were law.

In sum, the king had power, both legal and extralegal. But he didn't always get his way. As many a U.S. president has learned, power is often limited, even for potent leaders, by the sheer inertia of government. I met one foreign consultant to the Iranian government who counseled the removal of some ministerial functions to cities outside Teheran. "His Majesty has already ordered that, two years ago," the official in charge replied, and then added dejectedly, "but it's not being carried out. The bureaucrats refuse to leave the capital." Such frustrations reinforced the Shah's determination to be tough. "When everybody in Iran is like everybody in Sweden," he said, "then I will rule like the king of Sweden."

The constitution provided Iran with a dominant prime minister and the usual cabinet of other ministers, as well as a parliament and a judiciary, and the Shah ruled through all these branches, but the governmental institution closest to the king was one that derived from tradition and was not mentioned in the constitution: the Ministry of the Imperial Court. Unlike the workaday other ministries, scattered through downtown Teheran, the court ministry was headquartered at a building inside the leafy Saadabad Palace compound, within a couple of minutes' walk of the king's audience room. (As I was admitted through the Saadabad gate, a well-dressed man offered to lead me to the ministry, and I asked him if he was an official of it. "No," he replied. "I am His Majesty's carpet dealer; I sell carpets to be used as official gifts. My name is Guity, *G-u-i-t-y*. Not *G-u-i-l-t-y*.") The three-story building, marble-faced but plain, stood among gardens of marigolds and geraniums. Inside, crystal chandeliers hung from fifteen-foot ceilings, and furniture in classical French styles stood against beige brocade walls. Only the carpets, as big as volleyball courts, on the parquet floors were Persian; all else, including many enormous oil landscapes, was European. Rich tapestry lined the entire interior of the little elevator. Outside the offices sat modish secretaries, elegantly round-shouldered and booted in suede, drinking from small glasses brought by creaky, black-suited "tea boys," aged upward of fifty.

In this ministry one encountered in full measure the sycophancy that helped bring the Shah down. Working on a budget of $30 million a year, the ministry was in charge of palaces and protocol, salaams and celebrations, glitter and glamour. Cabinet ministers came to the palace in plumed hats, gold braid, and sashes, and kissed His Imperial

Majesty's hand on patriotic holidays. But the ministry was concerned with far more than royal pomp, as I heard during an informative hour with the redoubtable Amir Assadollah Alam, who at that time had been minister of the imperial court for more than a decade. (He later retired, and died in 1978.)

"In the old days, the kings of Iran always had a minister of the right hand and a minister of the left hand," Alam told me, referring to the formal grand viziers, and the more personal chamberlains, of shahs past. "Nowadays the prime minister is the minister of the right, and we are the ministry of the left." He hurried on to explain what he meant by "left." As applied to the court ministry, it connoted, I gathered, something of shadow government, something of supergovernment—the right ministry didn't know what the left ministry was doing. But it also connoted, Alam said, the political kind of left, though nothing anywhere near (shudder) Communism. Alam thought of the Shah and himself as relatively advanced in their concepts of labor's rights, social justice, and the need to narrow the gap between rich and poor. In sum, Alam considered himself to occupy the liberal position in his influence on the Shah, even though in fact his position was well to the right. "But as minister I do not have the power to execute the ideas we develop," Alam explained. Such ideas had to be accepted by the Shah and carried out by the other ministries.

The Ministry of the Imperial Court served as a channel—and evidently a poor channel—for the Shah to hear and respond to public opinion. "In this country, with its 2,500-year history of monarchy, the Shah is the father—everything is referred to him, and he has got to be aware of the problems," said Alam. His Majesty's Private Bureau, a division of the court ministry, received petitions of all kinds, recommended action at the bureau chief's audiences with the Shah every other day, and functioned as the monarch's liaison with his government and people. The ministry's protocol division arranged the Shah's audiences, his daily program, and state visits. The whole operation was computerized, and linked by fast communications.

> To want anything contrary to the wish of the shah would be equal to playing with your life. If he calls day night, you should simply say, "Behold the moon and the Pleiades."
> —The poet Saadi, ca. 1250 A.D.

It was a given condition of the Iranian monarchy that Their Majesties had to be eternally visible to the subjects. There were eighteen statues of the Shah in Teheran, and twelve of his father; *all* of them were toppled by Khomeini's mobs. In other towns and cities, nearly every main intersection contained a statue or a monument or a sculpture of one or the other of these worthies, as common as those aluminum busts of Lenin in the U.S.S.R. The first three words that a child learned in an Iranian school were: God, Shah, Country. The title of the national anthem was "Salaam to Shahanshah." The Shah in high-collared uniform was shown on the 50-rial, 100-rial, 200-rial, 500-rial, 1,000-rial, and 5,000-rial banknotes, and when you peered through the unprinted window of each bill, you saw a blurry watermark of the same face.

In the grand lobby of Rudaki Hall, Teheran's luxurious modern opera house, a painting eighteen feet long and eleven feet high depicted the coronation of Mohammed Reza and Farah Pahlavi; it reminded one of the huge murals of ancient shahs and their courts in the Pavilion of the Forty Columns in Isfahan. Paintings of the king, queen, and crown prince also hung in the offices of all cabinet ministers and other high officials; these men seemed to vie in showing loyalty by the quality of their icons. Each of these dignitaries had to decide, and did according to his own concept of idolatry, whether to hang the paintings as a backdrop to his desk, thus embellishing the official as viewed by callers, or on the opposite wall, as a presumably continuous source of inspiration. Paintings of the royal trio also hung in restaurants, hotel lobbies, railroad stations, airports, oil refinery control rooms, and over the proscenium arches of all theaters. Lesser offices, store windows, buses, and shops usually displayed colored or black-and-white reproductions of photographs of Their Majesties. All classrooms showed the threesome, and I recall a school in Baluchistan where the corridors were literally covered with royal photos framed in stretched yarn.

In *Persia the Immortal Kingdom,* the renowned French archaeologist Roman Ghirshman speaks of the sculptures of kings at ancient Persepolis as "art in the service of power." So, in his reign, did the Shah use painting and the camera and the printing press in the service of his power. Iran was stamped and plastered and ultimately overwhelmed by portraits, effigies, and sculptures of the king, the queen, and the crown prince. They became so banal that one scarcely saw them, but they still subliminally planted the message: "Mohammed Reza Pahlavi is your king, and Farah is your queen, and Crown Prince Reza Cyrus, with that lock of hair dangling boyishly over his forehead, is the future king, who will carry on the unending and omnipotent Iranian monarchy." The overmuchness of this message was not, ultimately, something that a sensitive man could accept without feelings of resentment and humiliation. Much of the jubilation of the 1978–1979 revolution came from tearing down the Shah's iconography.

Yet a thoughtful foreign observer could not help but feel—at least until 1978—that Iran was steeped in the concept of monarchy, and that the great majority passively accepted it if for no other reason than that Iran had always had it. Iran was to the monarchy born, imbued with what historian Frye calls "the charisma of the king of kings." Since the ascension of Cyrus, Iran had had ninety-two famous kings and a large number of obscure ones. Though they might in reality have been of different bloodlines, Iranian mythology always found a way to relate them. Thus, writes Frye, "the founder of the present dynasty, Reza Shah Pahlavi, was a poor army officer, who, according to many tales, had royal blood in his veins, some even saying that he was a true descendant of the Sassanians [224–651] or the Safavids [1501–1736]." The Pahlavi dynasty, with two kings, was the shortest in Iranian history, but only to foreigners and some Iranian dissidents did it seem parvenu or illegitimate; most of the Shah's subjects until lately did not question that he occupied the throne by right.

The predisposition of Iran toward monarchy, however, only made the Shah's job feasible, and he had to be clever and alert to keep power during his long reign. He used a number of techniques.

One was patience. The Iranians tell a folk tale about a foolish fellow who claimed to speak Arabic and was put to the test by being asked to give the Arabic word for "cow." He answered correctly, and was then asked for the word for "calf." He did not know, but would not admit it. "The Arabs are patient people," he replied smoothly. "They wait until their calves grow up and call them cows." The Shah's style was to wait until his opponents grew up, and call them friends. He cited the precedent of King Cyrus: "He would pardon the very people who had fought him, treat them well, and keep them in their former posts." Examples abound. At the Ministry of Information I met a prospering young employee who confessed that several years before, as a university student, he had often heaved rocks through bus windows to demonstrate his opposition to the Shah.

While co-opting some people, the Shah manipulated others. He was in effect surrounded by power points, military, political, and economic, and his genius as king was to keep them in tension with one another so that none could grow as strong as he. Men are ambitious, even in a monarchy, and none must be allowed to become too powerful. One trap that an Iranian could fall into was accumulation of too much wealth, for money is power, and power was the king's business. Take Habib Sabet, who from interests in Pepsi-Cola, Revlon, Phelps Dodge, and thirty-eight other companies made himself Iran's richest businessman. He built for a residence a copy of the Petit Trianon which outshone the Shah's own palaces. Featured in an article in *Fortune,* Sabet became too conspicuously important, and when I tried to find him for an interview I discovered that he had deemed it prudent to take up residence in South America (he now lives in Paris).

Of politicians, the political scientist James Bill wrote: "The stronger and more capable a particular individual is, the shorter will be his term of office." An example was Hassan Arsanjani, minister of agriculture in 1963. His job gave Arsanjani the popular task of carrying out the Shah's land reform by turning over the soil to thousands of peasants. At length Arsanjani staged a great Congress of Rural Cooperatives, gathering to Teheran 4,700 delegates, who praised "the selfless efforts and sacrifices of Dr. Hassan Arsanjani." Within weeks, Arsanjani became Iran's ambassador to Italy. I had a series of interviews with a prominent businessman who ended our talks with a plea for anonymity: "I don't want the Shah to think I'm trying to sell myself."

The Shah also ruled by teaching, persuading, cajoling, insisting. Without ever admitting that Iran had any defects, he ceaselessly urged that they be repaired. From apathetic laborers he demanded "a sincere love for work. You must try to climb a step further up every day. I expect you to increase your skills on a day-to-day basis." He had many a trick up his sleeve. In the early 1960s, when his leftist opponents were accusing him of excessively close links to the United States, he demoralized them by bringing about his own personal détente with the Soviet Union. He paid intense attention to detail—failing to see the forest for the trees may have contributed to his downfall. Touring the provinces, he might order the peasants to stop raising goats and start raising sheep. "The Shah decides piddling things, like the transfer of one single airplane from one base to another," one American official told me. The Shah, comparing himself to his father, wrote: "My father's inborn characteristics served his country better then, but notwithstanding my admiration for him, I think that mine are of greater service to it now."

What the Shah considered—with a good measure of self-delusion— to be the principal results of his thirty-seven years of kingship was the society-ripping set of changes that he called the White Revolution. The most important change was land reform, which, despite many shortcomings, destroyed the centuries-old feudal ownership pattern, decimated the landlord class, and took an immense amount of terrain away from the Islamic church. Some of the other reforms of the White Revolution's original dozen were merely administrative, but a number of them altered Iran in interesting and significant ways. Profit sharing. Woman suffrage. Peace Corps-like "armies" of young men and women to fight illiteracy and improve public health. Houses of justice—simple local courts, shorn of legalistics, that served to adjudicate misdemeanors and minor civil suits in the villages.

The Shah also undertook three important measures of nationalization: the state assumed ownership of all of Iran's water, range lands, and forests. All of Iran's water is not much water, which heightened the need for the state to control it. The amount of rain that falls on the dry Iranian plateau is a small and fixed quantity, and "clearly every drop of it belongs to the nation," said the Shah. As for pastures, the Prophet Mohammed had long before decreed that "Moslems have equal rights to water, fire, and pastures," but rich landlords had managed to seize ownership of the range lands, and exacted high grazing fees from the poor shepherds upon whom this mutton-eating, wool-clad land depends. Now they graze their animals cheaply on government land.

Iran used to have large forests; eleventh-century travelers wrote about them. But the forests' private owners cut them down, mostly for charcoal to be used in cooking and heating and smoking opium in a hookah. Now the government is conserving the remaining trees and planting new forests. In many parts of the country—on the outskirts of Isfahan, for example—one can see government registration numbers painted serially on every last tree, a measure that makes chopping down the nationalized trees more detectable and difficult. And around Teheran, a vast green belt of young pines is growing up in what used to be desert, while between Shiraz and Persepolis little pines by the thousands stand in straight rows. Irrigation gets these trees started, but they are soon able to subsist on the available rainfall.

In 1975 and 1977, the Shah proclaimed seven further reforms, and added them to his White Revolution. The thirteenth principle required corporations to let their workers share ownership by purchasing an aggregate of 49 percent of the stock. The fourteenth was a crackdown on profiteering and a set of controls over prices in an effort to stop inflation. The fifteenth relieved students and parents from paying any of the costs of education clear through college (this principle was rammed through just as university students were getting up a mass protest against tuition fees). The sixteenth committed the government to assure good nutrition for pregnant women and children up to the age of two (the Shah held that this period is crucial to the proper formation of brain cells). The seventeenth proclaimed universal social security insurance, including retirement benefits for farmers. The eighteenth controlled land price speculation, and the nineteenth required high public officials to disclose their wealth.

As the diversity of these measures suggests, the White Revolution was an assortment of separate cures for separate ills, lacking articulation and underlying principles. "In one respect this policy may coincide with the principles of capitalism and in other respects either with socialism or even communism," the Shah himself wrote. In any case, the Shah took a quietly belligerent pride in his accomplishments. "What is going on here is epoch-making," he told me. "There's never been so much change in three thousand years. The whole structure is upside down. Every one of the White Revolution's points is a small revolution in itself. It shows that if you think that it is only through bloodshed that you can make a revolution, you are wrong."

By intention and inclination, the Shah in public was always stern, stiff, remote, unbending, humorless. For Pahlavi charisma, he depended on his wife.

Empress Farah has starry eyes, and the role she played was starry-eyed. She was the symbol of the good, the spiritual, the uplifting. "She is sensible, open, caring, and loved," one prominent newsman told me—and I would add the adjectives "serious" and "appealing." Educator Ehsan Naraghi pronounced her, during a conversation I had with him, to be "a devout Moslem by her education, profoundly honest, and very proud to be an Iranian." Speaking of the queen, people offhandedly gave her credit for astonishing accomplishments—for example: "She stopped the destruction of Isfahan." And of course it turns out that she did work hard and successfully to preserve the aesthetics of that marvelous city. While her husband flogged Iran toward industrialization, his Shahbanou (consort), without openly contradicting him, said over and over that human values must always come ahead of mere materialistic gain.

Talking with me, the queen dwelt on the example—"exahmple," in her pronunciation; she speaks the cultivated English of a person who has been taught a British accent after first learning French—of a worker on an assembly line in an automobile factory, a new kind of job in Iran. "This sort of worker is undoubtedly happy to have good medical care, good schools for his children, and good housing," she said. "The work itself reminds me of Charlie Chaplin in *Modern Times;* I've told the factory manager to get a sociologist and try to humanize it. But the worker feels that his life is better. The danger is that he will simply want more and more of these material rewards, and we should not accept 'more and more' as the proper path. It has all come too quickly; we must not get too materialistic.

"Of course, that does not mean that I think anyone should remain poor and make up for it by being philosophical," Farah went on. "I am leading a very easy life, too easy for me to be recommending poverty for others. But more money for such a worker may go for things of little value—clothes, appearances, which only create jealousy among others. An attractive outside and an empty inside. I think people have to be educated on how to spend money, or how to save, perhaps for a worthwhile holiday."

She praised "old values": religion, morality, and Persian traditions that persist "even in the minds of illiterate people, villagers who can recite our epic poetry for hours." And she deplored people who could read but did not read, not even newspapers. She thought it all very well for Iran to be rich in oil, but "it can't last forever" and the nation's real wealth is its "valuable human beings" who are in a "period of renaissance after the Qajars, and could be an example to the world."

In public, her exhortations were so urgent and earnest that sometimes the newspapers, frantically attempting to reflect her thoughts in their reports, produced comically surreal headlines the like of which one does not see in other countries. Sample:

HUMAN ASPECT OF PROGRESS
MUST BE KEPT IN MIND

The queen was also sensitive to the perils of idolization, and impatient with it. One day while I was in Iran, she personally placed a telephone call—something monarchs rarely deign to do—to Seyyid Hossein Nasr, the eminent writer, historian, and president of the Imperial Academy of Philosophy. "There are too many streets in Iran named after members of the royal family," she told him, "and the street that most urgently needs a new name is Avenue Farah. Can you suggest a better name?" Shortly afterward, workmen swarmed into that prominent boulevard in the Abbasabad section of the city, ripped off the signs that offended the queen, and replaced them with new ones reading "Avenue Sohravardi." After due consideration, Dr. Nasr had decided that the honor should go to this seventeenth-century mystic, long ignored but lately rediscovered by Iranian nationalists. "Just right," said the queen; but the people of Teheran went right on calling the street Avenue Farah.

On another occasion, Farah fumed at newspaper sycophancy, saying, "Why must I be regarded as a medical expert if I visit a hospital? Or as an art expert if I go to an art gallery?" The next day the newspapers adulated her for rejecting their adulation. On her thirty-seventh birthday, October 14, 1975, one paper produced a four-page, four-color section headlined FARAH IS THE MOTHER OF THE NATION, while buses everywhere displayed her portrait. But if the queen was leery of idolization, she did enjoy the perquisites of monarchy. A couple of years ago, she returned from a three-week Paris vacation in her own jetliner—and right behind it flew an Iranian army Boeing 707 carrying three tons of French marble for Farah's new swimming pool.

The Empress seemed to accept a responsibility to keep in touch with grass-roots Iran, and traveled extensively. Not long ago, for example, she went to "the Kavir," the central desert (or more properly, to the habitable towns on the edge of it), and traveling by jeep and helicopter, talked to hundreds of rural people, including a ten-year-old girl who tearfully asked Farah to help her prevent her parents from getting divorced. A couple of years ago, touring Ahvaz, Farah managed to walk the streets for two hours more or less incognito and accompanied only by the chief of her Private Bureau. A bit later, in a hamlet in the Zagros Mountains, she laughingly baked a slab of Iranian bread during a village festival.

Farah Diba's father and mother came from well-off provincial families, who lived, respectively, in Azerbaijan in the northwest and in Gilan on the Caspian coast. Diba—the name means "silk"—graduated from the French military academy at Saint Cyr, but he entered the diplomatic service. Farah was born, in 1938, in a hospital that became the American Community School in Teheran. She attended the Italian School in Teheran until she was ten, when her father died of tuberculosis. Her mother then enrolled her in Teheran's Jeanne d'Arc School and later the Razi School, both of which taught not in Persian but in French. She got her first glimpse of the Shah when, as a fifteen-year-old Girl Scout, she dipped a flag during a parade in honor of his thirty-fourth birthday.

In 1957, an uncle who was an architect proposed that Farah should capitalize on her demonstrated artistic talent by studying at the École Spéciale d'Architecture in Paris. The next year Iran's ambassador to France invited her and a number of other young Iranians studying in Paris to meet the Shah, who was there on a private visit. Farah brazenly took the opportunity to complain to His Majesty that Iran's currency restrictions were making life hard for students abroad. A year later, in Teheran on vacation, she made the same complaint to Ardeshir Zahedi, then director of Iran's overseas student program. That night, at dinner in the palace, Zahedi, who was then married to Princess Shahnaz, the Shah's daughter by his brief marriage to the Egyptian Fawzia, mentioned the importunate young lady. "Astonishing," said the king, recollecting his own experience with her. All of which led Zahedi, and more particularly Shahnaz, to arrange a new meeting between Farah and the Shah. They had tea, and he proposed. On December 20, 1959, they were married at the Marble Palace, with the Imperial Guard band on hand to play the cancan from *La Vie Parisienne*.

The new queen's first assignment was to produce a male heir, something that neither Fawzia nor the Shah's second wife, Soraya, had been able to do. The Shah had had Farah's forebears checked out for any signs of congenital sterility, and (after the suspicious childlessness of a certain great-aunt had been traced to an unfortunate accident suffered by her husband just before their marriage) the future queen was pronounced quite probably fertile. Reza Cyrus, the male child essential to the continuation of the Pahlavi dynasty, was born on October 31, 1960. Farah subsequently gave birth to Princess Farahnaz (1963), Prince Ali Reza (1966), and Princess Leila (1970).

Farah thus overfulfilled her role as childbearer, and began to explore the other possibilities that go with being a queen. She threw herself behind the concept that city parks should have children's libraries, and now, behold, many do. I visited several of them; one, in Teheran, is an exquisite many-arched building containing well-lighted reading tables, kindly librarians, fifty thousand volumes in Persian, Arabic, and English, and even young people reading books. To get her orders carried out, Farah had a $5-million-a-year budget and a staff of forty.

But sometimes the queen gave orders that did not get carried out, because they were silly, ill-defined, or boldly ignored. Once she ordered people to play more tennis, and later she ordered the government to stop "imports of all articles of bad or worthless design." She spiritedly opposed construction of a big hotel in Teheran's Farah Park, but developmental impulses prevailed. Realizing her limitations, the queen often fell back on stratagems, persuasion, and example. Unable to stir the Ministry of Culture and Arts into effective activity, Farah created her own organization for the support of the arts. Upon learning that the streets of a poor section of the capital had been paved in anticipation of her visit, she remarked, rather resignedly, "If I knew that any place I visited would be asphalted, I would inspect several every day." One of her causes was the cure of leprosy, and when she visited the northern village of Raji, where cured lepers live, she accepted kisses and hugs from deformed victims of the disease as a way of showing that they should "realize that they are no longer lepers and that they must work, learn new skills, and do business like all other normal, healthy people."

Many gave Farah credit for sharpening the Shah's interest in social justice and hence for his White Revolution. But among the women around the Shah it was not Farah who served as his closest adviser; it was his twin sister, Princess Ashraf. The two women were by force of circumstance cast as unfriendly rivals—Farah as the young, beautiful, quiet-voiced, somewhat uncertain and inexperienced queen who would nevertheless rule Iran if the king were to die; Ashraf as the case-hardened royal confidante long trained in affairs of state, who might have had a chance to be queen herself but for Iran's male-chauvinist constitution.

Ashraf is energetic, courageous, intelligent, and volcanic. Her parties are sparkling; her *mots* are *bons,* her will is ferrous, and her furies famous. "A real man!" one of her admirers told me, although in physical stature she is five feet one and wears size eight. Way back in 1946, the Shah, who had learned to appreciate his sister's brains and strength, sent Ashraf to Moscow to confront Joseph Stalin over the Soviet Union's threatened seizure of Azerbaijan. Expecting ten minutes with the Russian dictator, Ashraf got three hours, and her flashing amber eyes and impassioned speech persuaded Stalin that Iran would not be such a pushover as he had thought. "A true patriot," he said as she left, and he gave her a fur-lined coat.

Ashraf's enemies accuse her of many scandalous crimes, opium-running and heavy gambling being among the milder charges. I heard in various parts of Iran that this or that factory or business was "Ashraf's," and she apparently used her position to make a fortune.

The princess has been married three times, and her first two marriages had something to do with her passion for women's rights. The first took place in her teens, when her father, the strong-willed Reza Shah, brought to the palace two young socialites and announced Ashraf's engagement to the better-looking of the pair, the other being assigned to her older sister, Shams. On the evening before the double wedding, Shams, the apple of her father's eye, demanded a switch of grooms. "Nothing could be easier," said the old shah, and the next day, Ashraf had to marry the second-best. Eventually her father let her get a divorce, but he also picked her next husband, an Egyptian. After another divorce, Ashraf happened, while sipping espresso at a sidewalk café in Paris, to meet an attractive Iranian lawyer named Mehdi Bushehri. They married and, she says, "Love between us ripened and blossomed into friendship."

The Shah's father had four wives and eleven children, so besides the king and Ashraf there are lots of other Pahlavis. By a cousin who died in childbirth in 1904, the old shah fathered a daughter, whom he later married to his personal physician. By the mother of the twins, Mohammed Reza and Ashraf, he also sired their older sister, Princess Shams, and a brother who was killed when his plane crashed in 1954. The old shah's third wife gave birth to Prince Gholam, and his fourth to Princes Abdorreza, Ahmed, Mahmud, and Hamid, and the Princess Fatemeh. In such a large family, it might seem that the question of the succession, which kept Iran and the royal family on pins and needles for many years until Prince Reza Cyrus was born, could not have been so hard to solve. But the constitution insisted that the crown must go to a male, and that no one with the blood of the previous dynasty, the Qajars, might succeed, which eliminated all the children of the old shah's third and fourth wives, both Qajars (he did not mind marrying into the family he overthrew). What with marriages and remarriages (almost all Their Imperial Highnesses have been divorced at least once), and the resulting children and grandchildren, the people whom the Shah could call relatives or ex-relatives numbered in the scores. When he was on the throne, they led lives of wealth, leisure, travel, sports, hobbies, social work, and moneymaking. "Some member of the Pahlavi family has a direct and legitimate voice, by dint of ownership, in the operation of nearly all commerce and industry in Iran," wrote Marvin Zonis, a well-informed American student of Iranian society, in *The Political Elite of Iran.* But they had little political power—never served, for example, in the cabinet. They were neither close nor particularly loyal; each lived in his own separate palace, and the Shah's spies kept tabs on his siblings as they did on everyone else.

When he was king, the Shah and his family lived in two palaces, one owned by the state and one by themselves, and they had rights to use a third for ceremonies. I never got to tour any of the palaces thoroughly, but I did get a few glimpses. What's a palace supposed to look like? Golden, moated, turreted, set on a hill? With one treasury for the crown jewels and one for the solid-gold dinner service? Does one see any dogs around a palace?

It is velvety dark on Christmas evening (a time of no special significance in Moslem Iran) when my car lets me out at the gate of the high iron-picket wall around Niavaran Palace in northeastern Teheran, just where the Elburz Mountains begin to rise. The guards look at my passport and make a phone call; then I walk alone, under tall poplars, past glowing lawn lamps and a few drifts left over from a recent snowfall, toward the newest and grandest of the Pahlavi palaces. It looms as a three-story cube of marble, capped by an overhanging thick flat roof. All is silent. At the ample, glass-doored main entrance stand a relaxed-looking army officer, a tail-coated butler, and a Scotch terrier. After only a moment to glance at the lofty atrium of the building, glittering with crystal chandeliers, I am led to the right and planted alone in a gray overstuffed chair in a mini-museum, whose glass cases display decorative Qajar-period jewelry boxes, and pottery and artifacts from ancient Persia. As the butler opens the door to bring me tea in a cloisonné cup with a gold spoon, I hear the echoing bark of the terrier.

On his next visit, the butler, a multilingual personage who has plainly dealt with hundreds of people of grander lineage than mine, leads me up a wide staircase of gentle curve and gradient, and along an ample corridor hung with abstract and Impressionist paintings. He opens a door and with an inclination of his head informs me that I may enter. The room is small, creamy, rich, with an ornate desk near one wall, a sofa and chair against the opposite wall, a bowl of white carnations on a table. The décor is French, except for the *de rigueur* Persian carpet. And in the center of the carpet, all alone, stands a slim and elegantly beautiful woman with a half-smile that dimples her cheeks. She is wearing a floor-length black evening sheath, with filmy black lace to cover the shoulders and arms. The soft sweep of her reddish-brown hair nearly hides her diamond earrings. Her good Persian eyebrows are plucked and subtly made up.

When my audience with the empress Farah had ended, I walked to the sweeping staircase and started down. Out of the corner of my eye I glimpsed a slim figure in black. It was the queen, hurrying up the next flight of the staircase to the third floor. My audience with her was the day's last; her work was over; now it was time to dine. The only other visible person besides myself in the brilliantly lighted palace, she seemed for a moment like a lonely little girl.

Niavaran, built a dozen years ago, was the Shah's response to his desire to get clear out of the claustrophobic and none-too-secure old Marble Palace (now a museum) in downtown Teheran. Niavaran occupies only about ten acres, contiguous to a lovely, formal public park. Farah herself, a former architecture student, conceived the design of the principal building, the royal residence. It is a clean, modern structure, and the interior manages to be intimate on a grand scale, if such a thing is possible. The décor and furnishings are unrestrainedly opulent. Detail: the gold-leafed spigots in the royal bathtubs are shaped like dolphins, with precious stones for eyes, jade for his and amethysts for hers.

State-owned Niavaran was the royal family's "winter" palace—its location puts it in the same climate as the "summer" palace, but it has good central heating. The summer palace was old Reza Shah's response to sweltering in the Marble Palace. On a foot-of-the-mountains site a few miles west of Niavaran, he built Saadabad (Place of Happiness). It amounts to a 300-acre walled estate, surrounded on three sides by the rich houses of the suburb called Shemiran. One approaches the estate on Saadabad Avenue, canopied by tall trees, and the palace grounds themselves are similarly cool and shady—an expanse of forest and grass broken by pools and flower beds. Ten or twelve broad granite steps lead up to the doors of what the minister of court, as we walked toward it together, called "the little palace." The building, facing west at the top of a slight slope, is boxy and cream-colored, with one colonnade set on top of another in the façade.

The Shah's office was on the ground floor, right off the alabaster-floored central hall on the far side from the entry. Since I had taken care to be early for my audience with him, I was seated to wait, alone, in a nearby reception room, about forty by forty feet in size, walled in nubbly saffron silk. The morning sun streamed in through high draped windows, picking out a television receiver and a complete set of Voltaire. The décor included a small Klee, a small Léger, a large Biblical-looking tapestry over a fireplace, a glass case full of porcelain birds, small portraits of the king and queen in which fancifully painted crowns and clothes had been added to photographic faces, and a full-length painting of Farah (by "MacAvoy '73") with a Persepolis cityscape and her children in the background and a Persian rug in the foreground. A servant brought me tea in a cup of peacock design, and set a bowl of gardenias on a coffee table.

Neither at Saadabad nor at Niavaran could I see the "Peacock Throne"—that journalistic metaphor for the Iranian monarchy. In fact, the phrase is more metaphor than reality. The original Peacock Throne was undoubtedly the one that the Iranian conqueror Nadir Shah seized when he captured the Red Fort in Delhi in 1739, and he created the initial confusion by ordering Indian workmen to make him a divan in the same bebaubled style. He brought both Peacock Thrones back to Iran, and soon lost them in a war against the Kurds, who distributed the jewels as spoils. History refers vaguely to the Peacock Thrones (perhaps reproductions) of a couple of subsequent shahs. Lord Curzon in *Persia and the Persian Question* (1892) says that a late-eighteenth-century shah found the Peacock Throne of Nadir Shah "in a piecemeal condition" at Mashhad and rebuilt it as the piece of furniture, more bed than throne, now displayed in Golestan Palace (of which more in a minute). But this same divan is also attributed to the genial Qajar Fath Ali Shah (reigned 1797–1834), who had Isfahan artisans make him a Throne of the Sun and then bedded a comely girl named Tavus, or Peacock, upon it on their wedding night. To confound confusion, the Iranian crown-jewels museum displays a chair-style throne of such blinding splendor that many viewers refuse to believe that it is not the Peacock Throne. In actuality, it is a Qajar reproduction of Nadir Shah's original, and was used by the two Pahlavi shahs at their coronations.

Just as the Shah did not own his winter palace, he did not own the crown jewels, because they were long ago converted into the security for the national currency—a sort of Fort Knox in gems. The Shah and the Empress could borrow some of them for the highest state occasions—though the former empress Soraya wrote that she found the Central Bank to be tiresomely fussy in demanding receipts for the jewels, and in insisting on their prompt return. As anyone can see by visiting the bank's museum, the crown-jewel collection surpasses anything of the kind in the world, including Topkapi. In crowns, tiaras, scepters, necklaces, and brooches, or simply heaped up in trays, these gems are the fabulous loot of uncounted shahs from times past. What passes for the Peacock Throne displays 26,733 jewels, and the Pahlavi crown, with egret-feather crest, has 3,380 diamonds. The collection also includes the 191-carat Daria-i-Noor, one of the largest cut diamonds in the world.

When the royal family had occasion to borrow some baubles, the setting for the event was likely to be their third, and purely ceremonial, palace: Golestan, down near the bazaar. Built by the early Qajars, Golestan—Rose Garden—remains a stunning place. It stands amid pools, fountains, and trees of great girth in an area of government ministries, still in use, which testify to its former importance. The Shah gave Golestan to the nation in 1971; it is now chiefly a museum whose main exhibit is itself, though it does contain some curious and valuable gifts—Sèvres, Japanese, and Russian malachite vases, ornate mechanical clocks, something that looks like a model of a Jules Verne submarine—presented to various kings in the past couple of centuries.

If gaudiness is magnificence, Golestan is magnificent; in any case it is irresistibly delightful to the eye. Painted tiles, mostly in blue and yellow, showing roses, lions, castles, and pastoral scenes, cover the façades. In a large portico there sits a divan carved from alabaster and marble, with fire-breathing chimeras and other grotesque monsters as motifs. Inside, mosaic mirrors cover the walls; the secret of their bedazzlement is that four small triangular pieces of glass are set to form a low pyramid, and these pyramids, repeated endlessly, reflect light in all directions, with diamond-like effect. In the throne room, where tail-coated diplomats would pay their respects to the Shah at his New Year salaam, the floor is covered with so many carpets that they overlap like shingles.

But to return to the question, What *is* a palace? In retrospect, a palace seems to be a place where a king can hide himself from reality, a place that overwhelms and silences messengers bringing the truth, a place of excessive opulence upon which the subjects can concentrate their hatred.

The Shah's own wealth was obscenely large. The fortune derived from the two thousand villages his father had seized (sometimes by murdering their owners) in the richest farm country of Iran, bordering the Caspian Sea. Upon taking the throne, the Shah found himself to be the lord of 236,000 virtual serfs in the crown lands, which were worth $60 million. During the late 1940s, the Shah returned some of this domain to the original landlords. In 1951, when wily Prime Minister Mohammed Mossadegh threatened his reign, the Shah distrib-

uted the land attached to 584 villages directly to its tillers, who pros-
trated themselves and kissed his feet. Mossadegh, who had a land-
reform scheme of his own up his sleeve, pronounced this to be nothing
but a grandstand act, and forced the Shah to put his land under government supervision. After Mossadegh fell, the Shah got it back, and during the late 1950s, to the smack-smack of a great deal more kissing
of boots, he turned over all the rest of the land to its cultivators.

But not for free. Rather, the new owners had to pay for it in twenty-
five annual installments (which, to be sure, were smaller than what
they formerly turned over as sharecroppers). This money went into a
new Development and Rural Cooperative Bank, later known as the
Bank Omran, or, colloquially, as "the Shah's bank." The Shah combined
the bank's wealth with other vast funds derived from his father, who
founded the Pahlavi custom of cutting himself and his near and dear
into any profitable private enterprise in Iran. For starters the Shah
got into cement factories, oil tankers, and hotels. In 1961 he put most
of his assets into a newly created Pahlavi Foundation, an institution
now familiar to anyone who has ever stood at the corner of Fifth Avenue and Fifty-second Street and viewed the skycraper belonging to
its Manhattan offshoot.

This charitable endowment and family trust fund gave a none-
too-conspicuous variety of benefits to Iranians: artificial limbs, fuel
for the poor, aid to students, and—unabashedly—piles of money for
relatives of the Shah. Mr. Pahlavi's foundation did not win a reputation
for altruism to equal Mr. Ford's—but then altruism itself is not in such
good repute in Iran as it is in the United States. What the Pahlavi
Foundation seemed chiefly concerned with was defending and enlarging its assets. Its investments included a tire factory, a publishing venture, sugar factories, the Imperial Teheran Hilton Hotel and the Hyatt
Regency Hotel on the Caspian, a computer marketing enterprise, an
oil-well drilling company, and two casinos by the Caspian Sea—which
contributed to the Shah's downfall by identifying him with gambling,
anathema to devout Moslems. The foundation probably ranked just
after the National Iranian Oil Company and the Industrial Mining
and Development Bank of Iran (and the government itself) as the most
powerful economic force in Iran. The Shah himself ran it, as custodian,
and gave it close attention, right down to selecting minor beneficiaries
for its charities. To put up the New York building, he hired lawyer
William P. Rogers, Nixon's first secretary of state, to set up an American
subsidiary of the foundation and get tax exemption on the ground that
the building's earnings would go to support Iranian students in the
United States. Bank Omran became part of the Pahlavi Foundation's
portfolio when the foundation was created, and its contribution to char-

ity in America was investment in a $500 million complex of office buildings, hotels, and apartment houses on the banks of the Mississippi in the French Quarter of New Orleans. Another American asset of the Pahlavi Foundation was, curiously, 5 percent of the First National Wisconsin Bank of Milwaukee. Robert Graham, for some years Teheran correspondent of the London *Financial Times,* estimated the total value of the foundation at $2.8 to $3 billion.

Apart from that, Swiss bank sources say, the Shah had yet another billion in personal wealth, and his brothers and sisters (particularly Ashraf) and nephews and nieces are rolling in money from years of cutting themselves into other people's business in return for royal favors. In mid-1979, the revolutionary government had announced plans to confiscate the Pahlavi Foundation. Getting the assets within Iran seemed easy. Whether the government could grab the Shah's riches outside Iran, and make him a pauper, seemed less likely.

PART
TWO

THE IRANIANS

6

"Drown Him, Even If I Drown Too"

❋

Conceivably the Shah sometimes wished that he ruled over a land as benign as a South Sea island and as fertile as Argentina, and over a people as cooperative as the Swiss and as dutiful as Germans; but such blessings were not his. Except for its oil, Iran is a spare and forbidding country, and its individualistic, hard-to-govern people do not shape readily into the molds of modernization.

Approached from the Indian Ocean, Iran presents a wall of mountains that rise directly from the water. Approached from Iraq, on the west, Iran is an awesome snow-capped range lifting up from the Mesopotamian plain. From the north, from the Soviet Union's low-lying Turkmenistan, Iran appears once more as lofty mountains creating a formidable barrier. And from the east, from Pakistan, one comes to Iran through the range that forms the western wall of the Indus valley.

The land contained within these rims, which average 10,000 feet in elevation, is also high, in many places (including most major cities) nearly a mile above the sea. It is as though the mountains formed a deep dish filled almost to the brim with stones and salt and sand. This high Iranian tableland, bigger than France plus Spain plus Germany, or the whole American South, does not stand quite completely in isolation, for on the northwest it adjoins mountainous Turkey, and on the northeast it adjoins Afghanistan's Hindu Kush highlands, which rise up into the Himalayas. Nonetheless, Iran is unique as a plateau nation, much bigger and better defined than its North American geographical counterpart, the Great Basin of Nevada and Utah.

Oil and other underground riches have had to be Iran's salvation, for what is on the surface is bitterly minimal. The jagged, narrow Elburz Mountains roughly border the north of the country; the broad, harsh Zagros Mountains, which touch the Elburz range in the northwest, sweep desolately south and then east. The dead heart and center of the country, the deserts called Kavir (Salt) and Lut (Sand), are empty and unspeakably barren. Starting near Teheran, a camel caravan could travel eastward for four hundred miles without crossing a single road. Even apart from this Iranian outback, the rest of the country, mountains and all, looks like desert from the air, although, to be sure, about a twenty-third of it is cultivated and greens up with sprouting wheat or barley in spring or fall. Only the fingernail of land along the Caspian coast is well watered, forested, and verdant with rice and fruits. Averaged out across Iran, only ten inches of rain fall in a year, as compared to the world average of forty, and in the central deserts the average rainfall is only two inches. "Snow is worth more than gold," say the Iranians. To Westerners envious of Iran's oil, the Shah used to reply: "Give us your rain. Rains will come until the end of the world. Oil will be finished in twenty-five years' time."

As singular as the land are the people, distinct from all their neighbors in race, culture, and history. The misconceptions of many Westerners to the contrary notwithstanding, Iran is in no way an Arabic country. You do not see the *kaffiyeh* in Iran, nor hear the lilting Arabic tongue. Iran is Iran, a distinct nation; and the Iranians are Iranians, a distinct people. Broadly, the distinctions are these: the Iranians

• Descend mostly from Aryans, the ancestors of present-day Northern Europeans, rather than from the Semites who are the forebears of modern Arabs and Jews, or from the Turkomans who fathered today's Turks.

• Speak Persian, the modern version of the language the Aryans brought with them, a tongue close in structure and vocabulary to English, and unrelated to Arabic or Hebrew (except that it is written in Arabic letters and uses a lot of Arabic words).

• Relate themselves, as friends, allies, travelers, and students, to Western Europeans and Americans rather than to their physical neighbors. Even poor farmers compare themselves to Belgians or Italians more naturally than to Pakistanis or Arabs.

• Belong, as Moslems, to the Shiite branch of Islam, which differs in many substantial ways from the Sunni branch prevailing in Turkey, the Arab countries, and Pakistan (as well as in Bangladesh, Malaysia, Indonesia, and much of black Africa).

• Cherish a vast and poetic literature, and their own traditions in music, architecture, painting, and food.

National character is, as Sir Walter Scott once wrote, hard to define, something whose "existence we are all aware of; and proposing to travel, consider it as certain, nearly, that we have peculiar advantages to hope for, and dangers to guard against, from the manners of a particular region, as that we shall enjoy peculiar pleasures, or have to face peculiar inconveniences." Elusive as the concept may be, the national character of the Iranians clearly contains two historical determinants that make this people distinct from the peoples of other nations. The first is the Iranians' guileful, many-centuried struggle to preserve their culture and identity while falling before military attacks by all the great conquerors of Eastern Hemisphere history—Alexander, the Arabs, the Turks, Genghis Khan, Tamerlane. The second is the acute schizophrenia of embracing (as a consequence of the Arab conquest) a religion that holds Persia's glorious ancient history to be pagan and despicable.

The contradictions created by these historic tensions live in every Iranian, and affect his life and behavior. "We have always been trying to survive in the face of some invading power," a wise and meditative deputy of the Iranian National Assembly, Mahmud Ziai, told me a while back. "We are the reverse of the Japanese, who were never invaded. If we had not been invaded so much, we'd be like them." A young businessman whom I met in the provincial city of Ahvaz capped a long disquisition by saying that "so many defeats make a people noncommittal, reserved, unenterprising." As the revolution suggested, Iranians seem to feel that they are good people, but being good people has not done them much good. An American diplomat serving in Iran pointed out to me that "there's a difference in perspective between Americans and Iranians. We're used to stability, and can count on it. Iranians still see life as teetering on the edge of a dark abyss." Deputy Ziai invoked the rare ups and numerous downs of Iran's history to show that "America—young, classless, formed by people who rejected the old country, or were rejected by it—is diametrically different from this country." History tells the Iranians that you always lose in the end, something that Americans do not yet have reason to believe.

And these feelings are only heightened by the national split personality that results from the second historical factor, the conflict between the heritages of the two halves of the nation's history—between the Iran of the ancient Medes and Persians and the Iran of Islam, between the Zoroastrian god Ahura Mazda and the Mohammedan god Allah, between Persepolis and Mecca.

Parents agonize over whether to name their boy children Hormoz, a contraction of Ahura Mazda, or Mohammed, for the Prophet; Jamshid, for the Persian mythical hero, or Abdul, Arabic for "servant of." It is a source of pride to be called Hushang or Leila, from mythology, or Ardeshir or Mandana, from ancient history. But it is also respectable to be, or claim to be, a descendant of Mohammed, and bear the honorific title Seyyid to prove it; to have made the *hajj* (pilgrimage) to Mecca, and bear the honorific title Hajji to prove that. With half of their beings, the Iranians still treasure their pre-Islamic past, the times of the Persian Empire and the Parthians and the fabulous Sassanian kings. With the other half of their beings, Iranians express their devotion to Islam, in particular to the Shiite sect of it—greater devotion, they often say, than that of the Arabs to their Sunni belief. So one half of the Iranian past is at war with the other half, and modern Iranians, seeking identity, are torn in two directions.

"There is in the heart of every Iranian, even the illiterate, this conflict between his Persian heritage and his imposed religion," Ziai told me. "And more and more the conflict is in the open and the ancient culture comes to the fore. Arabic words that crept into our language, for example, are being cast out by most writers and replaced by authentic Persian words from our ancient tongue." Scholars dig into history to rediscover pre-Islamic Persia, "to prove that Persians were great people before the Arabs came." These scholars readily uncover the ever renewable fascination and psychological impact of Persian mythology, so interesting and valuable that young nations with short mythologies (such as the United States) have reason to envy Iran. But these scholars must also face such facts as Persia's need through history to borrow culture, which is "something in the nature of a confession of weakness," as one historian puts it, and helps to explain some of Iran's failings. The 1979 revolution clearly exemplified this strain. By many acts—such as naming his personal guard the Ten Thousand Immortals after the guard of the emperor Cyrus—the Shah allied himself with ancient Persia. It was quite natural that his opponents took as their leader Ayatollah Khomeini, that quintessential Moslem.

Yet, not so strangely, double identity is better than no identity, and Iran adds up to an authentic and distinct nation, like France, Greece, or China, and not an ersatz conglomerate, like Lebanon or Canada. The conflict in Iran is within individuals, and not between classes, nor between religions, nor (with fast-disappearing exceptions) between tribes or races. The effect is to put every individual on his own, not feeling strong ties to his society as a whole (as the New Zealanders or the Japanese do), or to a substantial part of it (like the Scots or the Texans). The vicissitudes of history teach Iranians the importance of a man's survival, of looking out for himself; the same history diminishes the concept of a united society working toward a glorious national destiny. To this kind of interpersonal disunity the Iranians add deep skepticism (born of past defeat) over the potentialities of working together toward common goals. Obviously, no one can say whether this attitude is better or worse than the submission of the individual to society of, say, the Germans or the Russians; but it is a distinct attitude.

It struck me as illuminating, when the Shah was in power, that amid the pressures to conform that are part and parcel of a strong-arm monarchy one found a people whose most visible characteristic was concentration on self. Watching a military parade for the visiting Sheik of Qatar, for example, I saw plenty of men break through police lines to cross the street—no awe for authority was going to stand in the way of their me-first desire to get to the other side. I kept asking myself: "Is this a monarchy or an anarchy?" The answer seemed to be that if Iran were not a monarchy it would be an anarchy. The Shah might well have argued that his preeminent function was to unify and discipline the Iranians. He once wrote, with a figurative sigh, that "Persians have always been pronounced individualists. Neither invasions nor foreign domination nor other adversities have ever quenched the average Persian's determination to express himself in his own way." He made the point that Rastakhiz, his wholly owned political party, was created to take on "the task of preventing the individualistic and selfish mentality from dominating the whole of society." Ironically, the Shah did in the end unite the Iranians, if only momentarily, in hatred of him.

In its mildest form, this excessive individualism works out as unwillingness to collaborate. Team sports are weak in Iran, which goes in for weight lifting, wrestling, horsemanship, tennis, and skiing—in fact, the Persian language used to have no word for "team," and had to borrow it from English.

In its more harmful form, excessive individualism brings envy and malice, exploitation and manipulation, rascality and guile. A motorcycle rider, bulling his way illegally through a throng on a sidewalk, grows furious rather than apologetic if a child steps in his way. Unwillingness or inability to help a fellow human brings pleasure rather than concern. Several times I was greeted at our local post office with joyous cries of "No stamps! All gone!" In supermarkets, me-firstism leads to endless little tussles among line-jumpers in the checkout queues, and blasting one's way through the five-items-or-less counter with, say, two dozen articles is regarded as a delectable victory of the individual over the collectivity. An American businessman who had been in Teheran for many years remarked to me, rather sweepingly, that "the missing element is love, human compassion. Particularly between men and women, the relationship is usually exploitation. They do love themselves, though," he added sardonically.

"Drown him, even if I drown too," says a little Persian proverb. In losing a war to Afghanistan during the nineteenth century, each Persian general took delight in the defeats of the others. Some Iranians told me that their fellow countrymen's individualism was a powerful barrier to Communism. "The appeal of capitalism is strong here even to the poor," one explained. "Each thinks he has a chance of acquiring a Mercedes-Benz, and would rather go for that than be leveled out by socialism." Added another: "People are interested in getting things, and if somebody gets something, each person feels, 'I must have that thing.' "

The order of priorities in most Iranian minds, as many people to whom I talked pointed out, is: first, self; second, family; third, the nation. Patriotism is not a flaming passion in Iran. Since excessive nationalism has probably caused the world more violence than excessive individualism, these values may well deserve some admiration. But the consequence, as the tactful scholar John Marlowe puts it in *Iran: A Short Political Guide,* is that "Iranian nationalism appears to have little of that air of common purpose, of that sense of dedication, which have given such an irresistible impulse to the national movements of other and less well-endowed peoples." Deputy Ziai observed to me that "it's very difficult to persuade people that they must sacrifice."

With such individualists as constituents, politicians strive vainly to form a consensus. When I interviewed the mayor of Teheran, I asked, as my opening question, "How many policemen are there in this city?" He reacted as though stung by a bee. "Why do you want to know that?" he demanded in alarm. He picked up his phone, and in Persian barked what I took to mean: "Who let this spy into my office?" I withdrew the question, but added that the number of policemen in New York, London, or Tokyo is not a military secret but an easily ascertainable fact. He began to understand my point, and then explained his position. "If I revealed the number of policemen in Teheran," he said, *"nobody* would be pleased. Half of the people would protest that there are too many, and half would protest that there are too few."

Because well-organized and collaborative societies count heavily on interpersonal trust in order to function, it follows that a nation of self-interested individualists should be tinged with mistrust—and Iran is. Iranians mistrust their accomplishments, their future, and one another. Brothers demand collateral before lending money to sisters. The Ministry of Economic Affairs and Finance, says the newspaper *Kayhan International,* assumes "that all taxpayers are guilty of understating their taxable income until proven innocent." Businessmen mistrust their partners; parents mistrust their children; professors mistrust their peers; fellow employees mistrust one another. In a poll a few years ago, a majority agreed that "most of my associates would stab me in the back if it meant that they could get ahead faster that way."

Another Persian proverb says: "Conceal thy gold, thy destination, and thy creed." If concealment implies lying, the Iranian must and does stand ready to lie. In Iran lying is so commonplace as to cause perennial public concern. In a bas-relief among the ruins at Persepolis, a messenger reporting to the emperor Darius about 500 B.C. is depicted tugging his beard, a gesture that was supposed to reassure the king that the man was not lying. To judge from his famous stone inscription at Behistun, Darius had a lot of problems with prevaricators, and he ordained that "the man who is a liar, destroy him utterly." For ages the Sunni Moslems, who dominated what is now Iraq, required Iranian Shiite Moslems to profess to be Sunnis in order to make pilgrimages to Shiite shrines there, and the Iranians habitually did so, for this was honorable practice of the act of *taqiyah,* dissimulation.

Dishonesty and its variants—deception, cheating, hypocrisy, guile, duplicity, pretense, knavery, fraud, mendacity, and corruption—are the stuff of a great body of literature on the Iranians, the most accessible book in English being *The Adventures of Hajji Baba of Ispahan.* The author was the British diplomat James Morier (1780–1849), who, having traveled lengthily in Persia, resolved to do for Persia what Lesage had done for Spain in *Gil Blas,* and the result is a classic worthy of comparison. Poking affectionate fun at the Persians from the first paragraph, Morier baptized his picaroon with the honorific Hajji for having been born when his mother, not he, was making a pilgrimage to Kerbela, not Mecca (just as not every modern Iranian who calls himself Hajji has actually made a pilgrimage to Mecca). In the course of eighty chapters, Hajji Baba rises from barber to robber to doctor to executioner to high official of the state.

In his ascent Hajji Baba encounters, among hundreds of characters, a caravan guard who "enjoyed a great reputation for courage, which he had acquired for having cut off a Turcoman's head whom he had once found dead on the road." He meets a poet proud of having written a verse about the lord high treasurer that "he in his ignorance mistook for praise [because] he thought that the high-sounding words in which it abounded (which, being mostly Arabic, he did not understand) must contain an eulogium [and] did not in the least suspect that they were, in fact, expressions containing the grossest disrespect." He meets a doctor "who calls himself a staunch Musselman" but "makes up for his large potations of cold water and sherbet abroad, by his good stock of wine at home." He meets a mullah who boasts: "None pray more regularly than I. No one goes to the bath more scrupulously, nor abstains more rigidly from everything that is counted unclean. You will find neither silk in my dress, nor gold on my fingers. My ablutions are esteemed the most complete of any man's in the capital, and the mode of my abstertion [wiping the rectum] the most in use." The mullah proposes that Hajji Baba procure whores whom the mullah (for a fee) can marry to lecherous men, and divorce an hour later, in a sanctified form of prostitution.

Morier's English readers took the novel to be a satire, which surprised him, for he insisted that he had tried to write a carefully balanced picture of the Persian psyche. He swore, for example, that he actually heard a Persian soldier say, "If there were no dying in the case, how the Persians would fight!" His judgment of his book was vindicated by the Persians themselves. Then and now, they have read *The Adventures of Hajji Baba of Ispahan* as a straight and psychologically accurate account of the national character. Some have insisted that it was originally a Persian book, and merely translated into English.

Clearly, the charge that dishonesty is rampant in Iran can easily be overdrawn; Iranians do not vary greatly from human beings elsewhere. Nevertheless, the fact seems to be that dishonesty is built into the system. The Koran supports taqiyah. Children are brought up to be deceitful. "My mother taught me to lie," an Iranian who now lives in the United States told me. "She said lying was clever. I was amazed to find American mothers teaching their kids to tell the truth. My mother told my father, who was a colonel, that he ought to rip off part of the soldiers' ration allowance." His mother argued that "everyone else did it," but Iranians have profounder rationales than that for lying. The poet Saadi held that "well-meaning falsehoods are better than a truth which leads to a quarrel." In his novel *A World Full of Nightingales,* Leo Vaughan has one character say of another: "Attacking Dr. Marvasti for not being honest is like criticizing a cat for not barking. It's only single-minded people like Anglo-Saxons who think honesty is even possible, much less desirable. A [Persian] has a more complicated mind; he sees so many sides to every issue he knows you can't be strictly honest about anything, anyhow, so often he doesn't bother to try." And Marvasti himself is made to say: "One can only afford to be truthful about things when the truth is bearable."

"Iranians get into one another's favor by any means," said Deputy Ziai sadly, commenting on the guile employed in fawning upon superiors. "Let it stay between you and me" is the customary way to start revealing what one has sworn not to pass on. One function of walls around houses is to put a poor front on a rich interior, deceiving various kinds of supplicants. For a journalist, accumulating facts in Iran is a maddening process, since few sources can be relied upon. "My advice," says one old Iran hand, "is: always ask at least three people."

The historical lesson that you can't win, so why try, together with a benign absence of the Puritan ethic that keeps so many American noses to the grindstone, makes work an activity of no great seriousness to many Iranians. "For centuries people have not been interested in doing their jobs," a professor of history told me. One of my first puzzlements upon reaching Teheran was the much-repeated sight of sidewalk cabinetmakers hacking through wood with dull saws; my Anglo-Saxon formation decrees that a sharp saw gets the job done faster and gives its user more satisfaction. A note I made in Tabriz reads: "Man at airport mopping floor—floor still dirty when he's done—he seems to feel that his duty is not to clean the floor but merely to move the mop around."

It's a bit banal to draw examples of sloppy work from among restaurant waiters, but since Iranians with whom I dined suffered the same peccadilloes as I did, I assume that I can be objective. Waiters tend to appear in mismatched trousers and jacket, whisk the crumbs from the previous meal into your lap, and take down orders that only vaguely match what they finally bring. The bill always requires scrutiny, for what you ordered may grow in price between the menu and the tab, and the addition may be imperfect. I knew an Englishman who sent a waiter back three times to add up the bill, got three different sums, and then maliciously whipped a calculator out of his pocket to produce the authorized version.

Iranians can make a transaction like buying an airplane ticket into an operation approximately as time-consuming as negotiating an end to a major war. The attendant cracks pistachio nuts, interrupts for a long personal telephone conversation, then disappears to discuss the ticket perplexedly with a superior, as though this were history's first sale of an airplane passage. Many cabdrivers are similarly sloppy. They are good at filling the air with cigarette smoke and radio music, they do not mind making the passenger wait while they gas up their perennially empty tanks, they overcharge to the limit, but their knowledge of major streets and routes and destinations has only been brought down to the beginning of the century. Workmanship of all kinds tends to be mediocre. Plumbers seal joints with grass, rather than compound, and pipes leak. Tangerine-pickers jerk the fruit from the stem, causing it to spoil quickly. In two successive hotels I found the shower head broken and dangling from its pipe, unnoticed and unrepaired. Time seems to mean nothing (in fact, clocks are rare in offices and public places, and where they are to be found they are often wrong). Bank clerks take an hour to sell a book of traveler's checks. When I was in Teheran people were complaining that a new building for the post office, under construction for nine years, was still a couple of years from being finished. Professionalism, it seems, has little repute and few rewards.

In this century, the Iranian personality, already split between its pre-Islamic and Islamic psyches, has had to endure another division: Westernization. Adoption of the forms of parliamentary government, of electricity, and of Western dress were early steps, and sufficiently traumatic in their time, but then the influx of Westernization became torrential. It came to Iran in the form of books, consumer products, movies, and fashions. But mostly it came in technology, and in the persons of thousands of foreigners living in Iran to apply the technology. And besides accepting the inflow of Westernization, Iranians went out and energetically acquired it by living abroad and attending European and American universities. As a consequence, for example, English became the indispensable second language in the armed forces and the universities. Herodotus wrote that "the Persians of all nations are the most ready to adopt foreign customs," but the overwhelming impact of Westernization in recent years made many Iranians to whom I talked doubtful, worried, or even angry. The Persian character has resisted invasion for several millenniums, they said in effect, but can it resist this one?

"The half-Eastern, half-Western Iranian—he's a torn man," one observer remarked to me. Another said: "Any Persian who gets through high school nowadays is an alienated person. The old verities are gone. He won't trust his father and he won't trust his teacher." The social and sexual freedom of the West, for example, though appealing to Iranians who had experienced it, collided head-on with Islamic law. One common consequence of the fear of Westernization was to put down the West; I heard many Iranians deplore Western crime rates and "permissiveness." On the wall of a vocational school I saw a slogan that expressed paranoia against and reliance on Westernization all in the same mouthful: "We are an independent nation and don't fear foreigners and since we are the equal of any other country, cooperation with other nations is easy for us."

A century ago Japan deliberately undertook a process that was often called Westernization, adopting even such out-of-place frills as fancy-dress balls and sewing circles. But later the Japanese rejected the excesses, and went on to achieve a remodeling better described as modernization; they adopted parliamentary government, for example, and heavy industry, without altering the essential Japanese character. In Iran, too, modernization can be distinguished from Westernization, and modernization seems to be both inevitable and beneficial: Iran needs steel, copper, railroads, hospitals, secular schools, even cars. It is Westernization seen as cultural change—or more precisely, "Westernization at the cost of our culture," as one professor put it to me—that perturbs the Iranians.

"Our top government people are all educated abroad, and don't even know Persian history," a historian complained. "The expatriates compare things here with things in Indianapolis, and wind up criticizing everything Persian," said a parliamentary deputy. Western-educated Jamshid Amuzegar, the former prime minister, predicted to me that "in ten years we'll have an enormous amount of Western culture here. I hope we can differentiate between the bad and the good."

In the *Tehran Journal* a couple of years ago, publisher Farhad Massoudi quoted the advice of a sage who once told Iranians: "To foreign culture open both the windows of thy house—then let foreign culture seep in through one window and leave from the other." It was a pity, Massoudi went on, "that many of our people have forgotten to open the other window to let foreign culture, streaming in the front window, pass through.

"They have made the life in the West a pattern to build their own lives on. Ever since they were born they have watched the turquoise skies and the beautifully tiled buildings of Iran, but they seem to like nothing better than the violent and suffocating Western architecture; the first language they learned was the tongue of their ancestors, but today when they talk, what comes out is a mixture of English, French, German, and Persian words; they learned thousands of beautiful and intricate Persian couplets at school, but now, when they wish to argue a point, quotations from foreign experts come more freely to them." (Of course, Massoudi, writing in English, only proved his own point: all the Iranian elite speak at least one Western language, and speak it well. A Persian story tells of a mouse in a mosque who was afraid to come out of his hole because he heard a cat meowing, but confidently emerged when he heard a dog barking. The cat snagged him. "Where did the dog go?" asked the dismayed mouse. Replied the cat: "Don't you know that in Persia anyone with good taste speaks two languages?")

Massoudi saw "danger to national identity" in Iran's indifferent acceptance of foreign influence, citing the use of "foreign names and terminology for shops, buildings, and in our daily life. Today, there are perhaps more shops and business houses bearing foreign than Iranian names," and not only in Teheran but throughout the country. Worse yet, "some Iranian parents are so oblivious to the beauty of their language and literature as to choose foreign names for their offspring. This must be stopped."

A less fearful and more profound view of the consequences of Westernization came from Ehsan Naraghi, director of Iran's Institute for Educational and Scientific Research and Planning. Dressed in a shapeless old bathrobe, he received me one morning at his large, much lived-in family house in central Teheran, and genially thrust into my hand, to read while he bathed, a copy of a speech he had delivered not long before to a symposium of Iranians and Americans in Persepolis.

In this paper Naraghi ignored, presumably as not worth much concern, all the supposed defects of the Iranian national character, and argued that its overwhelming merits shape a collective psyche that not only should not, but cannot, be Westernized. He recalled that one of the leading reformers early in the century openly declared: "We must Westernize ourselves, body and soul." Today, he said, "among the new generation of poets, writers, and artists hailing from the most diverse schools of thought, not one wishes to become Western 'in body and soul.' " Why? Because Westernization is too rational and objective to deal with the human condition, and one of the greatest merits Naraghi quite correctly found among Iranians was their humanity. How odd, he thought, that Westerners, "having exalted rationality to ensure human happiness [had] to invent a special discipline—psychoanalysis— to cure the ills arising from an over-rationally organized life which is deprived of its basic relationship with the non-rational." In truth, psychiatry is rare in Iran, and Naraghi knew why: "Since psychoanalysis itself is the outcome of a rational and objective approach, it has been unable to fulfill the task it set itself." Passionately, he asked: "Why should cultures like ours, in which man is considered in all his aspects, be deprived of all their substance by following a so-called rational course at the end of which lies the vast expanse of the non-rational and the impossibility of receiving an answer to our questions? Why should this wealth of feeling and emotion which has reached us after centuries of tradition and mystical-poetic experience, and which is one of the outstanding features of the Iranian personality in history, have to be considered as something shameful and subjective that we must rid ourselves of?"

Naraghi concluded that "if only for our survival, we cannot do without science and technology in order to make the best possible use of our resources and enable our people to accede to material well-being in conditions of dignity and equity. However, this does not mean that we should regard this material well-being as the sole objective or bestow on it the same forms as it assumes in the West. . . . Our principal concern might be to interrogate other societies on their various experiences." And not only that. The West, too, "must gradually become accustomed to interrogating other cultures and other societies instead of seeking to make them like itself."

As we talked after Naraghi returned from his bath, he paused to answer the telephone. Finishing the call, he remarked, "That was the son of a cousin of mine. He's making nine thousand tomans [$1,350] a month and he wants his employer to raise his pay to fifteen thousand.

That's the kind of materialism the Americans have given us!" The feeling that Iran is losing its soul while it gains the world runs deep. Editor Amir Taheri, deploring "Westoxication," suggested that the West has culturally conquered Iran where the Arabs, Mongols, and Turks could not. He heard an Italian remark that Iran needed "a Reformation, a Renaissance, and a revolution"—advice so gratuitous as to make him respond, with dripping sarcasm, "This is truly charming!"

As his observations suggest, Naraghi found merit among the Iranians chiefly as the expression of a mystical spirit that moderates materialism and values the past. The Iranian experience has formed a people of some cosmic understanding, far less concerned than Westerners over ids and egos. They are animated in argument; they are passionate; they laugh; they kiss; they bow and gesture; they speak in body language; they compliment one another with a courtesy so exquisite, says one American, as to "make me seem like a coltish sophomore." Certain forms of courtesy even take precedence over me-firstism: men still rise and give their seats to women on buses. Nature and bodily contact appeal to Iranians. Vaughan writes of "soldiers and policemen . . . strolling down the street in pairs, holding hands and sniffing roses." Iranians adore water for its taste and its sparkle and its babbling sound. They genuinely prize their heritage of artistry—no one admires the beauty and workmanship in a Persian rug more than the Persians. "Our cooking is the same as it was 2,500 years ago," someone proudly pointed out to me—and Iranian cooking is not only old but also excellent.

As the Iranians themselves stand ready to tell you at any time, they are also a hospitable people. The fact that they boast of it implies that they are hospitable for show or other insincere reasons, such as fishing for a return invitation. "Hospitality is you scratch my back and I'll scratch yours," says one disillusioned foreigner. I heard of many warm invitations extended without specifying a time or a place for the occasion (not unlike, to be sure, the we-must-have-lunch-one-of-these-days turn-off practiced in London and Manhattan). One Iranian returning from his first visit to Moscow pronounced, with cynicism and mathematical exactitude, that "the Russians are five times as hospitable as the Iranian." But there is substance as well as unction in the Iranian proverb that says "The guest comes from God." Hosts serve food in quantities plainly too large for all the guests to consume and in varieties too numerous for any guest to try everything. I was told that "if there are five guests there must be food for twenty." I heard many stories of foreigners enjoying uncalled-for hospitality from poor families in remote villages. "The more rural, the more hospitable," one beneficiary reported. "Anything for the guest—kill the fatted chicken. The guest must sit in the best part of the room, and he's given the finest cushion. The host is supposed to offer tea and food several times, and the guest is supposed to refuse several times before accepting." Another man, an American professor, told me of wandering into a village, where he met a peasant who took him home to a "one-room house, poor except for the rugs and the TV. The lunch was served by his agreeable and candid wife, and then from somewhere the host brought in musicians with flutes and drums, and everybody danced."

"The Persian character comes from a long and turbulent history," said Deputy Ziai, summarizing his fellow subjects. But Ziai, a melancholy, intelligent man whose eyes look right into yours, believes that the Iranians can survive the turbulence of the past. "We always adapt," he said. "We do not believe that just because our forefathers lived in a certain way, we must live that way now. Even if our style of life changes, our tradition does not. Industrialization will not affect that. In fact, our growing literacy and awareness will make people more conscious of the past."

He concluded with what sounded like a bit of good advice. "People who understand Persians do not get frustrated by Persians," he said.

Teheran.

"Nightmarish," London's *Financial Times* calls it. A Yugoslavian composer wrote a loud and dissonant symphony *(Tehrana)* to the city's "total aggressiveness." An Air-India stewardess who stops in Teheran on the London run reports that no passenger ever exclaims, "It's so nice to be back in Teheran!" American servicemen called the place "grungy." During World War II, Roosevelt wrote Churchill that he would be glad to see his British colleague, "even in Teheran."

Architecturally, Teheran has about as much allure as Tucson, Arizona. The city's murderous taxi drivers are entitled by law to kill jaywalkers, and if they don't always succeed, it is because the streets are bottled up with the world's worst traffic jams. Nothing in art, literature, restaurants, or professional skills is truly first-rate. In this ancient land of Iran, Teheran even lacks history, having grown up mostly in the last two hundred years. After the 1979 riots, Teheran also looked a little like a war-struck city, with burned-out banks and cinemas on every hand.

But to see Teheran only through grim-colored glasses is a mistake. For if the city is difficult and problematic, it is also intriguing and astonishing. To begin with, though it is built on the dry clay-sand-and-stone of the high Iranian desert, Teheran is not a sere and desiccated city. "We have lots of water and we use it lavishly," the head of the parks department told me. Channeled from the nearby snow-capped mountains, abundant water grows tens of thousands of blossomy gardens behind the walls that surround all houses. Fountains spout in the public squares. The streets, too, are verdant: in the 1920s Reza Shah armed the soldiers of the Teheran garrisons with watering cans and poplar seedlings, and sent them out to line the streets with trees, under the order "If the tree dies, *you* die!"

This city that is green is also clean. It collects its garbage daily, and during the night men with brooms sweep the streets and even the expressways. Every morning, in front of the stores, boys wash sidewalks with water from candy-striped hoses.

Teheran is a large city, twenty-first in the world, the biggest between Cairo and New Delhi. It is growing fast, having reached a population of 4.5 million from only half a million thirty-five years ago. It overwhelmingly dominates Iran, not only as the capital but also as the home of 14 percent of the population, 23 percent of the manufacturing workers, 63 percent of the students, 76 percent of the automobiles. But so far Teheran strives in vain to achieve the stature of a great city; it lacks not only Tokyo's pace and Washington's stateliness, but even Cairo's antiquity and Delhi's humanity. It needs a Seine, a subway, a center, a spirit, or something.

The modernizing influences of the past few decades still fight in Teheran with its village values. Though Reza Shah banished camels from the city's streets, Teheran still tolerates the sheep. On fine new avenues, shepherds from the countryside drive bands of these utilitarian animals, meat on the hoof, to sell directly to householders, who butcher them. Once, as I rode somewhere with a city government official who was extolling Teheran's sophistication, the car ahead of us stopped and compelled us to wait and watch (my companion wretched with embarrassment) while its driver extracted a bleating sheep from the trunk and took it into his house for subsequent consumption. Another time I saw a peasant sell a lamb on the sidewalk in front of the Central Bank. One comes to understand that a sheep in the city, however innocently he may be nibbling the grass at the side of a street, will be shish kebab in a matter of hours. Occasionally I saw a sheep butchered in the street, blood draining into the gutter and the carcass pumped up with air to make it easier to skin. In this village of four million I also saw strolling ducks and turkeys, and from the eighth-floor office of the interior minister heard roosters crowing.

Like any village, Teheran rises early. I sometimes went out at seven to buy bread, hot from the ovens of any of four or five small bakeries within several blocks. By then the banks, the bric-a-brac shop, the fruit stores, the groceries, and even the (none-too-villagy) Mercedes-Benz showroom were open in the morning sunshine. A wispy old man who did an unbelievably large business in stovepipes could be seen, facing Mecca, at his prayers on the floor of his tiny shop. From the windows of upper floors of apartment houses people dropped refuse in buckets suspended by ropes to the five-man crew of the garbage truck. Every few blocks, I could see steam rising from a pipe that ran under the sidewalk from a shop to the gutter—the exhaust of clothes-pressing machines in dry-cleaning shops, which abound in Teheran as a consequence of the bourgeois Iranian man's insistence on wearing a proper suit at all times.

Similar small commerce proliferates in all the main streets of this fifty-square-mile village. Sidewalk peddlers sell freshly stolen Seiko watches, peacock tail feathers, balloons shaped like animals, floor mats for cars, brooms and mops, Persian melons. Near one of Teheran's main intersections, I saw side by side stalls selling, respectively, men's jockey shorts and prettily veined sheep livers. Newsstands and grocery stores peddle cigarettes one by one. Old women sit beside bathroom scales on the sidewalk, weighing people for two rials (three cents). On Ferdowsi Avenue you can Master Charge a hookah, a carpet, or a sheepskin coat. Beggars are few, except for the blind: an old flutist led by a ragamuffin six-year-old girl, an albino playing an accordion, a grizzled grandfather gently guided by a little boy.

Before the revolution, one charm of Teheran—at least to foreigners—was the naming of stores in English. This practice was intended not only to lure the visitor, but also to provide a cachet impressive to the Iranian shopper. The store signs were bright-colored plastic creations of Roman letters rendered (and often misspelled) in Persian Art Nouveau. What the signs said was by turns engaging and baffling. Some samples:

STORE HEN AND EGG
BARBER SHOP NICEMAN
ANAL CO.
EYEBALLOPTIC
GENERAL BABY
TAILOR SMORT MAN
ESKANDARIAN'S BED
PAYTON PLEACE BOUTIQUE
HILTON SHOOK ABSORBERS
LOCOMOTIVE AUTOMOBILE SHOWROOM
PARADISE INTERNAL DECORATION
ABDY DIAPER SERVICE AND INSURANCE CO.

Sophistication to most Teheranis seems to be things that sparkle. Dozens of stores sell nothing but crystal chandeliers. One store is four stories high, a fabulous sight when ablaze with white light in the evening. This love of light does not mean that Teheran is a neon city, at least so far; the preference is for incandescence. On the tall iron picket fences of the numerous ordnance depots and other military installations, pretty blue and green lights, arranged in star shapes, glow in the night. Mirrors abound in restaurants, theaters, private homes.

In such a village-city, life is largely lived at home, and in Teheran privacy is a mania. The expression of it is mud-brick walls—walls around houses, gardens, and every vacant lot. In some parts of the city you can wander for a long time in small winding streets between walls ten feet high, and only occasionally glimpse a garden through a momentarily opened door. But there is a way, though foreigners rarely use it, to invade the privacy and discover the beauty and tranquillity behind the walls. The view from the upper story of Teheran's British Leyland double-decker buses (fare, seven and a half cents) is a panorama of private lives.

The sounds of Teheran are village sounds, too: the cries of human voices. *"Cot-e shalvari!"* bellows the rag picker from the street—"Coats and trousers!" After him comes the lottery-ticket vendor, the scissors grinder, and the salesman of house plants. Off in the distance, marching high school students count out: *"Yek-do-se-chahar . . . Yek-do-se-chahar."* In the parks strollers carry Japanese-made shortwave radios, and listen to music from afar; on the sidewalks, youths sleep a siesta to the accompaniment of Persian sounds from transistors in their laps.

In still another way is Teheran village: it is, in essence, an oasis. It stands on the desert and could not live but for the water from the mountains that it abuts on its northern boundary. These mountains are part of the Elburz range at their most impressive heights, and they supply Teheran not only with water but also with a presence, a sense of raw nature, almost of dread. Mount Demavend, a few miles east of the city, is Teheran's Fuji, a volcanic cone that rises to 18,600 feet (which is more than 6,000 feet higher than Fuji). In the summer the mountains are dirty yellow, forbiddingly rocky; in the winter they shine with snow that rises in plumes when high winds blow.

For three days in March the mountains turn green with short-lived grass. In smog or dust storms, the range is ghostly, half invisible, a stony cloud high in the sky. But in these mountains, storehouses of the snowmelt that waters Teheran, are green valleys and cold streams which make climbing and camping a pleasant, practicable sport for Teheran's many mountaineers and boy and girl scouts.

Teheran itself, stretching away from the foot of the mountains, is a town on a tilt. Starting from the northern edge, right where the mountains begin their steep rise, one could coast on a bicycle, without pedaling, for twenty miles to the city's southern outskirts, descending in the process from 5,000 feet elevation to 3,000 feet. In the upper stretches of the tilt the grade runs between 3 and 4 percent; north-south walls step down three bricks in about twelve feet of run.

This tilt is the great fact of life in Teheran's geography; it produces concrete consequences in climate and water flow. Teheran's latitude (35°41'N) is about the same as that of Gibraltar, Memphis, San Francisco, or Tokyo—sufficiently near the Tropic of Cancer to guarantee hot summers. And of course Teheran is dry—eight inches of precipitation a year. But what shapes life in Teheran more profoundly than latitude or rainfall is the well-known fact that elevation changes climate. The rich, as elsewhere, pick the best of everything and leave the rest to the poor. In Teheran, the rich have chosen the cool northern sections of the city for their houses and have left the sweltering south to the poor. The middle class, appropriately, lives in the middle elevation. True, in winter, the rich end is colder, but its residents see the winter through with central heating, while the poor shiver around kerosene stoves. On summer weekends, the poor go by the busload to the cool parks and foothills in the north; the rich almost never go to south Teheran for any reason at all. The climate of Teheran thus varies according to who describes it. At a middling elevation, which includes the main business districts, annual average temperature is 61.3 degrees Fahrenheit, with a summer maximum of 102 degrees and a winter minimum of 9 degrees.

In midsummer, the heat is enervating. From my midtown penthouse I saw people sleeping all around on the flat rooftops, to escape hot rooms and enjoy the starry night. Yet often a breeze makes the heat more tolerable, and any shaded place is pronouncedly cooler than a sunny one. The chance of rain, until late fall, is zero; the air is so dry that contractors store mortar cement in uncovered mounds at construction sites. This dryness makes it feasible for houses to have simple, sensible coolers that work on the principle of evaporation (rather than the principle of refrigeration used in air conditioning), and they are a commonplace blessing. From spring through fall, the sky is mostly so clear that the Pan Am pilot on whose plane I arrived announced: "We can see Teheran now from 130 miles away."

In late September come some lightning flashes and sprinkles. October is a fine month, but toward the end you notice that upper-class women have begun to wear gloves, and in early November the more Westernized girls appear in boots. Crowds hurry homeward in cool autumnal air as the sun sets at 5 P.M., but the poplar trees still wear green leaves in spite of a touch of frost that turns the ivy red. At the end of the month the Teheran winter sets in. Once or twice comes that antithetical phenomenon of the desert, the cloudburst. Usually the weather is cloudy or drizzly. One day you rise to see the Elburz Mountains sheathed in white. At the royal family's deserted summer Saadabad Palace in northernmost Teheran, the boughs of the trees bend under several inches of snow—a fairyland sight. Cars traveling down the tilt carry thick snow on their roofs to the business district, where the snow is only a light dusting, and on to the south, where there is only the wet of snow that turned to rain before it landed. Leaves fall heavily from the poplars, and millions of noisy, noisome sparrows take their place. Ice forms in the gutters, and mechanics repairing Paykans (Iran's little locally assembled cars) on the sidewalks and curbs outside small garages burn used motor oil in makeshift stoves to keep their hands from turning numb.

So the winter goes, with an occasional bright, warm day, until the spring equinox. Then trees take leaf, gardens bloom, and the brassy sun again travels the sky.

Sunsets in Teheran are monotonously brilliant and slightly terrifying. The bloody-orange color comes from air pollution. A blanket of smog of varying density covers the city most of the time. Though not perceptible if you look straight up through it, the smog makes a dirty ring all around the horizon when you view it laterally from some high place. This pollution comes mostly from cars and trucks, filling the air with carbon monoxide, nitrogen oxide, sulfur, and lead. More comes from five hundred industrial plants on the fringes of the city, which burn oil-derived fuels. Besides man-made contamination, the wind from the desert carries dust that deposits itself on every flat surface in and out of houses, and on all foliage. Many car-proud owners cover parked vehicles with shrouds to protect them from dust that can become as thick as velvet in a week or so. Sometimes the Elburz Mountains cannot be seen for the dust. Shirts suffer seriously from ring around the collar.

Even a decade ago Teheran was too primitive to concern itself much with pollution, and its growth since then has outstripped its growing capacity to fight pollution. One of the more aggravating problems is the slow pace of the congested traffic; cars crawling in low gear and idling for long intervals produce much more pollution per mile than cars moving fast. On Teheran's streets one's eyes often sting from gasoline exhaust and diesel fumes, particularly during the temperature inversions that sometimes come during June, July, and August and make the sky a grayish-yellow roof of gases. Still, the government has made some progress. Brick kilns have been forced out of the city. The new green belt of pines around Teheran reduces dust. Circumferential industrial plants are slowly being required to shift from burning oil to burning cleaner natural gas. Some public vehicles are switching from gasoline to propane.

The gratifying presence of water in desert-surrounded Teheran comes partly from the charming eccentricity called the *jube,* the little concrete-lined ditch, a foot wide and maybe eighteen inches deep, that makes a gutter on each side of every Teheran street. The Teheran tilt comes ready-made to run water south through the jubes, and clever engineering—the Iranians excel at channeling water—connects the southbound jubes with laterals in the cross streets. Water flows from mountain sources down through all of Teheran, finally sinking into the desert south of the city. Some mastermind in the city's water department orchestrates the flow by valves and dams, drying one jube temporarily to send a cleansing surge into another, letting one trickle and another gush, rarely allowing overflows and always providing a path for the lapping liquid. Every street has its babbling creeks. Often the jubes tinkle musically from the sound of a stray bottle rolling along the bottom.

Jubes originated as a supply for household water; they carry on, now that Teheran has piped water, as a storm-sewer system, a street-cleaning system, and a tradition. A century ago, before Teheran grew north to touch the mountains, man-made underground canals called *qanats* carried water to the jubes, which distributed it to cisterns under houses. Householders took care to divert water into the cisterns at midnight, when it was running clear, and they disinfected it with lime. Jubes were not, and are not, open sewers; it is bad form to throw garbage in the jube. Jubes still supply water for many gardens; and the trees that line the streets get their water from jubes, often through a small hole that someone has thoughtfully smashed through the channel's bottom. Men wash cars with jube water. Small boys sail boats in jubes. Jubes carry away fallen leaves. At intersections jubes flow under streets and sidewalks; elsewhere people sometimes step into them and come up wet. Drivers often run a wheel into the jube while attempting to park parallel.

Since jubes do not carry sewage, what does? Except for several small areas, nothing. Village Teheran still depends on septic tanks under every house or apartment building. The closest thing to a sewage system is an ever-postponed plan for one. When and if it is built, the jubes will still run. Teheran loves them.

Four main avenues in Teheran—Hafez, Saadi, Ferdowsi, Khayyam—are named for famous Persian poets, and the new opera

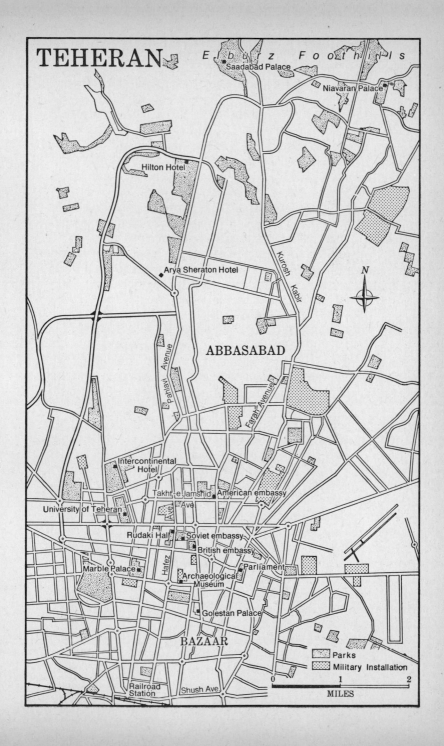

TEHERAN

E l b u r z   F o o t h i l l s

Saadabad Palace

Niavaran Palace

Hilton Hotel

Kurosh Kabir

Arya Sheraton Hotel

N

ABBASABAD

Pahlavi Avenue

Farah Avenue

Intercontinental Hotel

Takht-e Jamshid Ave.

American embassy

University of Teheran

Rudaki Hall

Soviet embassy

British embassy

Hafez

Parliament

Marble Palace

Archaeological Museum

Golestan Palace

BAZAAR

Parks

Military Installation

0   1   2

Railroad Station

Shush Ave.

MILES

house is named for a fifth: Rudaki, a tenth-century composer of odes and elegies. Set in a fountain-filled park on Hafez Avenue in the heart of modern Teheran, Rudaki Hall is a bejeweled triple horseshoe of red velvet, where from their blue-draped royal box the Shah of Iran and his Empress could look at portraits of themselves above the golden proscenium arch. In the top floor of a building that connects to the black marble theater is the Rudaki Restaurant, frequented by some of the most famous conductors in the world when they visited to perform in Iran. From this creamy, glassy place one can view everything that counts in Teheran.

The city plan, laid out by Reza Shah, is a grid of roughly parallel north-south and east-west avenues, forming blocks about 800 yards square that are filled in with lesser streets and narrow lanes—well-paved ones, you may be sure, in this petroleous land, and endlessly interesting places in which to wander. What one sees looking north from the Rudaki Restaurant is the main growth area of Teheran. Only recently it was empty land. I met a woman in her thirties who recalled that as a child she was sent to this area by her teacher to collect desert plants for a biology class. East-west Shahreza Avenue, just north of Rudaki, was in its first incarnation, many years ago, an irrigation ditch; then it became part of the city wall, and later the main boulevard. But now it has been left behind in prestige by Takht-e Jamshid, the next avenue north; and Takht-e Jamshid is in turn giving way to the avenues called Karim Khan Zand and Takht-e Tavus, even farther north.

Takht-e Jamshid starts on the west at the University of Teheran, runs in front of such power points as the International Bank of Iran and Japan, the headquarters of the National Iranian Oil Company, and the black, glass-walled high-rise of the Iranians' Bank (topped by a golden lion), and ends not long after passing the United States Embassy. It is a broad, thronged street, a wall of ten-story buildings fronting sidewalks made of ceramic tiles, with cinemas, hospitals, hotels, restaurants, and stores. On Takht-e Jamshid you can buy emeralds, jackhammers, English-language books, Czechoslovakian milling machines, Yashica cameras, sausage slicers, chain saws, caracul coats, surveying instruments, microscopes, Mikimoto pearls, masonry hammers, badminton rackets, and models of the human anatomy made for medical students.

The American Embassy, invaded by revolutionaries one day early in 1979, fronts on Takht-e Jamshid by an accident of history: the compound was there before the street. In the early 1920s, Envoy Extraordinary and Minister Plenipotentiary Hoffman Philip, seeking to remove his legation from the turmoil of old Teheran, bought a piece of land a mile north of the city from a Persian aristocrat who had won it on a turn of the cards. The minister paid $60,000; the present 25-acre plot, based on the going rate of $500 a square meter for downtown real estate, is now worth nearly $50 million. The merit of the place was the qanat that brought water from the mountains. For years U.S. diplomats struggled to keep upstream water rustlers from sinking shafts into the American qanat; finally the State Department bored some deep wells. In 1953, after Takht-e Jamshid Avenue was platted to run a little south of the embassy, the city of Teheran bought the strip of land between the compound and the street and gave it to the United States government. The compound now contains a large brick chancery, residences for the ambassador and the deputy chief of mission, eleven apartments for transients, a commissary, a restaurant, a power plant, three swimming pools, and two tennis courts. The ambassador's office provides a grand view of the Elburz Mountains, and his residence, surrounded by pines and marble-walled inside and out, glows with fireplaces.

All that is Oriental, exotic, and mysterious in Teheran comes in the area a mile or so south of Rudaki Hall. Four hundred years ago, this was a walled town, and even after 1779, when the Qajar rulers began to use Teheran as their capital, they chose to build their Golestan Palace within the walls just north of the bazaar. Not until 1874 did a Qajar shah replace the old wall with a new one, about a mile in every direction outside the original one. It reached what is now Shahreza Avenue on the north and defined Teheran until Reza Shah, removing all the walls, extended the avenues and added new ones in the 1930s.

In the color and excitement of its bazaar, Teheran does not have to concede points to any other city in the Middle East. The bazaar starts as a plunge: down stone steps from Buzarjomehri Avenue into a maze of passages—six miles of them—between dusty two-story brick buildings set close enough together to support zinc roofs over the lanes. Inside light comes from rather un-Oriental ring-shaped fluorescent tubes dangling by their wires. The bazaar has a rough system: in one passageway the stalls sell nothing but jewelry; in another, shoes; in another, clothes; in another, rugs. But elsewhere it's a jumble of merchants side by side selling abacuses, samovars, T-shirts, compasses, perfume, prayer beads, barber's shears, toys, grocer's scales, and suitcases made out of beer cans. The traffic, when it doesn't annoy or infuriate you by its jostling, danger, and sheer infeasibility, astonishes you. Motorcycles push through lanes jammed with people. Sheep go by on their quick little hoofs. Men serve as beasts of burden; I saw one wiry old human donkey so far bent over under a mountain of attaché cases that he required a small boy to lead and guide him.

You may notice that many merchants, especially rug dealers, seem uninterested in selling their goods, and this is a clue to a startling fact about the bazaar: more than a retail merchandising operation, the bazaar is a money market, a bank, and a wholesale import-export business with worldwide connections. BUSINESS IS BRISK AT THE BAZAAR, headlines the newspaper *Kayhan*, and among other evidence the story relates the sale of 250 tons of raisins to Britain at $595 a ton, as well as big deals in apricot halves, wool, pulse, and vetch. The shabby-looking rug merchant in a small stall may well have just cabled a sales offer to Amsterdam or Philadelphia, and his personal wealth probably exceeds that of most American small businessmen.

Such a *bazaari* can move money anywhere. A rich citizen of Teheran who wants to sneak funds out of the country (as so many have lately) can turn over rials to a bazaar merchant and recover them two days later in the form of Deutsche marks deposited to his account in, say, Bremen by a German importer, who thus pays for the carpets he imported from the merchant—and neither the Iranian central bank nor the German Central Bank knows anything about the transaction. Wholesale trading within the bazaar goes on with a maximum of haggling, suspicion, and distrust, but a deal is struck with a handshake and a code of total trust governs all money transactions. This trust lets the bazaar create its own currency in the form of personal checks, which are not cashed or deposited, but simply endorsed as many as thirty times and used as money. The bottom signer is the liable one, and if the check were to bounce he could return it to the endorser who preceded him; but in practice checks never bounce, because anyone tempted to write a bad check knows that he would be run out of the bazaar.

A bazaar merchant may also create money by banking. Typically a rug merchant uses his stock as collateral to get a bank loan—that's why he does not want to sell the rugs. He relends this money to another bazaari against a promissory note. In turn, he uses this note as collateral at a bank for a loan (equal to 80 percent of the note), which he lends out for another promissory note to get another loan—and so on until his original funds are extended many times. Collecting 36 percent a year on all these loans, he can easily pay the 12 percent bank interest and earn 24 percent profits—all because the bazaar's code of trust assures him that his borrowers will repay him. Getting around the Koran's ban on interest is easy—the bazaaris call their profits a "service charge."

The borrowers do not resent the high interest: they use the money as working capital for slightly shady deals, which no conventional

banker would finance but which make large profits. Bazaaris, for example, know how to bribe customs inspectors at bottleneck ports in order
to release imported merchandise and turn a fast rial. A young bazaari
may borrow the $10,000 he needs as startup money to lease a choice
stall from which to clean up on, say, turquoises sold to tourists—who
may nevertheless get such bargains that they can resell the gems in
their own countries for fat markups. High-interest loans also provide
starting money for small industries, which often grow to become large
industries and leave the bazaar. One of Iran's leading hub-cap manufacturers started as a copper-pot spinner in the bazaar; indeed, most of
Iran's leading business families, though now separated from it, have
their roots in the bazaar. Even after breaking away, they may still use
bazaar money. "No study of Iran's capital market is complete without
investigating the forces of the bazaar's moneylending operations," says
a high official of the Central Bank. "Approximately 20 percent of the
total working capital of all companies in Iran is financed by the bazaar
moneylenders."

For all these reasons, the bazaar is "a society separate from the
rest," said a business professor in Teheran who had grown so fascinated
by this institution that he studied it constantly ("It's wild in the middle
of the night"). Bazaaris are among the most devout of Moslems; they
respect their mullahs and in their stalls they put up likenesses of Ali,
first saint of the Shiite branch of Islam. Teheran's oldest and religiously
most important mosque is right in the middle of the bazaar. Bazaaris
all make the hajj to Mecca—"and stop in Beirut on the way back to
stare at the Christian girls' legs," said the professor. In semisecret
places among the dowdy buildings of the bazaar, there are great libraries of rare and valuable Korans and other Islamic works. Yet minorities
of bazaar merchants are not Moslems but rather Jews and Armenian
Christians. They honor the Moslem holidays, and the Moslems in turn
respect Yom Kippur and Christmas.

Because the bazaar, not only in Teheran but throughout Iran, is
so deeply traditional and so profoundly grounded in Islam, it has historically been a focus of opposition to shahs. In 1978 and 1979 the bazaars
reemerged in this role. When Ayatollah Khomeini called on the bazaaris to strike, they faithfully obeyed, and thus worked powerfully
to bring down the king.

South Teheran, the expanse beyond the bazaar, is *terra incognita*
to most upper-class Teheranis, which is one reason they did not foresee
the revolution. My three maps of Teheran do not even show this pov-
erty-ridden half of the city, but instead end in the south at the dividing-
line railroad.

One of my notes from *la ville basse* reads: "*Lots* of idlers, *lots* of motorcycles, *lots* of mullahs, *lots* of small industry, *no* women not wearing veils, *no* tourists." South of the tracks one sees Mack trucks and horse carts and pushcarts that run on wheels made from automobile wheel bearings. Barbers shave their customers on the sidewalk; shoemakers occupy an entire street; women fill pots at street-corner faucets, and wash clothes and dishes in the jube, occasionally glancing up at some Boeing 747 curving in low to land at Teheran airport. Beyond the city limits stand the needlelike stacks of the brick kilns, and beyond them, in the exurban town of Rey, is the golden pointed dome of a famous mosque, hard by the severe and monumental tomb of Reza Shah.

To build the boxy three-story apartment house that is nearly standard in Teheran, workmen dig a basement—sometimes with machinery, often with shovels and wheelbarrows—and pour concrete footings topped with steel flanges. A truck brings a load of light steel I-beams, about six inches by six inches in cross section, and welders fabricate them into columns about forty feet long.

Then a tall crane visits the site. Its hook picks up a column by one end, and dangles it vertically over one of the concrete-embedded flanges. Welders close in and fuse the foot of the column to the flange. The crane operator drops his hook a little; it comes free of the column, and, incredibly, the column stands! It, and the other columns, stand like wheat stalks, swaying gently in the wind, a miracle of balance.

The crane raises horizontal steel beams, and the welders swarm up the columns to fasten them in place—first floor, second floor, third floor, roof. Now the columns are steady, the cube formed. When the structure is finished, the steel will support it, but at this stage it looks like nothing more than a three-dimensional drawing of the building. Between the beams, at intervals of about three feet, the workmen weld I-beam joists. Masons appear on the site, along with loads of mortar cement, sandy dirt, and bricks. Barelegged men with long-handled shovels mix mortar in a heap on the ground—often they work some straw into the mud. They carry the mortar to bricklayers, who thereupon produce another miracle: they lay the brick horizontally between the joists to make a floor.

It is not in the nature of brick to form an unsupported horizontal surface; the essence of brick is its incompressibility, which makes it serve so well in vertical walls. But Iranian masons have a secret. They form the bricks between the joists into slight arches, with a hump of about two inches in the three feet of run. These flat arches turn the downward weight on the floor into sideward pressure against the joists. The slightly curved spaces at the sides on the top of the arch, and in the middle on the bottom, are filled in with mortar to make level surfaces, and the result is a solid floor above and a flat ceiling below. The masons then brick in the exterior and interior walls. They face the front with handsome tan brick, stucco, marble, or, occasionally, white stone brick laid without visible mortar. The interior finish is plaster, with ceramic tiles for bathroom and kitchen walls, and terrazzo or tiles on the floor. Buildings constructed this way are not limited to three floors; they sometimes rise as high as six.

With monotonous frequency, newspaper stories tell of the collapse of these buildings, sometimes during construction, sometimes after. Often the cause is jerry-building, but the construction method itself is flimsy by American standards. One suspects that in many blocks the buildings do not collapse only because, built side by side, they hold one another up. What an earthquake might do to Teheran—and Iran is earthquake country—is too frightening to think about.

Because Teheran grows so fast, construction is its major industry. The kilns near Teheran manufacture 3.2 billion bricks a year, and that is not enough; another 2 billion are imported. For lack of timber, brick is overwhelmingly the commonest building material in Teheran and throughout Iran. Even for a temporary barrier around a building site, contractors run up a brick wall. Considering the antiquity of bricklaying in Iran, though, the workmanship is often poor: lumpy, gray-yellow brick laid with an unnecessary excess of mortar, which itself is little better than mud mixed with lime. But all that brick at least makes for a fairly fireproof city. Teheran has never bothered to put in fire hydrants; when, rarely, a blaze breaks out, firemen bring water in tank trucks.

The quality of architecture is not much higher than the quality of bricklaying. Many buildings seem mere exercises in geometry. Afterthought cool-air ducts, running down the sides and into the windows, ruin the appearance of thousands of buildings. However, some of the new skyscrapers—Teheran has half a dozen in the twenty- to twenty-five-story range—are sleek and elegant, and a few buildings that draw their arched, adobe-look architecture from the Iranian village caravanserai are also pleasing.

But in consequence of a rare piece of luck, Teheran in the future may become a true metropolis with a distinct and distinctive center. Just where its heart should be, now that it has expanded so extensively to the north, is an empty wasteland, more than two square miles in size. This area, called Abbasabad, originally served for military maneuvers, and although the army sold it cheaply to military officers two decades ago, the city grew up around it, leaving it a patch of empty desert, stony dunes of soft brown and yellow, inhabited only by occa-

sional hikers and jube dogs. By means of thirteen thousand land transactions, the city has now acquired all of Abbasabad. One of the grand
projects set aside in 1978 as too grandiose was a plan to build a great
city center here; perhaps it will eventually come to pass.

If I were to compress into one impressionistic, imaginary movie
all the horrors that I have seen through the front windows of taxis
in Teheran, it would unreel something like this:

We are careening down Cyrus the Great Avenue at eighty kilometers an hour, having just missed a jaywalker who is serenely crossing
the traffic while carrying a sheet of window glass measuring about
three feet by eight. Our driver dodges carts full of garbage, men pushing
dead cars, boys darting into the avenue to retrieve soccer balls from
sandlot games. Going through a green light, we neatly avoid hitting
a school bus that came out of a side street against a red light. The
near-miss is all the more praiseworthy for the fact that our driver
could hardly see the school bus because of the decorative tassels that
hang around the taxi's windshield. What's that ahead? A dump truck
has smashed into a soft-drink truck-trailer! Cyrus the Great Avenue
is awash with Pepsi-Cola, a minefield of broken glass and rolling bottles. We roar through it—and through a red light, too. Our driver believes that green means go and red means go faster.

One of the passengers in this communal taxi seems a little faint;
he mumbles something to the driver, who, without losing speed,
reaches into the glove compartment and hands over the cab's only
window crank, so that the indisposed man can lower the glass. The
drivers around us seem as mad as ours, except for one fellow who is
staying in lane, paying attention, and keeping to a moderate speed—
in sum, doing everything right except that he's driving in reverse, for
he forgot to turn off at a side street several blocks behind him. Oh-
oh—there's a funny one. A car has just bumped a jaywalker who was
carrying about two gallons of yogurt; both the pedestrian and the car
are coated a dripping white from top to bottom, and a crowd has gathered to laugh. We pass a no-hands bicycle rider, but that's nothing:
our driver has removed his hands from the wheel to clap with glee
over the yogurt spill.

An oncoming car makes an illegal U-turn right in front of us, and
as he speeds away we see that he is a student in a driver-education
car, learning one of the standard maneuvers of motoring in Teheran.
Now the traffic is thickening; our driver plays bump-'em cars with
the others for a while, but when the going gets too slow he crosses
the double yellow line and shoots down the avenue against the oncoming traffic, which squeezes to the right, out of our way. (Teheran drivers

hold to the prudent opinion that a sideswipe is preferable to a head-on crash.) A car stopped in the middle of the street while its owner changes a tire gives us a chance to break back into our proper lanes.

Up ahead are a couple of policemen, whistling madly and waving two lines of cars into collision with each other. Our driver avoids that trap by driving on the sidewalk for a block, as pedestrians press their backs to the storefronts. By the tactic known as the Three-Inch Miss, our man avoids hitting a car that shot out of a gasoline station at right angles to six lanes of traffic. Up ahead is a motorcycle carrying so much freight that it ought to have a "Wide Load" sign. It crunches through the broken glass left by some newly crashed cars. We swerve left in front of screeching cars and come to a stop. I gratefully turn over fifty rials to the driver. He got me where I was going, perhaps through good luck brought by the kewpie doll with lavender hair that blocks the view from his rear-view mirror.

But the streets of Teheran often present more somber scenes: the inert body of a woman whose body veil, whipped off when a car killed her, lies in a crumpled heap a few feet away; the motorcyclist who arcs through the air to his death after hitting a car broadside. "My husband saw two fatal accidents on the day we arrived, and refuses to drive a car," one Englishwoman told me. Car accidents kill about five people a day. But even though the late racing driver Graham Hill once remarked that Teheran could be turned into a realistic simulation of Indianapolis just by painting numbers on the cars, the traffic often inches along in gigantic jams, and the death toll is not high for such a big city.

The psychological explanations offered for all this bad driving are various and none too convincing. A big factor, doubtless, is mass inexperience: Teheran's car population has grown from fifteen thousand ten years ago to 1.1 million now, which implies that most drivers learned to drive only recently. One theory says that Iranians are so naturally polite that they would Alfonse-and-Gaston endlessly at intersections for each other to go first, so they refuse to look at other cars and charge ahead. Another theory holds that Iranians work on probabilities: if a driver can run a hundred red lights without a collision, he figures that he can try for a hundred more. The *Tehran Journal* remarks that the capital's drivers "are as careless behind the wheel as to think as if they have been insured by the Providence against accidents." (Teheranis rarely use seat belts, or even have seat belts in their cars.) Closer to the mark, maybe, is the theory that driving is an expression of Iranian individualism, or a way of working out aggressions against the totalitarian state. Often I saw a driver tie up an intersection so that neither he (or she—women drivers are just as balky) nor any other driver could move, rather than back up a few feet. One Iranian friend amusedly suggested to me the thoughts that go through the heads of two drivers just before they crash at a corner. Mercedes-Benz owner: "If that guy thinks he can stop me just because he's driving a cheap little expendable car . . ." Paykan driver: "If that fat cat thinks he can stop me just because he's driving that big foreign tank . . ." Near the collision, each yells at the other: "Son of a dog!" Then, *bang-smash-crunch.*

After the crash, my friend related, comes a predictable drama. The drivers jump from their cars, shouting recommendations as to a certain course of action that should be taken in regard to each other's sister. Fists fly, but do not connect—for to the relief of each of the combatants, someone in the gathering crowd has undertaken to restrain them. The shouts die, and the bystanders begin to mediate, their criterion being that compensation should go to whoever is injured, and does not necessarily have to come from whoever was at fault. "Mr. Mercedes-owner, have mercy on Mr. Paykan-owner. You are rich and he is poor and has eight children." The Paykan-owner, who this informal court judges to be in the wrong, proffers 100 rials to the Mercedes-owner, who accepts. They part, smiling and shaking hands, or even kissing, as the crowd disperses.

The commonest kind of taxi in Teheran is the orange-painted Paykan shared by several passengers. The cab starts out toward the destination of the first passenger who boards. As he travels, the driver listens to the shouts of other possible riders standing at curbs, and if anyone yells the name of a destination on or near the route to the first passenger's destination, the driver will pick him up. Soon he assembles a group all going the same way. Each passenger notes the meter-reading as he boards, and subtracts that from the reading when he alights; the difference, plus perhaps ten rials for a tip, is his fare, usually quite low. Filled with five passengers and a driver, the little Paykan is overcrowded (the driver can hardly manipulate his gear shift, which is invariably topped by a bejeweled knob), and a little dangerous. As one driver told me, in rough but vivid English: "Chevrolet very good—Paykan no good. Accident, finish. Going cemetery."

7

The Veiled Society

❀

"Today marks the 40th anniversary of the abolition of the veil," noted the Teheran newspaper *Kayhan International* in an editorial a few years ago. "Decreed by Reza Shah the Great in 1936, [the abolition] was a measure with wide-ranging implications [because] Reza Shah also meant the measure as a symbolic one: a pulling down of the walls that kept women confined to the home and cut off from the larger society; a thrusting aside of barriers that prevented the fuller realization of the potential of the individual woman."

Many Iranians told me of their pride in parents who helped abolish the *chador,* which is what Persian women call their full-length body veil. "My mother was among the first to give up the chador. Now she's eighty and she has never worn one since then except in a mosque," one upper-class woman recalled. A doctor in Tabriz related that his father had joined Reza Shah's campaign against the chador with such enthusiasm that the mullahs sent a message to the king: "You kill him or we will." (On Reza Shah's advice, the father reined in his anti-chador zeal for a while.) One of Iran's women senators, Shams-ol-Moluk Mossaheb, said a while back that had not Reza Shah's wife, Taj-ol-Moluk, and his daughters, Shams and Ashraf, so bravely appeared in public without veils, "Iranian women would still be cursed by the chador."

Yet . . . as anyone who has eyes can plainly see, more Iranian women wear the chador than when it was "abolished."

The most striking sight for the foreigner upon first reaching the modern and Westernized city of Teheran is that more than half of all women move about the streets under what appear to be tents, most of them black. Out of Teheran, the proportion of women in chadors grows to more than three fourths. What they wear covers the body almost completely. The classic chador consists of something like six or eight yards of cloth cut so that a woman can drape it over her head to cover all but her eyes and nose, and then clench a couple of folds of the open side in her teeth (or hold them over the mouth by hand) so as to make the garment sheath her already well clothed body clear down to the floor or pavement. Reza Shah's abolition of the veil lasted only until his abdication. His son, ascending a throne badly weakened by the events of World War II, felt too shaky to oppose the forces— chiefly the mullahs—that favored restoring the chador. In the late 1970s, as revolutionary fervor heightened, the chador became not only a garment but a symbol of political opposition.

Historically, the chador gets authority from the Koran, which says: "Good women . . . guard their unseen parts because Allah has guarded them." Many people support this logic; I heard often of the lascivious, "animal-like" life Persians supposedly led before the Islamic conquest in 637, and of the Prophet's accurate perception of a need to instill sexual morals. The Koran's encouragement of chaste appearance, implying that any display of a woman's sexual attributes will excite men beyond their capacity to restrain themselves, suits the purposes of many Iranian men. "If a girl is dressed in a sexy way, how can you ever get to appreciate her mind?" one man asked me. A journalist explained that "A man's wife's chador assures him that no one can ogle his wife. And the chador on another woman makes it impossible for him to ogle her. It greatly mitigates the jealousy that Iranian men are so prone to feel." Once, at a pleasant outdoor restaurant near Teheran, I nodded toward a group of women standing in the garden and asked my hostess, a thoroughly modern woman, why one member of the group felt obliged to wear a chador amid friends all wearing dresses. The answer: "Because her husband makes her wear it. Not because of religion. Her husband thinks that if another man sees her he will covet her." Back of all this fear of adultery, one man told me, was "the Moslem man's suspicion that his sexual performance will be compared unfavorably with his predecessor's." In any event, a voluminous black chador worn to expose only the eyes and nose is unquestionably a fast turn-off for seducers—particularly if, as I noticed more than once, the nose has a large wart on it.

But many women deny that they put on veils for religio-puritanical reasons, and they prove their point by wearing chadors that are filmy, ghostlike, colored in tans, blues, or even pinks, patterned with flowers or squares, revealing the whole face and neck, and somehow adjusted to give an occasional glimpse of an elegant ankle and calf. Pretty chadors combine tradition and grace, almost like the Indian sari; they "equalize beauty and give ugly girls a chance," as someone told me. The wearers of such veils are usually up-to-date women; I recall seeing one with her veil flung wide so that she could photograph a mosque with her Instamatic. Obviously, chadors can even be seductive, leading to feverish passages in novels like F. M. Esfandiary's *Identity Card:* "She slowly let her veil drop, showing more of her face, then suddenly she opened up her entire veil, revealing her naked body." More prosaically, I heard from many Iranian women, the chador is a handy garment to throw on over an old housedress when one has to hurry out to buy a melon.

Except in novels, chadors are always worn over clothes: dresses or slacks or jeans for modern women, dreary black skirts and baggy black stockings for rural or elderly women. Deeply religious women wear chadors indoors and out; others only on the street. Tradition-minded parents require even their small daughters to wear chadors, though more often patterned ones than black; but at playgrounds little girls throw their chadors into neglected heaps to get sufficient freedom to play on the slides and swings. The flowing chador is not an easy garment to manage—often I saw taxi doors close on the hem, leaving part outside to whip in the wind.

A chador makes a good disguise for all kinds of chicanery. A friend of mine had his pocket picked by two men in chadors; and when the police showed him a thick file of known pickpockets, he could not identify those who had robbed him because he had seen only their eyes and noses. Former Queen Soraya recalls that in 1954 two policemen spotted an odd figure in a chador in the Teheran bazaar. "Do you notice how strangely that woman walks?" asked one of the cops. "Yes, you might think she was a man," replied the other. They parted the chador at mouth level and discovered a luxuriant beard. They opened the shopping basket and found dynamite. The man in the chador was Huseyn Fatemi, a well-known opponent of the Shah, who had gone into hiding.

The wearing of the chador correlates clearly with social class: to drive from upper-crust northern Teheran to the poor and industrial districts in the south is to see the proportion of chadors rise from perhaps 10 percent to nearly 100 percent. Few women who have taken college degrees and traveled outside Iran wear chadors except to mosques—but for this purpose all these sophisticated women own at least one chador. In offices, on elegant shopping streets, or at jet-set parties, one sees few chadors.

The chador, or more exactly the chador mentality, efficiently mutes public sexuality in Iran; only once did I see a man walking with his arm around a woman in a chador (while passers-by glared in disapproval). And by all accounts this reticence pervades private sexuality as well. Religious and moral objections to sex before marriage, so largely abandoned in the West, still prevail with full force for most Iranians. "Even friendships between boys and girls is not customary," writes the Teheran psychologist M. H. Saheb-ol-Zamani, deploring "pent-up sexuality," which leads to masturbation ("often causing great sorrow and guilt feelings"), prostitution, homosexuality, molesting of women, and "anonymous telephone annoyance: the man keeps dialing telephone numbers until he gets in contact with a woman who is willing to engage in an erotic conversation."

Sex after marriage also has plenty of hang-ups. "The wedding night is of special significance for most Iranian families," writes Reza Baraheni, a poet and professor. "The bride carries to the bedroom a white handkerchief called *dastmal-e-zofaf* (a defloration handkerchief), which is soaked in the defloration blood and handed to the women and men waiting outside. This is evidence that the girl had not been touched by any man before her husband." If the woman is not a virgin, the man can cancel the marriage contract. Some brides resort to plastic surgery on the hymen to appear virgin. Baraheni and other writers also report that anal sex with wives is commonplace. Says one Iranian psychologist: "Women accept sex as submission to the man. There is little foreplay and no question at all of giving pleasure."

Among the well-to-do internationalized Iranians, however, morals match those of Europe and the United States. In this set birth control by the pill and the IUD is as acceptable as it is to most Westerners. These Westernized people also display affection in public without any chador-mentality restraints. "Fourteen years ago it was unthinkable for a boy to touch a girl's hand," one professor told me; but now, on the more sophisticated streets of northern Teheran, young couples stroll with arms around waists just as they do in Paris, and the girl may well be wearing not a chador but tight jeans and a tight sweater. Many mullahs profoundly disapprove, and Islam's comeback works to reverse this trend. But in March 1979, when Ayatollah Khomeini proclaimed that all women should wear the chador, thousands of modern women took to the streets for five days and forced him to put out the word that "modest dress" would be sufficient.

"A woman should ask her husband three times a day what to think, what to say, and what to do," says a Persian proverb. Though feminism gained ground in Iran under the Shah, sexism remains powerful. By law, no woman may receive a passport to go abroad without her husband's permission. Even an Iranian-born woman with an American passport, acquired by marrying an American, must prove that her husband will allow her to leave the country. For most women, though, the practical problem is not leaving the country but simply leaving the house. Women commonly go out daytimes to shop or work or take children somewhere, but "in the evening," a pretty, young, American-educated woman told me, "a woman is not supposed to go out alone." And even if she has a male friend or a husband, a woman often finds that he will not take her out at night. In such a place as the Rose Restaurant in Isfahan, I noticed, nine out of ten diners at night were men. At parties, many men appear without wives—and even those who bring them tend to group themselves away from whatever women are present. One woman, explaining to me the custom of filling houses with potted plants, said ingenuously, "In Teheran, nearly all the wives are at home nearly all the time, so they have plenty of time to tend the flowers."

The Shah, though taking pride in sponsoring such equal-rights measures as woman suffrage (he noted that not so long ago in Iran those deprived of the right to vote were customarily defined as "beggars, lunatics, murderers, thieves, and women"), often slipped into sexist talk, pronouncing, for example, that women are "built in such a manner that they could be employed usefully in many intricate industries such as electronics." An Englishwoman teaching English to adults in Tabriz asked her class, "Are men superior to women?" The men *and the women* in the class all cried, "Yes." She then asked her class to estimate what proportion of teachers in Iranian schools were women. The class guessed about half. "Doesn't that prove women are as good as men?" Replied the class, again unanimously: "No." A professor in Ahvaz told me, of his students: "The girls agree that girls are inferior, and the boys are absolutely certain of it." One journalist even contended that Iranians go further than Arabs in keeping women inferior. "The scorn may be covered up among modern men," he said, "but it comes out fast if, for example, a woman succeeds at a man's job. He and his colleagues will try to destroy her." Attempting to come to terms with feminism, the newspaper *Kayhan* seemed to be gritting its teeth as it urged men to "ingrain our minds with the inevitability of the equality of men and women." One consequence of sexism in Iran, a country that needs workers of all kinds, is that only 16 percent of women work (versus 50 percent in the U.S.), and they mostly hold low-paying "female" jobs: handicrafts, weaving, and secretarial work. Of twelve thousand doctors, only a handful are women. Paradoxically, many Iranian terrorists and anti-regime guerrillas are women.

The family is Iran's strongest social institution, the locus to which these individualists give their loyalty if they give any at all. Some Iranians argue that it is within the family that the downtrodden woman comes into her own, running the house and raising the children. I recall once watching a woman in a black chador with her husband

122 **THE IRANIANS**

in the semiprivacy of a hospital room, at ease and garrulous, slapping
his knee and laughing. But in the final analysis fathers run families.
I met one middle-aged man who had taken a degree in architecture
at MIT, and who also liked to write and illustrate children's books.
His aged father had ordained that he should put aside these talents
and administer the family factory, and that was what he was doing.
"Sons here rarely reach the point of despising or disobeying their fathers," one professor told me. As for mothers, one gets the impression
that they mostly lack the force and influence that the American mother
has won for herself. Once I complimented a young man in Mashhad
on the character of his aged mother, and he replied wearily, "You
can have her!" On the other hand, I met a professional woman ("the
most liberated woman in Iran," she called herself) who said, "I am
the one who decides what we do in our house." She worried that her
son would be "dumb, like his father."

Her child and most other upper-class children are lightly disciplined, often by threats not carried out—no punishment, no demands
for responsibility. But they are pushed from the age of four into intensive schooling, including a foreign language that will let them travel
and study abroad at high school or college age. For the children of
middle- or lower-class parents, the coming of universal education is
improving a life that used to be, and in backward places still is, awful.
Thousands of them, terrorized by overly strict fathers, denied play and
entertainment, must still go to work on farms and in cottage industry
at the age of eight, even though the laws forbid child labor. Partly
from the need for strong workers, but more broadly from the conviction
that women are inferior, boy children are prized over girls, and mothers
who produce only girls suffer all the more for that.

Many great, tight-knit, dynastic families—according to some esti-
mates, about two hundred of them—still prevail in Iran. The Afshars,
the Alams, the Qavams, the Akbars, the Samiis, the Mansurs, the Am-
inis, the Mahdavis, the Dibas: families like these influence the nation
out of proportion to their numbers. The most remarkable family may
be the Farmanfarmaians: thirty-three brothers and sisters from a father, a "prince" of the old Qajar royal family, who had three wives.
No fewer than seventeen of the children have earned Ph.D.'s; there
are Farmanfarmaians in architecture, law, banking, engineering, government; one is a professor at the University of Texas.

I met some members of one family who claimed descent from Shah
Abbas, and, further back, from the prophet Mohammed himself. Royalists to the core, of course. They said that Shah Abbas had passed on
the advice that his descendants must be educated both in the broad,
liberal arts sense, and in a specific art; so even now, besides being

intensely literate, well informed, and active in government, education, sports, and writing, each member of the family is a passably good painter or sketcher.

Families, grand or small, work to the benefit of their own members at the expense of other families, which leads to famous feuds. One American businessman related that he took five long years to get his firm going because he unwittingly made friends with a family whose enemies included families important to his business, who automatically became his enemies, too.

An essential function of families is to take care of their aged; Iran, doubtless fortunately, so far has only one "rest home" for old people. Strong, institutional families require carefully arranged marriages, marriages that subordinate love to such more consequential motives as security, the creation of links between important tribes, the carrying on of the family name in fitting dignity. Modernization has been changing the nature of marriage in Iran at a furious pace, though perhaps the revolution will turn the clock back. Only fifteen years ago, parents arranged almost all marriages, often picking a girl as young as thirteen to marry a man twenty years older. The consequences of such "unsuitable marriages," as M. H. Saheb-ol-Zamani calls them, were old bridegrooms watching over "their still childlike brides with the greatest jealousy" and an absence of "real partnership, a deeper community of feeling, or for the wife, sexual satisfaction"—which, as the husband grew older, tempted many wives into adultery. Polygamy was allowed, following the Koran's instructions that "you may marry other women who seem good to you: two, three, or four of them." In practice, only about 7 percent of men had more than one wife, because only the well-to-do could afford extra spouses. But divorce, similarly condoned by the Koran, was common, leading to many remarriages; also common was the Shiite Moslem custom of *siqeh*, temporary "pleasure marriage" or "marriage for a limited period of time." Taken together, polygamy, remarriage, and siqeh created large numbers of half-brothers and half-sisters—something like 40 percent of Iranian siblings were the children of the same father but different mothers. Saheb-ol-Zamani regards this factor as a prime cause of the Iranian traits of "self-doubt, daydreaming, indecision, solitude, uncooperativeness, and overpowering jealousy."

In recent years, young Iranians have been more and more marrying for love rather than to carry on a dynasty. One of my Iranian friends guessed that in Teheran 90 percent of marriages are motivated by love, even among the conservative middle and lower classes; another friend more cautiously estimated 50 percent of all Iran, and added the condition that young people who pick their own spouses must still obtain their parents' consent. The age of women at marriage now averages more than nineteen, and they commonly marry men in their mid-twenties. Polygamy is virtually outlawed by the new Family Protection Act (which Ayatollah Khomeini denounces as counter to Islamic law). At weddings many brides have taken to wearing white Western-style bridal gowns. Dowries, which used to consist of quantities of gold coins, are rare nowadays except among some of the hinterlands tribes. Single women are relatively rare in Iran: 98 percent marry before their child-bearing years are over. Khomeini deplored modernizing trends in marriage and as one way of fighting them he changed the minimum marriage age for girls to 13 from the 18 decreed by the Shah.

Because so many Iranian men go to college in the United States or Europe and meet local girls, thousands of marriages in Teheran are made up of an Iranian man and a Western woman. Such wives have severe problems. "American women often have to fight off excessive affection," one such wife told me. "They are never left alone; they never get any solitude; there is no privacy except privacy within the family." These women have a club, the American Wives of Iranian Husbands, which one American man who lives in Teheran analyzes as "a kind of Alcoholics Anonymous. They come to one another's aid when nervous breakdowns occur from the pressures of living here— chiefly from mothers-in-law or other family members." A number of American wives have returned to the United States, where their hapless husbands visit them whenever they can. Any American Christian or Jew proposing to marry a Moslem Iranian must convert to Islam in order to get a marriage license, but the conversion can often be accomplished by a simple telephone call to a mullah.

The growth in the rate of marriage for love has not reduced the divorce rate; instead the rate has risen, to about one in three, the same as the United States. Divorce is "usually a catastrophe for the young woman because her chances for remarriage are much more limited than for a man," writes Saheb-ol-Zamani—in fact, statistics show that her chances are less than one third as good. Worse yet, if she has children she must give them up, because Iranian law requires that they go to the father.

The population of Iran includes tribes mostly descended from Turkic races, plus some leftover Arabs, and some Christian Nestorians, Armenians, and Jews, but the basic stock is precisely what history served up: the descendants of the Medes and the Persians, the Indo-Iranian branch of the Indo-European family of peoples. They are a race like no other. "A Persian is a Persian like an Irishman is an Irish-man," an Irish resident of Teheran told me admiringly.

The archetypical Iranian looks like an Iranian and not like anybody else. He does not look like an Arab or a Turk; he does not look like an Indian or a Chinese; he does not look like a Russian or a Spaniard. He looks Iranian, which is to say that he, or she, has pale skin, narrow-set, dark liquid brown eyes, thick, black, arched eyebrows that join or nearly join in the middle, abundant, curly, brown-black hair, and . . . a nose. Not your little Western or Oriental button that seems designed merely for inhaling or exhaling. Far from that. The Iranian nose starts from a peak well up there where the eyebrows join, and skis downmountain on a straight but long and leisurely course to fetch up at base camp somewhere just above the upper lip. The bone is sharp, the skin taut, but there is no outthrust Roman bridge, and never a ski-jump tip—in fact, the effect is a little like that of the prow of an overturned whaleboat. In the male, the proboscis is apt to end its run in front of, and partly hiding, a great shrubbery of mustache, making a striking contrast between white skin and black hair. Although the Iranian configuration of molten dark eyes, lush eyebrows, and strong nose makes for seductive-looking women, the kind you see in Persian miniatures and Qajar paintings, it is the bearded male who brings this physiognomy to perfection. His beard begins high up on the prominent cheekbones and, thick as crabgrass, covers all his face except the forehead and the pallid area adjacent to the noble nose. The mouth, though hardly visible, is straight and unsmiling, to complement the stern and virile—even fierce—expression of this whole work-of-art face, seemingly modeled on the sculptures of ancient warriors at Persepolis.

Of course, some of the blood of all Iran's conquerors is mixed into this race; not everyone has the classic Persian face; and one may fancy that he sees the features of Greeks, Arabs, and Turkomans in many people—especially the ruddy, sunburned complexions, contrasting to the Persian pallor, of "those impassive, soulless Turkoman faces which are so appropriate to a people engaged in an unremitting battle with life, a people which regards any action as permissible if it helps it to go on living," as novelist Sadegh Hedayat puts it in *The Blind Owl.* The Mongols, strangely, did not leave much of a mark; the slanted eye is to be seen only in the northern provinces of Mazanderan, Gorgan, and Khorasan, and not often there. A few blacks live in the south, the part of Iran nearest Africa.

Nomadic tribesmen, who constituted a rebellious third of all Iranians during the heyday of Reza Shah, now form a meek one eighth of the population, having been tamed and "detribalized" at a fast rate in recent decades. Fifty years ago the tribes were virile, proud, and so independent that their sheikdoms formed enclaves barred to other

Iranians. Moving in caravans of camels, horses, cattle, and sheep, they pitched their tents high in the mountains during the summer, and in warmer lower valleys during the winter. The sheep provided them with meat, wool, hides, casings, and milk—in sum, a symbiotic life and a self-reliant value system that made them contemptuous of, and opposed to, the humble sendentary peasants and the central government that represented them. In the years just before World War II, both the British and the Germans kept agents at work among the tribes to use them for military gain of one kind or another, such as tying up Reza Shah's forces.

In recent years, newly created schools, making tribal children literate and in many cases well educated, have been turning them into middle-class Iranians. But thousands of Bakhtiaris still traipse back and forth from lofty and pleasant valleys in southwestern Iran, the men in baggy black trousers, black-and-white-striped tunics, and high, brimless felt hats. The Turkic-speaking Qashqai migrate three hundred miles from south of Shiraz to the border of Isfahan province, the women dressed in layers of skirts and embroidered blouses (nomadic women do not wear chadors). Near Kermanshah and Hamadan, the remainder of the Lurs live much as they did three thousand years ago. It is probably nowhere near as romantic a life as it sounds: the death rate among children, for example, is high as the caravans move across the land.

The big handsome Kurds form the largest tribal nation, though it overlaps parts of Iraq, Turkey, Syria, and the U.S.S.R., as well as Iran's western province of Kurdistan. The Kurds are Aryans by descent (probably from the Medes) and speak a language like Persian, but profess the Sunni faith of Islam rather than Iran's Shiite faith. They yearn for a state of their own, and fought the Iraqis to a standstill in the early 1970s; but the Shah's withdrawal of support doomed the Kurds' already unlikely chances of becoming independent. For these dashing horsemen, whose turban ends fly in the wind as they ride, it's all very sad. In Teheran in the winter, one frequently sees bands of ragged men, sticking together and looking out of place, a sight that led me once to ask a companion who they were. "Kurds," he said. "There is no work for them in Kurdistan at this time of the year, so they come here to get construction jobs, sleeping in the same buildings they are putting up."

The Arabs of Khuzistan (once called Arabistan) form the largest non-Aryan segment of Iran's population, but they are disunited menials who are losing their language and other culture to the economically dominant Persians. The big, tight-knit, minorities are the Jews and the Aryan-descended Christian Armenians, about eighty thousand of each.

Dating back to neo-Babylonian and Achaemenian times, the Jews, centered in Hamadan, Rasht, and Teheran, have mostly enjoyed the traditional tolerance of the Iranians for other races, but they sometimes suffered from Islamic fanaticism, and may now be vulnerable to a new dose of it. A young woman who was brought up in superdevout Mashhad says that "in school I was never asked about my religion, but I was sure that I should not tell that I was a Jew." She felt obliged to wear a chador, like the Moslem girls. In general, Jews have stayed apart from the Iranians socially. One Jewish man says of his youth: "I went to a Jewish school. My family relations were with Jews. My friends were Jews. I saw the non-Jewish people as out of my private world. I know Iran as a Jew who knows that he is Jewish and nothing else."

The Armenians mostly live in Teheran, Tabriz, and Isfahan. They speak Armenian, and in the streets of Tabriz one occasionally sees signs in the neat, squarish Armenian alphabet, much in contrast with the Arabic swashes of the other signs. Though the Armenians, too, are neither ghettoized nor looked down upon in Iran (quite the reverse; they are well-to-do and admired), they also stay apart from Iranian society.

A smaller minority are the Nestorians, who descend from the Assyrians and speak Syriac. Once concentrated on the western shore of Lake Rezaiyeh, they were removed by Reza Shah to Teheran, Hamadan, and Kermanshah. This uprooting was so distasteful that many of them migrated to the United States, and only about 35,000 remain.

Taken together, the Iranians numbered 33.6 million in 1979, and with a growth rate of 3 percent, one of the highest in the world, were increasing by a million a year. The growth has come fast: in 1900 the population was fewer than 10 million, and in 1956 not quite 19 million. According to demographer Mohammed Hemmasi, of Pahlavi University, "the birthrate has remained high and stable, around 45 to 50 births per thousand population per annum" throughout the century. Meanwhile, the mortality rate has dropped from some high but unknown figure to the present low of 13 per thousand per year. "Improvements in means of transportation and the possibility of interregional grain trade, particularly during severe drought and crop failures, improvements in general health conditions especially through malaria eradication, and achievements in socioeconomic developments are responsible for the observed downward trends in mortality," writes Hemmasi.

The life expectancy of Iranians at birth, which was a scant 40 years only fifteen years ago, has shot up to 55, which compares to 41 in India, 73 in the United States, and 75 in Sweden. The decline in the death rate here, as elsewhere, is mostly a decline in infant mortality;

once a person gets past infancy, his chances of survival to old age increase sharply. In other words, because there are many children, life expectancy rises. The effect of this recent demographic shift is to make Iran a nation of young people: 45.5 percent of the population is less than 16 years old; the whole age range from 16 to 64 comprises just 51.5 percent, and those over 65 merely 3 percent. Many people, especially women, look old, but that is because they age rapidly in appearance, and look 60 or 70 when they are still in their 40s.

Professor James Bill, in *The Politics of Iran,* distinguishes nine social classes in Iran: the ruling class, the bureaucratic middle class, the bourgeois middle class, the cleric middle class, the new professional middle class, the traditional working class, the peasants, the tribesmen, and the new industrial working class. But I think that if the Iranians had to be divided into only two classes, the fault line would be an economic one, that which divides the well-to-do from the poor.

When Iranians are rich, they are very, very rich. Not long ago, a sidewalk thief in London snatched an Iranian woman's handbag and discovered $500,000 worth of jewels in it. One woman reportedly gambled her way through $20 million in London casinos in five years. The parents of brides in Teheran think nothing of paying $150 for their daughter's bridal hairdos and makeup. The favorite car of the rich is the biggest Mercedes-Benz, which costs $60,000 in Iran; I heard of one tycoon who owns 123 M-B's of various sizes. Newspapers advertise "superb heavily gold-plated bathroom fixtures." When the London owners of Tramp, a discotheque, excluded a rich Iranian named Sahrab Eshragi, he retaliated by coolly buying the building that housed the joint. As the Shah teetered and toppled, rich Iranians exported billions of dollars and moved into sumptuous houses in London and Los Angeles.

The rich do not know the meaning of philanthropy. They are generous to the poor on a one-by-one basis, helping those in need whom they personally knew. They seem to think that impersonal charity should be left to the government. The Red Lion and Sun, the Iranian equivalent of the Red Cross, receives many private gifts but relies for its survival on a government subsidy. Until the revolution, Westerners and the Iranian upper classes paid little attention to the fact that effective charity in Iran was in the hands of Khomeini's mullahs, who received great sums of money from bazaar merchants and gave it, in return for devotion and gratitude, to the authentically needy.

In the form of society that prevailed under the Iranian monarchy, every individual had to make his peace with the fact that he was a subject of the Shah, that his life would be shaped by the decisions of one man at the top. By the nature of the system, every subject had to relate himself to the Shah, had to remain conscious of the Shah, had to give some time every day to thinking about the Shah. Subjecthood would be intolerable for Americans, as they proved in 1776, and many Iranians found that it subtracted from their humanity. "It is an indignity for every Iranian to live under a half-mad king," fumed Abolhassan Banisadr, an economist whom I met when he was in exile in Paris and who in January 1980 was elected first president of Iran. In point of fact, it was not necessarily the Shah himself but rather monarchy as a form of government that inspired the nearly perpetual grumbling. It is an unhappy situation for an individual to be dominated by a ruler even if he thinks the ruler is doing the right thing.

In what they read in their newspapers, full of puffery for the Shah, Iran's educated people were treated like little children, their intelligence insulted and degraded. Every subject of the king had to carry an official document that was not only an identity card but also his birth certificate and a record of his marriage and of the birth of his children. This document was issued at birth, renewed at the age of eighteen with the addition of the holder's photograph, and renewed once again at the age of forty. A computer did the work—Big Brother computerization of personal information was a *fait accompli* in Iran. The fine for losing the document was seventy-five dollars. As *Kayhan International* pointed out, the document was "needed as a means of identification to cash a cheque. It has to be produced, and a copy made, every time the holder wants to make a trip abroad, participate in a major transaction or even undertake something so simple as buying a car." In a word, the document served as a continual reminder of one's subjecthood. Some observers believed that this dinned-in feeling of loss of ego was a major cause of the Iranians' aggressive driving and other hostile public behavior.

However, thousands of the king's loyalists subordinated loss of ego to pride in collaborating with their monarch for the greater good of Iran. Shapur Shahbazi, the archaeological curator at Persepolis, had, when I met him, just received the decoration of the Order of the Royal Favor from the Shah, and he was plainly grateful for it and proud to be in a spot where he could serve the king. Many professional men— I recall, for example, a mining engineer met on a plane, and a computer expert in a university—seemed to feel that they and the king were fellow pros, mutually appreciating one another's work.

A great many other people put aside problems of subjecthood because they saw no choice between the stable institution of the monarchy and the presumable chaos of any alternative they could think of. But other thousands of loyalists—virtually the whole top rank of the Ministry of the Imperial Court, for example—were blatant fawners. The Ministry of Information man whom I met in Ahvaz was an uninformed, boastful fool, who tried to make up for his defects by overpraising His Imperial Majesty.

The question of whether to be a subject or a citizen poignantly anguished thousands of Iranians who had gone to Western nations for higher education and learned firsthand what freedom is. Hormoz Farhat, whose name is familiar to every ethnomusicologist in the world, is a case in point. Starting with a B.A. in music from the University of California at Los Angeles in 1953, he took a Ph.D. in ethnomusicology at the same school, taught there, composed the scores for six motion pictures, and married an American woman. He wrote the *Grove's Dictionary* article on Persian music. In 1968 he went back to Iran on a six-month sabbatical to do research on the traditional Persian musical drama. "In the course of my stay I became so moved by the dynamism and the motion of the country, by the renewal of childhood memories, by being reintroduced to my homeland, that I asked myself, why not try to do what I can for my country?" He became a professor of music at the University of Teheran, chaired the department for five years, and stepped up to the vice-chancellorship of Farabi University. Divorcing his American wife, he married an Iranian. As far as I could tell, he had accepted subjecthood, though he did confess to "feelings, mixed feelings, for America."

A young sculptor who had returned to Iran after training in the United States and taken a job teaching for a semester at the University of Teheran told me that he liked working in Iran. "The opportunities for a sculptor are better. There's lots of support. But I'd have to do my military service. I think I'll go back to America."

Kings seem to think that subjects like being subjects, even though history since the Magna Charta argues otherwise. The Shah's arrogant misperception of the indignity that he inflicted on intelligent people was an important cause of his downfall.

Compared to the burden of subjecthood, putting up with the foreigners that the Shah imported was a less profound reason for Iranians to rise up against their king, yet one tinged with so much emotion that most foreigners finally fled. Many, perhaps most, Iranians and foreigners would probably report that they had friendly relations with one another, but nevertheless resentments ran high. As is their custom when abroad, the Americans mostly stuck with other Americans, usually other employees of the breadwinner's company. They did not learn Persian, as a rule, and sent their children to "American" schools (where, nevertheless, more than half the pupils were Iranians).

The Americans and the Iranians irritated each other in many ways. American women sometimes dressed in too sexy a way (no bra, for example), causing old chador women to strike them and young men to ogle, paw, jostle, and stroke. (I heard of three American women who counterattacked one of these "phantom squeezers" by grabbing his arms to immobilize him, and he indignantly complained to the police.) Some American personal habits repelled Iranians. "Loud sniffling and nose blowing, for instance, when you are with an Iranian, is just about as rude as breaking wind generally is," wrote Mary Catherine Bateson in her guidebook *At Home in Iran*. Richer than they had ever been at home, Americans hired house servants and created what was often a desperately unhappy relationship. "My *badjis* steal my food, my clothes, my keys—I have to keep my Nescafé in my filing cabinet!" one American man fumed to me, unaware that *badji*, the word universally and condescendingly used by Americans to mean female servant, is not even Persian, but rather Turkish for "big sister." I should add, though, that hundreds of Americans did learn Persian, acquired Iranian friends, and appreciated the culture.

The cumulative irritations of life in Iran (high rents, language hassles, school problems) often built up to broken contracts and furious departures for home. When I was in Iran, 140 instructor pilots for Bell Helicopter angrily walked off the job, complaining of impossible conditions, and 100 of them eventually pulled out of Iran. Others left for a different reason: they talked too freely of their work, and the Iranian secret police, who spied closely on the Americans, put them on an outbound airplane. A good many of the military technicians were former servicemen who fought in Vietnam. "Guys who liked Saigon," says one Bell official, "are the midlevel fellows who don't know any other way of making a living." They tended to fill up on Coors beer, start fights, race motorcycles into mosques, call the Iranians "ragheads" or "a bunch of monkeys." They took in as much as $120,000 a year. For their part, the Iranians, by the nature of the training contracts, were put in the unhappy position of pupils taking orders and, more broadly, of seeing their country invested by foreigners who often lived in enviably better circumstances.

These factors left the Iranians with little love for the thirty thousand Americans (including eight thousand military advisers) among them, and with the revolution most of them had to flee the country in undignified haste.

On the other hand, as Bateson explained, "There are many walls in Iran, walls you can see, around houses and gardens, and walls you cannot see, but feel." The foreigner was a *khareji,* an outsider. The

Iranian traits of dissimulation and cynicism, experienced, for example, in bad relations with gouging landlords, quite understandably offended the foreigner. An attractive young American woman told me that she disliked hailing taxis because so many single men in private cars would try to pick her up. To help foreigners with problems, the government set up a Foreign Residents Advisory Bureau, run by an energetic woman named Shirin Mahdavi. One of her first crises concerned an American man who had married an Iranian woman nine years earlier in the United States, and found upon reaching Teheran that his marriage was invalid because it had not been registered at the Iranian Embassy. To remarry his wife, he had to prove to the mullah that he was circumcised. Would he have to get a medical certificate to that effect? he asked Mahdavi. She solved the problem boldly. "Just let the mullah take a look," she said.

One of the first of the Shah's men to be executed by the Khomeini revolutionaries was General Nematollah Nassiri, the same man who years before the Shah had sent to arrest Mossadegh. His crime: heading up SAVAK, the brutally repressive secret police whose job—the Shah apparently thought—was to bring into line those few Iranians misguided enough not to love their king. But far from protecting the king, SAVAK stirred up so much hatred that it became a major factor in the king's fall. Even more ironic, SAVAK as an intelligence agency failed to detect or report to the Shah that Iranians in general wanted to topple him.

Until the revolution disbanded it, SAVAK (an acronym of the Persian words *Sazeman Etelaat va Amniat Keshvar*—Security and Information Organization) was one of the world's harshest secret political police forces—doubly sinister because it had "a higher number of Ph.D.'s than any other government organization in Iran," as one knowledgeable American told me. For its organization and training, SAVAK had technological assistance, including methods of forcible interrogation, first from the CIA and later from Shin Bet, the legendary Israeli secret service. As a secret police force, SAVAK tried to stay out of sight. Its headquarters was a group of buildings in north Teheran, identifiable not by any plaque or sign but by its many antennas. Branch offices in the capital were buildings originally put up to be apartment houses, looking just like their neighbors. A French lawyer who investigated SAVAK reported that it employed 20,000 people plus 180,000 informers. "Is it true, as I've heard, that one in every thirty Iranians is an informer?" I asked Parvis Radji, at that time deputy prime minister. "I'd take that with a grain of salt," he replied. "On the other hand, *all* Iranians *should* be spies if they happen to hear, for example, of some bombing plan being made." Certainly I got the impression of spooks everywhere. Once, interviewing a provincial governor, I became irritated at a pesky fellow who stuck like glue to this official and even undertook to answer many of my questions. "Who's he?" I asked my interpreter. The reply: "He's the SAVAK man, though he told me not to tell you that. He says he doesn't want to be in your book." I ultimately realized that in many, but not all, of my interviews with government officials, including several cabinet ministers, some shadow insisted on listening in. An important part of SAVAK's job was watching the government's own people. SAVAK, like the CIA, also stationed men under cover titles in Iran's embassies, to spy on Iranians wherever they are.

Every university professor I met told me that he assumed that one student in each of his classes was a SAVAK informer, and every business firm had to expect that at least one employee would be a spy. One American businessman told me amusedly that he had long since learned not only to spot the spies in his organization but also to welcome and appreciate them. One in particular was skilled at digging up hard-to-get information—he obviously had good connections. Ultimately the businessman fired him. But not because he was a spy. The fellow had an intolerable case of body odor.

SAVAK also kept a sharp eye on airports and plane travelers. One day at Kerman I boarded an aircraft in the company of an Iranian engineer whom I had met by chance a few minutes before in the lobby. At the gate, a watchful, long-haired young man in a blue suit checked our tickets against identification, and after the passengers were aboard he scrutinized the luggage as it was loaded, speaking all the while into a walkie-talkie. "Who is he?" I asked, glancing out the window. "Oh, he's a friend of mine. He's the SAVAK man," the engineer replied.

Curiously enough, SAVAK was not invented by the Shah (though he came to cherish it). Quite the reverse: the Shah had to spend many years gaining control of SAVAK from its founder, who gradually grew ambitious to topple the monarch; and in a drama worthy of Sophocles, the Shah ultimately used SAVAK to rub out its own founder.

This ambitious man, the Shah's most serious challenger after Mossadegh and until Khomeini, was General Teymour Bakhtiar. Son of a noble khan of the Bakhtiari tribes, educated in French lycées and at Saint Cyr, the dashing officer—always clad in splendid uniforms and a Robert Taylor smile—came to the Shah's favor in 1953 by skillfully deploying his tanks against Mossadegh's mobs. As military governor in Teheran after that, he mopped up Tudeh resistance and took charge of army intelligence, positioning himself to be the first chief of SAVAK when Parliament, responding to American pressure, enacted the secret police law in 1956. Building up dossiers on every important Iranian, Bakhtiar pulled into his own hands power that grew even as the future of the Pahlavi dynasty came into question because Queen Soraya could not provide a son. The American Embassy and the CIA liked Bakhtiar; dispatches to Washington mentioned, with equanimity, the possibility that he might topple the king and create a Republic of Iran. Presidential candidate John F. Kennedy received Bakhtiar and enjoyed his gallantry and charm. It came to be that no appointee for a government job dared accept without getting Bakhtiar's permission. By torture that he took pleasure in observing personally, the smiling general fought for the landlords, whom he adored, against the "Communists," whom he abhorred, coming eventually into collision with the Shah's newborn White Revolution, which Bakhtiar saw as a dangerously left-wing exercise. Meanwhile, by blackmail and embezzlement, Bakhtiar built a huge fortune; the Shah had to grit his teeth as he drove from his Marble Palace office to his Saadabad residence and observed the construction of a million-dollar house for Bakhtiar. Recollecting his noble tribal ancestry, Bakhtiar finally decided that he had more right to rule Iran than any upstart Pahlavi.

Separating Bakhtiar from SAVAK turned out to be easier than the Shah foresaw, for in his first decades as king he often underestimated the power of monarchy. The Shah caused his prime minister to denounce officials with "too many millions in Swiss bank accounts," then summoned Bakhtiar and fired him. For a replacement he chose General Hassan Pakravan, a pipe-smoking, piano-playing intellectual of unquestionable loyalty. But Bakhtiar did not lie down and die. In 1962 he engineered, from behind the scenes, an intentionally excessive military attack on antigovernment students at the University of Teheran. "I have never seen or heard of so much cruelty, sadism, atrocity, and vandalism," wrote the chancellor later. "Some of the girls were criminally attacked in the classrooms by the soldiers." Four days later the Shah told the general to get out of Iran on the next plane. For five years Bakhtiar lived in the Swiss villa he had built in case he was exiled, but he boiled with rage against the Shah. In 1967 he supplied the bombs and radio for a remote-control car directed, by a dissident Iranian student and with no success, against the Shah during a royal tour of West Berlin. The Shah responded by getting his Office of Military Prosecution to confiscate Bakhtiar's wealth and to sentence him to death for treason. When Bakhtiar then surfaced in Lebanon and got thrown into jail on a gunrunning charge, Iran demanded extradition. Lebanon refused, backed by a motley chorus of Bakhtiar defenders who ranged from Pope Paul VI to ex-Queen (and Bakhtiari tribeswoman) Soraya to Jean Paul Sartre. Bakhtiar moved coolly on to Baghdad to put his knowledge of Iran at the disposal of the Iraqi government, which was then fighting its Kurdish rebels and thus indirectly the Shah.

The Shah of Iran was death on hijackers, and in all the recent history of this kind of offense, only one set of criminals has ever managed to make off with an airplane in Iran. On a flight out of Teheran, two dastardly men rose from their seats one day in August 1970, brandished pistols, and forced the pilot to go to Baghdad so that they could join Bakhtiar's fight against the Shah. Bakhtiar welcomed them joyfully, and a few days later all three went off on a companionable hunting expedition in country only twenty miles from the Iranian border. There one of the hunters put a bullet through Bakhtiar's body, and he died two days later. The hunters fled back to Iran.

Thus, by a rather simple piece of trickery, did SAVAK kill its founder.

When SAVAK was at its worst in the mid 1970s, it confronted opponents of the regime with a series of possibilities that were all dreadful. If the National Police (who usually handled arrests after SAVAK fingered someone) managed to surround a suspect in his hideout, the chances were high that he would not escape alive. The police preferred a shootout, in which the quarry actually or allegedly pulled a gun or a grenade and the policemen shot him, or her, dead. Alternatively, the police liked to pretend that the hunted person accidentally killed himself. With unbelievable frequency the government reported that some cornered terrorist had stupidly blown himself up with his own hand grenade—the public assumed that some of these deaths were suicides carried out to avoid facing SAVAK tortures.

When the police arrested a suspect, SAVAK took on the task of investigating the offense and preparing the file that formed the entirety of the prosecutor's case at the trial. Both the arrest and the detention were gloomy times for the defendant. The arrest was often a disappearing act—the offender simply vanished, and might not get in touch with his family or friends, much less a lawyer. Thousands of Iranian families had the doleful experience of losing contact with a son or a brother, or a daughter or a sister, and going for months without knowing where the relative was.

Where the vanished person was, however, could usually be narrowed to the cells of SAVAK's own prison, Evin, not far from the Royal Hilton in northwestern Teheran. In this pink, brick-walled compound, with bright yellow corridors, SAVAK agents, often without informing the prisoner of the charge against him, built their cases, mostly by extracting confessions. It was the use of torture for this purpose that won Iran disrepute as one of the world's ranking users of institutional-ized torture.

This shame embarrassed Iranian officials, but one of them defiantly admitted to me that "if someone is guilty of throwing bombs, you may be sure that SAVAK doesn't offer him caviar and vodka." Indeed not. What SAVAK often did offer was a soft-drink bottle forced up the rectum. Other tortures were equally sadistic. The novelist Reza Baraheni was whipped: "It was like a huge, hot charcoal, live, burning and tear-ing at the soles of the feet, crippling the whole legs. I was screaming at the top of my voice." Some victims were tortured less by the pain inflicted than by the helmets clamped on their heads, which magnified their own screams. In the chamber where he was kept, Baraheni saw electric prods (for use on the genitals), skull-squeezers, shoulder-break-ing weights, and the notorious Iranian bedspring torture device, on which the victim lay, tied, while the wires were heated from warm to hot to searing. Some years ago at a trial, an observer from Amnesty International was taken by surprise when the defendant "suddenly pulled off his sweater in front of everyone and showed me appalling burns on his stomach and his back." About the same time an engineer named Samavati was forced to watch SAVAK torture his two children (but he did not break), and in 1976 a colonel named Veziry, allegedly caught plotting a coup, reportedly had to look on as his wife and three children were tortured at Comite prison (in her case, to death). Rape of both men and women was routine: Baraheni once saw a benumbed girl of thirteen introduce her torturer as "my rapist." Torturers not only broke their victims' bones, but, in a chilling refinement, broke them again once they partially knitted.

Torture is torture, and any torture is too much. Nevertheless, some of the Shah's critics apparently got carried away in contending that most arrested political prisoners—that is to say, tens of thousands— were tortured. In *Chronique de la Répression 1963–1975,* a booklet pub-lished by the Paris-exiled heirs to Mossadegh's National Front, the compilers made a conscientious effort to assemble the names of all persons jailed, tortured, or killed by the regime; and although the au-thors believed that they might not have discovered more than 10 per-cent of names of the arrested, the number of those provably tortured came to no more than 170. Similarly, London-based Amnesty Interna-tional, the world's leading tabulator of violators of human rights, pru-dently refrained from inflating the number of victims. But in one signif-icant sense, whether the tortured in Iran numbered in the hundreds or in the thousands is irrelevant. The mere existence of torture as an instrument of government humiliated, degraded, and repressed the

Iranian people. They all lived with this national atrocity plucking at the edge of their consciousness.

The consequence was a spiritually gray, oppressed, unhappy police state. The psychological impact of sensing that SAVAK knew everything, that it had a dossier on you, that your cousin might be a spy— in sum, that the government had no faith in the people—was profoundly demoralizing. When I went into an English-language bookstore to buy Professor James Bill's mildly critical *The Politics of Iran,* the bookseller told me that he had stopped stocking it because "it's against the government. It's all true, but the secret police won't allow it." The bookseller had good reason to be cautious. Some months before, SAVAK men had raided his store, ransacked his stock, and confiscated a children's history of Russia as Communist literature. "This is not a free country," he told me sadly.

In private, people told bitter jokes like this: The Shah learns that for $10 million a minute, the telephone company can put through a call to heaven. Eagerly he asks to talk to his father, person to person. The operator cannot locate Reza Shah in heaven, but finally finds him in hell. When, after a long conversation, the Shah is finished, he asks for the charges. Operator: "Ten cents." Shah: "So cheap?" Operator: "It was a local call."

Professors avoided teaching *Hamlet* because it dealt with the killing of kings. A British woman teaching English to adults told me of her difficulties in finding subjects for conversation: "You get onto some sensitive subject, and suddenly the whole class falls quiet—no one will respond." Most professors spoke to me with apparent freedom, but one fellow in Tabriz said in a rattled tone of voice: "You must go to the government to get your information. We always receive a letter from the Ministry of Science and Higher Education before we talk to people. I am not allowed to talk to journalists."

A foreigner visiting Iran would almost certainly meet someone (as I did) who would say something like this: "One of my brothers is a student, doing well. Another is already a teacher, and very happy about it. A third is getting along fine as a government employee. And the fourth [face falls, voice trails off] has disappeared. . . . We don't know where he is." The inquiring journalist encountered both timidity and defiance. When I asked the governor of Mashhad to tell me how big the population was, he called in a consultant—the SAVAK man, maybe—to inquire whether this sort of information could be divulged to the press (it could). But a chance acquaintance in a restaurant, after hearing of my projected book, hissed: "Keep your eyes open! Don't be afraid! Write the truth!" And a taxi driver in Isfahan obligingly indicated a big prison that we were passing by removing his hands from the wheel and crossing his wrists as if manacled. This prison reportedly contained a thousand mullahs and other political prisoners.

The ultimate irony is that SAVAK failed in its mission to appraise the strength and nature of the opposition to the Shah, and thus failed to head off his fall. In its zeal to ferret out the "Communists" that the Shah thought were his enemies, SAVAK did not hear the bubbling discontent in the mosques. Worse from the U.S. government's point of view, SAVAK, relied upon to exchange intelligence with the CIA, couldn't warn the Americans any more than it could warn the Shah. And CIA men in Iran didn't try very hard to uncover the truth themselves because SAVAK was spying on *them*.

8

The Case of the Hidden Imam

And the signs for his appearance are many,
So know you when He comes. For first will come
the Dajjal, a one-eyed man who is skilled in magics.
　　Shouting there will be, in the sky,
　　like thunder: "The Righteousness is come."
Then will a man of pure lineage be murdered
in Mecca, and the sun shall eclipse the moon
and the moon the sun, at the end of Ramazan.

Such signs are definite, but these are probable:
Many earthquakes will there be, and killings
in the world; the sky, the whole sky will be
red, and the rain will pour down on the desert.
In the East a star will come in the shape
of a moon. And men will sin, and women even
will dress as men.

The mullahs and the ayatollahs of Iran abominated SAVAK as much as anyone else did, and were also in conflict with the Shah because he greatly reduced the clergy's revenues from church landholdings, and because his modernization brought with it such "immoral" offenses as coeducation and pornography. But the basic conflict was theological: Islam holds that religion and government should be identical in Iran, and that the Shah's secular monarchy was therefore illegitimate. Worse, theology says that the nation's true leader *exists,* although he is in "occultation," in hiding. In fact, he has been in hiding for centuries, but he will reappear, with the sky red and the rain pouring down upon the desert, and he will rule Iran.

　　The religion of Iran is the interminglement of belief that resulted from the conquest of a strong native faith, Zoroastrianism, the creation of the great sixth century B.C. Iranian prophet Zoroaster, by a strong foreign faith, Islam, the creation of the great seventh century A.D. prophet Mohammed. To accept another culture's religion at the point of a sword does not make for pride; the Iranians responded by keeping the oral tradition of the Zoroastrian creed alive, and ultimately Ferdowsi recorded it in his epic poem, *Shahnama*. When it came time for the Iranian kings to choose an interpretation of the Islamic heritage that would accommodate their pre-Islamic tradition, they deliberately adopted the Shiah sect of Moslem belief to distinguish themselves from the Arabs' Sunni sect. The central distinction between Shiah and Sunni is Shiah's belief in a messiah—a great "imam" who will someday, no one knows when, bring about the triumph of justice and good, just as the world nears its end. This imam, last of a bloodline of twelve, disappeared in 874 at the age of four or five. But Shiites believe that he lives to this day, unrecognized by his fellow men, somewhere in Iran. The powerful and mystical concept of a Hidden Imam is the force behind faith and devotion in Iran today—and behind religion's opposition to the Shah.

When the prophet Mohammed died in 632, two parties contended for religious and political domination. The majority, who argued that Mohammed had designated no successor, elected Abu Bakr, the prophet's chief lieutenant, as the first caliph (spiritual *and* temporal leader). Following Abu Bakr's death two years later, the holy warrior Omar claimed the caliphate, and spent a decade expanding the Arab empire to western Persia, Syria, what is now Iraq, Egypt, and the North African coast, until he was stabbed to death by a Persian slave. Another elected caliph succeeded Omar; then the minority faction, the legitimists, put over the idea that a relative of Mohammed should be made caliph to start a bloodline succession from the prophet. Hazrat Ali, the "Lion of God," Mohammed's cousin and the husband of his favorite daughter, Fatima, took power. Soon he, too, was assassinated, and the faction that supported election of caliphs, now given the name Sunni—Right Path—replaced him with one of their luminaries. Moving the empire's capital to Damascus, they founded the line of caliphs called the Omayyad dynasty. The losing faction took the name Shiat Ali—Partisans of Ali—thereby giving their sect of Islam its modern name of Shiah.

The Sunnis increasingly persecuted the Shiites, mainly for protesting the worldliness of the Damascus rulers. The most infamous persecution occurred at the death of the dynasty's first caliph, when Husain, a son of Ali married to a Persian princess, disputed the Sunni successor at the famous battle of Kerbala, south of Baghdad. Husain died bravely with his eighty-odd men, endowing Shiah with a martyrdom that is

THE CASE OF THE HIDDEN IMAM   141

commemorated today in Teheran with much passion. Shiah became a clearly separate branch of Islam. But its believers were scattered throughout the Arab empire, not only in Iran, and they remained ineffectual until the Shiites of Khorasan, Iran's northeast province, helped to overthrow the Omayyads in 750.

At the beginning of Islamic history the Sunnis and the Shiites shared in a common understanding of the word "imam": the person who stands before the congregation to lead the prayers. As the Arab culture became more international, the Arab term took on an honorific dimension signifying a religious leader. But in a parallel usage of the word, Shiite theologians began to apply "imam" to the leaders of their sect who descended from Ali, embodying the spiritual reality of the Prophet. Down through the two centuries after Ali's death, these holy men formed an imamate of exactly twelve. The first, Ali himself, ranks nearly as high in Iranian reverence as Mohammed. The second, his son Husain, the preeminent martyr, is seen (echoes of Christ) as having sacrificed himself in atonement for the sins of mankind. The sixth, Jafar, was a scholar of such power that his particular exegesis of Shiah is constitutionally the official religion of Iran. The seventh, Ismail, was so fond of alcohol that his father, Jafar, transferred the succession to another son; yet Ismail was so charismatic that a sect of Shiah, now called the "seveners," broke away to become the international faith that is now headed by Aga Khan IV, the Indian playboy. Other seveners were the Druses and the Assassins. The eighth saint was the fabled Imam Reza, the martyr entombed in the shrine city of Mashhad. The twelfth was the one who put an end to the imamate by disappearing as a boy of four or five. Four stand-in "lieutenants" succeeded the missing boy, until the last of them declined to name a successor; this period came to be known as the Lesser Occultation. The much longer period since then is the Greater Occultation.

Lacking any more unoccultated imams, Shiite Islam developed into a faith without a church. It has no pope, no centrally administered hierarchy of archbishops, bishops, and priests. Mohammed stipulated in his teachings that there must be no intermediary between Allah and man. Nevertheless, a clergy grew up to interpret the laws and customs of Islam. This clergy divides into a common priesthood of about ten thousand mullahs, and a higher rank of about a hundred *mujtahids,* distinguished by superior piety, learning, and wisdom in interpreting the Koran. From time to time a mujtahid achieves such respect that his peers by consensus raise his rank to ayatollah ("reflection of Allah"), and sometimes the ayatollahs choose one of their number to be leader of the Shiites throughout the world and temporary surrogate for the Hidden Imam.

From the end of World War II until his death in 1962, the gentle and learned Ayatollah Borujerdi held this position. After Borujerdi died, the front runner was the holy man whose name later became familiar to all the world: Ruhollah Khomeini. He had been born, as Ruhollah Hendi, in 1901 in the town of Khomein, from which he later took his present name to distinguish himself from a brother arrested as a leftist in 1930. He studied at the holy cities of Qom and Najef, Iraq. His opposition to monarchy may have begun when the mayor of Khomein killed his father in some clash. As early as 1944 he was denouncing the Shah in his writings. He married twice, fathering two sons and three daughters. In 1963 he led demonstrations against the beginnings of the Shah's modernization program, particularly confiscation of the clergy's land, and made himself the leading symbol of no-holds-barred opposition to the Shah. When the Shah arrested Khomeini, crowds rioted for three days in Teheran, Qom, Mashhad, Isfahan, and Shiraz, and soldiers—in a preview of 1978 and 1979—savagely killed thousands of protesters. The following year the Shah exiled Khomeini to Najef, and thereby made him the martyr who, deploring the Pahlavis as a "family of looters whose arms are sunk to the elbows in the blood of the innocent," finally brought down the monarchy. He discovered that by sending tape cassettes he could preach fiery sermons to thousands in Iran's mosques, and by 1978, when he moved to a white stucco house in the suburban Paris village of Neauphle-le-Château (not far from where Brigitte Bardot lives), he had made his communication network so effective that he could set Iran afire merely by saying a few words.

After Khomeini went into exile, another ayatollah, Sayed Ghassem Shariatmadari, gradually ascended to leader of the faith in Iran until Khomeini's triumphant return. Two years younger than Khomeini, white-bearded and frail, he opposed the Shah in less flamboyant ways. He saw Islam as a force against injustice, and in his view a major injustice was that Iran had never had free elections. As a result, the country got laws repugnant to Islam. "Alcoholic beverages are permitted," he pointed out. "There is gambling. There is illegitimate sex." He contended that banking without interest was feasible. Still, he favored science, technology, higher education for women as well as men (but in separate classrooms), and the vote for women (in separate booths).

If there is one city in Iran that comes close to being a Vatican, it is Qom (population 247,000), 96 miles south of Teheran. For some reason Qom adopted Islam with a special fervor, just after the Arab conquest, and it favored the Shiite branch of the religion long before most of the rest of Iran. When Fatima, a sister of the eighth imam, died

in 816 she was buried at Qom and her tomb became—and still is—
an object of pilgrimages to rival her brother's in Mashhad. Modern
Qom is a city of many mosques and shrines with dazzling domes, in
which infidels are not welcome. Religion is its business: Shiite Islam's
most respected theological seminaries are in Qom.

If a young Iranian receives a "call" to become a mullah, he usually
goes to school in Qom. The instruction is "decentralized to a fault,"
one scholar told me. The student picks his school, and on the basis
of reputation chooses a mullah to teach him. The way an instructor
might explain how he acquired his reputation, I was told, is as follows:
"There is a mosque. I sit down and open a book. You come and listen.
If I can keep my audiences, I announce that at 8 A.M. or 5 P.M. I will
teach. People come from other cities. This way I get to be an instructor.
After ten or twenty years I grow to be a great instructor. Then I begin
to let good students teach in my place."

The teachers use texts a thousand years old, but the heart of the
instruction is discussion. Sample topics: "Since the Koran says that
most people go to hell and few go to heaven, why did God create the
world in the first place?" "Can God create a stone so heavy he cannot
lift it?" "Why did God choose a Prophet who was illiterate?" (Answer:
God wrote the Koran using Mohammed's hand.) Theology dominates
the course, but the student may take some science, such as astronomy,
and some classes are taught in English.

The product of such an education is the commonplace mullah of
the cities of Iran. Often looking rather seedy in his turban (white for
commoners, green for descendants of Imam Reza, black for descendants of the Prophet) and brown or black robe that flies in the wind
like a bat wing, he doesn't necessarily look impressive. He may even
be a figure of fun—witness the story of the mullah Nasruddin, who
called the people to prayer from a minaret and then ran down and
away "to see how his prayer call sounded from a distance." Narrow,
rote-learned, their only foreign language Arabic, the bottom ranks contain much deadwood.

Yet people prize their mullahs. I heard from one woman who hired
a mullah to perform a memorial service for a dead relative: "The mullahs are much better educated than they used to be. The oration turned
out to be well written, sincere, not overflattering, and touched with
philosophy." And it was mullahs, interested in the secular as well as
the spiritual well-being of their followers, who played the vital role
of disseminating the revolution that felled the Shah.

Those mullahs who rise to become mujtahids take on serious theological tasks. Ministering to laymen, who seek them out, they provide
the religious guidance and counseling that makes many Iranians boast

that they have "no need for psychiatry." Most mujtahids write books that interpret the Koran to apply it to particular situations, and though the layman may consult the mujtahid personally from time to time, he can read the book for instruction even on such detailed points as "how to wash the arms," as one woman told me. "Ah, the consolations of a good mujtahid!" she exclaimed. The mujtahid, who is in effect a doctor of religion, must also try to update Islam according to divine wisdom that (mujtahids believe) the Hidden Imam communicates to him. A slightly flippant example, given to me by a mujtahid's son, is this: "The old texts say that if you possess forty camels you must give away one. So if you have forty airplanes how many do you have to give away?" A more serious example: "How should the texts on slavery be changed to accommodate the disappearance of slavery?"

The fact that the Shah opposed the Moslem clergy and feared basic Shiite doctrines did not mean that he painted himself an atheist, or that he neglected to try to build support by linking himself to the faith of his subjects. He once wrote that when he was a small boy, stricken with typhoid, he dreamed that he saw Ali, Mohammed's son-in-law. "Ali had with him his famous two-pronged sword, which is often seen in paintings of him. He was sitting on his heels on the floor, and in his hands he held a bowl containing liquid. He told me to drink, which I did. The next day, the crisis of my fever was over." But, the Shah added: "Although I was still only seven, in my childish way I recognized that the dream and my recovery were not necessarily connected." A little later, "my family and I made an excursion to Emamzadeh-Dawood, a lovely spot in the mountains above Teheran. To reach it one had to follow a steep trail on foot or on horseback; and since I was so young, a relative who was an army officer placed me in front of him on the saddle of his horse. Some way up the trail, the horse slipped, and I was plunged headfirst onto a jagged rock. I fainted. When I regained consciousness, the members of the party were expressing astonishment that I had not even a scratch. I told them that as I fell, I had clearly seen one of our saints, named Abbas, and that I had felt him holding me and preventing me from crashing my head against the rock." Another vision came still later, "while I was walking with my guardian near the royal palace in Shimran. Our path lay along a picturesque cobbled street. Suddenly I clearly saw before me a man with a halo around his head. . . . As we passed one another, I knew him at once. He was the Imam or descendant of Mohammed who, according to our faith, disappeared but is expected to come again to save the world." The Hidden Imam! The Shah saw him!

The Shah's opponents laughed at these stories. "Yes, indeed, he

gets divine guidance from Ali in his dreams once a week," Abolhassan Banisadr told me derisively. And the Shah himself was careful
to take a tentative tone when he wrote: "I have felt that perhaps there
is a supreme being who is guiding me."

The Shah sometimes made a pilgrimage to the shrine of the Imam
Reza in Mashhad, but only rarely did he otherwise enter a mosque.
He often conferred with Ayatollah Borujerdi, but when the Shah's land
reform in effect deprived Islam of the rewards of owning property,
Borujerdi refused to continue the relationship. Nevertheless, the Shah
maintained a prestigious personal mullah, Seyyid Hassan Emami, the
Imam Jomeh of Teheran (Imam in this case meaning prayer leader,
and Jomeh—the word for Friday—signifying his identification with
the holy day of the week). The Imam Jomeh—"the Shah's boy," some
called him—took his degree in Lausanne, speaks French, wears European clothes, breeds parrots and parakeets, and performed the Shah's
second and third marriages.

The Imam Jomeh was on hand at the Iranian New Year's Day
celebration on the spring equinox of 1976 when the Shah, in an intriguing speech, struck the balance of his relationship with Islam on
the fiftieth anniversary of the Pahlavi dynasty. After praising "the great
Iranian nation . . . whose inexhaustible power has once again come
to the fore," he said: "May the God of Iran help us all along this glorious
path." When, in the distance, a *muezzin* called all Moslems to noonday
prayers, the Shah fell reverently silent. But for this renewal of the
"eternal covenant" between himself and the Iranian people, he point-
edly chose a pre-Islamic holiday, and his specific message was that
"we, the Pahlavi dynasty, nurse no love but that for Iran, no zeal but
that for the dignity of Iranians, and recognize no duty but that of serving our state and our nation." With such words did the Shah help
build his downfall.

The secular conflict between the Shah and the clergy came from
Islam's aspiration to be a religion that embraces all aspects of life
and controls all the attitudes and actions of its believers. Religion *is*
government. Religious law is *the* law. One of the most astonishing
writings ever set down in Iran is not poetry or fiction but rather Article
2 of the constitution, as imposed ("In the Name of God, the Compassion-
ate, the Most Merciful!") by the powerful clergy in 1906. Stressing the
influence of the Hidden Imam (here called Imam Mahdi), it purported
to put a religious arm lock on the National Consultative Assembly,
now Parliament. In its entirety, it reads:

> Art. 2. At no time may the enactments of the sacred National Consul-
> tative Assembly, which has been constituted with the aid and favor
> of His Holiness the Imam of the Age (Imam Mahdi, the Twelfth Imam),

may God immortalize His reign! and under the supervision of the learned doctors of theology, may God increase their number! and by the whole Iranian people, be at variance with the sacred precepts of Islam and the laws laid down by His Holiness the Best of Mankind (the Prophet), may the blessings of God rest upon Him and His descendants! It is plain that the learned doctors of theology, may God prolong their beneficent lives! are charged with the duty of determining any contradiction between the laws made by the Assembly and the principles of Islam. It is, therefore, solemnly laid down that at all times there shall be constituted as follows a body of at least five devout doctors of Islamic law and jurisprudence who shall at the same time be conversant with the exigencies of their age: The most learned doctors of theology in Islam who are recognized as such and whose example is followed by the Shiites shall nominate to the National Consultative Assembly twenty doctors of theology possessing the above qualifications; the members of the Assembly shall choose five or more of them, according to circumstances, by a unanimous vote or by drawing lots, and shall recognize them as members so that they may carefully discuss and deliberate the bills proposed in both Houses, and reject any that contravene the holy principles of Islam, so that they shall not become law; the decisions of this body of doctors of theology on this point shall be followed and obeyed. This clause may not be modified until the Advent of the Imam of the Age, may God hasten His reappearance.

In practice, the learned doctors of theology never—until now, perhaps—managed to veto legislation, but Islam only slowly let go of its control over law. Even under the Shah, *Shariat,* religious law, still dominated four areas: marriage, divorce, adoption, and last wills and testaments (including inheritances); the civil code was based mostly on Islamic law. (The whole religio-civil legal relationship was roughly like Israel's.)

The theology behind this secular conflict involved the relationship between the Shah and the Hidden Imam. The theologians contended, in effect, that the Imam was the head of state; and since he was hidden, rather than dead, the Shah's rule was illegitimate; but since somebody must run the country until the Advent, the mujtahids could, if they were of a mind to, authorize the Shah to act for the Imam. They didn't. Their attitude, said one observer, "combines a denial of legitimacy with a quietistic patience and abstention from action."

From this theology, this polarization of the Shah and the Imam, came the concept of the Islamic Marxist, a synthesis of right and left, which at first blush seems so contradictory that the Shah's propagandists happily mocked it—how could a good Moslem be a Marxist? Upon examination, the idea of Islamic Marxism gains some credibility. The Baathist parties of Iraq and Syria, though indisputably far to the left, have never rejected Islam. The Koran teaches many "communistic" ideals. "As a matter of fact, we did not have to go through Marxism or Leninism to reach concepts of brotherhood and justice—we had them already," one explicator of Islamic Marxism told me. "Our ideas are much more dangerous to the Iranian Establishment than simple Marxism, atheistic and deprived of religious power." Upon his return, the Hidden Imam, carrying a sword, will kill all the corrupt, and the leftists certainly included the Shah among the corrupt.

To all of which the Islamic Marxists added one final explosive thought.

The Hidden Imam, they suggested, is not a man. What man could live more than eleven centuries? He is, instead, a *concept,* the concept of revolution, the ideology for a coup d'état. The Idea-Imam's time is near; no one needs to wait for a *man* to appear. In a sense each Iranian is the Hidden Imam, and must act for God.

Who was behind this theological rebellion? My informant, speaking before the Shah fell, shrugged. "God spread it." Upon consideration: "We don't know who is pushing the idea. It seems that some of the oldest and apparently most conservative of the clergy are among the most radical. But there are no leaders. The idea does not have to come from one man."

Still, one clearly identifiable revolutionary (though anti-Marxist) philosopher in the 1960s and 1970s was Ali Shariati, who altered Islam's traditional preaching of surrender to fate. He preached and wrote that a man should determine his own fate and that if he did so correctly Allah would bless him. He singled out the Koranic concept that those who die in a holy undertaking live forever—which may well explain the bravery in the face of death of thousands of revolutionaries in the 1978–1979 revolt. For dangerous ideas like these, the Shah predictably deported Shariati. He went to London, and one night in 1977 he suddenly died, though shortly before, he had been pronounced to be in good health despite chain-smoking. Shariati's preachings were widely distributed in Iran through tape cassettes, but perhaps the most important dissemination of his thought was through his books, soaked up by thousands of Iranian students in the United States and Western Europe. "In Iran, if one such book was found in your house," said a student, "you might go to jail for three years. In the United States, we could read everything."

Clearly, the concept of the Hidden Imam was not the sole contribution of Islam to the humbling of the Shah. Islam also provides a faith that is now enjoying a worldwide revival, and an organization—a framework of mullahs, mujtahids, mosques, and money. Ayatollah

Shariatmadari says: "Religion used to be considered marginal—apart from the mainstream of events. Now it has become much stronger than before."

Part of the faith's attraction is its purity. Many a mullah, to be sure, is selfish, reactionary, or corrupt, but the learned mujtahids are by definition men of integrity, simplicity, and merit. The half-dozen ayatollahs live with a lack of ostentation that contrasted sharply with the ugly showiness of the Pahlavi family. When the Ayatollah Borujerdi died, it was said that his possessions consisted of one samovar.

Islam prizes all of the great prophets, including Christ, whom the Koran praises. But it does not contend that Mohammed is God, as Christianity equates Christ with God; therefore Mohammed, as a man with human failings, becomes an easier model for the faithful to follow. Islam exalts nature—flowers and water. It comforts young men in college who—never having seen their mothers or sisters dressed in anything but the floor-length chador—are disturbed over sitting next to unveiled girls in classes in modernized universities, and therefore agree with the mullahs' stand against coeducation. Even one of Iranian Islam's darker aspects, self-flagellation on the anniversary of the death of Husain, is helpful: Iranians mourn not only Husain but also their own oppression, and in this way religion provides a safety valve.

The mullahs are said to have "the power of poverty," a reference to the fact that land reform cost the church most of its wealth. Actually the priests, and particularly the mujtahids, control plenty of money. A practicing Moslem donates one fifth of his disposable income to whatever cleric he regards as his priest. Bazaaris, who count among the most devout of Moslems, not only contribute faithfully but also have lots of disposable income, being usually richer than they look. The mullah or mujtahid can use this money for living expenses, but he usually receives much more than he needs and customarily gives the excess to needy people under his care—the victims of shooting by soldiers, for example. In their skirmishes with the Shah, the mullahs did not suffer for lack of money.

Taken together, the mullahs and the bazaaris have one other strength to contribute to overthrowing a government: communications. The Shah may have controlled the media and suppressed announcements of antigovernment demonstrations, but word-of-mouth in the mosques and bazaars proved more effective than prime-time television might have.

When the theological, human, and financial strengths of Islam are added up, the Shah's ambition to be the first monarch in Iranian history not to collaborate with the clergy seems all the more foolhardy. But he tried that and more. In the 1960s and 1970s, his police and troops harassed mujtahids, jailing many, and torturing one ayatollah, Hussain Ali Montazeri, atrociously, causing him to lose most of his hearing. In 1978, soldiers raided Shariatmadari's house and shot one of his followers before his eyes. To be deputy grand trustee of the Imam Reza's shrine in Mashhad, the Shah named a tough general who was close to the secret police—an appalling affront to Islam. (Iranians joked that the imam rose from his sarcophagus and joined his sister in her tomb in Qom.)

The power of Islam to make a revolution in Iran in 1979 is, historically speaking, ironic, for Iran received Islam on the points of Arab swords, and in doing so cast away a religion that was not only native but also one of the world's foremost faiths. This was Zoroastrianism, and the essence of it, in the words of Zoroaster himself, was this:

> I will speak of the two spirits
> Of whom the holier said unto the destroyer at the beginning of existence:
> "Neither our thoughts nor our doctrines nor our minds' forces,
> Neither our choices nor our words nor our deeds,
> Neither our consciences nor our souls agree."

Shaping the myths of the Indo-Aryan tribes, Zoroaster postulated two distinct realities, Good and Evil, which exist separated by a vast void. In the first period of three thousand years, the benevolent deity Ahura Mazda creates all that is good. He creates seven immortals or archangels to reflect aspects of his perfection and to act as intermediaries between the worlds of spirit and matter. Then he creates the sky, water, earth, the tree, the animal, and last of all, man. The spiritual forms of all these are united with material forms during the next three thousand years, and the will of the deity is reflected only in goodness.

Another period of three thousand years follows, during which the archdevil, Anahita, and his demonic cohorts assault the Good World with the sole purpose of destroying it. Each heavenly immortal finds an opponent in the underworld of demons and does battle: Good Mind against Wrong Mind, Truth against Deceit. But only the all-wise Ahura Mazda can grant material forms to his spiritual ideas; the devil and his company are entrapped in Ahura Mazda's world of spirit and matter as spirits who can infiltrate matter but never take visible form. This will ultimately mean their destruction.

Zoroaster's birth in 618 (?) B.C. coincides with the commencement of the last period of three thousand years, during which the forces of evil were to be defeated. From his birth he could commune with God. At the age of 30 he experienced the first of eight visions in which God revealed his mind. Then Zoroaster went in search of converts.

The new religion spread throughout the Iranian plateau. The prophet married, fathered three children, and lived until his seventies, when he was murdered by enemies.

Unlike such roughly contemporary thinkers as Lao-Tzu and Confucius in China and Buddha in India, Zoroaster was not a philosopher as much as a prophet. He organized the polytheistic beliefs of a tribal society based on revelations he received from an all-wise God. He constructed the first cyclical interpretation of history, which Nietzsche followed in his own treatise on historical method, *Thus Spake Zarathustra.* And most important for the Christian world, he introduced the idea of man's redemption through the efforts of a savior. Zoroastrian revelations predicted that three saviors would appear during the last period of three thousand years. Each was to be a son of Zoroaster born from a virgin who had bathed in a lake that preserved the prophet's semen. The first was to appear one thousand years after their father's birth, the others to follow at thousand-year intervals. Each was to assist Zoroaster in carrying mankind toward his ultimate triumph over evil. It was an optimistic religion—God made men to help him—and by its dualism it neatly side-stepped the question that the theologians of such monotheistic religions as Christianity and Islam have never been able to answer: How could a good God create a Satan?

On several reliefs at Persepolis there is a winged figure hovering above the king of kings in procession. Many scholars have accepted this figure as the symbol of Ahura Mazda, the god of Good and Light whom Zoroaster described in his hymns. Inscriptions on some of the buildings at Persepolis suggest that Darius believed in Ahura Mazda. By the coronation of Darius's son, Xerxes, in 485 B.C., the Zoroastrian faith had been established throughout the Achaemenian kingdom. Following the victory of Alexander at Persepolis in the fourth century B.C., Greek and Roman gods overwhelmed Zoroastrianism among both kings and the populace. But it resurfaced under the Parthians (171 B.C.–227 A.D.), and during the Sassanian period it once again became the imperial religion. For the first time the Avesta, a collection of hymns and prayers which makes up the Zoroastrian scripture, was written down in an ancient Iranian dialect akin to Sanskrit.

Zoroastrians believed that fire symbolized the spirit of Ahura Mazda, giving forth light to dissipate the insidious darkness of the devil Anahita. Thus, high up on mountains, they built fire temples—one of them can be seen a few miles west of Isfahan. Keeping the sacred fire lighted was the task of the mountain-dwelling Zoroastrian priests known as the Magi. And since Zoroastrians believed that death (along with disease, poisonous creatures, and pestilences) was the work of Anahita, a manifestation of evil, they left their dead in towers, also on mountaintops, where the sun and the wind, not to mention vultures, could dispose of the corpse without defiling the elements of the earth created by the all-good god.

When the Arabs conquered Iran with a new religion, the Zoroastrian defenders believed their god had abandoned them. According to their computations, the first savior should have appeared by 400 A.D. Zoroastrian historians were compelled to revise the cyclical theory of their millennial religion, and in so doing they identified the invaders as the cosmic demons assaulting Ahura Mazda. They cautioned the people to persevere in their faith, because soon a savior would be born to assist God in overthrowing the devil and all his demons. Nevertheless, thousands of believers fled to India, a country whose Hindu religion embraces many features of Zoroastrianism because both religions developed from the same Indo-Aryan source. Their descendants are the Parsees (equals Persians) of Bombay. Today about 36,000 Iranians in Yazd, Kerman, Isfahan, and Shiraz, plus a few in Teheran, still follow the Zoroastrian religion. Many are renowned gardeners and businessmen. Since Zoroastrians will not accept converts, the sect seems destined to stagnation.

Zoroastrianism, writes historian Yahya Armajani, was "without doubt the most significant contribution of the Persians to the world." Zoroastrianism in the third century B.C. fathered Mithraism, through the teachings of a Christ-like figure named Mithras, and Mithraism slowly spread to as far away as Ireland and Japan, becoming the major competitor to Christianity in the Roman Empire in the second and third centuries A.D. On circumstantial evidence, Zoroastrianism supplied Christianity (directly or through Judaism) with most of its precepts and adornments: a savior or messiah, angels, saints, heaven, purgatory, hell, a beginning and end of the world, mysteries, intercessors, atonement, a millennium, a day of judgment, and even the halo. And Zoroastrianism's offspring, Mithraism, probably provided the concepts of the mass and the mother of God.

Persian history and legend suggest, furthermore, that the Wise Men of the New Testament were Zoroastrian Magi. Star watching had been going on ever since Zoroaster prophesied that a bright sign in the sky would announce the coming of a savior. Zoroastrian records say that the Persian Magi kept a two-week vigil for the star every year on top of an Iranian mountain. Archaeologists have located this mountain in Sistan, in southeastern Iran. An ancient fire temple remains there, as well as some brick buildings that belonged to the Iranian king, Surena Pahlav, who a few months before Christ's birth defeated the Roman armies and marched victoriously into Jerusalem to depose King Herod. But his victory was short-lived, because he was murdered by jealous rivals and the Persian army left Jerusalem to return home. The Romans then returned and Christ was born on territory ruled by a Roman emperor rather than a Persian one. Perhaps this contact gave the Magi some knowledge of Jerusalem. At any rate, popular legend in Iran relates that the Magi started their journey to Bethlehem from Sistan after sighting the star from the mountaintop. They passed through Kashan on the edge of the Kavir desert and Saveh, a small trading center near modern Teheran, before turning west. Since religious rules forbade them to defile water, they traveled by land along an old caravan route. Iranian children today still love to reenact the visit of the three wise men to the crib of Jesus.

On top of all this, Zoroastrianism, blended with Buddhism and Christianity, was the inspiration of the Persian prophet Manes (A.D. 216?–276?), founder of Manicheanism, a major heresy of both Zoroastrianism and Christianity at the time. In the realm of politics, Zoroastrianism bequeathed the concept of a theocratic state whereby religion and royalty coexisted but did not coincide. The Achaemenian and Sassanian monarchs depended on the Zoroastrian priests for counsel, but only counsel.

Islam drove Zoroastrianism underground and caused Iran to develop the Shiite branch of the faith, with its doctrine of the Hidden Imam. Neither the Sunni nor the Shiite branch of Islam is much given to theological exegesis, the Hidden Imam concept being the main exception. But as the centuries passed after the twelfth imam's disappearance in 874, some thinkers in Iran did elaborate on their faith, and finally some of them devised the strange dervish sect called Sufism. Its credo:

> I am neither Muslim nor Christian, Jew nor
> Zoroastrian, I am neither of the earth
> nor of the Heavens, I am neither body nor
> soul; yet, I am all of these, at one and
> the same time.

The mystical poet Rumi, who wrote these lines, was born in 1207 into a traditional Sufi family who descended from Abu Bakr, Mohammed's companion and Islam's first caliph. Until he was eleven, Rumi was educated by his father in his birthplace, then a religious center located in northeast Iran. But the ruling king turned against the Sufis, who historically have opposed the worldliness of political power. In 1218 the boy was compelled to flee with his family, fortunately just before the onslaught of the Mongol invaders.

For ten years Rumi and his father lived peripatetically in the lands west of their homeland. They received instruction at Sufi centers in Damascus and Baghdad. After making the Moslem pilgrimage to Mecca, they finally settled in Konya, Turkey.

When he was nearly forty, Rumi was inspired by an itinerant ascetic to express his religious ideas in poetic couplets. Choosing the pen name Rumi because it signified "light" in Persian, he produced many volumes of poetry, which continue to inspire Islamic believers. Persians still call his literary works "the Koran in the Pahlavi tongue" and devotedly visit his grave in Konya.

The Sufis sought a oneness with God in the most direct way possible. They chose an ascetic way of life that would transcend the material. To the Sufis, if the center of a circle is God or the True Reality and the circumference is the Shariat or Moslem law, then the radiuses are the various spiritual paths to God. This means that there are many paths to God within the circumference of Moslem law, and even outside it. Scholars who have studied the ninth-century Sufi cave dwellers in the northeastern province of Khorasan have discovered that they even came under Buddhist influence from neighboring India. (Conversely, Freemasonry, introduced to an English king in the tenth century, has been traced to Sufi fraternities.) The Sufis also adopted elements of Christian monasticism, Neoplatonism, and even Zoroastrianism.

Whatever its origins, Sufism began to jell during the Seljuk period, when this Turkish dynasty reunited the lands of Islam from the Mediterranean to Central Asia and spread what Richard Frye calls "a new Iranified Islamic culture." During the twelfth century many orders of Sufis developed. When a Sufi became advanced in his mystic understanding he would be sent to other lands to proselytize. Because he lived as a mendicant, he was called by the Arab term *fakir,* meaning "poor." Some of them also became known as dervishes, mystics who danced and chanted their prayers until they reached a peak of ecstasy. Rumi himself founded the order of whirling dervishes of Turkey. Other Sufi saints spread their religion to India, Central Asia, and Africa, but the Persians were more active in the mystical interpretation of Islam than other peoples and their poets planted the garden of Persian culture with seeds from Sufi thought.

It is to these sources that a number of disillusioned intellectuals in Iran are returning nowadays to find inspiration and renewal for the future. They propose that Iran must reembrace tradition and mystical poetic experience as "an antidote to the risk of isolation and emotional indifference today threatening Western society."

Currently in Iran, four orders of Sufis guide a few thousand people who practice this esoteric interpretation of Islam. Sufis in the past have sometimes been revolutionaries, the prime example being the aforementioned Ismail. But modern Sufis seem to adopt their mysticism as an escape from an otherwise too rigidly controlled society. As one Moslem from Shiraz told me, "It's frustrating to live in a country that is in a sense totalitarian, so Sufism offers a needed emotional outlet."

However, one small group of these intellectuals, calling themselves Neo-Sufis, have set about actively and publicly to combine Iran's modern goals with its more spiritual heritage. The foremost of them is Hossein Nasr, one of Iran's leading philosophers. His scholarly essays in English have clarified for Western readers many of the esoteric beliefs of Iranian Islam. He believes that Western philosophers err in confusing intellect and reason. "Sufis believe intellect is that instrument of knowledge which perceives directly," Nasr has written. To explicate Sufism in the context of Iran's modernity is one of the intellectual tasks assigned to Teheran's Imperial Academy of Philosophy, which Nasr directs.

With the founding of the Shiite Safavid dynasty at the beginning of the sixteenth century, Shiah finally became the established religion of Iran, and the faith of 90 percent of its people. It still is. About 8 percent of Iranians are Sunnis (the Arabs of Khuzistan, plus many Kurds, Baluchis, and Turkomans); 2 percent more are Christians or Jews. The remainder are Shiites. To say Shiah is to say Iran: about four fifths of the world's Shiites live there (the rest are mostly in Iraq, Afghanistan, Pakistan, the two Yemens, and India). Worldwide, Sunnis outnumber Shiites about fifteen to one. From Africa to Indonesia, there are about 600 million of them, including 60 million in China.

But in Iran, as elsewhere, statistics cannot reveal the depth of belief, which in turn is a function of what the faithful are supposed to believe.

The central belief of Islam is strong monotheism, expressed in the muezzin's cry (now usually tape-recorded) from the top of a minaret: *"La-ila-ha Il-lal-lah"*—Arabic for "There is no God but Allah." It follows from this that the believer should accept, submit to, and commit himself to God alone; the word *Islam* means "surrender." "Islam's attractiveness is its black-and-whiteness—you know where you stand," a Christian minister in Teheran remarked to me. Yet many of Islam's beliefs, as defined in the Koran, are borrowed from, or adapted from, the Biblical religions; the Koran lists seven commandments similar to the Old Testament's ten (though it allows for some special cases: "Do not interfere with the property of orphans except with the best of motives, until they reach maturity"). Similarly, Islam proclaims a heaven, but one modified to its prejudice in favor of men, a place of shade and water and seductive girls. Islam stresses morality.

I met two teen-age boys in Teheran who told me: "We saw a movie showing the atomic bombing of Hiroshima. Our religion would not permit us to do bad things like that." A high school teacher said: "Our people regard the United States as corrupt, and our own religious traditions as strong and moral."

Though merely recommending moderation in smoking and such lesser temptations, Islam seriously opposes alcohol. A deputy minister told me: "My driver quit because I ordered him to buy me a couple of bottles of whiskey. He wouldn't even touch the bottles." Islam is against abortion and, traditionally but less resolutely, birth control. The governor general of Sistan and Baluchistan told me of his efforts to cajole or browbeat the local mullahs into preaching that the pill was desirable; he succeeded in the end by "simply giving the mullahs a small salary." But Islam also opposes celibacy (which is, one believer told me, "like having an arm and not using it"). Almost all Moslem men are circumcised, and circumcision is an initiatory requirement for converts.

Many big theological issues of Christianity, such as predestination versus free will, do not much concern Islam. One scholar in Mashhad told me that "Islam has never been against science, like Christianity," and a devout Moslem in Khuzistan argued that "Islam early on was a little more scientific, for example in its advocacy of the sun as a germicide, or in its opposition to water pollution—we're forbidden to spit in water." In fact, water is an Islamic obsession. Every mosque provides a courtyard pool where men clean up before prayer; they cup their hands and splash water over faces, heads, and arms. The Koran stresses the cleanliness of running water. One American I met in Teheran claimed that his maid used a bottle of detergent a day washing dishes under the faucet rather than in a sink. Unluckily for dogs, Islam deems them unclean, and the mutts in the cities and villages live miserably. Luckily for Persian cats, Mohammed was a cat lover, and he exempted felines from the fate of canines. Besides banning pork and shellfish, Islam's dietary restrictions prohibit consuming blood, as well as the flesh of animals that die naturally or by strangling, beating, goring, falling, mangling by other beasts, or sacrifice to idols (which, incidentally, is not a Moslem practice).

Mohammed decreed that every good Moslem must pray five times a day: at dawn, midmorning, noon, late afternoon, and after dark. Not by a far cry does prayer time bring Teheran to a halt—only a tiny minority publicly prostrate themselves on prayer rugs facing Mecca. Yet prayer is on the minds of the millions of men, from cabinet ministers on down, who carry prayer beads at all times. One such believer told me that he possessed two of these rosaries. One, with thirty-four beads, was "to hold in my hand." It is the nervous habit of uncounted Iranian men to clutch a rosary constantly, counting the beads over and over by pushing them along with a finger. For serious praying, my informant told me, he used a rosary, made by himself from coral, that had a hundred beads, divided into thirds. This system guided him to say "God is greater than I" thirty-four times, "God is good" thirty-three times, and "God can do no wrong" thirty-three times. One hundred, incidentally, is the number of aliases used by Allah, the hundredth of which is unknown to man.

Good Iranian Moslems make a pilgrimage to Mecca once in a lifetime, if they can afford it; and so many can that Mehrabad airport has a special Hajj Terminal, which is thronged by pilgrims in the last month of the Islamic lunar year. The Red Lion and Sun Society, Iran's Red Cross, makes a big effort to provide health care for Iranians in Mecca. The Iranian faithful also demonstrate their devotion by occasional family gatherings in homes, presided over by a mullah, who offers thanks to God for some prayer answered, or marks the anniversary of a death. The majority of Iranian marriages take place in storefronts run by mullahs, some of them licensed as notaries public so that they can marry couples both religiously and legally. As the signs over the storefronts show—typically, MARRIAGE AND DIVORCE BUREAU NO. 29—the mullah can split couples as well as join them.

When an Iranian dies, he is usually underground in short order, in compliance with the Koran's ruling that burial must take place in twenty-four hours or less. To make such speedy interment possible, the government of Teheran operates the efficient cemetery called Behesht Zahra (Paradise of Zahra, who was one of Mohammed's daughters). When a body reaches Behesht Zahra, it goes at once to a mortuary for washing and swathing in a white shroud; meanwhile the men of the family that brought the body register the death at the cemetery office, and the women, usually in black chadors, wail and keen. At any of a number of small mosques, a mullah says a prayer, and cemetery workmen place the shrouded body (coffins are not used) in a waiting grave and cap the grave with a six-foot slab of stone, upon which they engrave the name and dates of the dead person. Three days later the family attends another eulogy at a mosque, and forty days later the family gathers at home for a final ceremony, which includes a bountiful meal. It was in Behesht Zahra that thousands of dead rioters were buried in 1978 and 1979, and a visit to this cemetery was Ayatollah Khomeini's first act upon returning from France.

Behesht Zahra, one and a half square miles in size yet a dignified place with its rose gardens and minarets beside the main gate, is surrounded on three sides by miles of low colonnade. Back of each small arch thus formed lies an aboveground crypt with room for as many as twenty-five bodies. Here rich clans can leave the bodies of their dead without condemning them to the obscurity that is the fate of those many thousands buried under side-by-side slabs in the more than square mile of graveyard. For the more devout among the rich, however, not even crypts are enough; they bury their dead in cemeteries at the holy cities of Qom or Mashhad. Islamic law does not allow the quick obliteration that comes from cremation, but on the other hand, it permits the authorities to demolish tombs thirty years after a cemetery has been filled and closed, and the bodies decomposed, and reopen the area to other uses.

One day, in my presence, a British journalist asked an Iranian bureaucrat to join him at breakfast the following week. The Iranian accepted, then stopped short. "Next week will be in Ramazan," he said. "I'll be having my breakfast at 3:30 A.M. that day." Ramazan (the Arabs say Ramadan) is the ninth month of the lunar calendar, and while the moon goes from slender crescent to full to slender crescent again (according to the sightings of a designated mullah in Qom), the faithful Moslem does not eat during daylight, and he drinks only as much water as will leave him with his thirst unsatisfied. Further, according to some young men I happened to meet, "You cannot look at girls, and if you are married you cannot have sex between sunup and sundown." Moreover, it is bad form to eat or drink in front of someone who is fasting. There are many exceptions to Ramazan's rules: boys under sixteen, girls under nine, the aged, travelers, and just about anyone who chooses not to obey. Still, it is a mostly joyless month, and to signal to everyone the end of the fasting, the traffic policemen in Teheran, on the first day of the next month, wear wreaths around their shoulders.

To rituals common to all Islam, the Shiites add some of their own. In the first ten days of Moharram, first month of the lunar year, they stage passion plays to reenact the battle of Kerbala. The plays, stirring deep emotions, cause considerable self-inflicted bloodshed. Heeding street signs that say, "All believers are summoned to take part in the flagellations in observance of the murder of Imam Husain," overwrought paraders slash their own scalps and beat themselves with chains; a few years ago a mourner killed himself by cleaving his skull with a hatchet. Black flags fly everywhere. The anniversary of the murder of Husain's father, Ali, the first imam, does not set blood to flowing, but everything closes down, and people, avoiding the temptation to picnic, stay home and pray. Similarly solemn is the anniversary of the death of the great imam Jafar. In the Shiraz bazaar, where I happened to be that day, the merchants hung black flags over their shops and paraded through the passageways chanting, "The sixth imam has been killed! His father is very sad!" while alternately striking their heads twice and their hearts twice. The Moslem revolutionaries used all of these occasions in 1978 and 1979 to stage demonstrations that helped bring down the Shah.

The Mecca of Shiah Islam, the shrine city of Iran, the goal of seven million pilgrimages a year, is Mashhad, capital of the northeastern province of Khorasan. The city's center, focus of four boulevards, is a circle 390 yards across that contains the most dazzling complex of religious buildings that I have ever seen in a life of traveling. Western infidels do not know about this shrine because they have historically been barred from entering it. Even now, with rare exceptions, it is not open to foreigners as mosques elsewhere are; I had the luck to be one of the exceptions.

The story of this shrine, and the story of Mashhad, starts with a figure straight out of the *Arabian Nights,* to wit, Harun al-Rashid, the caliph who (though the book makes him seem more fictional than real) actually ruled the Arab empire, including Iran, from 786 until his death in 809. The genial caliph naturally favored the Sunni, or Arabic, sect of Islam, which set him against the Imam Reza, eighth in the line of the great Shiite saints who claimed, against Sunni dogma, to be Mohammed's earthly spokesmen. When Harun died, he was buried in an impressive tomb at Sanabad, a village standing on the present site of Mashhad. Harun's son and successor, the caliph Mamun, renounced his father's stance and converted to the Shiite faith. He agreed to a request from Reza that the imam be buried, whenever he died, next to Harun, as an eternal reproach to his late enemy. Then Mamun, reverting to the Sunni faith, made sure that the Imam Reza would indeed have to be buried by killing him with poisoned grapes one day in 817. Tongue in cheek, Mamun carried out his promise to entomb the imam next to Harun. This ironic juxtaposition inflamed the emotions of devout Shiites, and they began to speak of the imam's tomb as Mashhad, meaning "Place of the Martyr." Approaching to pray at the imam's tomb, the faithful would pause long enough to deliver a stout kick at the caliph's. With this activity, Mashhad became Khorasan's capital, replacing Tus, which had been the main city from times immemorial (and is now scarcely a village).

Genghis Khan's men, and later Tamerlane's, leveled and sacked Mashhad; the tombs supposedly not only survived, but were rebuilt in more elaborate form after each destruction. Thus grew the cluster of mausoleums, mosques, and seminaries now collectively known as the Shrine of the Eighth Imam. Some of the tilework dates from the twelfth-century Seljuk dynasty. The biggest single contribution is the mosque built in 1418 for Gowhar Shad, one of the few forceful and creative women in Iranian history. She was the wife of Shah Rukh, Tamerlane's son, who ruled Khorasan and Afghanistan from Herat during a period when Iran was sundered into various parts. A century and a half later, Shah Abbas, from Isfahan, ordered the construction of the mausoleum of the Eighth Imam to build up Mashhad as a shrine at a time when Mecca was in the hands of the enemy Ottomans; when the work was done, Abbas walked six hundred miles across the desert to view it. Nadir Shah, and the last century's Qajars, and this century's Pahlavis, have all added repairs or embellishments to the shrine as it now exists.

The irregularly shaped complex of religious structures does not fill the circle created by the ring avenue around them, and historically the fragments of space between the street and the buildings' walls were the site of the Mashhad bazaar, a labyrinth of twisting alleys, cubbyhole stores, and turquoise-cutting shops. Now this screen of hovels is gone, the shops removed to a new bazaar, revealing the high, continuous, unadorned masonry that encloses the shrine, a pattern of interior and exterior corners, set off by grass where the bazaar once stood, all strikingly visible from anywhere on the ring avenue. Floating above this massed architecture are the luminous turquoise dome over the sanctuary of the Gowhar Shad mosque and the blinding gold dome over the mausoleum of the Eighth Imam, with accompanying minarets.

By arrangement, I entered the shrine one evening and was met by a member of the administrative staff, dressed in a sober black suit. My guide asked me to remove my shoes, and parked me for a moment in the small mausoleum of some minor ecclesiastic, a room walled and ceiled with mirrors. From overhead hung mirrored pendants three feet long, forming dividers for a pattern of large square looking-glasses. I was stunned at the splendor, not realizing that this was only an antipasto for mirrors to come.

We moved on to a glittering, high-domed room carpeted with carpets that were carpeted with pilgrims. I began to appreciate that simply as a practical matter, non-Moslems cannot be allowed to tour the shrine, for it is already jammed day and night with Moslems. The worshipers at the shrine are mostly segregated; this was a holding room for women, veiled women with babies at the breast, sick women seeking cures, all waiting to visit the imam's coffin. A minute later, through an arch, I caught a tantalizing look at this shining sarcophagus in the secret center of the building. But my guide steered me, through carpets hung as curtains, out into the shrine's New Court—so called, I gathered, because it contains contributions from such a recent dynasty as the Qajar, specifically a bizarre clock-tower minaret with a little onion dome. Through a dim passageway, lined with small shops, a little bazaar inside the shrine, we then went to the Old Court, where pilgrims were washing hands and faces in an elaborately geometrical pool. Going through a lofty ivan back into the nested chambers near the sacred heart of the shrine, I again glimpsed the great mysterious tomb; but rather than approach it, my guide once more detoured, and we circled it through one room after another, each blazing with mosaic mirrors, each shaped like an upended bullet, that is, of a height to dome ceiling much greater than the diameter of the roughly circular floor. Some of the masonry that divides these chambers is thirty feet thick. In one room a mullah related to a small group of men the age-old story of the assassination of the Eighth Imam, a narrative that always ends with the audience in disconsolate tears, or in downright hysteria. I picked my way among dozens of little prayer tiles, made of Mashhad clay, on which the faithful, kneeling facing southwest, can rest their foreheads. The noise of praying, weeping, singing, and clerical instruction on the Koran echoed from the hard glass of the mirrors on the walls—fragments set to form stars and pyramids reflecting light at cunningly calculated angles.

The encirclement of the tomb chamber led us for a moment into the courtyard of a mosque named for the lady Gowhar Shad. For mosquely splendor, Iranian connoisseurs rate this one just behind the Royal Mosque and the Friday Mosque in Isfahan. The tiles that cover every square inch of the arcades around the courtyard mix blues and tawny reds; the dome is solid blue except for inscriptions near the base in Kufic, the archaic squared-off form of the Arabic script that was used in the original writing of the Koran.

Finally the guide, his build-up finished, took me to the tomb.

The room is an explosion of mosaic mirrors, shaped as octagons, crosses, and stars. A two-ton crystal chandelier hangs in the middle, with smaller ones around it, giving white light that flashes from mirror to mirror. The room's plan is square, but high up, squinches—arches that jump across a corner—make it into an octagon that supports the circular dome. In the dome the mirror mosaics are colored, so that one looks upward into dim jeweled heights. All this glass is flawlessly clean and bright. Here, surely, the possibilities of the mirror have been carried to the ultimate.

The sarcophagus lies under a canopy of chased gold and silver, supported by twelve slender golden columns with grillwork between them, the whole forming a small house. The goal of the pilgrims is to worship and adore this structure. As I watched, people circled the tomb with arms spread out, walking sideways, sliding their hands along the grill, fervently kissing the metal. What the pilgrims thought of such a blue-eyed infidel as me among them was hard to tell; they observed me with obvious interest but impassive faces. Soon the guide whisked me away. My last glimpse was of some new doors to the chamber, gold-plated silver sheathed in protective plate glass, gifts of Empress Farah. The pilgrims were kissing the doors.

I met the governor general of Khorasan, Abdol Azim Valian, not in his provincial government headquarters but rather in the executive offices of the holy shrine—a circumstance that turned out to be highly significant. Valian (a much-hated general who has since been replaced) was deputy grand trustee of the holy shrine of Imam Reza, the Shah being the grand trustee. Valian's role as deputy grand trustee was more important than his role as governor general, because the shrine administration is more powerful than the provincial government. He was governor general because he was deputy grand trustee, not the other way around. And therefore he was most likely to be found at the shrine.

The shrine's importance comes from what it owns. For a thousand years landowners in Khorasan and elsewhere commonly bequeathed their estates to the imam, until the shrine ultimately owned *vaqfs* (church estates) more extensive than the government lands, or the pre-land-reform royal estates. Most of Khorasan became shrine land, and so did parts of Azerbaijan and Kerman, and even Afghanistan. In his war with the mullahs, Reza Shah secularized the shrine land, which meant that some of its income went to social projects such as hospitals and water supplies, but he did not dare expropriate it. Neither did the recent Shah, who exempted the shrine from losing title to its estates during the 1963–1974 land reform. The shrine was, however, forced to rent the land cheaply: 10 percent of crops in the countryside and fifteen cents a year per square meter for lots inside Mashhad. Farmers get ninety-nine-year tenure, city-dwellers ten-year tenure; both can renew tenure rights or sell them, and can build on the land; but residual ownership stays with the shrine. Officials of the shrine say that farmers approve of this arrangement because "they don't want to take the land away from the imam." If anyone disputed the shrine's ownership of a given piece of land, the deputy grand trustee was empowered by the Shah to take it for the shrine without recourse for the other claimant. The shrine—which perhaps surpasses the Vatican in riches, although no outsider knows for sure how much either owns—has also inherited thousands of priceless Korans and art objects and jewelry, some of them on display in its new museum, which is open to everyone.

The religion business keeps Mashhad bustling all year round, but most pilgrims come during Ramazan and Moharram, those floating months of the Islamic lunar year set aside for fasting and mourning. A proper pilgrim, making what will probably be his only visit, brings a homemade rug to sell for enough money to stay ten days, in order to do the whole round of prayer and fasting. But Mashhad also observes between seventy and eighty religious or civil holidays a year, and many pilgrims visit then. At busy times twenty thousand people arrive and depart every day; half a million may be present at any given time. They used to stay at two hundred lodging houses in the old bazaar; Valian demolished these warrens and when I was in Mashhad ten replacement hotels were going up. Twelve thousand private houses also stand ready to take in visitors. The Hyatt Omar Khayyam puts up the richer pilgrims. Afghanistan and Pakistan supply thousands of Mashhad's pilgrims.

As residents of a holy city, the Moslems of Mashhad fought particularly hard against the Shah's soldiers in 1978 and 1979, and hundreds of them were killed. Many died crushed by the treads of army tanks as troops attacked the home of an ayatollah, who fled. A SAVAK agent was hanged in public.

Cyrus the Great set an enduring precedent when he proclaimed a policy of toleration toward all races and creeds. Over a span of 2,500 years Iran's monarchs have occasionally persecuted Christians and Jews, but such attacks have been few compared to those of European and Arabic history. When Cyrus conquered the ancient Babylonian kingdom, he allowed the exiled Jews to return to their homeland and he ordered the reconstruction of their temple in Jerusalem. In my interview with the Shah, he reminded me that one of the Iranian kings married a Jewish woman. For love of Esther, Xerxes I in the fifth century B.C. retracted an order to kill all Jews in the Persian Empire. If the Islamic revolution now turns violently against Jews, it will be a break with history.

Teheran is a Moslem metropolis that traffics easily with other religions. The 2 percent of Iranians who are Christians are mostly Armenians (270,000) and Nestorians or Assyrians (32,000); but Western sects of Christianity are also present and prominent. Several places in the capital are distinguished by the formal façades of Christian churches: the Greek Orthodox church on Roosevelt Avenue, the Iran Mission of Seventh-Day Adventists on Pahlavi Avenue, and the Protestant Community Church in Saltanatabad. There are also churches for Baptists, Lutherans, Anglicans, and Roman Catholics. Protestant and Roman Catholic ministers adapted to the Islamic week by holding services on

Fridays and Sundays, but Orthodox priests stick to Sunday masses on what is otherwise a busy Moslem weekday.

Christmas in Iran is—or at least has been—a festivity that brings joy to the Christians and profits to the Moslems. The merchants and hotelkeepers stock up with large quantities of trees, tinsel, and turkeys, and the Christians good-humoredly pay inflated prices for them. But Teheran's ecumenical spirit might best be illustrated by newspaper advertisements for Transcendental Meditation. Moslems, Jews, and Christians all agree that living in Iran's largest city is maddening. So Maharishi Mahesh Yogi appeals to all faiths when he promises reduced anxiety and fatigue to all those who practice TM.

I was waiting for a bus one cold November day in Teheran when the driver of a Mercedes-Benz pulled up and offered me a lift. During the next twenty minutes I learned that my benefactor was an air force general and, intriguingly, a Bahai. As late as the 1950s the resentful mullahs were still able to keep Iranian members of this newest of Persian religions from gaining entrance to the government. But by 1966 the Shah's cabinet reportedly contained seven Bahais. Today in Teheran there are 30,000 Bahais, and another 30,000 live in other cities.

The Bahais, now a worldwide religious organization, originated from Iran's historic quest for a messiah. Particularly in the mid nineteenth century, after forty years of the despotic and degenerate Qajars, many Iranians hoped for the appearance of a new prophet. In 1844 a precocious young man from a Shiraz merchant family announced to a Sufi sect there that he was the Bab, the Arab word for "gate," who would make known the grace of God. After a satisfactory initial success in attracting followers, he came right out and claimed to be the Hidden Imam, reappearing to give the world universal love and a just government. Iranians from all classes—aristocrats, merchants, and poor farmers—found the Bab's religion of universal brotherhood an escape from the oppression of the Qajar autocracy. The growing membership of Babis, as the members of the new religion were called, so incited the mullahs, who feared the loss of their privileges, that they spurred the government to have the Bab executed in Tabriz. His martyrdom at the age of twenty-five only redoubled the fanaticism of his followers.

When a fervent disciple of the Bab attempted to assassinate the shah in 1852 to avenge his leader's death, thousands of Babis were killed or thrown into prison. One of the imprisoned was Husayn Ali, a young man from a rich Teheran family who had elected to follow the Bab from the beginning. He grew so ill in prison that he was allowed to leave after the officials were satisfied that he was not implicated in the assassination attempt. But he was exiled to Baghdad, where for the next ten years he directed the reorganization of the Babis as they fled from Iran. In 1862 Husayn Ali declared himself Bahaullah, Glory of God, whose coming the Bab had foretold nineteen years before.

Bahaullah never returned to Iran; in fact, the Iranian government conspired to force him and his followers to go to Turkey. In and out of prisons and houses of detention, he spent the last years of his life in Bahji, a town in Palestine, then controlled by the Ottoman Turks. Writing and teaching, Bahaullah gathered around him a devoted coterie of followers. One inspired visitor from England, Edward Browne, wrote in *The Persian Revolution* of being taken into Bahaullah's presence: "I bowed myself before one who is the object of a devotion and love which kings might envy and emperors sigh for in vain." At his death in 1892, the Bahai organization (the word is the first half of Bahaullah's name plus the suffix *i*, "adherent of") had already succeeded in spreading the new religion beyond the boundaries of the Middle East. Today the Bahais boast a worldwide membership in three hundred countries.

As a heresy of Islam, the Bahai sect does not enjoy the tolerance that orthodox Moslems accord to other religions. In particular, they cannot accept that the Bab was the Hidden Imam. The Shah's custom of appointing Bahais to high office—former Prime Minister Amir Abbas Hoveyda was said to be an example—was among the inflammatory causes of the Islamic revolt against the king in 1978. Ayatollah Khomeini denounced Bahai "missionary centers" that alienated people from their religion, and demanded, "Is it not our duty to demolish these centers?" At the end of 1978, the Bahai community in Iran had practically gone underground. Whatever may have become of the air force general who gave me a lift I do not know.

9

The Iranian Way of Life

❃

It is hard to remember, when a nation is going through a revolution, that its people remain intensely interested in what they eat and drink, how they dress and furnish their houses, how they play, kiss, bathe, and get high. Yet because it is what a revolution is all about, a nation's way of life is vitally important in understanding the revolution—particularly in the case of Iran, where the concern of the revolution is to preserve some age-old cultural values that the Shah, in his hurry to turn Iran into Sweden, lost track of.

Rice in Iran? Of course not. Rice is the dish of China, Japan, India, Southeast Asia. Everyone knows that. But the plain fact is that barren Iran, making use of that thin strip of well-watered land along the Caspian coast, grows rice of longer grain and finer quality than any other nation, and the Iranians cook it more skillfully than anyone else. Yet the rice is only a staple to go with a delicious cuisine: scores of savory dishes combining meat or fowl and vegetables with the special Iranian touch of fruits and fruit juices.

The Iranian housewife goes through fourteen steps to make a bowl of *chelo,* crusty steamed rice. Starting with two and a half cups of her good long-grain rice, she washes it and rinses it three times in lukewarm water. She soaks it overnight, covered, in heavily salted water. The next day she sets two quarts of water to boiling with two tablespoons of salt, and adds the drained, soaked rice in a stream. She boils the rice for ten or fifteen minutes, stirring it once or twice, then puts it in a strainer and rinses it with lukewarm water. Next she melts half a cup of butter, and puts a third of it in a cooking pot, to which she adds two tablespoons of water. She spoons the boiled rice into the pot so as to make a cone, and pours the rest of the butter evenly over it. She covers the pot with a folded tea towel, to make the rice cook evenly, and then puts on the lid. She cooks it for ten or fifteen minutes over medium heat, and for forty-five more minutes over low heat. She places the pot in cold water, to make the rice come free from the bottom of the pan. She turns it out so that the golden crust on the bottom, which is the specific asset that makes Iranian rice the world's best, flecks and accents the whole fluffy mound of distinctly separate grains. She puts two or three tablespoons of rice into a dish and mixes in a tablespoon of saffron. She pours the colored rice over the rest, and she is done.

This rice tastes heavenly all by itself, but the commonest way of eating it is in the Iranian national dish, chelo kebab. In each serving of rice the housewife makes a depression big enough to hold one raw egg yolk. She tops that with a kebab, and sprinkles a teaspoon or two of sumac over the whole dish. Kebabs are basically the same as kebabs anywhere, meat broiled on a skewer and pulled away from it upon serving, but the Iranians have a way with them. Perhaps the best kebabs are those made of strips of lamb fillet (though leg or shoulder will do), marinated in grated onion mixed with yogurt (alternatively, with vinegar, onions, and oregano), and forced tightly onto the skewer, to be broiled over charcoal. In another form, ground lamb, or beef, or camel meat, is rolled with onion and egg into a shape like a bread stick, and threaded onto the skewer.

An even more savory way in which Iranians combine rice and meat is to top the rice with one of the many types of stewy sauce called *khoresht*. Making khoresht is an exercise of the imagination, but broadly each khoresht contains four kinds of ingredients: meat or fowl, fresh or dried vegetables, fresh or dried fruits, and seasoning. The results approach the exotic. Wild duck with pomegranates. Lamb with prunes seasoned with cinnamon. Ground beef with spinach and orange juice. Iranians say that the secret is in the seasoning, the right combination of salt, pepper, vinegar, nutmeg, garlic, parsley, and cinnamon; certainly cinnamon is characteristic and common. But I came to believe that the secret was in the fruit: tart apples, reduced pomegranate juice, green plums, rhubarb, peaches, sour cherries.

Many of these same ingredients go into soup, usually also with yogurt, that healthful curdled milk that Iranians believe lends longevity, fends off ulcers, and even (as a lotion) soothes a sunburn. Yogurt with barley, onions, oil, and mint makes thick, hearty soup. Another soup, *ash anar,* omits yogurt, but still makes a meal: meatballs, plums or pomegranates, barley or rice, spinach, green onions, mint, and cinnamon in a lemony broth. The Iranians also like a range of noodle and ravioli soups. Appetizers, served with soup, are usually *dolmehs*—grape or cabbage leaves around meat (hot) or rice and currants (cold). Two common desserts are baklava, made much as it is all over the Middle East, and halvah, a Turkish delight with an Iranian touch in the addition of rose water. Making halvah, which is a peanut-butter-like sweet containing flour, is not easy. An Iranian friend told me that "out of one hundred cooks, only one can make halvah, and out of one hundred who can make halvah, only one can make it right, and out of one hundred halvahs that this cook tries, he gets only one that is superb." In Shiraz the favored dessert is *paludeh*, a fruity ice. In fact, the Iranians, using snow from mountaintops, started making good dessert ices centuries ago; *sherbet* is a Persian word. Another Iranian specialty for dessert is simply a crisp leaf of romaine dipped in a sweet-and-sour syrup.

As breakfast, as a simple lunch, and as a substitute for rice in places distant from the Caspian, Iranians eat a lot of bread and goat cheese. Most of the bread comes from neighborhood bakeries, where fast-moving men, using a mushroom-shaped trowel, plaster a slab of unleavened flour and water against the inside walls of a beehive oven heated by the furious orange flames of a diesel burner, and bake it for a few minutes. Millions of Iranians go out just after dawn to buy these delicious and nutritious disks, about the size of large pizza, and eat them not ten minutes out of the fire. Other varieties are slightly raised, and quilted, or topped with sesame seeds.

A piece of slab bread, torn off and folded, used to be the implement Iranians employed to pick up food for eating. Westernization brought the fork and spoon, but not the knife, into common use. The fork, held in the left hand, which is unclean in Moslem belief, holds down meat to be cut with the edge of the spoon, and pushes rice onto the spoon. Lunch is usually the main meal, and bountiful. One Iranian hostess served me fried chicken, meat loaf, a celery-chicken khoresht to go on rice, salad, radishes, broiled pumpkin, cake, tangerines, tea, and orange juice. We helped ourselves from a low buffet and sat in living room chairs or on the carpets, because, like most Iranians, my hosts did not use a dining table and chairs. They move a lot while eating, not to form conversation groups—for they concentrate on the food—but rather to get small second helpings and desserts.

The whole cuisine grows out of excellent raw materials. Cucumbers are so good that Iranians eat them like fruit; once when I was working in a library, a young woman kindly peeled one and gave it to me as though it were an apple or an orange. The Persian melon, with unribbed rind and orange flesh, sold cheaply from street-corner mounds the size of a Volkswagen, lives up completely to its worldwide reputation. The tomatoes are bred not to be picked by machine, like Florida's, but to be eaten; thin-skinned, red, and ripe. The word for peach in English, French, German, and Russian derives from ancient words meaning "Persian," for the peach is a Persian original. Pomegranates abound. You knead the fruit, nick the skin with a tooth, and suck out the contents. The skin makes a red dye for carpets, and the seeds, I was told, prevent constipation and dysentery. Orchards in Khorasan grow a delectable black cherry. In winter street vendors in Teheran serve steamed beets from charcoal braziers, a nice sidewalk snack. A long list of good materials for salads includes a sweet and perfect purple-edged onion. The Iranians say that it takes four persons to make a salad: a generous man to add the oil, a stingy man to add the vinegar, a wise man to add the seasoning, and a fool to mix it well. Yet another Persian word is *pistachio,* and pistachio nuts are plentiful—fortunately, since one cannot stop eating them once one starts. One Teheran meat-packer puts pistachio nuts in bologna: appetizing! (To complete the list, the English words "orange," "spinach," "candy," "syrup," and "caviar" are also of Persian origin.)

Religion imposes two main taboos on what Iranians eat: pork and shellfish are deemed unclean. During the Islamic calendar's fasting month of Ramazan, true believers do not eat or drink anything during daylight, but they usually have good breakfasts before sunrise and hearty meals after sundown. Perhaps a fourth or a third of the population ignores the Ramazan restriction, or makes plenty of exceptions: business at restaurants declines but does not die. The consumption of fish is not a religious matter, and in fact fish are sold commonly and eaten as a holiday food; but for some reason the Iranians do not prepare it with the attention they give to meat and rice.

Do Iranians drink, in spite of the Koran's prohibition? Under the Shah, they did. At the end of a meal, a restaurant table was likely to be littered with empty vodka bottles. About forty firms distilled hard liquor, made wine, or brewed beer. "Your drinking pleasure is our business," said the label on bottles of Caviar brand vodka. I liked Pakdis vodka both for the price (three dollars for a 700-cubic-centimeter bottle) and the low proof; one can drink it neat, for it lived up to the Iranian saying that "good vodka should be like a ghost." In the hinterlands men bootlegged arak, a kind of raw brandy. Persian wines have always been better in poetry than in practice, but there were some drinkable rosés and dinner wines. The Iran Malta Company produced a Scandinavian-style beer called, naturally, Skol.

Under Ayatollah Khomeini, the Koranic ban is back with a vengeance. One day in 1979 millions of cans of Skol were dumped into an empty lot and crushed by a bulldozer. About the same time, the $1.2 million wine cellar of the Intercontinental Hotel was destroyed.

But even when they drank, the Iranians drank with great moderation. Bars were uncommon. The street drunk, Bowery style, was not to be seen. Beyond the objections of their religion to liquor, many Iranians are uninterested in this kind of drug, or fearful of it. "Alcohol wastes your time. One drink follows another," one woman told me, and a young man whom I met said: "It seems to be bad for the Persian stomach."

What seems to be good for the Persian stomach is tea, tea in small glasses with plenty of sugar. Every visitor to every office gets a glass of tea, a kindly custom. Tea in someone's home includes pastries and apples and oranges. Tea from a samovar in a restaurant garden, under a willow tree, becomes a languorous occasion that may go on all afternoon. Tea in some bazaar's glazed-brick tearoom, drunk while one reclines on rugs and pillows, is as Oriental as Oriental can be; usually one's neighbors are smoking hookahs, and in a corner a tearoom flunky is chipping sugar lumps from a white cone, the form in which much sugar is sold in Iran. Despite this sense of tea as a tradition, tea drinking dates only to the nineteenth century, when the custom came in from Russia. Before that Iranians drank sooty black coffee, the way the Turks do, and coffee remains common. With chelo kebab the standard drink is *doogh*, yogurt thinned with cold artesian water or soda water and flavored with salt—a drink that makes the mouth feel clean and refreshed.

Still, the Westernization of Iran entails a good deal of Westernization of its food. Big granaries and bakeries now compete with the neighborhood producers of slab bread, and the raised breads they bake—rye, whole wheat, substantial white—equal European breads and surpass American. Coca-Cola and its consorts have wiped out once-popular drinks made of violets, pomegranate juice, vinegar, sugar, cucumbers, and garlic in various combinations. In supermarkets one sees Hamburger Helper, frozen German chicken (with dates and rice), Rumanian cream cheese, Danish luncheon meat, French's onion salt. Potato chips sell well. Meat comes plastic-wrapped with a printed label giving "price per kg," "net wt per kg," and the date it was packed.

When I think of the houses I visited in Iran, I think of doilies. One may wish that Iranian houses were tiled and vaulted like mosques or caravanserais, but the fact is that urban homes are—apart from the ever present Persian rugs—about four fifths Westernized, in décors that run from French provincial to Victorian to art nouveau to Danish—or all of them together. I saw, in various houses, a coffin-shaped coffee table, a blatantly big television set, a collection of dolls, elaborate glass candleholders, hot-water radiators, crystal chandeliers, reproductions of European paintings, a lace tablecloth covered with a sheet of clear plastic, fireplaces, pianos, pictures hung with no sense of arrangement, chairs upholstered in zebra-striped fake fur, an Italian enamel miniature of a nude, a Coleman heating stove, and ornate cornices under blue ceilings. The furniture stores that supply the Iranian home display some authentically hideous pieces.

But the carpets always make up for the clutter. They are all beautiful and they are used lavishly, filling the floors to the corners, overlapped if necessary, sometimes three or four deep; and as tapestries they often cover the walls as well. In one house the carpets rose from the floor to upholster the benchlike sofas, an agreeable effect that reflects the use of the carpeted floor in humbler houses for eating (from tablecloths spread picnic style) and sleeping (on unfolded quilts and mattresses), much as the Japanese use their tatami mats. In fact, the true, old, un-Westernized Persian house, like the Japanese house, has no chairs, and the tables, if any, are low ones.

As with furniture, so with clothes. Bright turbans, big as beehives and accented with a thumb-size emerald, are long gone. Apart from the chador and the tribal costumes, the only traditional clothing in use is the cotton shirt, baggy blue cotton pants tied at the ankle, and long blue cotton coat of some farmers and laborers, together with the black trousers of their wives. Reza Shah's stern orders that Iranians must take up Western dress had the absurd effect of putting most laborers into business suits; and so they are today, rather shabby, dusty from work, and sans necktie, but nevertheless looking a little as though they were headed for the office. Among white-collar men who really are going to the office, the necktie is as essential as the suit, and they wear both tie and jacket throughout the torrid summer. But minor functionaries, such as clerks in banks and government offices, get by on the job with sport shirts and open collars, even blue jeans and denim jackets (the worldwide fad prevails here, too), and like cabdrivers, they seem to shave one day in seven.

At their best, though, Western clothes as worn by Iranians follow the styles of Paris and London, and look well on an already handsome people. Concealed in little streets and arcades in Teheran are a surprising number of fashionable boutiques with up-to-date, tasteful, and costly clothes for women. Children are dressed, above all, warmly; wool caps appear at the first chill of fall.

Sports is one of the disaster areas of the Iranian way of life. The Iranians love sport, both as participants and spectators; crowds of 95,000 come to see soccer games at Teheran's Aryamehr Stadium. They particularly like the sports that pit one individual against another, or against the record book: wrestling and weight lifting (they are good

THE IRANIAN WAY OF LIFE

at both), skiing, horsemanship, gymnastics, boxing, fencing, tennis and table tennis, track, bowling, and karate, as well as the games of backgammon, bridge, and chess. They also play some Western team sports, most enthusiastically soccer, but also basketball, polo and water polo, cricket, and hockey, though little rugby and no baseball.

They play everything with bravado, eagerness, intelligence, daring, and the heroic impulse; they have strong muscles and coordination; they are willing to take on all comers from other nations. But they fatally lack rigor, perfectionism, stamina, coolness, and heart. In the sense that even an amateur should be professional, they are not professional. They train unpersistingly; they coach poorly; they make excuses; they collaborate grudgingly in team sports. The results, in such a typical period as the Olympic year of 1976, are predictably dismal. From the Summer Olympics in Montreal, Iran, with a team of 120 members, brought home only one silver medal and one bronze medal. The country's best heavyweight, Parviz "Killer" Badpa, who had skipped training because of "differences" with officials of the local boxing federation, lost by knockout in the second round. High jumper Teymour Ghiassi, who against his custom had to wear a shoe on his left foot because the track was wet, failed to qualify and complained that "God was a little unkind to me" in having allowed the rain. The cyclists could not complete the course. The soccer team beat Cuba, but lost to Poland and the Soviet Union; a well-trained Japanese threw Iran's best welterweight wrestler; Italy trounced the Iranian water polo team by 12 to 1. In the same year, Iranian skiers "dominated the bottom places" at the Innsbruck Winter Olympics despite having the best equipment and most fashionable clothing; the skiers, wrote *Kayhan*'s Husang Nemazee, were "known to avoid rigid training schedules."

In Manila, early in 1977, the national cycling squad lost its Asian road title because one rider quit eighteen miles from the finish; a little later, in a trial ride near Teheran, half the horsemen did not finish because their mounts were not fit; at a marathon through the streets of the capital, "the start was a shambles of pushing and shoving." One of the leading soccer teams lost a game because two players, known to "hate each other's guts," refused to pass to one another. The coach of the national youth soccer team noted that most of his players were "too tense before big games. They feel overburdened by the responsibility of representing their country in an international match."

To some extent the tension was the Shah's fault. Like other aspects of Westernization, most sports are relatively new to Iran, which did not even take part in the Olympics until thirty years ago; to expect mastery so soon is too much. But the Shah wanted to put Iran on the map in sports as in other fields, and poor showings displeased His

Majesty. The Shah was impressed during the Montreal Olympics by Nadia Comaneci, the sensational Rumanian gymnast, who trains four hours a day; he recommended that Iranian athletes model themselves on her.

As in other areas of human endeavor, the Shah counted on foreign technology to help Iran in sports, and after the Olympics defeats he ordered more reliance on foreign coaches. But even before then, Iranian sports clubs had been employing many foreigners: Irishmen, Englishmen, Russians, and Yugoslavians for soccer; Italians for cycling; Germans for track; and for badminton a fellow from India, where the game originated. After Montreal, the head of the wrestling federation, saying flatly, "We don't want an Iranian coach," arranged to hire a Russian.

The ancient Persians invented polo (and backgammon, too), but the only uniquely Iranian sport, if such it is, that is now much practiced is a kind of show-biz gymnastics performed in a club called a *zurkhaneh,* meaning "house of strength." There are zurkhanehs in all cities and towns. The best-known one in Teheran, a major tourist attraction, is the one across from City Park which is run by none other than Shaban Jafari, the "Brainless" who helped Kermit Roosevelt overthrow Mossadegh. The typical zurkhaneh is square or polygonal, about twenty feet across, and half underground, because according to tradition, this paramilitary form of exercise began as secret cells of resistance to the Arab conquerors. The dozen performers, mostly just average jobholders who have ham-like muscles, come on to a thumping drumbeat, dressed only in knee-length embroidered pants. While spectators watch from a raised ring around the pit, the gymnasts swing, with both hands, clubs as big as their thighs, spin like dervishes, heave heavy chains while reciting passages from the *Shahnama,* and for a finale wrestle one another.

Zurkhaneh's centuries-old stress on sweaty anatomy presumably accounts for the relative success of Iranian wrestlers and weight lifters in international competition. They have won all the medals that Iran ever collected in the Olympics—four gold, nine silver, and fourteen bronze. The most outstanding of these athletes is the pint-sized weight lifter Mohammed Nassiri, who is either the world's smallest strong man or strongest small man. Four times world champion flyweight, Nassiri can jerk (raise from shoulder level to high above his head) a 300-pound barbell. The shout that he makes with each lift is an appeal to the Imam Ali to give him strength.

History, in the form of riders galloping out of the north to conquer Iran, gave the country another of its most cherished sports: horsemanship in its various forms. The basically Turkoman horse of Iran, together with the Arabian, was crossed two centuries ago with British mares to make the English Thoroughbred. Though Turkomans cannot beat Thoroughbreds in races, they remain a strong, fast animal, capable of further breeding, and sound stock for racing, jumping, and trail riding in Iran. And the Turkoman men themselves, in caracul hats and belted tunics of stripes and tartans, still stand out as the most skillful among Iranian riders. A couple of years ago they won the Pahlavi Cup when the stethoscopes of the veterinarians showed that they got their mounts through the tough, mountainous, four-day trail ride from Alasht (birthplace of the first Pahlavi) to Teheran in best condition. Such trail rides have lately become popular activities in Iran, and are not confined to rich and horsy people. The entries in a ride early in 1977, who followed a trail that matched the route of Reza Shah's 1921 march on Teheran, included Kurds, University of Teheran students, members of the Royal Hunt Club, policemen from the National Gendarmerie, soldiers from the Shiraz Armored Corps, and one mullah in clerical garb.

The mostly desert land of Iran might seem an unlikely place for good skiing, but the mountains just north of Teheran providentially offer fine slopes that are snow-covered four to six months a year. The closest, Ab-e Ali, a beginners-and-family sort of place, is only forty minutes away from the capital. Shemshak, an hour away, and Dizin, two hours, are alpine spots with two good hotels and restaurants at each. Shemshak's slopes are for skilled skiers; Dizin has runs both fast and gentle. The lift fees are low by U.S. standards. Iran might also seem an unlikely place for the game of cricket, but a valiant, though small, league of amateur teams competes annually in the All-Iran Open Cricket Challenge Shield.

The big league in Iran is pro soccer, sixteen teams in three divisions that play from March through December. Private companies sponsor most of the teams, paying players sign-up fees of as much as $30,000 plus salaries of $1,500 a month, and often providing company jobs as well. When a Turkish club a couple of years ago tried to hire away Iran's best player, Parvis Qelitchkhani, the Shah ordered the government to match the offer and keep that talented fellow (who is often the national team's captain) at home. The most popular clubs, judged by gate receipts, are Persepolis (a Teheran team, despite the name) and Taj (also of Teheran), even though they are not always the league leaders. Most clubs are named for their home cities' industries: Abadan Oil, Isfahan Steel, Ahvaz Water and Power. The devout city of Mashhad fields a club called Abu Moslem. The industrial city of Tabriz supports both Tabriz Tractor and Tabriz Machine Tools. A club called Ararat plays on behalf of the Armenian colony in Iran.

Iran's National Team (which is also the Olympic team) draws its players from the best men of all the league clubs. Playing teams from everywhere for the World Cup, they manage frequent wins from Kuwait, Syria, Iraq, and Taiwan, regularly taking the Asian Nations Cup. In 1978, having defeated Australia, Iran won entry in the World Cup finals in Argentina, but lost to Holland and Peru; the coach blamed the referees.

Iran's entries in the under-23 Asian Youth Cup tournaments do well. Iran not only won the cup four times running, but also beat the Soviet Union's youth squad in 1976.

Kisses. Baths. Siestas. Pastimes. The calendar. In their daily customs, the Iranians are sometimes unique and sometimes eclectic.

"Teheran's another New York—we all get up in the morning ready to kill each other," a businessman remarked to me. Actually, Teheran may be in the process of becoming a Middle East New York, but the pace of Iranian life (though tensions from personal relations often seem high) is still far slower than New York's. Especially in hot weather, everyone takes a siesta after lunch, and to provide time for this rest, store hours are typically 9 A.M. to 1 P.M., and 4 P.M. to 7. Laborers and other people caught away from home unself-consciously nap on cots on the sidewalks, as pedestrians pass by.

Kissing upon greeting in Iran is done the French way: men kiss women's hands, and kiss one another on both cheeks. When the Sheik of Oman visited Iran in late 1975, the *Tehran Journal* reported that "The Shahanshah and the sheik embraced and kissed each other at the planeside." Yet the Western-style handshake is gaining, and may now be more common than the kiss of greeting, both between men and between men and women. Still, women kiss one another a lot, and they overwhelm children, even strange children, with kisses.

If kissing is rather Gallic, shoe customs are a bit like the Japanese: in operational, as opposed to historical-monumental, mosques, one must tread the carpets stocking-footed; and in walking on the carpets in their own dwellings, many people do the same, for cleanliness and comfort. Another custom reminded me of the ways of still a third foreign community, the Latin Americans: Iranians politely screen the operation of picking their teeth by holding their left hands in front of their mouths while their right hands do the work.

"Persian" is a word that mates most naturally with "garden"; sometimes Iran seems like a nation of gardeners, out at dawn to hose their salvia and hyacinths and their bountiful, lovely roses, whose colors often blur off from red and pink toward orange and yellow. If a housing development springs up to add a hundred acres of desert land to any of the cities, the gardens that go with the houses, even apartment houses, will be mature and luxuriant within four years. This obsession must come from an atavistic urge to make something orderly and beautiful out of hostile nature; and it may be the same urge that sends people off on another Iranian obsession, the Friday picnic in some mountain meadow or beside some pleasant stream that contradicts the barrenness of most of the country.

The bathhouse in Iran is fighting a losing battle with the bathtub and the shower, but the older parts of the cities and the villages still provide places where a man can get a scrub and a shave and a massage amid steamy luxury and harem-like opulence. The baths are mostly more than a century old, and one in the Kerman bazaar, now a museum, supposedly goes back three hundred years. I visited this bath and another working bath in the same bazaar; both illustrated the main characteristics of the Persian bath. The baths are, to begin with, mostly underground (though fitted with skylights) to make them easy to heat and to get water from a qanat—the one feeding the old bath at Kerman is 26 miles long. Big cisterns receive the water, and distribute it to various shallow pools of temperatures ranging from cold through tepid to hot. Architecturally, the baths are congeries of alcoves and arches and passages, topped with vaulted ceilings; but each bath has a large entrance room where the clients undress and leave their clothes. The floors and wainscot are greenish marble, the walls and ceilings mosaic, with tiles depicting birds, lions, hunting scenes—in the bath that is still operational, there's one picture of Rustam killing his son, and the entrance murals show pretty girls passing out cologne.

A bath takes two or three hours, and the chief functionary is the scrubber. Seating the customer in an alcove, the attendant first massages him, then wets him with hot water and scrubs him with a rough glove and soap. For the feet he uses a special cleansing mud. Then he goes over the body with a spongy, abrasive volcanic stone, sloughing off all dead skin. When the client is immaculately clean, he can enter the pools, the hotter the better, to relax. After he dries off, he may stay in the entrance room, smoking (including, sometimes, opium) or praying, before he dresses and departs, feeling marvelously renewed. (Women too have bathhouses, but I didn't visit one.)

The toilet of Iran is (except among Westernized Iranians, or in places frequented by Westerners) the standard floor-level squat toilet of most of Asia. In plumbed bathrooms, a corrugated steel hose with a nozzle (and in unplumbed bathrooms a ewer) supplies water for cleaning after defecation; traditional Moslems regard toilet paper as unsanitary. Since the left hand is used in this process, custom decrees that the left hand should not be used for handling food or giving gifts.

In their daily lives, Iranians must deal, for various purposes, with three distinct dating systems.

The oldest is the Islamic calendar, reckoned on the phases of the moon, with 354 days to the year plus eleven days added in leap years spaced out over a thirty-year cycle, to keep the calendar in pace with the moon. Any given date on this calendar thus comes about eleven days earlier year by year in terms of any solar calendar, such as the Gregorian calendar used by most of the world; and after the passage of thirty-three years of Gregorian time (12,053 days) the Islamic calendar has measured thirty-four lunar years (12,048 days), and any given date on it returns to about where it was thirty-three solar years before. The effect on the average Iranian (or any Moslem) is to keep him constantly calculating how much earlier, in sun time, the holy month of Moharram and the fasting month of Ramazan will fall in any given year as compared to when they fell the year before. In Iran's Shiite Moslem belief, there are ten holidays in the Islamic year serious enough to be general public holidays; they include, typically, the anniversaries of the death of the Prophet and of the birth of Imam Reza.

The Iranians lived with this calendar for most of their Islamic history, but in 1925 Reza Shah decided to put Iran on solar time, and created a calendar with six months of thirty-one days followed by five months of thirty days and one of twenty-nine (thirty in leap years), all coming out at the 365¼ days a year that the sun allots. He dated it, like the Islamic calendar, from the Hegira of the Prophet Mohammed in 621–622 A.D., but changed the span of time since that event from lunar years (then 1342) to solar years (1303). Reza Shah placed New Year's Day on the spring equinox, as the Achaemenians had done, and gave the months the names they had in pre-Islamic times; he chiefly intended to make the calendar match the seasons, but was also interested in putting down the mullahs. This is still the official calendar of Iran. The correspondence of the Iranian and Gregorian calendars is as follows:

FAVARDIN	MARCH 21–APRIL 20
ORDIBEHESHT	APRIL 21–MAY 21
KHORDAD	MAY 22–JUNE 21
TIR	JUNE 22–JULY 22
AMORDÁD	JULY 23–AUGUST 22
SHAHRIVAR	AUGUST 23–SEPTEMBER 22

MEHR	SEPTEMBER 23–OCTOBER 22
ABAN	OCTOBER 23–NOVEMBER 21
AZAR	NOVEMBER 22–DECEMBER 21
DEY	DECEMBER 22–JANUARY 20
BAHMAN	JANUARY 21–FEBRUARY 19
ESFAND	FEBRUARY 20–MARCH 20

Many thousands of people in Iran have to keep this correspondence with the Gregorian calendar always in mind, since Western dating is essential to all international communication. Businesses use desk calendars showing both the Gregorian and the Islamic solar dates. But calculating Western dates from the Islamic solar calendar remains a continual small headache, because the years start two and a half months apart. An Iranian friend is likely to tell you: "I graduated from high school in [long pause, while he figures in his head] 1936!"

In March 1976, the Shah suddenly shifted the base date of the Iranian calendar to the coronation of Cyrus the Great in 558 B.C. What was to have been the Iranian year 1355 abruptly became the year 2535. ("That means that if you were born twenty years ago you're now twelve hundred years old," cracked an Iranian friend of mine.) The Shah intended this change to put down Islam and play up Iran's Persianness and monarchical heritage, which he naturally loved to stress. Psychologically, it was one of his worst mistakes, clearly demonstrating that he was arrogantly out of touch with his people. As the end of his reign neared in late 1978, he apologetically shifted the calendar's base date back to the Hegira (and the twenty-year-old man became twenty again).

The Moslem month may have been officially supplanted in Iran by Reza Shah's calendar, but the Moslem week lives on. Friday is the day of rest. To the Westerner living in Iran, Friday soon takes on the traits of Sunday; and, therefore, Saturday seems like Monday, and Thursday is the day that begins the weekend (exception: the American Embassy takes Friday and Saturday off). The foreigner quickly gets to think nothing of phoning his Iranian colleagues on business at 9:30 A.M. Sunday. It was on a Sunday morning that the Shah received me. Sometimes the transfer of the days' identities becomes so complete that it produces utter confusion. One Western woman told me how she unthinkingly invited guests to a "Saturday-night supper," and was dismayed to be left with a lot of uneaten food when they failed to appear on Thursday evening. Iran's week corresponds with the week in the Arab countries, but many other countries with large Moslem populations, such as Pakistan, India, Malaysia, Indonesia, and the African Moslem countries, influenced by the old British Empire, make Sunday their day of worship. And being out of step with most of the world is a handicap. One reason Teheran never became a world money market is that its banking work week would overlap that of the major financial centers by only Monday, Tuesday, and Wednesday, not enough for trading in commodities and currencies whose quotations change fast.

The great nonreligious holiday on the Iranian calendar is Now-Ruz (New Year), three days off work at the spring equinox—combined, for many workers, with a bonus of a month's wages. To prepare, Iranians clean their houses, buy new clothes, and plant seeds of wheat or lentils in a bowl. The New Year's Eve banquet table, when laid according to tradition, holds a mirror and candles flanked by a Koran, unleavened bread, nuts, fruit, candy, colored eggs, chicken, fish, and a tray containing seven items whose Persian names begin with the sound of *s:* wild rue, apples, garlic, vinegar, malt grain, greens, and sumac (*sumaq* is an Arabic-Persian word). Amid all this is a bowl of water with a leaf floating in it; legend holds that the leaf will move a little at the exact moment the sun crosses the equator. On the following days, people call on one another in great numbers; but the thirteenth day of the New Year, thought to be an unlucky day, puts an end to the celebration. People throw shoots of wheat or lentils into the street, and go off to picnic in the country, carrying with them, away from their houses, the day's burden of bad luck. To get out of their houses for the day, people will, if necessary, pitch tents and spread rugs in city parks and boulevards. In one recent year, 116,000 cars poured out of Teheran to the countryside.

"The United States has a rapidly growing drug abuse problem and a fully developed economy. Iran has a rapidly growing economy and a fully developed drug abuse problem," writes Frank Johns in his master's degree thesis on what amounts to Iran's greatest behavioral weakness. What alcohol is to Americans, opium is to Iranians. Cutting the use of opium is difficult because smoking it is a grand old tradition, an accepted—and far from sinister—idle amusement. "We do not think of opium addiction as an illness because for centuries our forefathers have used this drug with the notion that it is good, particularly after the age of forty," says University of Teheran psychologist Valiollah Okhovat (though he himself opposes its use). Smoking opium is so common, writes Johns, that "there is a general drain on the nation's ability to function efficiently."

Opium may have been introduced into what is now Iran by the Sumerians sixty centuries ago; in any case, the Arabs, who fed opium to their camels as well as to themselves, brought the drug with them in the course of their conquest. Not only did Iran like the poppy; the poppy liked Iran—the plant grows rapidly in Iran's desert climate and produces the world's best opium. In Isfahan's time of glory, the sixteenth and seventeenth centuries, the Safavid courtiers liked to drink opium mixed with wine. Smoking opium came later, copied from Europeans smoking tobacco (who of course copied American Indians in this habit). At this point some fastidious Persian developed the more or less standard opium pipe, an egg-size, decorated porcelain bowl on the end of a stem turned from mesquite or cherry wood; the smoker uses tongs to hold a glowing coal close enough to the opium to make it bubble and fume. Iran came to be one of the world's biggest exporters of opium, particularly after the invention of the hypodermic needle in 1853 made the opium derivative morphine a commonplace medical sedative, and after the derivation in 1898 of heroin (from morphine) made this hallucinogenic popular. Iran grew the opium that the British East India Company used to narcotize the Chinese in its commercial conquest of China. By 1924 opium production earned Iran a quarter of its export income (apart from oil), and supplied the government with a tenth of its revenue. Reza Shah, who liked a pipe of opium himself, tried to regulate poppy growing, but let Iran export opium to the Japanese army, which also used opium addiction as a tool to subjugate the Chinese.

Within Iran, opium abuse, causing loss of vitality, weight, memory, and will, came to be seen as a serious problem, although the Iranians stayed away from morphine and heroin and the use of the needle. World War II, cutting off exports, flooded Iran itself with the drug, causing the most widespread addiction in history. The Anti-Opium and Alcohol Society in 1943 counted a million addicts, twelve hundred opium dens, and five thousand opium-induced suicides a year. After the war, shipments resumed, with Iran supplying as much as three fifths of the world's legal imports, around a hundred tons a year. Nevertheless, in 1955, with addiction up to a million and a half, the Shah decided to declare war on opium by banning the cultivation of poppies.

The ban demolished a $60-million-a-year farm industry, and cost Iran $30 million a year in export income, while reducing the number of addicts by two thirds. But, like Prohibition in the United States, the ban created a fresh new problem: the smuggling of opium from Turkey and Afghanistan. At first these neighbors half-heartedly collaborated with Iran in trying to stop smuggling, but in the end they succumbed to the profits to be made in supplying Iranian addicts. To get the drug across the border, smugglers killed Iranian gendarmes. After thirteen years, the Shah pronounced the poppy ban a failure. Iran resumed controlled production of opium in order to end smuggling, to supply legitimate medical needs for the stuff, and to ration the drug for its own certified addicts aged sixty or older. But again the law did not work. Authorities carelessly or corruptly issued opium-purchase coupons in large quantities to unentitled people, who black-marketed the coupons or the rations themselves. Opium smoking became—and remains—a sign of high living and distinction. Jahanshah Saleh, who was minister of health during part of the poppy-growing ban and later, as a senator, led the battle against the drug, says that coupon peddling reached the point that "opium was openly available in every pharmacy shop, and few receptions would be complete without gracious provisions offered for opium smoking to the guests." Currently around half a million people—about 1.5 percent of the population—are addicted, and Turkey and Afghanistan still send opium to Iran in spite of a death sentence for smugglers, which resulted in the execution of sixty of them in six months a few years ago. Recently drug squad cops near Isfahan arrested a smuggler transporting opium inside children's dolls. An Englishman living in Tabriz told me that opium pushers there are "'tried' and shot in three days." Every so often in Teheran, the police raid and close down opium dens—one of which, according to the newspapers, was protected by "guard snakes"—but Senator Saleh says that many dens remain. And drug users are turning more and more to morphine and heroin; about twenty thousand people now prefer these opiates. They still largely avoid the needle; the common way to take in these drugs is to place a small cone of the stuff on tin foil, heat it, and inhale the fumes through a paper tube. Though hashish created paradise on earth for the Assassins of the twelfth century, modern Iranian drug users find no sense of well-being in it (or the other hemp drugs, such as marijuana) to compare with opium, and they smoke only a little of it. In spite of Saleh's stress on the upper-class cachet of opium smoking, the addiction runs through all classes, and the biggest users are probably able-bodied laborers.

10

The Great (Illiterate) Civilization

❀

In Iran's 1978 budget, the last presented under the Shah, expenditures for the military ran to more than twice those for education. In effect, defense from illusory foreign enemies got a two-to-one priority over the crying need to cut Iran's illiteracy to something less than 55 percent of the population. Of course, pouring in money doesn't necessarily cure any social problem, but the Shah's reservations about schooling seemed to reflect a certain ambivalence: he wanted a population sufficiently well trained to man the factories and offices of his so-called Great Civilization, but not sufficiently smartened up to overthrow him. What he got was the reverse.

Illiteracy is a plague and a scandal in this ancient birthplace of civilization. Though the percentage of illiterates declines, the total number of them rises (because of population growth), so that fifteen million a decade ago have become eighteen million now. In the hinterlands, as few as eight women in a hundred can read and write. In airport waiting rooms, you can tell Westerners from Iranians by distinguishing those who are passing the time by reading from those who are merely sitting and staring.

Excruciating problems stand in the way of transforming Iran into a literate nation. The first is history. The government-operated public school is relatively new to Iran. The Qajars and previous dynasties were quite content to leave education, such as it was, to the Moslem mullahs, who in ungraded elementary schools called *maktabs* taught a few lucky pupils such reading and writing as was necessary to understand the Koran, and in upper-level *madressahs* gave select students the elements of the Arabic language, religious law, and rhethoric. In 1911, for example, only one child in a thousand attended school. Reza Shah encouraged public schools, and tried to make government and military people literate. He ran up against stonewall obstacles. "Fathers said, 'We did not go to school, so why should our children?' " a Central Bank economist recalled when I talked to him. The people almost universally believed that educating women was "unnecessary." Horace Mann was in his grave almost a century before the Shah became secure enough, in 1956, to turn his attention to the problem of making all Iranians learn to read and write, the census that year having revealed Iran to be 85 percent illiterate.

But in spite of these odds, the Shah told me: "The day is coming of 100 percent literacy." And he was right. The public schools are rapidly making most children literate, which makes higher literacy largely a question of waiting for adult illiterates to die.

Looking over the history of Iran's fight to reduce illiteracy since 1956, I distinguished about a dozen separate governmental efforts, each kicked off as a "war" that would put an end to the problem or to some part of it. The major "wars" resulted in the establishment of three organizations that have endured and have effectively fought illiteracy even if they have failed to end it. They are the Literacy Corps, the National Committee for World Literacy, and the National Center for Adult Education.

The Shah founded the Literacy Corps in candid recognition that the Ministry of Education was by itself not up to the job of erasing Iran's illiteracy, that "no basic solution to the country's problems was possible by ordinary methods." The country's universal conscription law gave him a powerful lever to get the Corps going: high school graduates willing to teach in villages would be spared from military service. Since then a hundred thousand young men and women have chosen to take teacher training for six months and then work for eighteen months in remote and primitive parts of the country. The Shah quickly expanded their duties from combating illiteracy to Peace Corps-style projects: building roads, planting forests, demonstrating farming methods, dredging qanats, building schools and public baths, and even repairing mosques. Some of the corpsmen got so involved in their communities that they never returned to the cities. When asked, "What is the most important thing you have ever done in your life?" they are likely to make such an answer as: "The well I dug in my village."

I spent an hour in a Literacy Corps school in the village of Baghak, not far from the Afghanistan border. The young women teachers, under a pretty, blue-eyed principal, wore the heavy khaki wool of the Imperial Army's winter uniform. The school, an old building of mud brick, contained three classrooms, each big enough to hold only twenty pupils, all six-year-olds. An aisle down the middle between the desks divided the boys from the girls—the local parents insisted on that, one teacher told me. All the girls wore scarves on their heads. In photograph form,

His Majesty looked down from the wall upon the hopeful, serious little Baluchi faces. As the teacher stood by, one boy, standing in the front, led the recitation, and the others, following paperbound textbooks, read the answers in unison. The school is on a passable gravel road, and the teachers live in nearby Zabol, commuting to work; other Literacy Corps schools in the area can be reached only by camel or helicopter.

This effort, touching and valiant, gives a little hope for future literacy in backlands Baluchistan and provinces like it. Corpsmen, who number about twenty thousand at any given time, have been teaching about 15 percent of Iranian first-graders, but they carry only a tenth of children who start through the fifth grade. The Corps' task is too big for it.

To try another attack on illiteracy, the Shah in 1964 founded the National Committee for World Literacy. (The word "World" in the title stemmed from the Shah's rather wistful hope that Iran's experience in the methodology of teaching reading and writing could benefit other nations.) A thoughtful—indeed, concerned and none too optimistic—educator named A. Faryar was running the Committee when I called at its offices on a pleasant, California-like street in mid-Teheran. He told me first of one of the Committee's undoubted successes: literacy for members of the armed forces, including the gendarmerie. "All draftees have to learn to read before they get demobbed," he said. "This program works 100 percent. We have a captive audience." Hulking men in fatigues sit like children on benches in front of blackboards in the open courtyards of their barracks, and, as Dr. Faryar says, "under army discipline and free from family ties or responsibilities, which frequently act as a deterrent to study," they learn to read—nearly 300,000 of them so far.

With guidance and some funds from the secretariat, the Ministry of Education offers evening literacy classes for children who "do not attend school for various reasons and are thus in danger of becoming adult illiterates"; so far several hundred thousand of them have learned to read and write. Working in another direction, the Committee supports and advises the Ministry of Labor and Social Affairs in teaching reading and writing to about 600,000 illiterates who work in urban factories, with classes right on the job during thirty minutes of work time every day. By law, factory managers must give a 5 percent pay raise to any worker who passes the course. The first six months go to basic reading and writing; the second six months go to expanding this base while learning more about the job and the tools of the trade. But many manufacturers refuse to allow time off or give raises, law or no law. "They don't all collaborate," Faryar said, with a melancholy shake of his head.

Finally, working with the Ministry of Cooperatives and Rural Affairs, the Committee devised a new technique to reduce illiteracy in the same area where the Literacy Corps operates, the backward villages. In this effort, bright, literate young men and women from the villages themselves take twenty months of training at ten centers, in small provincial cities, funded by the Committee. Besides learning how to teach reading and writing, these youths study agriculture and animal husbandry, individual and public health, and vocational schooling. Then, motivated not only by "roots" in their villages but also by high salaries, they go back and found "Houses of Culture," to a planned total of one thousand. The House of Culture is a combination of school and library, but it does not have chairs. "I was against that—too formal," said Faryar, who, though a modernized man with many years of living in the United States behind him, feels that "we Iranians are more comfortable sitting on the floor."

Besides collaborating with ministries, the Committee guides the Women's Organization of Iran in the bitterly necessary job of helping women catch up to men in literacy. Men in rural Iran often refuse to let their wives and daughters attend classes. Husbands particularly find it unthinkable that their wives might surpass them in education. For their part, the women are often apathetic. Their concerns, as identified by the Women's Organization, are those that arise from marriage at ages as early as nine, and from pregnancies spaced between twelve and eighteen months apart. Reading and writing are not much on their minds. (Iran's Family Planning Instruction Society reports, incidentally, that illiterate couples have an average of nine to twelve children.) Even when they agree to attend classes, women are timid. "They won't come to a literacy class unless the teacher is a woman," one provincial governor told me. The Women's Organization, in devising teaching programs, found that they "must include religious content and recognize the strong religious sentiments of participants."

The teachers are volunteer women aged between twenty and forty-five, mostly not even high-school-trained; the state of education in Iran is still such that the organization has to settle for primary schooling as sufficient training for teaching. But all this effort is far short of what is needed. The rate of literacy among women in rural areas is still no higher than 10 percent. Even in Teheran, where the general literacy rate is 80 percent, the rate among women runs much lower than among men. Often one sees a chador-wearing woman on the street pathetically asking a passer-by to read aloud the words of a letter or a sign.

One huge task of the Committee is providing new readers with material to read, in words simple enough to be understood. Of its one hundred publications, about half are primers, in editions as large as

25 million. The other titles deal with a surprising range of topics: *Job and Jonah, Iranian Petroleum, The Seven Adventures of Rustam, Car Mechanics, Jesus Christ, Growing Alfalfa, The Prophet, Poultry, The Holy Koran, Local Dishes, Adam and Eve*. And, at least until lately, *Two Thousand Five Hundred Years of Monarchical History*. Of the books on Moslem and Christian saints, Faryar, fingering his prayer beads, noted that "you can't trample on religious books, and this spreads respect for all books." The secretariat also publishes, and circulates free, the weekly newspaper *Ruz Now (New Day)*. "To a villager a newspaper has usually been something with which to fix a broken window," Faryar said. "Now we use the newspaper to 'fix' the reading habit. If we don't keep the new literates reading, they relapse into illiteracy."

"I don't believe in the battle against adult illiteracy," Chancellor M. Mashayekhi of Iran's main normal school told me. "We ought to start with the six-year-olds, teach them all, and teach them well." Many Iranians agree that teaching grownups to read and write is a lost cause. But the considered view of the Shah was that ignorant adults were worth saving from the tragedy of illiteracy, even though all the efforts up to 1974 made only one million adults literate. In that year he started a new "war" by founding the National Center for Adult Education. Under pipe-smoking Dr. S. Fattahipour, the center has imported UNESCO and United Nations Development Program experts to concentrate on the astonishingly difficult and unresearched questions of the technology of teaching adults to read and write.

To begin with, what are literacy and illiteracy? "Is some shepherd illiterate who can't read or write but can recite thousands of verses from the poet Ferdowsi?" asks Faryar. "Perhaps his memory works *better* because he's illiterate." All those scholars with doctor's degrees who lead the fight against illiteracy have a hard time putting themselves in the shoes of the illiterate, and they know it. But they have learned that literacy defined merely as the skill of reading and writing is unreal; the teaching of literacy has to relate to and include vocational, cultural, and social education—"the whole life" of the student. The education of an adult must be a substitute for the education he missed as a child, and it must fit him to provide a literate environment and example for his children (which is a powerful reason why adult education cannot simply be by-passed). He is supposed to become a "productive worker and an informed citizen." These goals are different from what schools do for children, and for achievement they need scientists, not educators. In its research laboratories and libraries, the Center relies on economists, statisticians, sociologists, psychologists, linguists, and demographers (plus a predictably overstuffed bureaucracy).

The overriding obstacle seems to be that adult illiterates suspect the authorities who say that they should learn to read and write. The government's motive in trying to teach them, which at bottom is to make them better workers, does not carry much appeal even if literacy brings higher wages. To be a grown man, sitting, tired, at the end of a workday, in front of a fresh-faced high school graduate scrawling on a blackboard the mystifying loops and dots of the Persian alphabet is perhaps not wholly enticing. If a man has got along without reading for thirty or forty years, the joys of literature may be hard to perceive. Bad examples abound, too. Village chiefs and councilmen notoriously will not deign to take literacy courses. Iran cannot yet afford to make literacy a condition of election to public office. As incentives for people to get literate, the secretariat has tried radio propaganda, compulsion for illiterate government employees, baby-sitting for illiterate parents, convenient class hours, and priority for jobs, but resistance remains strong.

And if it can be said that the students are reluctant, it must also be said that the effort to teach them is flawed. "The campaigns are sometimes not very serious," one official of the National Center for Adult Education told me. "The attempts are scattered. The whole thing needs mobilization." The Iranian trait of considering a project accomplished because it has been announced that it will be accomplished shows up conspicuously in the field of combating illiteracy; a few years later the same project is reannounced, and a couple of years after that announced again.

Taken as a whole, Iran's effort to beat illiteracy is serious and earnest, doomed to many future disappointments, but capable, ultimately, of achieving the modest goal of reversing the present increases in adult illiterates in absolute numbers, reducing the percentage of them among the rising number of Iranians, and finally achieving universal literacy as defined in the West.

The most elegant of ministry buildings in Teheran belongs to Education, a deconsecrated mosque with attendant structures set in an estate-like compound a few blocks from the Parliament. The ministry administers only the lower schools, leaving the universities to the Ministry of Higher Education. With 300,000 teachers and staff, the Ministry of Education forms Iran's biggest bureaucracy, half the civil service. Of late it has expanded convulsively, roping 8.5 million pupils into a school system that had to handle only 2.5 million fifteen years ago. In effect, a big slice of the Iranian population are the ministry's charges, for the recent reduction in infant mortality has made the number of children under sixteen nearly equal the number of people older than that. Two million children turn six every year. Each is lawfully entitled to five years of primary school (the three R's plus history, social science, geography, civics, and science), followed by three years of "guidance" school and four years of secondary school. Guidance schools teach amplified forms of primary subjects, but they also try to discover a pupil's aptitudes and aim him toward some kind of specialization. This judgment determines whether he enters a general-education secondary school or a technical-vocational secondary school.

The expansion of schools appears to be one of those cases where the Shah, by decreeing universal primary education, pushed an institution beyond capacity, on the theory that it is better to demand too much than too little. To heighten the pressure even more, the Shah decreed that some of his new oil wealth should go toward providing a midday meal of fruits, biscuits, dates, and nuts, or of bread and cheese, for all pupils in grades one through eight, creating an astonishingly effective inducement for poor parents to send children to schools. And he abolished the tuition fees that public schools formerly charged, removing an obstacle that had kept thousands of poor people from enrolling children. The resulting growth rate in the school population, anticipated to be 6 percent, turned out to be 11 percent. The ministry, moreover, now sternly warns all parents to stop preventing children from attending school.

The effect is that the schools are swamped, and the quality of education, always parlous, is poorer than it was. Constructing new schools set the Ministry of Education into rough competition with industry for Iran's already short supplies of skilled builders and building materials. The only way to absorb the children has been to put schools on double or even triple shifts, with as many as one hundred pupils to a class. "We are spread too thin," one top educator told me. "Quantity has made quality suffer." Yet the normal schools produce only twenty thousand teachers a year, against a demand of forty thousand now and a total of half a million by 1983, for 14 million pupils.

The worst defect of Iranian lower education, both pre- and post-expansion, is a heavy stress on memorization, accompanied by no stress on thinking. Empress Farah herself worried about "cut and dried" instruction, and said that "reading lessons and doing homework faithfully cannot take the place of a real understanding of life where individual creativity and intellectual ability form the true basis of education." An American businessman observed that "there's nothing in the curriculum to teach children to think comparatively. The teacher says, 'Follow me.'" The ministry apparently cannot create exciting textbooks. "*Old* teachers write the *new* textbooks," the businessman noted. As a consequence of this pedagogical dullness, many teachers hate their jobs. They call teaching "eating chalk," and prefer to work on the administrative staff of the ministry. Among other shortcomings, the teachers have so far failed to provide guidance in their guidance schools, for lack of any understanding of the concept. But there must be many exceptions to the dull and disinterested teachers. My wife one day happened to meet a secondary school teacher of Persian literature who also speaks French, German, and English (his favorite writer in English: Jack London). He reported that his students were keen readers and enthusiastic composition writers. "They like to write about their feelings, and about the stars, and about the moon," he said.

The lack of schools for about 10 percent of the school-age population remains a nagging problem: the illiterates of the future. "The ministry has reached all villages of two hundred people or more," one official told me, "but it's a big country and we have not reached those villages of, say, five or ten families." Another big class of children missing school is dropouts, 20 percent of primary-age children, 50 percent of guidance age, and 70 percent of secondary age. Most drop out to work, at parental insistence. The third class of children out of school consists of girls, mostly rural girls. In every statistical table showing school enrollment in Iran—totals for all schools, for kindergartens, for vocational schools; every kind of education except teacher training—the number of girls runs substantially lower than the number of boys.

Amid all these shortcomings, there is one astonishing success in the Iranian education picture: the tribal schools that teach the country's seminomads so well that 90 percent of tribal high school graduates pass university entrance examinations.

The credit for this success goes mostly to a Qashqai tribesman named Mohammed Bahman-Beigui, and when I was in Shiraz I looked him up. He would have been illiterate himself, he told me, but for a blessing in disguise more than thirty years ago: the Shah exiled Bahman-Beigui's trouble-making father to Teheran (mistakenly, Bahman-Beigui says, for his father was not all that important). "My father, instead of blaming the government, said, 'This is a chance to educate my child,' and he put me clear through law school at the University of Teheran. I came back to Fars province and fortunately selected tribal schooling as my life's work."

Under government pressure, the tribes in Iran have been gradually settling in one place in recent decades, but "we did not wait for settlement," Bahman-Beigui told me. "We established a school that moved with the nomads. We pitched a white tent among the black ones at the winter grazing area. At the beginning most people thought that such a program would not work. But it did. And why? Enthusiasm, hard work, cutting out red tape, but mostly because we picked teachers from among literate young tribesmen, men who could pitch a tent and ride a horse. It took only a few years to establish the value of the migrating school, especially the quality of its education. We set up more tents, and they became better schools than the elementary schools of the big cities.

"In 1956 we established a normal school in Shiraz, and it now graduates more than a thousand teachers a year, including five hundred girls. Girls!" he said in an aside. "A few years ago it would have been considered a dream to educate girls from the tribes and send them out to teach. In 1951, and again in 1958, I went to the United States to trade experience with others who were running tribal schools. I spent two six-month periods among the Indians of New Mexico, Arizona, and Utah. Until six years ago we ran schools only in Fars, but considering our exceptional success, we were ordered to contribute to other parts of the country, and now, in collaboration with the Ministry of Education, we send teachers to tribes in Kurdistan, Elam, Luristan, Khuzistan, Kermanshah, Kerman, and Baluchistan. The whole effort now adds up to 3,800 teachers and 85,000 students, one half in tents and one half in buildings—buildings because the tribes are settling."

Bahman-Beigui, a big-bodied, swarthy man with wavy hair brushed straight back from a high forehead, also built the tribal secondary school in which we sat as we talked, a building that would not be out of place in Pasadena. Girls in gaudy Qashqai costumes work there in first-rate chemistry labs, and chat with the boys in the surrounding gardens. A dormitory houses students whose parents are nomads or residents of distant villages. Again Bahman-Beigui boasts, with justification: "This is the *best* high school in the country. It's hard in Iran to get into a university right out of high school, but fifty out of fifty-two of our first graduates managed it. The enrollment is now nine hundred, and eventually thousands of our students will go to universities. They will become *somebody*—doctors, military officers, judges." One of the last American Peace Corpsmen from the operation, which is now phased out in Iran, happened to be with us the day I talked to Bahman-Beigui. "He's right," said the corpsman. "This school is better than my high school back in Oregon. And the tent schools are just as amazing. All five grades in one tent. They learn arithmetic so well that some can add a column of ten four-cipher figures in a glance."

Although Bahman-Beigui's bright boys may well deserve their college education, what Iran needs is less stress on universities and more on vocational training. An elitist notion that every secondary school student should strive for college entrance has virtually deprived the

country of vo-tech schools. Less than a tenth of all secondary students
are taking vocational training. In spite of the rarity of vo-tech schools,
I managed to find and visit one in Zahedan. The first scene that greeted
my eyes was a class in carpet-making for girls about ten years old,
all in chadors, and all in tears as well. The director of the school,
Hossein Aalam, explained that student carpet-makers get only pocket
money from the rugs they weave, because they make many mistakes
and the product has little value. The girls nevertheless wanted more
money, and it was his refusal that had turned them tearful. "After
six months they will become competent weavers, and they can work
for money at home or for the local carpet company," said Aalam. Child
labor is a touchy question in Iran; theoretically it is banned for children
until twelve, but by some legal fiction they can work if not forced—if
they do it "voluntarily."

Most of the 420 students are boys, sent by their hinterlands parents
to sleep in a barracks-like dormitory, eat corn and beans and stew in
a self-service mess hall, get short haircuts from the school barber,
attend the school's own supermodern mosque ("the mullah instructs
the boys not to tell lies," Aalam said), and learn to weld, to repair
cars, and to operate machine tools imported from India together with
Indian instructors. The school is new, and its architecture is all of a
pleasing modernized traditional, the buildings being surrounded by
arcaded porches buttressed at the ends. The students are of all ages,
some adult, mostly secondary level, some as young as seven or eight—
brave little boys cut off from their rural parents. Aalam tries to father
them, and see that the instructors treat them well. "A sympathetic
word from the teacher brings the student to school even on Friday,"
says a motto in the auto shop.

Since the quality of public schools in Iran is low and declining,
college-educated parents respond, if they can afford it, in the same
way that Americans or Britons do if they distrust government-operated
schools; they flee to private schools. The choice of the rich is often to
send children abroad. A guess is that 25,000 Iranian children go to
Western preparatory schools, public high schools, and even grade
schools as a solution to the problem of getting a good education. Other
well-to-do and international-minded parents send their children to any
of a dozen kindergarten-to-twelfth-grade schools in Teheran that are
run by foreign communities to teach their children in their own languages, with tuitions as high as $3,000. Three of them, until the revolu-
tion upset everything, were American-oriented: American Community,
Teheran American, and Teheran International Typically, Community's enrollment of about 1,500 was only 20 percent American; another
20 percent were other foreigners, and all the rest were Iranians. One

of Community's teachers, an Iranian, told me the standards were so high that the students stood a grade ahead of their peers in the United States. To get their children into these Western schools, Iranian parents had in effect to select what foreign culture their children would take on—French, German, British, American—and have them tutored in its language. I met parents far more interested in having their four- or five-year-olds learn their ABC's than learn the *Alef, Beh, Peh* of the Persian alphabet. "We can always teach our son Persian later," said one father. Another solution was to send children to any of 160 private Persian-language schools, which strive for high standards and teach subjects not given in run-of-the-mill public schools, such as higher math, advanced French, or classical music, as well as the standard subjects.

All Iranian schools are supposed to teach English beginning in the seventh grade; in practice many do not, for lack of teachers who know English. In his dealings with the Iranian man on the street, the English-speaking foreigner cannot count on finding many who speak English, although an English-speaker always seems to materialize from somewhere when really needed. Over and over, in parks and public places, I met students poring over English readers, and they often asked me questions about the language ("What does 'comic strip' mean?"). In a communal taxi a girl once engaged me in a serious discussion of the poetry of T. S. Eliot compared to the Persian poets. In short, English, replacing French, was becoming Iran's second language.

Perhaps most significantly, a knowledge of English admits the Iranian to the realm of books. For several reasons, book publishing in Persian is not a healthy business. Writers in Iran must get a "license for publication" for their books, and at least until lately the Ministry of Culture and Arts denied licenses for anything its timid bureaucrats deemed controversial.

The wry result is that the big, impressive bookstores of Teheran offer only books in foreign languages, chiefly English. They carry an immense variety of trade, technical, and cultural books in hardback and paperback. They also stock a type of book that is something of an Iranian speciality: pirated editions, photocopied and printed in Iran, which does not subscribe to the international copyright convention.

The first time I walked through the main gate of the University of Teheran—later to be on the world's television screens as a focus of the Iranian revolution—four policemen closed ranks in front of me and turned me back. The universities of Iran, at least those I visited, were walled and guarded, locked and barred on Fridays and between semesters, accessible at other times only to teachers and students with proper identity cards and to visitors with letters of authorization. Such rigid control, so out of keeping with academic freedom, makes a university a laughingstock. A British observer, driving by the University of Teheran and noting the institution's high green steel-pike fence, wise-cracked, "That's not a university, that's a jail." I met one U.S.-educated Iranian professor, newly hired for the university, who got through the main gate only with a hassle and encountered barred doors when he tried to enter the central library; he quit within a week and went back to his old job at the University of Washington.

But police-statism was not—and is not—the only defect of Iranian universities; indeed, they are racked with even more troublesome problems of maladministration, noncooperation, incompetence, waste, and obscurity of goals. As in the case of the public schools, the low quality of Iranian higher education comes partly from explosive growth. The first Iranians to seek higher education, a dozen or so, were sent to Europe in 1811, when Harvard was already 175 years old. In 1851 the shah of the time set up, with Austrian advice, an institution to train men for government service, but it was more high school than college. The first real university, Teheran, goes back only to 1934. Tabriz, Isfahan, Mashhad, and Shiraz did not get universities until 1949 and 1950, and the first private university, National in Teheran, did not come along until 1957. But a burst of building since 1971 has raised the total to fifteen, and five more are in gestation.

In an amazing accompaniment to the growth of universities, 129 two- and four-year specialized colleges have sprung up. In some years, the Shah increased the budget for higher education by a fourth or a third. In the process of growth, as Clark Kerr, former president of the University of California, pointed out in a speech in Teheran in 1976, Iranian higher education has transformed itself from an antiquated purveyor of tradition (theology and the classics) to a modern supplier of science and service to the industrial society. Enrollment has risen from 1,550 in 1935, to 5,500 in 1950, to 28,900 in 1965, to 150,000 in 1978, and the goal for 1988 is 270,000. Despite expansion, the colleges and universities cannot keep up with the market created by the flowering of secondary schools.

I met an Iranian businessman who, upon visiting the offices of Hitachi and Sumitomo in Japan, was astonished to discover that these firms recruited their staffs exclusively from Japanese universities. "In Iran," he said, "we don't want people who graduate from the University of Teheran; they have got to come from some good foreign university." Teheran, which has seventeen thousand students now and is growing toward fifty thousand, has its weaknesses. Modeled in the first place on French universities, it has strong autonomous faculties, which make administration a headache. The central library, although immaculately marbled, sheathed in faïence, and set against a stretch of fine-leaved grass, has only 146,867 books. Still, when not afflicted by riots and demonstrations, the university is a serious teaching institution, with prestige among the bureaucracies of government, and the campus, near the center of Teheran, is a pleasing arboretum dotted with three- and four-story tan stone-faced buildings. The students dress much like Americans, though the jeans look a little cleaner and a sizable number of the women, who make up about a fourth of the enrollment, wear chadors.

Teheran served as parent and model for Azarabadegan University in Tabriz, Ferdowsi University in Mashhad, and the University of Shiraz. Then, on orders from the Shah, Shiraz broke away sharply from the model. Renamed Pahlavi University (and re-renamed University of Shiraz after the revolution), it made a contract with the University of Pennsylvania that was designed to turn it into Iran's first "American" university. It got a board of trustees, A-B-C-D-E-F grades, deans, credits, repeat courses, mid terms, and instruction in English, not to mention a dramatic yellow-brick campus. The incompetence of undergraduates in English gradually forced the university to go back to teaching in Persian, except for the sciences. But over the years, Pahlavi has done much to accomplish its twin goals of encouraging Iranians to study in Iran and encouraging Iranian scholars abroad to return and work in Iran. Its occasional Pahlavi Lectures, bringing eminent scholars (such as Harvard historian Oscar Handlin in 1976) to speak in Shiraz, Teheran, or Isfahan, have helped keep the university near the forefront of learning. Four hundred of its 670 faculty members hold Ph.D.'s from American or British universities.

Pahlavi became Iran's prestige school, and the American model for a university became the favorite one. Among other advantages, it trains Iranians to go on to doctorates from American schools. Perhaps typical of the results is Tabriz's Azarabadegan University, which, though fenced like an ammo dump, possesses a lovely new campus of wide-spaced pink brick buildings and globular area lights. It teaches medicine, science, education, pharmacy, humanities, agriculture, and nursing, and like all universities except Teheran, holds itself to a maximum enrollment of eight thousand. In Ahvaz, the university with the euphonious name Jundi Shahpur reincarnates in its beautifully tiled new buildings what was the world's greatest medical center for several centuries in the Sassanian dynasty. Lately it has become strong in English, with—at least until 1979—thirty American professors in this subject and a library of fifty thousand English titles ("but we have no chalk or erasers," one of the American professors told me). Jundi Shahpur also offers medicine, dentistry, and science. The University of Kerman has lately occupied a new-built campus, and even far-off Baluchistan has acquired a university with a few hundred students spread among a maritime college at the naval base in Chah Bahar, a civil engineering school in Iranshahr, and a medical school in Zahedan. Kermanshah is getting a university named for the ninth-century scientist Razi. In Teheran, Empress Farah in 1976 inaugurated the country's first university for women only, and if that seemed like a step backward in a feminist age, it was quickly put about that it might eventually admit men. This school, then called (what else?) Farah Pahlavi University, plans to teach its women medicine and engineering, among other subjects.

Four universities that are just getting going undertake more specialized kinds of education. Abu Ali Sina Technical University (named for the eleventh-century physician and philosopher usually called Avicenna in English) at Hamadan (site of Avicenna's tomb) will reinforce Iran's capacity for higher education in technology, currently taught at Aryamehr University of Technology in Teheran and Isfahan and at various colleges. Abu Ali Sina's foreign guidance comes not from the United States but from France; even the near-square-mile campus is a design of Paris architect Georges Gandiliss.

Another European country that is guiding the founding of a new Iranian school is West Germany, which is assisting the University of Gilan in Rasht and will provide instruction in German. A third forthcoming institution, in Mazanderan, will give graduate and post-doctoral courses only, and try to make up for Iran's lack of research in universities. Harvard University, which ten years ago gave the Shah an honorary LL.D., was put in charge of this new school's design. And still another new school, Farabi University, with a village-like campus under construction at Qaraj, just west of Teheran, will tackle all the arts: music, drama, cinema, television, design, graphics, painting, architecture, and urban planning.

The ten biggest universities enroll 43 percent of students who are in higher education; the rest attend the small and specialized colleges and institutes. Many of these began as free enterprises aimed at making big profits by ripping off tuition from desperate students who failed to get into the universities; the Shah tried to curb such ventures by putting them under university supervision. Now about a dozen of these schools would rank high anywhere in the world.

"Abadan Tech is the most successful institute in Iran," an American businessman told me, speaking of the refinery-based school that since 1939 has been training Iranians in the technology of petroleum. The National Iranian Oil Company, which got on its feet only with the efforts of Abadan Tech engineers, accountants, and administrators, recently expanded the school threefold. The school teaches in English only. Another creditable college in Iran is Demavend, a four-year liberal arts school for 720 "best-family" women which occupies a set of caravanserai-style buildings of tan bricks, designed by Wesley Peters, on high land northeast of Teheran. Here, too, the instruction is all in English.

The top business school in the country—"the main channel for bringing modern capitalism to Iran," as one professor puts it—is the Iran Center for Management Studies. Founded in 1972 by some Harvard-graduated Iranian businessmen and government officials, it teaches by the Harvard Business School case method, and had for a patron that prince of a Harvard man Abdorreza Pahlavi, the Shah's brother and look-alike. The school's architecture—madressah-style buildings around a large garden that centers on a modernistic library, with running water everywhere, and all isolated on a hilltop west of Teheran—is by Nadir Ardalan (Harvard '62), and it made his fame as an architect. Ardalan copied the pit-style classrooms of Harvard Business School, and done in sandy Iranian brick, they turned out to have splendid acoustics.

I attended a class led by James K. Owens (Harvard '71), a bouncy man who says "git" for "get" and who likes to climb the snowy Elburz Mountains in January for an overnight campout. The eighty students were mostly Iranian—lots of black beards—but included some Indians, Afghans, Africans, and Americans, and one or two with French and Spanish names. Seven students were women. The class followed Owens intently, and when he needed a percentage or an addition to explicate his case (should fictitious Western Fabricating Company finance itself in the long range by debt or by stock?), the students punched their pocket calculators and shouted the answers to him. The students live on campus ("to keep their families off their backs," Owens explained), in groups of eight who occupy four double bedrooms arranged around a common room. The course lasts eleven months, and the school expects the students to study as much as fourteen hours a day. So that qualified but moneyless students can enter, the center makes tuition loans, which can be repaid when the graduate steps into the job he is certain to get (or return to, if on leave), with pay of around $30,000. But occasionally, said Owens, "we ask people to withdraw for academic reasons—something unique in Iran." The library is intentionally small. "In the case method, you rely on your wits and not on books," explained Owens.

What most Iranian students want from higher education is a piece of paper. They want a degree, which is essential for a career in government, valuable for a career in business and industry, and prestigious in society. One gets a degree by passing examinations, and one passes examinations by memorizing knowledge. Professors possess knowledge, and their job is to spoon it out to the students. Various consequences flow from this line of reasoning. Students believe that there is an answer to every problem. If the professor suggests that there are several (and worse, that he does not know which is the preferable answer), or if he proposes that the students think out the answer, the class grows furious: he is holding out on them. Anything that stands between the student and the degree is a plot. One such barrier is to demand that the student read books; a class syllabus of no more than one hundred pages is thought to be sufficient reading. Seminars and essay writing are equally unnecessary barriers. Too much classwork is also deplored. "Three short stories and fourteen poems in one semester are all that my class will take," one teacher of English told me. The highest barrier is low or failing grades. A sheaf of low marks makes the class "bang on their desks and break glass," the same professor said. As a result, one journalist who keeps tabs on higher education told me, "the teachers give passing grades to keep the students happy," and therefore 95 percent of those who enter college get degrees.

In sum, a university or a college is supposed to be a route to a job rather than a possibly exciting adventure into the liberal arts—into thinking and debate and wonder. Stirring up enthusiasm for learning becomes pointless. Professors skip classes, take outside jobs, fail to update their lectures. Regarding their students as enemies, teachers make little effort to know them or communicate with them. "Professors do not like to work with students," one student told me. In science laboratories, a normal-school president told me, usually "only the teachers use the equipment. We Iranians don't like to use our hands. It's all theory." I asked him if the students were, on the whole, good. "More or less," he replied, with pursed lips. "They're selfish, and lack social responsibility, and don't like coordination and cooperation." For that matter, professorial ability can also run low. A while back, Teheran University Chancellor Ghassem Motamedi charged that 80 percent of college and university mathematics instructors are not well qualified to teach.

A college education long since ceased to be a privilege of the elite, but now almost every high school graduate wants to matriculate. In 1976, 300,000 of them vied for 34,000 freshman openings. To screen this mob, the government each year gives applicants a National General Record Examination of 240 multiple-choice questions, and asks them to list their preferences of schools and studies; a computer matches students to schools. As elsewhere, it is not impossible to by-pass the computer with a well-placed bribe.

Before the revolution, no fewer than fifty-nine American Universities were providing guidance to Iranian colleges or universities or to governmental entities. Bryn Mawr, Green Bay, Goucher, Florida State, Johns Hopkins, Lewis and Clark—they were all there. Pahlavi had brought in Kent State, feeling that some of its problems were more akin to a young American state university than to Pahlavi's old, established adviser, the University of Pennsylvania. In a valiant effort to upgrade itself, Ferdowsi University in Mashhad took for an ally George-town University of Washington, D.C. Massachusetts Institute of Technology helped Teheran's Aryamehr University toward its goal of becoming an Iranian MIT. The University of Teheran counted on collaboration from the universities of Illinois, Indiana, Alabama, Colorado State, and Utah.

All this cooperation ran dead against the Islamic grain of Ayatollah Khomeini's revolution, and the new government broke virtually all of the aid contracts.

Lincoln University in Jefferson City, Missouri, a once all-black and now half-black state school, was aboil with trouble several years ago, trouble caused by its Iranian students. Demonstrating against the Shah, they got into a factional scuffle that ended with twenty-seven of them in jail, where they continued the fight. Jefferson City's mayor was so angry that he gathered names and pictures of the demonstrators and sent them to the Shah, after some research on how to address this government-to-government communication. What the Shah did with the letter I do not know, nor is it the point of the story. The point is that there were—inevitably, it seemed—a hundred Iranian students in such an obscure American university as Lincoln.

They were part of a throng of 23,000 Iranian students in colleges and universities in the United States, a group larger than that of any other foreign nation (the runners-up are Taiwan, with twelve thousand, and Nigeria, with eleven thousand). The Iranian contingent in the United States was at the same time the largest of the groups of Iranians in foreign countries, although the United Kingdom had a big contingent, seven thousand, and sizable numbers studied in West Germany, France, Austria, and Italy. In smaller numbers Iranians went to Canada, Japan, the Philippines, and elsewhere. All told, they constituted about one fourth of all Iranians receiving higher education. It was quite feasible for Iranians, even those of low social station, to go abroad.

Like university students within Iran, those abroad could get a lot of help if they agreed to return and serve in the government or in industry. The sponsorship included tuition, a stipend ($225 a month in the United States), as much as 65 percent off on air fares, help in getting placed in foreign universities, and exemption or partial exemption from military conscription. The big hurdle for most students who aspired to study abroad was not money but poor preparation: secondary school education inadequate for passing entrance examinations, and inability to speak a foreign language well enough, even after the customary tutoring.

The Westernization implicit in all this foreign education did not appeal to the mullahs, and as the revolution went on it seemed certain that they would cut down on it.

11

On Literature, Lutes,
and the Chin of a Kitten

❀

بنگر ز جهان چه طرفه بر بستم ، هیچ
وز مال جهان چه مانده در دستم ، هیچ
من جام جمم ولی چـو بشکستم ، هیچ
شمع طربـم . ولی چـو بنشستم . هیچ

This is a verse from the *Rubaiyat* of Omar Khayyam, printed in the slightly modified Arabic alphabet that the Iranians use to write the Persian language. You read it from right to left. The dotted squiggle at the left end of each line is the word "nothing." This verse is one of many from Khayyam not to be found in the customary English translations by Edward FitzGerald and others, but its meaning might be rendered as

> Think! What good have I got from the world? Nothing.
> What of the world's wealth do I have? Nothing.
> I am the chalice of Jam, but what good does it do me? Nothing.
> I am the candle of Torab, but where have I sat? Nowhere.

Madar, pedar, baradar, and *dukhtar* are Persian words, and their resemblance to "mother," "father," "brother," and "daughter" is no accident; indeed, scores of Persian words resemble English and German words. Persian has had a long and adventuresome history, but it is fundamentally one of the Indo-European languages, tracing back to the dawn-of-man tongue that is the ancestor of Greek, Sanskrit, Germanic (and its derivatives, including English), Latin, and Slavonic.

The Afro-Asian languages, including Arabic and Hebrew, stand completely apart from the Indo-European, and as a consequence Persian bears no family resemblance in structure, grammar, or vocabulary to the tongues of Iran's neighbors to the west. "For European people Iran is more interesting than the Arab countries because they find here a branch of their own culture," Dr. Sadegh Kia, head of the Academy of Iranian Language, told me.

The language of Iran first became distinct as Iranian, which evolved into Old Persian, spoken until about 300 B.C. and written (sparingly—5,800 words of Achaemenian inscriptions are all that survive) in cuneiform (wedge-shaped) strokes. For commercial correspondence and royal communications, the Achaemenians used Aramaic, a Semitic language with a workable ideographic alphabet, which in those times constituted the major writing system in the Near East. When Old Persian, dropping gender and declension, evolved into Middle Persian (also called Pahlavi), the Aramaic language faded out but Aramaic ideograms were applied to Persian words. The Sassanian dynasties got along with Middle Persian for centuries, then gradually turned it into the New Persian spoken for the last thousand years. A famous work of literature, put down on paper as this transition took place, is *The Arabian Nights Entertainments,* which is not Arabian at all, but rather a collection of Persian and Indian stories, and more properly called *The Thousand and One Nights.*

At that point, as a blessing in disguise, came the Arab conquerors, bringing their Semitic language and insisting that the Iranians use it, at least for religion and government. Brought thus into close contact with the simple Arabic alphabet, the Iranians ditched the complex Aramaic ideograms of Middle Persian and began writing with phonetic letters. They also adopted thousands of Arabic words, which even today provide Persian with a wealth of vocabulary like the richness of words English got from the Norman Conquest's infusion of Old French into Anglo-Saxon. After a couple of centuries the Arabs gave up trying to impose their language on the Iranians, and Persian emerged, in the words of Indian scholar Firoze Cowasji Davar, "as a remarkable blend of vigour and elegance with a sweetness and melody that asserted itself effectively when handled by poets and authors of acknowledged merit." Persian replaced Arabic in official and diplomatic usage; Marco Polo spoke it at the court of Kublai Khan. Just as Latin served as the international language of the Roman world, so Persian was for centuries the language of correspondence among the Islamic nations.

By the tenth century the language was a sublime medium for poetry, and for five hundred years this art flourished as nowhere else on earth. The first poet was Rudaki, commissioned by the king to set into verse the glory of Zoroaster. After his death, Ferdowsi was called

ON LITERATURE, LUTES, AND THE CHIN OF A KITTEN

to the same court, and settled down to finish his *Shahnama*, the mythology merged with history that is to Iranians the core of their nationhood, "the whole soul of a people," as educator Ehsan Naraghi puts it. Unfortunately, its sixty thousand couplets prove to be too many for most foreigners to get through, even as translated by the nineteenth-century English essayist Matthew Arnold.

Next came the quatrainist Omar Khayyam, who in FitzGerald's translation delights the West, despite the fact that his contemporaries recognized him only as a mathematician and astronomer, and despite his traditionally low repute among Iranian literati. His quatrains (*rubaiyat* in Persian) mysteriously grew in number after his death, to total a thousand by the seventeenth century; the contemporary Iranian politician-scholar Ali Dashti contends that only 102 "could most reasonably be thought to have been composed by such a man." FitzGerald distilled his translation from about six hundred of what he supposed were Khayyam's quatrains, and, scholars admit, probably caught the authentic Khayyamic mixture of hedonism, pessimism, and fatalism:

> What, without asking, hither hurried Whence?
> And, without asking, Whither hurried hence?
> Oh, many a Cup of this forbidden Wine
> Must drown the memory of that insolence!

The talented poet Nizami broad-mindedly chose as the subject for one of his epics the conqueror who anciently brought Persia to heel, Alexander the Great; for another long poem he adapted the heart-melting Arabic love story of Laila and Majnun. The greatest delighter of all, in the opinion of many Iranians, was Saadi, who moved on stage shortly after Nizami and died in 1292 at the age of 108. Born in Shiraz, he filled his mind with anecdote and fable by traveling the world from Abyssinia to India, then spent his last three decades in the cell of a hermit, delivering himself of his experience in the form of books that mix prose and poetry. His *Rose Garden* is required reading for Iranian schoolchildren. "Never," he writes, "did I complain of my forlorn condition but on one occasion when my feet were bare and I had not wherewithal to shoe them. Soon after meeting a man without feet, I was thankful for the bounty of Providence to myself, and with perfect resignation submitted to my want of shoes." After Saadi came the whirling dervish Rumi, who attached himself, one after another, to three men he considered to be saints of the Sufi sect, and made his relationship with them ("two bodies with one soul") his muse. In *The Soul of Goodness in Things Evil* he writes:

> . . . 'Tis the love of right
> Lures men to wrong. Let poison be but mixed
> With sugar, they will cram it into their mouths.

Finally, Hafez: another man of Shiraz, whose assumed name means "the rememberer," because he learned the Koran by heart. His six hundred poems were mostly in the form of the *ghazal,* a sort of lyrical sonnet. According to legend, a line in one of them poked fun at Tamerlane, and when that conqueror took Shiraz, Hafez, summoned to the court, quickly invented a replacement line and pleaded misquotation. Hafez, like the other great Persian poets, depended for his living upon the patronage of the royal courts, but he lived in a century when princes and kings murdered and blinded one another with insane frequency, and the poet, though coolly keeping above the devastation, could hardly help adopting what the critic A. J. Arberry in *Hafez* calls a "philosophy of unreason" remindful of Khayyam's. In many of his odes he makes this point with a third-person reference to himself in the last few lines:

> I walked where tulips blossomed red,
> And whispered to the morning breeze,
> "Who are yon martyrs cold and dead,
> Whose bloody winding sheets are these?"
>
> "Hafez," he answered, " 'tis not mine
> Or thine to know this mystery;
> Let all thy tale of ruby wine,
> And sugar lips, and kisses, be!"

Hafez came so near perfection, it would seem, that no Persian since has even tried to surpass him. But as Goethe said, "One Persian poet equals seven Europeans," and by the time Hafez died, in 1390, Iran possessed not only a large body of poetry but also an oral tradition, an "acoustical culture" (as psychologist Saheb-ol-Zamani explained it to me), a public love of poetry as entertainment, which survives until now. In homes, on buses, in restaurants, over the radio, reciters recite. This is true in part because the poetry is so recitable. It has marked rhythm and rigorous rhyme; it utilizes alliteration and fanciful figures of speech; it has power, nuance, much meaning in single words. "With poetry, you can make a person cry," said a friend of mine in Teheran. "You can completely change his mood."

Thus history gave modern Iranians a rich and even ornate language. The authoritative Dekhoda Dictionary runs to forty volumes. Forms of polite address in Persian are as flowery and deprecating as a Hafez verse. "Excellency," says one's host, "this humble place is your own home. Please grace it with your footsteps." His sumptuous meal is "these few morsels of bread and cheese." If he does not say "I am your slave," he says "I am your sacrifice," and he hopes that "God will drown you in his compassion" and that "your kindness will never diminish." A plain military physician becomes "His Excellency Mister

Doctor Colonel Teherani." But the language is also well supplied with insults and obscenities. And it frequently adopts words from Western languages; *merci* has long been the commonplace word for "thank you," and Dr. Kia says that "every day, as we industrialize, we receive a new word from English." But, he added, "We also coin new Persian words for modern artifacts and concepts." His seven-year-old Academy of Iranian Language, concerned with "linguistics, not literature," keeps tabs on modern Persian, but its main purpose is scholarship in Old and Middle Persian, until now a neglected field. "This institute was the Shah's idea," one of the professors told me. "He wanted us to be proud of being Iranian, to believe in our history and our people."

Although schools and television are standardizing Persian throughout the country, dialects persist, and it is not always possible for one Iranian to talk easily to another. Apart from Azerbaijan's Turkic vernacular and Khuzistan's Arabic, various tribes and regions speak tongues that are cousins of standard Persian, with common ancestry going back to Middle Persian, Old Persian, or Iranian. Such variant dialects are heard in Kurdistan, Mazanderan, Gilan, Luristan, and Baluchistan. Soviet Turkestan also uses a Persian dialect, and Afghanistan two of them.

The thirty-two-character Arabic alphabet, which to some Westerners looks like Gregg shorthand, serves Persian well; Iran has felt no need, as Turkey did, to Romanize its script. A standard typewriter keyboard readily contains all necessary letters and their variations, as well as numbers and signs, and the only characteristic of the machine that is unusual to Westerners is the carriage's left-to-right movement. Similarly, Persian can easily be transmitted by Telex.

Putting Persian words into Roman letters is a rat's nest of confusion, and no standard system exists. How one *hears* Persian is part of the problem. The sounds for *g* or *gh, q* or *k,* and *kh* are confusingly alike. Qatar comes out "Guttar," and "Qom" comes out somewhere between "Goom" and "Hoom." The sound of the second *e* in "Teheran" represents an effort to duplicate the strongly aspirated sound that Iranians give to *h,* so many Westerners spell the city's name "Tehran" to indicate that the middle syllable should be nearly inaudible. Some Westerners hear "Isfahan," some hear "Esfahan," and some even "Espahan." Beyond that, transliterations into English and French vary—for example, Qajar and Kadjar. Scholars try to overcome the difficulties with underlines, overlines, macrons, and apostrophes, but succeed only in compounding confusion.

For that matter, precise usage of the words "Persia" and "Persian" often comes hard to foreigners. "The name of our country," writes Hormoz Milanian, professor of linguistics at the University of Teheran, "in our culture and language and from an official point of view has always been 'Iran.' What we have done, since the thirties, is to have asked the others also to call our country 'Iran.' If someday Germany wants to be called 'Deutschland' by everyone, does it mean Germans have changed the name of their land?"

Nevertheless, many Westerners, particularly Britons, persist in calling Iran Persia. The Shah wrote that Winston Churchill once told him, "grumpily but with a twinkle in his eye, that he, Churchill, would never be intimidated into speaking of Persia in any way except Persia." Strangely, many who inexactly call Iran Persia cannot bring themselves to say "Persian" in reference to the language, preferring *farsi*, which is the name for "Persian" in Persian. Says Milanian: "In English you should always use the term 'Persian' for the language and not *farsi*, for the same reason that in English you never say: 'He speaks *italiano.*'"

One last paradox about the world of things written is that the Arabic numerals used in Iran (not to mention the Arab countries) are quite different from what the West calls Arabic numerals, looking like this:

١	(1)	٦	(6)
٢	(2)	٧	(7)
٣	(3)	٨	(8)
٤	(4)	٩	(9)
٥	(5)	١٠	(10)

The numerals used in the West evolved from these figures, but in point of fact there is nothing very Arabic about either set. The idea of using numbers rather than letters (such as Roman numerals), an idea basic to all modern mathematics, originated in India, and passed to the Arab world and ultimately, in the ninth century, to Europe through the algebra texts of a great Iranian mathematician named Mohammed al-Kharazmi. (Wrote the British historian Edward Browne: "Take from what is generally called Arabian science . . . the work contributed by Persians and the best part is gone.") The exigencies of mathematics overcome custom in Persian script, and the numerals are written from left to right. Foreign travelers in Iran may neglect to learn the language, but they must learn to read the numerals (which is, obviously, easy) to find addresses, dial telephones, read prices, and so on. Conversely, Iranians have to learn the Western notation, because so many cash registers, car speedometers, and elevator control panels use it.

With literature and poetry in the doldrums, the principal purveyors of the Persian language nowadays are the newspapers. What they had to print, or felt they had to print, when the Shah was riding high had a lot to do with why he fell. For any literate and intelligent reader, the newspapers were a daily dose of sycophancy and lies—slap-in-the-face reminders of their subjecthood. Flipping through seventy-five typical front pages, I found the Shah's picture on all but fifteen of them (and the Empress or the crown prince were pictured on most of the fifteen). News of the Shah, the Empress, and publicity-minded Princess Ashraf sometimes filled three quarters of page one. When the Shah spoke, the editorial in one paper was likely to say: "Never before has such an important topic been so explicitly and comprehensively covered," and the editorial in another: "The Monarch has once again proved to the hilt that he is for the Iranian nation and the latter is for him." Writing such flattery must get tiresome, for the praise sometimes took on a weary tone. "It all goes without saying that all the progress and successes last year were due to the wise leadership of the Shahanshah Aryamehr," yawned the *Iran Oil Journal*. Headlines were servile to the point of becoming inane:

MAN'S EXPLOITATION BY MAN ABOLISHED—SHAHANSHAH

GREAT CIVILISATION MUST IMPROVE LIFE—EMPRESS

WORLD CAN LEARN LOT FROM IRAN—MONARCH

The newspapers had excellent reasons for printing what the government wanted them to. To begin with, the Shah some years ago showed his disdain for freedom of the press by closing down thirty-six dailies and weeklies—disreputable rags, to be sure, deriving income from blackmail, from selling news, and from government subsidies in the form of advertising, whose withdrawal was enough to kill them off. The effect was to leave two major newspaper companies, in debt to the government for survival and implicitly commissioned to be the government's propaganda machine, but at the same time magnificently positioned, as a joint monopoly, to make big profits. Without being told, their editors knew pretty much how to behave. "Defense and foreign policies are matters of state, not considered proper subjects for public discussion. We never editorialize on them," said one. The government, through the Ministry of Information and Tourism, passed down orders about what and what not to print, in considerable detail. When I was in Teheran, the newspapers were forbidden to print stories deploring bad traffic and city-government blunders. A public relations man for the National Iranian Oil Company told me forthrightly, "Our agreement with the newspapers is that we tell them the good side and the bad side of a story, and they print only the good side." As if all this were not enough, most government news was fed to the press from the Pars news agency, which was run by the Ministry of Information and Tourism. The Ministry of the Imperial Court also took a hand in censoring the press, particularly in the play given to photographs of the royal family and politicians. Backing up all this was a press law, which among many restrictions provided a punishment of three years in prison for insulting the king in print, and required newspaper publishers to be people "of good reputation." Of course, censorship is nothing new to Iran. Under Prime Minister Mossadegh, one journalist told me, the government posted a list of nineteen topics banned from mention in the press. Number nineteen was "et cetera." Ayatollah Khomeini, too, backs censorship of "certain things that would lead to the corruption or demoralization of man," and by mid 1979 he had virtually closed down the Iranian press.

Before the Khomeini revolution turned National Iranian Radio and Television into little more than a forum for exalting the glories of Islam, this government-owned corporation was one of the royal family's instruments of propaganda and rule, run by a relative of the Empress. Here, again, an idea backfired. NIRT politicized millions of Iranians by showing an appealing world outside Iran, while at the same time offending other millions of Moslems by airing shoddy Western entertainment.

The Shah's interest endowed NIRT with plenty of money, which among other benefits let it cover world news lavishly, through satellites over the Atlantic and Indian oceans. In small villages humble Iranians saw the events of the West and the East brought by NIRT's links with Eurovision, American networks, and the Asian Broadcasting Union. In simultaneous translation they might hear a man on the other side of the world say, "This is David Schoumacher in Washington"; or they might look at a colorful map and learn where Zimbabwe is. The entertainment programs also brought in the outer world—even Lucille Ball, miraculously made fluent in Persian. From within Iran came costume dramas, sports reports, and much music. NIRT held commercials to a total of one and a half hours a day, and considerately planted them not in but only at the end of programs. With 102 transmitters linked by microwave, television covered all Iran except the almost unpopulated central deserts.

The Shah also gave educational TV a real try, in response to the plain fact that the Ministry of Education could not adequately do its job as Iran attempted to get all school-age children into classrooms.

The goal was to put a television receiver into almost all classrooms of grades one through twelve—specifically, one hundred thousand of them—and let it serve "as a stimulating agent for accelerating and intensifying learning among the students." A satellite system, which Stanford University helped to install, broadcasted instruction, but the receiver could also use video cassettes, which the teacher could get from twenty-five "learning resource centers" all over the country.

The staff at NIRT's handsome new educational television building on a hilltop in Teheran had by 1978 developed most of the software for this system, and put it into use in thousands of classrooms of grades five to nine in Teheran and Shiraz. When I visited, eleven "educational technologists," chosen from among five thousand teachers who applied for the jobs, were busy "Iranianizing" American instructional material, helped by writers, artists, film-makers, and producers, many of them bright-looking young women. Some of the staff were Americans: besides Stanford, NIRT had enlisted the help of Michigan State University and the University of Southern California, both leaders in educational technology. This gallant—but to Moslems, offensively Western—effort was shut down by Ayatollah Khomeini.

In the middle of 1979, Khomeini pronounced all music to be "no different from opium," and—in one of his more fatuous and ineffectual moves—tried to ban it from radio and television. But Persian music has a long and honorable history of invention and refinement in spite of all Islam's efforts to suppress it as a licentious amusement. What most Westerners recognize as the Middle Eastern sound is historically Persian, the result of an intense development of musical theory between the ninth and fifteenth centuries. *The Great Book of Music* by Abu Nasr Farabi, the writings of Avicenna on harmonic consonance and dissonance, and subsequent works by others guided musical development not only in the Arabic countries, Turkey, North Africa, and India, but also in nations as far away as China and Spain (inspiring flamenco). The Sufis, heretical Moslems in more ways than one, embraced music ardently for their whirling dervish dances that brought them into union with Allah; and even the more orthodox Moslems acknowledged that they needed music for their passion plays. Semicovertly, all the royal courts, clear through the Qajars, amused themselves with music.

What modern Iran has inherited is a large body of its own classical music, and classical stringed instruments to play it on. Preserved over the centuries by ear rather than by notation, this repertory varies somewhat between one master performer and another, but in general its contents are organized into twelve groupings *(dastgahs),* each containing from ten to thirty classical melodies *(gushehs),* with titles that describe them or trace from place names. Most of these melodies have lyrics, specifically the poems of Saadi, Rumi, and Hafez. The scale used for this music is divided more finely but less exactly than the Western do-re-mi-fa-sol-la-ti. The Persian scale uses the same five whole tones and two half tones, but instead of merely dividing the whole tones in two with sharps and flats, it divides the whole tones into three or four microtones, and the half tones into two. Just how to divide them is the source of the inexactitude of the scale. Some performers divide them equally, some use an ancient Greek system of unequal divisions. Depending on who divides it, the Persian scale contains nineteen to twenty-four notes, as against the Western scale's twelve.

When an instrumentalist or a singer sets out to give a concert from the classical repertory, he has to call up all his creativity. First he chooses one of the twelve groupings, and thus commits himself to play its opening melody. But to play all the grouping's melodies would make an impossibly long concert; the performer selects four or five, which will run about thirty minutes. Now he runs up against the fact that each melody is not a hard-and-fast tune, but more like what Ella Zonis, in *Classical Persian Music,* calls "genetic material" from which the musician is expected to improvise a performance not exactly like any previous performance of the same piece. He must stick to certain fixed elements; but he must add his own embellishments, in the form of repetitions, grace notes, strumming, and trilling. "The melodic form of a gusheh is not something clear and tangible," says the musicologist Hormoz Farhat. "Rather it is a skeletal idea upon which the performer improvises. Only through much exposure and experience can one come to recognize the melodic form of each gusheh with any certainty." The performer also improvises the varying rhythms, but if the melody has a lyric, he usually sticks to the meter of the poem.

These rules of the game set the essential characteristics of purely Persian art music. The requirement of improvisation eliminates orchestration or ensemble playing, since all musicians improvise differently. Yet instrumentalists can, and do, play with singers. In fact, "vocal music in Iran can perhaps be considered as even more important than the instrumental," writes Farhat. For "it is in singing that the two arts of music and poetry blend into one; and, because of the splendor of Persian poetry, the result can be something truly magnificent." He adds that "Persian vocal music, with its trills, high falsettos and quasi-yodeling style, makes for a very singular vocal tradition."

Most hearers agree that classical Persian music is a sad music, and it is easy to assign the reasons for the sadness: Shiite Islam's concern with mourning and its antipathy to joy, Iran's history of disastrous invasions and long foreign occupations, the sadness of the dry and stony land itself. It is languid, contemplative music, lacking a driving beat and other excitements, though some of the melodies are bright and happy. Yet even on first hearing, the Westerner may well be stunned with this music's sheer beauty, its heavenliness, its subtlety (the result of that finely divided scale). Within its own definition of itself, it is an art form that has, one quickly senses, achieved perfection. In Farhat's words, "it is an expression of unsurpassed refinement and grace, an art that can transport its listener into a state of unawareness of time and the elements."

The six main instruments of Persian classical music nicely accommodate its demands. The *setar,* a long-necked lute with four strings and a belly in the shape of a half-pear, makes sounds so soft that it could be played in secret in the times when the mullahs most fanatically opposed music, and its movable frets adapt to the imprecise intervals of the scale. The player plucks it with the well-tended long nail of his right index finger. The *tar,* which is the most popular of the instruments, is a bigger version of the setar, nearly three feet long, with a double-bellied body and six strings plucked with a metal plectrum. The *santur* is a trapezoid-shaped dulcimer with eighteen rows of quadruple strings, played with small, supple wooden hammers. The player tunes it in advance to provide the notes needed on a particular melody. The last common string instrument is the *kamachay,* a fiddle with a blunt-ended spike extending from the bottom of the body, so that the performer, holding the fiddle vertically, can support it with the spike on his thigh. The sound box is covered with sheepskin; the neck has no frets. This rather primitive instrument is popular in rural areas, but in the cities the European violin has put it to rout in recent times, since the violin is well suited to Persian music. Irony here: most modern European instruments, including the violin and the dulcimer, descend from the same ancient Persian instruments that are the ancestors of modern Persian art-music instruments.

The wind instrument of the art-music sextet is the *nay,* a six-holed cane flute. "To blow the tones of the lower register," writes Ella Zonis, "the player holds the instrument against one side of his nearly closed lips. The notes of the upper register are produced by inserting the end of the instrument between the two upper teeth with the player's lips entirely covering the end of the mouthpiece. (By fortunate coincidence, or as a result of extensive practicing, most players have a space between their upper front teeth.)" The last instrument, for percussion, is the drum called the *tombak,* vase-shaped, carved from one block of wood, faced on one end with sheepskin, played with the fingers and palms while the drummer holds it in his lap.

To all of which it must be added that modern art-music players often perform on the piano, or the clarinet, adapting the melodies to the Western octave, at a loss of some subtlety. Moreover, under the influence of a great Iranian musician named Ali Naqi Vaziri, who is still alive in Teheran at the age of ninety-three, classical Persian music has been set down in Western notation, even though many musicians cannot read it, and still play by ear. After studying in Paris and Berlin between 1918 and 1923, Vaziri devised signs for half-sharps and half-flats that made notation of Persian music feasible, and published some of it. In 1963, the Ministry of Culture and Arts published the whole body of Persian classical music in Western notation.

Beyond these technical touches of Westernization in art music, most modern composition of serious music in Iran combines Persian themes, and often Persian instrumentation, with Western harmony, instrumentation, and orchestration. A leading composer in this mode is Emanuel Melik Aslanian, who learned Armenian, Turkish, Kurdish, and Persian music during his boyhood in Tabriz, then went on to study piano, particularly the music of Beethoven, in Hamburg and Berlin during World War II. He calls his music "overnational," and explains: "On its first hearing, overnational music doesn't seem to belong to any particular country. But if you study that music in depth, you will find out where the composer's roots lie."

Only the hairs from under the chin of a two-week-old kitten were fine enough for the brushes of the best of the Persian miniaturist painters of yore. Perhaps these artists would have preferred bigger brushes and bigger pictures. But painting small gave them a way to evade the Koran's restrictions on the representation of humans and animals: the faces in a miniature are patently too small to be mistaken for real-life figures, and hence raise no possibility of idolatry. Anyway, the Persians' Shiite branch of Islam has always been more lenient toward representation than the rigid Sunni branch: the Persians permitted themselves to enjoy representative art even when they still restricted themselves to commissioning Christians to sculpt their coins and paint their murals. And in the Safavid dynasty (fanatically Moslem, but touched with the joy of Sufism), the Persians began openly to paint portraits that were life-size or bigger. All these factors working together have bequeathed to Iran a vast body of mostly delightful painting, as anyone reading the fourteen volumes of *A Survey of Persian Art,* edited by Arthur Upham Pope and Phyllis Ackerman, can see. (Pope's collection is now housed at Pahlavi University in Shiraz.)

The Mongol invaders brought the inspiration for miniature painting from China, and many faces in these little paintings have a Chinese look. The Persians mostly applied the technique to illustrating books—*The Arabian Nights Entertainments,* or the mythology in Ferdowsi's

Shahnama, or Omar Khayyam's *Rubaiyat.* The eye feasts on gold and red and those two Persian blues, turquoise and ultramarine, in swirling pictures of battles, hunts, polo games, and—over and over—a downy-faced youth using one arm to embrace a thick-thighed girl and the other to ply her with wine. Some dealt with religion—for example, miniatures of Mohammed and Moses.

When painters finally felt authorized to do full-size figures and faces they did lots of them, mob-scene murals filled with bemustached soldiers and slashing scimitars in pictures of the tragic seventh-century battle of Kerbala, or of Nadir Shah subduing the Moguls at Delhi in the eighteenth century. From these big-picture beginnings came the entrancing world of Qajar art, chiefly portraits of that dynasty's decadent kings and princes, which nowadays bring as much as $400,000 in the European art market (with Iranians themselves among the most enthusiastic buyers). The Qajar-era court painters worked in warm, dark, thick oils, rich reds and golds. They paid no attention to anatomy or perspective, but devoted themselves to detail, outlining every pearl of the hundreds that lined the hems and belts of the royal gowns and covered their epaulets and crowns. The tops of the frames form triangles or half-circles. Apart from royalty, the favorite subject of Qajar painters was dancing girls. One famous picture shows a dancer-acrobat balancing upside down on the tip of a dagger that she holds with an outstretched arm, while her almond eyes peer languidly from under four-inch eyebrows. In other paintings, entertainers, some in gold-spangled dresses, some bare-breasted, play tambourines, castanets, and the tar. They all have small, seductive, contented mouths, with lower lips like bruised strawberries.

Ten years ago most Qajar paintings were hidden away in private collections, particularly those of two British diplomats, but Empress Farah managed to buy two hundred pictures and repatriate them. Two Iranian collectors added to the treasure by donating a number of works. Then, so that anyone who wanted to could see this art, the Empress set up, in what was once the residential palace of Reza Shah, the Negarestan Museum of Eighteenth and Nineteenth Century Iranian Art. Beautifully mounted and lighted, the Qajar collections ooze delight and humor; and for extra pleasure the museum has a rooftop restaurant.

But the Empress cared more about modern art (and as a former architecture student, modern architecture) than classical art. Establishing Negarestan turned out to be only a warm-up exercise for her. With counseling from Thomas Hoving, then director of New York's Metropolitan Museum of Art, she went on to build Teheran's new Museum of Contemporary Art as the keystone in her grand design of sct-ting up nine museums and an art library in Iran. The Teheran building uses four towering concrete "light scoops," something like the ventilators of a ship, to bring natural illumination into the galleries and to give the structure a dramatic profile. They also seem to invite a viewer to enter, and inside, smaller scoops and sinuous walkways repeat the invitation.

The museum shows modern art and design from everywhere, but there are enough capable contemporary Iranian artists to provide a respectable local contribution. Modern painting in Iran begins with Kamal-ol-Molk (died 1926), the first in his country to paint from observation rather than imagination. Much of his work hangs in the buildings of the lower house of Parliament, and the school that he founded still teaches his Diego Rivera-like style as basic training. After World War II, Iranians trooped to Europe and the United States and brought back all the modern international styles from Fauvism and Surrealism to Pop and Op. Adding their own wit, sensitivity, and sometimes cynical temperament, Iranian painters have handled these styles well enough to place work in the world's major museums and biennials.

Many present-day artists meld modern art and Persian motifs. Hossein Zenderoudi, seemingly heeding the dictum that calligraphy is the highest art because it is the means of conveying the contents of the Koran, uses the swashes and dots of the Arabic alphabet to create paintings sometimes reminiscent of Jackson Pollock's, paintings that seem to sing with luminous and colorful poetry. Marcos Grigorian, who sometimes works and teaches at the Minnetonka Center of Arts and Education in Minnesota, used to be an impressionist, and now favors abstractions in sandy and fibrous textures. Sculpture never flourished in post-Islamic Iran, for the Koran said that art in three dimensions amounted to taking over God's role, but now, freed of that restriction by the birth of abstract sculpture if nothing else, the bushy-haired welder Parviz Tanavoli has drawn on the alphabet to make a series of works called "heeches." *Heech* is Persian for "nothing," the word that ends the four lines of verse at the beginning of this chapter. The two-eyed squiggle-with-a-tail that starts the word (at the right) is the Arabic *h,* and in one form or another this motif appears in most of Tanavoli's sculptures (which include some jewelry). Tanavoli professes amazement at the "astonishing resemblance between a heech and a human being."

Mahmud Farschian draws miniatures with a difference: they are big miniatures, and they show scarcely any color. In swirling Art Nouveau-like lines, Farschian depicts stories from the Koran, the Bible, and Ferdowsi's myths. Fish swim in the manes of lions, Jonah sits yogi-like in the belly of the whale, a Christian girl seduces Sheik Sanan to depart so far from his Islamic vows that his mustaches ardently entwine the horn of wine. Farschian's *Birds in Winter,* part of the Empress's personal collection, surpass Dr. Seuss's birds in mad fantasy—and at the same time send out a feeling of chill.

Smothered in support from the Ministry of Culture and Arts and Her Imperial Majesty, Iranian artists under the Shah took care not to do anything that would offend His Imperial Majesty. But they were freer than the Russians, for Iran had no ideological strictures on what's good and bad in painting style; and social criticism in the content was acceptable to a point. Ardeshir Mohassess dealt obsessively with the master-slave relationship in savage pictures of human beings spiked along with documents on some indifferent bureaucrat's desk, or simian creatures in top hats leading their underlings around by cords tied to their tongues. The Islamic revolution, echoing Koranic suspicions of art, and leery of Western influences, may well repress artists more than the Shah did.

> Here in this carpet lives an ever-lovely spring;
> Unscorched by summer's ardent flame,
> Safe too from autumn's boisterous gales,
> Midwinter's cruel ice and snow,
> 'Tis gaily blooming still.
> The handsome border is the garden wall
> Protecting, preserving the Park within
> For refuge and renewal: a magic space.
> —Unknown Sufi poet

To weave a Persian rug, seat yourself in front of a loom strung with vertical woolen warp threads and pull one pair of them toward you. Grasp a short length of dyed woolen yarn and insert one end of it between the warp threads, under and around the right-hand thread, back between the two, and under and around the left-hand thread. Allowing three years for the job, repeat the knot 7,200,000 times to make a nine-by-twelve-foot rug. Less, if the rug is to be woven of coarse wool; more, if it is to be woven of silk. After each row of knots is complete, weave two thin weft threads in and out of the warp threads across the rug, and hammer them down tightly with a comb to the row beneath. With a sharp knife, cut off the knot ends at the length of the desired pile.

Naturally, the rug must have a design. Unskilled weavers in Iran work from graph-paper cartoons placed behind the warp threads, but expert weavers, making rugs of designs traditional to a family, a village, or a tribe, go by memory alone, switching intuitively from one color of weft thread to another with no need to count along the warp threads. It is an amazing skill: these microscope-eyed weavers can depict a curving hairline and outline it with border hairlines of a different color. And they work so fast, plucking yarns from banks suspended just over the weaving area, that no stranger could possibly learn the Persian rug knot simply by watching their flying fingers.

The poet writes:

Over and around the tendrils swing, each its separate way pursuing,
From coy entanglements they flee apart,
In sudden collisions find sweet embrace;
In rhythms enchanting, with stately pace
Or rollicking speed; emerging, retreating,
Reversing in peaceful finality
Their conflicts reconcile.

Rich in composition, exuberant in form, harmonious in color, Persian rugs may well represent, as one connoisseur puts it, mankind's "zenith of decorative art." Westerners dote on Persian rugs, but they are made less for export than to cover (and usually overlap on) the floors and sofas and often the walls of Iranian houses, rich or poor, providing Iranians with figurative oases of birds and flowers and geometrical delights to stand in contrast to the sere land all around. Patterns vary by regions; experts can distinguish at least two dozen types. The Tabriz area, for example, usually makes carpets with hunting motifs, but also turns out tendrilous garden-of-flowers rugs. Isfahan carpets often take designs from mosque domes. Kashan, one of the leading weaving centers, favors medallions centered on solid-color grounds surrounded by the wide borders characteristic of all Persian rugs. Baluchistan rugs, in browns, dark blues, and camel colors (from the use of undyed camel hair), generally employ geometric designs and include a representation of a mosque pulpit that can be placed in the direction of Mecca when the rug is used for prayer. Another cherished Baluchi motif is the tree of life, apparently a heritage of shamanism, the primordial religion of northern Asia. The Qashqai tribes in Fars use bird and animal motifs, together with stars and diamonds. The Kurds and the Lurs depict camels, horses, lions, goats, and even dogs, despite Islam's distaste for the canine. Turkoman rugs come from the area that spreads across northeastern Iran, northern Afghanistan, and a fringe of the Soviet Union; the Siberian ancestors of these people may have made the earliest known knotted rug, discovered in the Altai area after having been preserved in permafrost since about 500 B.C. These rugs, which include the famous Bukhara class, use a geometric motif called a *gul*, apparently an ancient flower design altered to conform to Koranic dictates. In practice, the combinations and permutations of designs are infinite; no two carpets are ever exactly alike.

The best dyes in Persian rugs still come from natural sources: rose petals, pistachios, madder, walnut shells, vine leaves, and roots. Red is the commonest, because it is the color of good fortune. Turquoise, Iranian weavers believe, wards off the evil eye. Green is rare, for no one must tread upon the color of the Prophet; when weavers make a green rug, they mean it to be hung. The qualities of a good rug are easily defined. The more knots per square inch the better. The back should look tight and the colors bright. The pile should protrude at an angle to the back, so that the side of the yarn, not the end, takes the wear. The best materials, in order of quality, are silk, silk plus wool from the chest of a lamb, Angora goat fleece, ordinary sheep's wool, and camel hair. Thickness is unimportant; good rugs can be thin. Similarly unimportant are small mistakes made in weaving, such as a little asymmetry, slightly different shades in corresponding parts of a pattern, and irrectangularity.

A few years ago a German tourist, arriving in Iran by car, found a fine Persian carpet lying on a heavily traveled street in Tabriz. With Teutonic propriety, he gathered it up and turned it over to the police. The police said: "Put it back where you found it and mind your own business." Rugs lie in the streets all over Iran, placed there so that cars can run over them. I heard two explanations for the practice, neither of them convincing. One is that the tires of speeding cars beat the dust out of a dirty rug, even though the opposite might seem to be the case. The other is that wear and tear makes a new rug look old, raising its value. Merchants told me that age does not count in rug quality; there are good old rugs and good new ones. Wear is not a big factor. Persian rugs in light use can last two hundred years, but when the warp begins to show, the value declines. Of course, old rugs acquire value as antiques, and in practice bring the highest prices. In London, Sotheby Parke Bernet put a starting price of $40,000 on a nine-by-twelve-and-a-half-foot rust-red rug, with blue medallions, and saw the bidding go to $200,000 before a London dealer got it.

One knot at a time, hand weavers in Iran produce nearly three square miles of rugs a year. Their products are sold everywhere from Kress's notions store in Honolulu to the great Mitsukoshi department stores of Japan, but the numberless carpet stores on Ferdowsi Avenue in Teheran provide the world's most select concentration. Prices are rising, but as little as $100 will buy a two-by-three Qashqai and $10,000 a ten-by-fourteen Tabriz. In Iran one can usually bargain the price down to about 70 percent of the dealer's first demand. Though far behind the front runner, oil, carpets are Iran's number-two export commodity, at about $120 million worth a year. Rugs make impeccable investments; prices rise faster than inflation rates. Banks in Iran commonly accept carpets as security for loans, storing them in large vaults.

Two factors are at work to keep rug prices going up: heavy world demand and shortage of weavers. The industrialization of Iran gives a weaver a chance to threaten to go to work in, say, a steel plant, unless weaving can be made to pay him more than the six dollars a day that he has been getting in recent years. And the universal education effort puts into schools children who formerly stayed home and worked on the family loom. "I'm buying carpets as fast as I can," one Teheran tycoon told me. "The people who weave them are going to stop. The children have to go to school, and they won't make carpets after they get educated." Reinforcing the drain of children to schools are new laws against child labor. "The carpet-makers used to buy small boys from their fathers and force them to work in basements until they got tuberculosis," a doctor in Tabriz told me. "Now the carpets are made by skilled men who get high wages and fringe benefits such as insurance." Of carpet-making, dealer Nader Ghermezian told me: "It's going to be a dead art in twenty years."

But such pessimism helps sell carpets, and perhaps the future of carpet-making will take a different turn. Machine looms in Iran, spitting out a rug in five hours, are now producing an eighth of the national output, and this industry is growing. They can make a nine-by-twelve imitation Kashan to sell for $500. Probably machines will fill the demand for rugs of Iran's growing middle class, yet leave a healthy market of well-to-do connoisseurs all over the world who want works of art made by those Iranian weavers for whom the manufacture of good carpets is still too much of a Persian passion, too much in the blood, to be forgotten. For as the poet writes:

> . . . this carpet fair.
> Its patterns were by angels wrought,
> Those ardent hues from the blood of flowers came.
> Of the Garden of Paradise
> 'Tis token and counterpart.

PART
THREE

PETROLEUM POWER

12

King Oil

✳

In the year of the Shah's coronation, oil production in Iran had topped two million barrels a day, worth more than $600 million a year. Compared to the $90 million a year of ten years earlier, that seemed like a torrent of money. But in the following ten years, production rose to six million barrels a day, and revenues to $22 billion a year. The Shah saw this wealth, enabling him to buy anything he wished, as confirmation of his destiny to remodel Iran the way he wanted it. Some of the money did go to build an industrial base that Iran will have to have no matter who rules it, for the oil will eventually run out. But many of the billions went for excessive weaponry, air-polluting, traffic-jamming automobiles, and other Western trappings—which brought with them unbearable corruption and inflation. The Shah took his billions and bought his downfall.

As if to acknowledge that oil money can't buy a happy Iran, the revolutionaries of 1978–1979 cut oil production back to 2.5 million barrels a day, later raising it to four. Iran may never return to the pattern of using a million barrels of oil a day and exporting five. Yet it remains one of the great petroleum reserves of the world, and oil will help mold the future as it helped mold the past.

When the drill bit bites through the cap rock in an Iranian oil field, what happens is akin to sticking an ice pick into a fire hose. Oil races up the well casing as though desperate to escape from an imprisonment that goes clear back to the Oligo-Miocene era. There are two reasons for the high pressure. In the first place, the oil occurs in sharply tilted anticlines, which give Iran the world's highest "oil columns," sometimes six thousand feet. But this gravity drive only adds to the existing pressure of gas associated with the crude. As a consequence, Iranian oil wells are sensationally productive. In the United

States, 500,000 oil wells, mostly requiring pumps, draw up an average of sixteen barrels a day per well. In Iran, the typical well spouts up, with no coaxing at all, sixteen thousand barrels a day, and such top performers as Wells 35 and 45 at Gachsaran field pour out 100,000 barrels a day, more than the entire consumption of many small nations. All of Iran's production comes from fewer than four hundred wells.

These generous wells make Iran the world's fourth-largest petroleum producer (after the Soviet Union, Saudi Arabia, and the United States), and second-largest exporter (after Saudi Arabia). Moreover, only Saudi Arabia, the Soviet Union, and Kuwait surpass Iran in proved petroleum reserves. Iran's reserves are nearly double those of the United States or Iraq, and what they may be beyond the admitted seventy billion barrels is one of the country's well-kept secrets. Probably its lament about running out of oil in twenty-five years is at least partly put on. But even if that's true, Iran will not be suddenly penniless, for exploration suggests that Iran may be the richest country in the world in oil's hydrocarbon sister, gas. (It has the second largest reserves, after the Soviet Union.)

Within Iran, oil is far and away the biggest industry. Although it is not labor-intensive, petroleum production normally employs 66,000 people, who work at everything from wildcatting and road-building to computerized research and sophisticated management. Indeed, one of the vital secondary tasks of the petroleum industry in this developing country is to supply job-trained employees for other industries; oil is a sort of university of modernization, and the industry literally runs some of Iran's best formal schools for technical and administrative training.

Besides providing the biggest industry, oil powers Iran itself. Per capita, consumption of oil is the highest in Asia after Japan. Kerosene, fuel oil, and bottled gas, replacing wood and charcoal as cooking and heating fuels, have reprieved Iran's remaining forests from extinction. Oil provides almost all of Iran's dollar earnings, 40 percent of its GNP, 76 percent of its governmental revenues. The National Iranian Oil Company is the second-largest industrial company in the world outside the United States; only the Royal Dutch–Shell Group surpasses it. It has been far and away the world's most profitable company; its 1976 earnings of $17.1 billion exceeded those of General Motors, Exxon, American Telephone & Telegraph, and IBM combined.

Given oil's power now, it is hard to remember that until 1951 Iran's oil might almost as well have been produced at the North Pole, for all that average Iranians benefited from it. Historically, oil in Iran was less an Iranian concern than a British concern, because it was a

British corporation owned by the British government that produced oil in Iran for more than forty years after a British subject, financier William D'Arcy, discovered it.

For D'Arcy, sensing that Iran had oil had not been hard: petroleum and gas seep to the surface in many parts of the Middle East. Such flows, ignited by lightning, were worshiped as fire gods by the first men who came to Iran, and later the Zoroastrians, venerating light, built temples around these eternal flames. A European a couple of centuries ago took note that the Iranians used crude petroleum "in varnishing and in painting, and Physick too, for the curing of raw cold Humors." Nevertheless, D'Arcy, the Australian who got the exploration concession in 1901, went through his own fortune (made in Australian gold) and a good bit of money promoted by the oil-thirsty British Royal Navy before he found oil. Finally, in 1908, one of his cumbersome cable-tool rigs pounded through the 1,180-foot depth and drove into the first of those famed Iranian high-pressure pools. The site was southwestern Iran, just where the narrow flatland along the Persian Gulf starts to rise into the Zagros Mountains. The success of the well, announced by black crude shooting high into the sky, signified the discovery of the world's most extensive oil field (twenty miles by four miles) to that date, and the debut of the history-making Middle Eastern oil industry. D'Arcy bought off the Bakhtiari tribal chieftains, Empress Soraya's uncles, who terrorized the area, and founded the Anglo-Persian Oil Company. Within four years, Anglo-Persian built the world's largest oil refinery, at Abadan on the Persian Gulf.

When the discovery well blew in, spattering camels and mules and turbaned Bakhtiaris, one witness was Lieutenant Arnold Wilson, commanding a contingent of British troops there without the shah's permission. Anglo-Persian was essentially a British military enterprise carried out in anticipation of World War I. In 1908, two thirds of the world's oil came from John D. Rockefeller's Standard Oil Company, and the rest from Russia's Baku fields on the Caspian, and from the Dutch East Indies. To get longer cruising ranges, the British admiralty desperately needed to burn efficient oil instead of bulky coal. Winston Churchill, first lord of the admiralty, put not only British troops but also British government money into the quest for oil in Britain's quasi-colony Iran, and by 1913 Britain, too, was a major power in oil. In 1914, just six days before the war started, the British Parliament enacted a law by which the government bought 51 percent of Anglo-Persian. Iranian production, growing to six million barrels in 1918, fueled the Royal Navy "to victory on a wave of oil," as Lord Curzon put it. The same oil served British warships equally handsomely in World War II.

D'Arcy's contract gave the Iranian government a royalty of 16 percent of Anglo-Persian's profits, but in this particular business, profits were determined by what the British company charged the British navy for oil. "It was never revealed what this price was nor whether the navy paid anything at all," writes the Iranian historian Yahya Armajani. "The Persians were never allowed to examine the books." In any case, profits were deliberately minimal, and the Iranians got peanuts. Between 1911 and 1951, the oil company paid out $615 million in profits, mostly to the British government, and $700 million in corporation taxes to the British government, but only $310 million in royalties to Iran. The company disdained employing Iranians in white-collar jobs, preferring Britons who had served in India, and until 1930 it even hired much of its unskilled and semiskilled labor from India, paying in rupees. In those days Iran had to earn its foreign exchange from carpets; less than one fifth of it came from oil. The company even balked at supplying petroleum and its products to Iran itself, which had to import them from Russia. Obviously, Iran grew increasingly unhappy with the deal. Reza Shah canceled the concession in 1932, but he was too much in awe of the British lion to talk tough, and the new agreement he made six months later gained almost nothing more for Iran.

Anglo-Iranian (as it became after Reza Shah decreed the national name change) was one of the oil companies that by means of the "seven sisters" cartel restricted oil production and divided up world markets during the 1920s and 1930s. In the Middle East the cartel's notorious 1928 Red Line Agreement—conceived by the Armenian oil financier Calouste Sarkis Gulbenkian, who red-penciled a line around Arabia, Syria, Turkey, and part of Iraq—in effect prevented the exploitation of what are now the great oil fields of Saudi Arabia and Iraq. World War II ended the danger of a glut of oil, and Franklin D. Roosevelt began to insist on the rights of American companies to produce Middle Eastern oil. The cartel then became a means of divvying up the profitable development of the oil on the western shore of the Persian Gulf. Anglo-Iranian got half of Kuwait and part of Iraq, but had to watch glumly as the other sisters moved in force into British-dominated terrain. Standard of California, Texaco, Exxon, and Mobil got almost all of Saudi Arabia. As the postwar Marshall Plan began to restore prosperity and the need for energy in Europe, no one wanted to trust the continent's fate to the Ruhr coal mines, dominated by Communist unions. The oil of the Middle East, including Iran, became the propellant for Europe's "petroleum takeoff."

In 1950, Iran was the world's fourth-biggest oil producer (after the U.S., the U.S.S.R., and Venezuela), and not at all pleased with the rewards this position earned for it. Two years before, a democratic government in Venezuela, having ousted a dictator long cozy with the oil companies, had forced the companies to pay Venezuela royalties equal to the companies' profits. This historic 50/50 split led Saudi Arabia to win equality, too. Iran's pittance from Anglo-Iranian became clearly a scandal and an injustice—which led Mohammed Mossadegh in 1951 to try to get a better deal than either Venezuela or Saudi Arabia. Inspired by Britain's own nationalization of steel and coal after the war, he took over the whole Iranian oil industry, in the world's second oil nationalization (after Mexico's).

Anglo-Iranian shut down the Abadan refinery, offered Iran a 50/50 deal, and (upon Mossadegh's rejection of it) rallied its sister oil companies to deny Iran tanker services and freeze Iranian oil out of the world's markets. When President Eisenhower sent Kermit Roosevelt into Iran to help topple Mossadegh, it was with the thought that if America pulled Anglo-Iranian out of the fire, Anglo-Iranian would have to let some American companies into Iran.

After Mossadegh's fall, Secretary of State John Foster Dulles sent oilman Herbert Hoover, Jr., to Teheran to talk to the Shah. For Iran's pride, the principle of nationalization had to be maintained, so ownership of the country's oil fields was turned over to the National Iranian Oil Company, formed a couple of years before in anticipation of this upshot. Naturally, it was also agreed that Iran would get the now standard 50/50 split of profits. But to operate the industry for NIOC, Hoover insisted upon a consortium of members of the seven sisters cartel. These companies were British Petroleum (the new, laundered name of Anglo-Iranian), which got 40 percent of the action; Royal Dutch–Shell, 14 percent; Compagnie Française des Petroles, 6 percent; Exxon, 7 percent; Gulf Oil, 7 percent; Mobil Oil, 7 percent; Standard Oil of California, 7 percent; Texaco, 7 percent; many smaller companies got the remaining 5 percent. The ironic net effect of Mossadegh's nationalization was to turn a good share of Iranian oil production over to American firms. "We kept it from falling back into British hands," an American Embassy official candidly explained to me.

A secret "Clause 28" in the consortium agreement (revealed by Senator Frank Church's investigation in 1974) authorized the participants to conspire to hold down production in Iran, if necessary to keep the price up. But the world market grew steadily in the 1950s and 1960s, and the consortium let Iran's output expand accordingly. The Agha Jari oil field, in the Zagros foothills, became one of the top half-dozen producers in the world. On the Ahvaz field, in the plain to the west, Well 6 came in one day in 1958 with a blaze that took sixty-five days to extinquish. Gachsaran, up in the hills 78 miles east of Agha

Jari, turned out upon intensive development to be a patch 4 miles wide and 36 miles long of record-breaking gushers. The year 1964 brought the discovery of the Marun field, Iran's biggest producer, with a capacity of 1.5 million barrels a day.

All these finds took place within the consortium's Khuzistan concession area, leading the Shah to wonder what could be discovered in the rest of Iran, and who might discover it. After Egypt humiliated Britain by taking over the Suez Canal in 1956, British influence in the Middle East declined so sharply that oil companies outside the cartel could consider shouldering into the area. The first man to try was Enrico Mattei, head of the Italian government's energy company, Ente Nazionale Idrocarburi. He offered the Shah the world's first 75/25 country/company profit split, and the Shah accepted all the more readily because the joint-venture pattern offered a way for Iran to begin to break out of the cartel's embrace. The Shah later said that what he called "attacks" against Iran from the West began right after he made this deal with ENI. "Mattei was killed," he said, referring to the Italian's 1962 death in an apparently sabotaged private plane, "but the attacks against our country continued."

ENI-NIOC found Iran's first offshore oil at Bandar Deylam in the Persian Gulf not far west of Gachsaran. NIOC then built up joint oil production ventures with various combinations of foreign companies, which came to produce about 10 percent of Iran's oil. The Shah found this expansion pleasing, particularly after some tattletale belonging to the Compagnie Française des Petroles informed the king, to his rage, of Clause 28. He protested to the U.S. Department of State, which beseeched the oil companies to raise output.

The cartel refused—and its refusal underlined the emptiness of Iran's nationalization. During his winter vacation at Saint Moritz early in 1973, the Shah fumed over this humiliation, and came to the conclusion that Iranian oil needed yet another emancipation. Returning to Iran, he decreed that NIOC should henceforth operate, as well as own, the Iranian oil industry.

The new agreement went into effect July 31, 1973, and the anniversary became Oil Day, a holiday. The members of the consortium were not forced to leave the country. Instead they formed, in precisely the same proportions, a new enterprise called Oil Service Company of Iran. The partners in OSCO got the right to purchase from NIOC and sell abroad oil in proportion to their equity shares and at a profit that amounted to roughly one fourth of the difference between production cost and the posted sales price. Not all NIOC's oil was to go for sale to the sisters, however; the government kept an increasing amount— more than 30 percent by 1978—and sold it abroad, taking all the profit.

Obviously, OSCO's partners could not lose; they were dealt in on a sure thing. In return they provided the latest and best technology, with the goal of expanding production in Khuzistan to 7.2 million barrels a day. OSCO's partners were also expected to accept service contracts (in contrast to the old rich concessions) for the discovery of more oil. They had to pay the exploration costs, but they got the right to buy half of the oil they discovered and resell it at a guaranteed profit.

Though they made billions, the consortium companies regarded their role as "vestigial." Only around five hundred foreigners remained in Iran to carry out OSCO's obligations, chiefly exploration. But they were conspicuous. When I was staying at the Royal Astoria Hotel in Ahvaz, I heard newly arrived American children shouting in the lobby while their mothers and their technician fathers drank vodka tonics and waited to settle into company housing. Such employees got $100,000 a year between salary and fringe benefits, stirring in Iranians envy that translated to Yankee-go-home xenophobia in the anti-Shah revolution. One OSCO executive was murdered, and a car belonging to the head of the company was bombed (without hurting him).

NIOC, a complex giant, contracted with eight other service companies besides OSCO (though they are much smaller). Some foreigners grumble that NIOC got so cocky that it always wanted the lion's share, but the Iranian company argued that it had to be exigent because it supplied the irreplaceable oil. "It's like a pig and a hen opening a ham-and-egg shop," one NIOC official told me jovially. "NIOC is the pig, and he says to the hen, 'You can go on laying eggs indefinitely, but I am 100 percent committed!' "

NIOC even added a neat final touch by undertaking some foreign ventures of its own. In 1975 the Iranian company went into partnership with British Petroleum, Standard Oil of California, and SAGA of Norway to acquire from the Danish government a concession to discover and produce oil on the continental shelf off western Greenland. NIOC had a part, with BP and others, in developing oil production in the North Sea. The Iranian company also operates joint-venture refineries with the Indian government and public in Madras. Supplying its own expertise, NIOC is building refineries in South Korea and Senegal. By itself and in a joint venture with British Petroleum, NIOC operates two million tons of tankers, including the 230,000-ton supertankers *Azarpad* and *Kharg*. NIOC and its tanker subsidiary have a 40 percent interest in the superport under construction in the Palau Islands, just east of the Philippines, which will distribute Iranian oil to Japan, North America, Central America, New Zealand, and Australia. The company hoped that these "downstream" operations would let it enter consumer markets abroad.

Within Iran, of course, NIOC owns the entire market, except that Shell and Exxon wholesale lubricating oil to the nation's twelve thousand service stations. NIOC franchises three fifths of these stations and operates the rest. To supply them and to fill the ever growing industrial demand, NIOC runs two large refineries in Teheran, and one each in Shiraz, Kermanshah, and Tabriz. Another is going up in Isfahan. The company took over the Abadan export refinery in 1973, and, by expanding it, made it again the world's largest, a versatile specialty plant that can turn out more than one hundred petroleum products.

The symbol, and the shame, of every oil field and every refinery in Iran is a plume of blazing gas. From the airplane descending into Ahvaz, one sees half a dozen flares near and far in a vast flat terrain—and within the city people stand in line to get propane bottles refilled. The south-facing rooms of the Abadan International Hotel glow orange all night long from the dancing flames of the great refinery. Over nearly seventy years, trillions upon trillions of cubic feet of gas have been burned to no better effect than to heat air that was already too hot.

In times past, the petroleum engineers in Iran had little choice but to waste this gas. They were forced to produce it, because it came up in solution with the Iranian type of crude, between 400 and 500 cubic feet of gas per barrel of oil. Lacking a market, it burned. But now NIOC, which controls gas through its subsidiary the National Iranian Gas Company, has four uses for gas: as a fuel for Iran and other nations, as a reduction agent in steel-making, as feedstock for petrochemicals, and as a means for forcing oil out of the earth when natural pressures decline. In fact, the markets could surpass the supply of petroleum-associated gas. Luckily, in the last decade Iran has made sensationally large discoveries of plain natural gas. Iran's reserves are at least 400 trillion cubic feet, and may equal the Soviet Union's 547 trillion cubic feet; they far surpass the reserves of the runner-up United States, 291 trillion. Oil remains Iran's big money-earner, but when it is gone, an NIOC official told me, "gas will keep us going for 230 years."

Most of the Iranian gas used as fuel normally goes to the Soviet Union. Even as the U.S.S.R. supported the Khomeini revolution, some of its citizens were shivering for lack of heating gas because of the strike Khomeini ordered. The southern U.S.S.R. has gas on both sides of the Caspian, but needs more. To supply it, Iran a decade ago created the Iranian Gas Trunkline, a 42-inch pipe running 700 miles from the Khuzistan oil fields to the Russian border. The trunkline can provide a billion cubic feet of gas a day for the Russians, and spur lines can supply another 600 million feet to Shiraz, Isfahan, Kashan, and

Teheran. Gas now fires many of Iran's ubiquitous brick kilns, ending bad air pollution.

By a separate trunkline, partly constructed from the oil fields to the Soviet border, Iran several years ago contracted, in effect, to supply 1.6 billion cubic feet of gas a day to Europe. Under the terms of a deal among West Germany, France, Austria, the U.S.S.R., and Iran, the Soviet Union was supposed to receive that much more gas from Iran and turn over an equivalent amount of its own gas to the European countries at the West German border. But in the middle of 1979, xenophobia was running high in Iran; the government canceled this sensible deal and cut down the supply of gas to Russia. Still, gas lines are spreading through western Iran—3,000 miles of them so far—to supply residences and industries not only in the cities but also in the villages. A discovery made right on the Afghanistan border now provides Mashhad with clean fuel and electricity; soon this same gas is scheduled to flow eastward through a 550-mile pipeline to bring its boons to towns en route and fire a 1,400-megawatt power plant at Neka near the Caspian Sea.

Several refineries in Iran already produce liquefied petroleum gas (propane and butane) for domestic use and export. Gas is replacing coal in steel-making, at direct-reduction plants in Ahvaz and Bandar Abbas.

As for petrochemical use of gas, the most striking fact about Iran is that the country itself urgently needs almost all the products of what is already the largest petrochemical industry in the Middle East, and will need most of what it is going to produce from the giant, integrated expansion of this industry now going on. Petrochemical technology is complex, but broadly the input is gas, salt, limestone, phosphate rock, and benzene, and the output is fertilizer, an array of acids and other industrial chemicals, and, ultimately, substitutes for such traditional commodities as steel, lumber, packaging materials, natural fibers, natural rubber, and soap.

Luckily, Iran has the gas and most of the other materials for the input, and a ravenous market for the output. But it is also true that Iran, so wrapped up in the oil and gas industry, is particularly aware of the economics of using hydrocarbons to manufacture materials rather than to burn as fuel. "It is a sobering thought that over 90 percent of the world's hydrocarbons are consumed in conventional energy used at low efficiency and that less than 5 percent of the hydrocarbons are used as petrochemical feedstocks," writes M. Towhidi of the National Petrochemical Company of Iran, another NIOC subsidiary. "If we could succeed in diverting only 10 percent of our total crude oil and gas production into petrochemical intermediates and final products from

Iran, the revenue from the latter would be more than double that obtained from the sale of the crude oil and gas as such."

The National Petrochemical Company runs four plants, one near Shiraz and the rest clustered around the gulf, and they are all being expanded. More importantly, the National Petrochemical Company is building a new plant that all by itself will exceed the entire existing industry. This complex, a joint venture with a combine of Japanese firms belonging to the Mitsui conglomerate, has been built under the guidance of three thousand Japanese workers at Bandar Shahpur, on the Persian Gulf, although the revolution postponed its start-up. With this project goes an oil refinery, as big as Abadan's, to make products for use in Iran and export to Japan. (Rather confusingly, a smaller Japanese-Iranian petrochemical company is operating at Bandar Shahpur. Mitsubishi Chemical Company is the partner.)

Whether it sells oil-associated gas as fuel or supplies gas for petrochemicals, the Iranian hydrocarbons industry at present still has too great a flow of this noble but hard-to-store stuff, which explains why flares continue to burn. But eventually this excess gas will all be used, and much unassociated natural gas as well, for the strange purpose of being injected back into the earth. As the pressure and reserves of Iran's oil fields decline, engineers are beginning to use reinjection as a way of forcing up the remaining oil. Luckily, 85 percent of reinjected gas eventually comes to the surface again.

One day when I was in Abadan I rose at 3 A.M. and at about four took off in a high-winged, twelve-passenger airplane for a 150-mile flight out into the Persian Gulf. We landed at five on a dot of land that has existed since only fourteen thousand years ago, when the coral of which it is built began to poke through the surface of the sea. This is Kharg island, Iran's 1958 response to the fact that the then new supertankers, drawing sixty or seventy feet of water, could not put in at the terminals along the coast.

I found that even apart from its mantle of oil-moving machinery, Kharg, two miles wide and six miles long, is intriguing. Though it is basically a barren hump of sandy white, with dramatic big boulders strewn here and there, nine hundred tiny deer manage to feed off some skimpy grass, with supplements of hay courtesy of the National Iranian Oil Company. Occasionally you see a tree, the temple fig, found only on Kharg, which has hanging roots to absorb the paradoxically high humidity of this sometimes torrid island. Kharg could use a lake, but an earthquake two hundred years ago cracked the rim of the only lake the island ever had, and emptied it into the sea.

Priests, pirates, soldiers; fire-worshipers, Christians, Moslems;

Greeks, Turks, Portuguese, Frenchmen, Dutchmen, Britons—all these have variously occupied Kharg in the past thirty-five centuries. A scattering of ruins includes some Zoroastrian temple steps, Palmyrene burial caves, a Nestorian church. The small standing Islamic buildings include a round-domed mausoleum and a beehive-domed *imamzadeh,* the shrine of an imam who fled from Iraq. Until Kharg became the beating heart of Iranian oil exportation in 1958, the Shah used it as a Devil's Island for "Communists" and the more unmanageable partisans of Mohammed Mossadegh.

Kharg was chosen for a deepwater terminal just after the Gachsaran oil field, 75 miles inland from the adjacent shore, came into full development. The premise was beautifully simple: the crude oil, placed by providence up in the mountains, would flow by itself over hill and dale down to and then under the sea to tanks on the island. Kharg was ideal. The neighboring sea was deep enough for big tankers but not too deep for the feeder pipe (which was welded together in sections on the shore, weighted with concrete collars, and push-pulled into position). The island had a hill 220 feet in elevation, high enough so that oil could flow from the tanks on it by gravity into the waiting ships.

Now, after much expansion, oil reaches Kharg in six underwater pipes, the biggest 52 inches in diameter. The crude comes from Agha Jari and other fields near sea level, as well as from Gachsaran, so where necessary it is moved by 120,000-horsepower pumps. The island's hilltop tank farm holds forty-five tanks, including nine with a world-record capacity of a million barrels each—which means that they are big enough to contain an entire football field. Tankers of up to 250,000 tons moor to a T-shaped jetty, and load in fifteen hours; standing on the wood-planked dock, you can watch them sink inch by inch into the water. Enormous VLCCs (very large crude carriers, including the 550,000-ton, French-built *Batilus,* the world's largest ship) moor, as many as four at a time, to "breasting dolphins" made of piles driven into the sea bottom, and oil reaches them through underwater pipes. At full tilt, Kharg can load 7.5 million barrels a day.

As I flew into Kharg's little airport in predawn darkness, I spotted some gas flares, flickering orange patches against the black sea and sky. The explanation for them was astonishing. Around 1964, well after Kharg became a loading terminal, somebody thought of drilling for oil there. The effort brought in eight gushing wells. What a prolific island! Added to the output of fields discovered before and since offshore from the island, Kharg receives several hundred thousand barrels a day apart from what the big pipelines bring. This oil carries up the customary associated gas, so in 1967 oilmen formed Kharg Chemical

Company to turn the gas into sulfur and liquefied petroleum gas. What is flared now is the unusable excess. From the T jetty, the flares and the stockpile of yellow sulfur against the coral hill make a harmony of warm colors reflected in the green gulf.

Fourteen thousand people live on Kharg. Four thousand work in the oil industry, a few thousand more hold military or other support jobs, and the rest are spouses and children. Technicians and managers occupy bungalows in areas made passably park-like by planting and diligently watering many young trees. Laborers live in three-room concrete-block row houses near Kharg village, an antiseptic little place with a grade school, a library, a couple of banks, small arcaded stores selling carpets and fruit, some donkey carts, and a few sheep and goats. The company provides swimming pools, and the shore provides two skimpy beaches.

Kharg has no farmland and only brackish water, so most food comes in by airplane, and fresh water comes from gas-fired plants that desalinate the briny sea. Despite these limitations, the islanders gobble up vast quantities of the best imaginable cucumbers, lettuce, eggplants, radishes, peppers, broccoli, tomatoes, and cabbages. These vegetables are grown in a two-acre plastic greenhouse designed by the University of Arizona and managed by a green-thumbed Englishman, who amid his beautiful edibles seemed to be the most contented horticulturalist on earth. The plants grow in a foot of sand, fed on a scientific mixture of nutrients and desalinated water, which is distributed through pinholes in hoses. The purpose of enclosing this garden is to keep the vegetables cool and humid, which is accomplished by fans that suck in air through radiators wet with sea water.

Life on Kharg is tolerable and healthy, except for the disease called "island fever." Because a big population would strain the water supply and otherwise "burden the infrastructure," the company will not allow employees to import any family except spouses and children, which bucks the Iranian desire to be surrounded by collateral relatives. One staff man told me that "Kharg is good for wives, because their husbands can't misbehave, and good for husbands, because their wives can't bring in in-laws." No tourists may visit, either. To cure island fever, company planes shuttle all employees, and their families, to the lovely mountain city of Shiraz. Each family gets off the island four times a year, for four days each time. The National Iranian Oil Company joint venture called Iran Pan American Oil Company, which runs one of the offshore fields, employs only bachelors, and gives them an entire week in Teheran after two uninterrupted weeks of twelve-hour days in the island. Sailors on the tankers that call at Kharg are not permitted, out of fear that they might be saboteurs, to go any farther ashore than the landward end of the jetty, where the United Seamens Service has a club.

Twenty years ago, near Qom in central Iran, far from the existing oil fields, an out-of-control exploratory well spewed oil three hundred feet into the air for eighty-two days, creating a large lake complete with waves that beat upon its shore—until the flow suddenly stopped. In the Caspian Sea, whose coastline Iran shares with the Soviet Union, the Russians are exploring for oil from a big offshore rig. In the northeast, not only Iran but also Afghanistan produce gas. These three facts are portents that Iran may yet contain a lot more petroleum. Even as Iran makes contingency plans for when it runs out of oil, it can hope for more.

Two factors suggest, though, that revolutionary Iran may never export oil in the quantities that the Shah did. First, Iran can't find new oil, or even produce old oil at full capacity, without Western technology and technicians, who for years will be wary of working there. Secondly, the whole idea of setting production to Western needs and buying Westernization with the dollars earned runs against the new Moslem tide. The Arab nations, too, have noted the Iranian example and are growing cautious of producing all-out. For the United States, the Iranian revolution seems to spell serious, long-term inflation and an ever weaker dollar.

13

Industrialization—So Far

❋

Not much mentioned in news accounts of the turmoil that came with the fall of the Shah was the fact that Iran is—as a consequence of the Shah's Western-oriented goals and dictatorial determination—the most industrialized of the Moslem countries. Besides oil and petrochemicals, it has steel, copper, hydroelectric and thermal power, an auto assembly industry, telecommunications, machine-tool capacity, airlines, arms factories, modern textile mills, and a great array of light industry. The purpose of industrialization is not only to produce goods for Iran but also to provide exports to earn foreign exchange after the oil is gone, thus preventing Iran from slumping back into a primitive economy.

But the industrialization of Iran has been planned and carried out so inefficiently, wastefully, and rapidly that by and large it is not productive enough to provide competitive exports. The country needs a government that can face up to and solve this problem. Religious leaders don't seem to be the men for this job, and the future of industrialization in Iran is one of the country's touchier questions.

The stenciling on the packing cases, the lettering on the engineering plans, the labels on the office doors—all are in Cyrillic, the alphabet of the Russian language. Here and there, you see broad Slavic countenances among the numerous narrow Iranian faces. This is the Aryamehr Steel Mill, built by the Soviet Union in exchange for Iranian gas—the heavy-industry showcase of Iran, apart from oil.

A half-hour drive southwest of Isfahan, Aryamehr stands on three square miles of land in the tawny valley of the Zayandeh River; abundant water, so rare in Iran, is a major reason for the choice of the site. Steel-making came late to Iran, and it came hard. Western nations refused to help. And although the gas-for-mill deal with the U.S.S.R.

was economically sound, it was an organizational nightmare. The construction, begun in 1967, threw together, on the banks of the Zayandeh, Russian metallurgical engineers who could not speak Persian, Iranian metallurgical engineers (a rare species) who could not speak Russian, the country's entire supply of Russian-Persian technical-language translators (five of them), and a work force of mostly illiterate and unskilled laborers from nearby farms. But some of the Russians learned Persian, and some young Iranian engineers went to the U.S.S.R. for training. By rail, the Soviet designers sent in plant equipment worth $286 million, mostly from Russia but some from East Germany, and six years later the mill was built.

Many of the Shah's foreign critics liked to label his development plans "grandiose," but what makes more sense than to trade Iranian gas for a mill that uses Iranian iron ore and Iranian coal to make steel for the Iranian market? Aryamehr gets its coal by rail from near Kerman, 440 miles east, and its ore from Bafq, 340 miles east on the same line. The mill's product is mostly reinforcing bars, I-beams, channels, and other construction shapes, for a market that reached 2.2 million tons in 1973, double that in 1975, and might reach 12 million tons in 1983. When the mill finally got going, after embarrassing delays that were eventually solved by importing West German coal to form one tenth of the mix for proper coking, it produced 600,000 tons of steel a year. Then its engineers, by now mostly Iranians, constructed a second blast furnace, twice as big as the first, from Soviet-supplied parts, and raised capacity to 1.9 million tons; in 1985, after two more furnaces are put up, Aryamehr supposedly will be able to produce 8 million tons a year.

When I visited Aryamehr early in 1976, it was operating two rolling mills, each one kilometer long, and the earth was being turned up over a huge adjacent area for more rolling mills. Nearby, a by-product unit, fired by gas, was making ammonium sulfide, sulfuric acid, and benzene for the petrochemical industry. I saw the thin red-yellow stream of molten iron pouring from the blast furnace. Big Mack trucks pulling long trailers hauled the finished products away to all parts of Iran.

Three miles from the mill, but cut off from it by a range of hills, stands the all-new city of Aryamehr, built for steelworkers and the service people whom the mill attracts. In contrast to the low, mud-walled village of rural Iran, this modern town shoots into the sky with five-story, ten-story, and seventeen-story apartment buildings, as well as with a ten-story hotel and a three-story motel. Newly planted pines provide a green belt. When I saw it, Aryamehr held about 70,000 people, but it is growing toward an eventual population of 300,000.

The cost of the city, the mines, and a pro-rata share of the railroad reportedly pushed government expenditure for Aryamehr to $1 billion, which makes the true cost of production high. Talking to me over lunch at the Engineers Club (a green spot beside a lake made by damming the river), one executive argued that "our income is not only from steel sales but also from the intangible assets of training. We have a big turnover in labor, and that is exactly the aim of the government—workers learn skills here and take them to where they are needed elsewhere. In fact, we run a formal school, a training center for seven hundred students." Besides, as they say in third world countries, "The most expensive kind of steel is the kind you don't have."

Big as it may grow, Aryamehr may ultimately constitute less than half of the Iranian iron and steel industry. With the deliberate intention of creating competition for Aryamehr's parent, the National Iranian Steel Company, the government established the National Iranian Steel Industries Corporation to exploit the new technologies whereby natural gas combines with ore to make iron. In a conventional blast furnace, hot air rises through a bed of burning coke to strip oxygen atoms from iron ore and make it into molten pig iron, suitable for use in open-hearth or basic-oxygen furnaces to make steel. In the new gas-reduction technology—developed in Canada and described by *Fortune* as "the next revolution in steel manufacturing"—gas combines with iron ore in hot revolving kilns to produce pellets of sponge iron suitable for electric steel-making furnaces without melting the ore. In 1977 the Shah inaugurated one of the world's first gas-reduction mills, built by Kaiser Engineers at Ahvaz for more than $600 million, and eventually capable of producing 2.5 million tons of sponge iron a year.

If all proceeds according to the original plans, by 1983 the new company will be running a similar-size mill at Bandar Abbas, and a smaller one near Isfahan. The new company's mine at Gol-e Gahar, south of Kerman, will fill the needs of the Isfahan plant and part of the needs of the Bandar Abbas plant, but the rest of the ore for the two Persian Gulf mills will come from Kudremukh, in India, where Iranian money is financing a new mine. When all the new mills are in production, Iran may turn out as much as 15 million tons a year (for comparison, the U.S. produces 136 million). Iran will have steel to export, earning revenue to replace some of that to be lost as the oil gives out.

Steel is basic, steel is sinew, steel is the without-which-nothing of industrialization. In the three-sector Iranian economy, steel symbolizes the *modern and future sector,* as against the engine of change, the *oil sector,* and the backward agriculture and carpet-making of the *traditional sector.* The modern sector's potential is significantly greater than that of all the oil-rich Arab states together. Iran has more than oil: it has size, it has other mineral resources, and (in contrast to other oil countries, such as Saudi Arabia) it has sufficient population.

Iran got moving about 1960, when oil revenues hit $285 million a year, and the government began to encourage import substitution—that is, the local manufacture of goods previously imported—by raising tariffs and lending money to entrepreneurs. Real gross national product grew an average of 11 percent a year (as compared to 4 percent in the United States), rising from $4.5 billion in 1960 to $26 billion in 1972. Then came the surge in the price of oil, and in 1977 GNP reached $68 billion. Official projections in 1977 said that it would touch $180 billion by 1985. High oil revenue let Iran invest in development without any such inconveniences as belt tightening, high taxes, foreign-exchange shortages, loss of reserves, or even the sacrifice of production of consumer goods in favor of capital goods. By 1975, with demand high for local and imported manufactures, the government could drop the import substitution policy, ending most bans on imported products and decreasing tariffs.

Such growth means that each individual Iranian's share of GNP, if it were divided equally, rose from $225 a year (about the same as Peru's) in 1960 to $2,220 in 1977, and on form would reach $4,500 in 1985; for comparison, America's per-capita GNP in 1976 was $6,441. "Obviously we must not deceive ourselves," the Shah said a few years ago, going on to point out the dominance in the GNP of oil, which uses little labor, over other labor-intensive industry. As a result, the per-capita income is high, but a large gap lies between the incomes of the rich and the poor, and only a tiny middle class receives incomes somewhere near the per-capita GNP. Moreover, through the 1960s and early 1970s, the gap actually grew—that is, the rich grew richer faster than the poor grew richer. According to the Iranian economist M. H. Pesaran, in 1974 the top 10 percent of households spent 38 percent of all money that went toward household needs, while the bottom 10 percent spent only 1.37 percent of the total. But since 1973 the gap has begun to close. And as Pesaran points out, even while the gap was widening, the incomes of the poor were rising, so that "the number of people below the poverty line in Iran has been declining." And Iran has already overcome the desperate kind of poverty of India or Egypt. Rarely does a beggar or an importunate peddler approach you in the street. This is the kind of backward economy where such conveniences as aluminum foil and detergent from plastic bottles are taken for granted by most people.

Pinning an exactly descriptive label to Iran's economy is difficult.

A long-time American adviser to the Shah mulled the question a moment and told me: "Public-sector management—maybe that's it." The economist Ali Fekrat observed that "the government has moved into center stage in leading the economy and in providing expanded social and economic service." Whatever the tag, though, the elements are clear. Heavy, basic industry belongs to the government; light, diversified marketing business and industry belong to the private sector. Steel, copper, aluminum, oil, electricity, railroads, airlines, telecommunications: these, said the Shah, "must be put at the service of all the people, and remain in their control." The government guides; private enterprise follows.

The government's main tool for guidance is the Plan and Budget Organization, which fills a palatial building on a hard-to-find small street near the Parliament, and utilizes the largest computer bank in the Middle East. Economic planning appalls laissez-faire capitalists in the United States, who see to it that the American government practices no such iniquity. But Iran finds no objection to copying the Soviet Union in respect to planning, at least, and the Plan Organization is a big factor in the life of anyone connected with business, industry, or government.

Abol Hassan Ebtehaj, a prominent Iranian banker, brought planning to Iran in the late 1940s when he was governor of the Bank Melli (the word means "national"—Bank Melli was at that time Iran's central bank). Ebtehaj ardently desired to rev up Iran's economy, and pulled in a group of American firms organized as Overseas Consultants, Incorporated. They proposed spending $58 million a year—all of Iran's then trifling oil revenues plus loans from President Harry Truman's Point IV aid program—for seven years toward specific development goals. The planners managed to expand cotton, tea, and sugar beet crops, build two cement factories, fight malaria, and construct roads, but overall the First Seven-Year Plan was a flop, because of administrative bottlenecks and Mossadegh's annihilation of the oil industry.

Ebtehaj himself took charge of the Second Seven-Year Plan (1955–1962), and the fur began to fly. Revenue from oil started to flow again, and the Plan Organization got 60 to 80 percent of it. Ebtehaj's widespread friendships among international bankers, such as Eugene Black of the World Bank and John McCloy of Chase, helped Iran get loans of $363 million, raising the Second Plan's total funds to an ultimate $1 billion. Ebtehaj built missing-link railroads which connected Teheran to Tabriz and Mashhad. He paved 1,700 miles of highway and constructed an equal length of secondary roads. "There was a Ministry of Roads, but it didn't build roads," Ebtehaj told me, with a chuckle. "The foreign bankers could not understand that. But I finally got them to see that if roads were to be built, the Plan Organization would have to build them. And we did." It it astonishing now to recall how unconfident many Iranians, paralyzed by centuries of national nonprogress, felt as recently as twenty years ago. When Ebtehaj proposed to build a dam on the Sefid River in northwestern Iran, local engineers, remembering earlier washouts, pronounced the task impossible. Ebtehaj not only had difficulties in hiring foreign engineers; he even had problems in hiring competent foreign advisers to tell him what foreign engineers to hire. Yet in the end, dam-building became the major accomplishment of his regime. The dam across the Qaraj River assured Teheran of the water and power needed to let the capital grow. The dam on the Sefid irrigated 940 square miles and generated more power. And before the end of his term, Ebtehaj got construction going on the dam across the Dez River in Khuzistan.

The Third Plan, spanning five years in the middle 1960s, spent $2.7 billion of mostly oil money in a much more integrated way: this was when the pipeline, steel, and petrochemical industries began to grow and fall into relationship. Moving more than before into social areas, the planners built schools and fought illiteracy. The Fourth Plan, with $10 billion to spend, advanced in heavy metallurgy, water conservation, electric power, domestic use of natural gas, and agribusiness—plus roads, ports, airports, dams, and housing.

The Fifth Plan, running from 1973 to 1978, started out with the unthinkably ambitious goal of investing $36 billion over five years—and within a year, after the price of oil went up, raised the target to $70 billion. Its sweeping goals were "to improve living standards and incomes, particularly of low-income groups; achieve continuous, balanced growth with minimum inflation; improve social services and spread social justice; protect the environment; distribute manpower resources more evenly; spread scientific knowledge and technology; increase domestic production and industrial imports; invest surplus foreign exchange abroad to create new sources of wealth for the post-petroleum era, and preserve and promote the national culture and heritage."

Abustle with economists, sociologists, horn-rimmed administrators, and typewriter-pounding secretaries, the Plan Organization weighs and balances its goals and then prepares the government's budget. In the $42-billion budget for the Iranian year 1978–1979, for example, the various goals received allocations as follows: economic development, $17.2 billion; the military, $10 billion; health, education, and welfare, $8.5 billion. Of the development funds, electricity got one fourth, followed by industry, oil, transport, and agriculture.

With such big goals, it seems, come big bloopers. In the windfall year of 1975, after oil income had risen from $4 billion to $16 billion, the planners managed to produce a government deficit when actual revenue fell below planned revenue by what the prime minister called "a miserable few billion dollars." The Plan Organization drew down criticism for insufficient stress on agriculture, communications, and literacy; for deficiencies in contingency planning; for waste, white elephants, and pet projects. Worse, its largely foreign-educated staff were what one Iranian sociologist called, in Persian, *masachuseti*—technocrats who might have graduated from Massachusetts Institute of Technology. Masachuseti, he thought when I talked to him, were homogenizing Iranians, neglecting religion, relying too heavily on bureaucracy, and were, in fact, Marxian in their faith in planning, growth, centralization, change, and preference for cities over villages. They were cold people, he told me: "They think about Iran as they would think about Ghana or Guatemala. Quantification is everything. Too much 'macroeconomy.' The horrible traffic in Teheran shows that they are wrong. I'm very happy about the traffic. It may bring down the technocrats." Certainly the Plan Organization's way of thinking was a major cause of the revolt against the Shah. There may never be a Sixth Plan.

High on a mountain not far south of Kerman, in central Iran, there lived, in the middle 1970s, a group of families from Butte, Montana. What Butte has in common with Sar Cheshmeh is that both sit on mountains of copper ore. The Anaconda Company, developer of Butte one hundred years ago, was the major consultant to the Iranian government's Sar Cheshmeh Copper Mining Company, which is about to begin producing 142,000 tons of blister copper a year, enough to put Iran among the world's half-dozen biggest producers.

In full operation, Sar Cheshmeh will form another of those surprising Iranian new towns, with 25,000 people in brick or prefab houses—"Copper City." About a third of the production of the mine and smelter will go for Iranian industry (wire, plate, tubing), with some of the fabrication right at the mine site. The rest will go down a yet-to-be-built railroad to the port of Bandar Abbas, and earn Iran about $200 million a year as an export.

At Sar Cheshmeh and in five other regions, scattered from one end of the country to the other, Iran has 400–450 million tons of copper ore. Its wealth in this mineral is only a small part of what's in them thar hills. There have been hints of this wealth for many centuries. Out on the dreaded Dasht-e Kavir desert, at Anarak, miners have long extracted silver, and more recently nickel and lead. A maze of galleries in the mountains near northeastern Nishapur has for ages yielded some of the world's finest turquoises.

Until two decades ago, Iranian mining technology consisted of a pick and a shovel in the hands of a man. Now lead, zinc, and chromite are mined by machinery on a big scale, and the government is building a large lead-zinc smelter. Bafq, source of Aryamehr's iron ore, has proved to have chromite, too. Coal, already plentiful around Kerman, has lately been found in big deposits where Iran bulges into the Soviet Union east of the Caspian. Iran also has gold, salt, lime, phosphorus, gypsum, marble, alabaster, clay for brick and firebrick—plus topazes, emeralds, sapphires, and carnelians. A couple of years ago, prospectors found at least 30 billion tons of coal in the supposedly worthless Kavir desert.

Iran also has uranium, at Anarak and near Hamadan, Isfahan, and Yazd. Someday this mineral may become a major source of Iran's energy, but the revolution put a stop to the construction of four nuclear reactors that the Shah had ordered.

"I'd like to know what kinds of problems are bucked up to you on a typical day," I said to Abol Gasem Kheradjou, managing director of the Industrial Mining and Development Bank of Iran (IMDBI), the largest private enterprise in the country. "What sort of things have you had to deal with since you came to work this morning?"

Kheradjou leaned back in a comfortable chair in his hushed and modern office. "Since this morning? Well, we talked about the glass industry, and furniture, and silkworms, and paper, and"—he brightened at the thought—"chickens! In Iran chicken-processing has not been very advanced. Chickens are killed by a man with a cleaver—beheaded." He made a throat-slitting gesture. "But we have a project, with the Agricultural Development Bank, to mechanize and modernize the whole process—killing, plucking, cleaning. Fifty thousand a day. All clean and healthy. I found it fascinating. This job I have is more interesting than any hobby. Very creative."

A man of massive jaw, deep eye sockets, and a big, heavy body, Kheradjou had for years been at the turbulent storm center of Iran's private sector. Born sixty years ago, he was the son of a merchant who died three years later. Kheradjou learned accounting and worked at the Bank Melli in the 1940s when Ebtehaj was governor. When Iran nationalized oil, Kheradjou became director of finance for the National Iranian Oil Company. During a year with the Plan Organization, he set up the government's Industrial Credit Bank. Then he put in a spell with the World Bank in Washington, where his work in the Far East Department gave him a chance to learn how Japan modernized itself. His English is more than fluent: he is a speech-maker with a flair for bringing out the drama in banking, and he was heard with attention in Delhi, New York, or Tokyo.

In action, IMDBI has been bold and freewheeling. Once again one sees how primitive Iran was only a few years ago, and how fast it has changed. In 1949 Iranian banks were reluctant to lend money to anyone who did not have at least an equal sum on deposit. To break into modern finance for private industry, the government contracted with Lazard Frères and Chase Manhattan to found IMDBI, matching 60 percent of equity from Iranian investors with 40 percent of their own. The contract, and with it foreign guidance, eventually ended, and Kheradjou came in as managing director. Iranian investors ultimately bought out all the bank's shares except 13 percent (which is owned by a score of foreign banks ranging from Chase to Barclays to the Bank of Tokyo). Selling shares presented a problem: Teheran had no stock exchange. So in 1968, Kheradjou and others plunged in and created one. Now nearly six thousand Iranian individuals and institutions own shares of IMDBI. Besides its capital and reserves, the bank's resources, totaling nearly $1 billion, come chiefly from World Bank loans, Government of Iran loans, and Eurodollar loans.

Before World War II, industry in Iran consisted of little more than a cement mill, a couple of sugar mills, and a few textile mills. Now the country has thousands of big enterprises, but most prominent among them are eighty-five large-scale operations promoted by IMDBI. Their products range from automobiles, diesel engines, elevators, bicycles, and water meters to asbestos, foundry sand, glucose, school milk, aluminum foil, poplin, blue jeans, and motion pictures. By spotting Iran's needs and opportunities and initiating industries to fulfill them, the bank made itself the architect and bulldozer for progress in the private sector.

As Kheradjou saw it, Iran in the late 1950s had most of the ingredients needed for its own small *Wirtschaftswunder:* stability; a growing, energetic, young population; an increasing flow of university graduates; a rising market; a base of roads, railroads, and electric power; unexploited natural resources; and a moneyed government eager to get the country moving. "Yet because of Iran being a late starter, the legal, professional, and institutional infrastructures were inadequate and slow-developing for an emerging industrial society," he said. Into this vacuum moved the bank. Its philosophy was to accept a contract with the government to promote private industry, but remain a private bank, which meant borrowing heavily from the government for resources while keeping the government out of day-to-day control of how the loans were used. "We are a client of the government because we borrow from it, and we are agents, or trustees, for the government, but we deal only with private companies, and we take care to make a profit," Kheradjou told me. "The government wants to provide incentives for business, credit being one and tax and other exemptions another. We give the credit."

But credit, for IMDBI, was more than loans. The bank actually bought shares in many of the new industries that it helped to start, and kept them through the start-up stage, when they yielded no dividends. This meant that the bank had to make itself expert in dozens of fields. "We have engineers of all kinds, analysts, economists—we're more like technical consultants here than a bank. A new enterprise in a new industry faces as many hazards as a newborn baby," said Kheradjou.

It was hectic: "The bank had to learn to run before it learned to walk." IMDBI made many mistakes. The annual reports are full of stories like: "Due to a technical defect in the kiln, poor quality chinaware was produced and was sold below cost and consequently the company incurred a loss." But the net effect of the effort was an unexpected success.

"Rising incomes and fast growth not only caused quantitative changes, but also brought about those qualitative changes that usually require decades and generations," Kheradjou said in one of his speeches. "Customs and habits changed; so did markets. An enormous market for durable goods, which usually develops at a much later stage of economic development, came very much sooner. Cars, televisions, refrigerators, air conditioners spread fast, especially in towns. Servants became scarce and ladies emancipated and, as a result, many kitchens as centers of food processing ceased producing and a market for processed food developed sooner than expected.

"Many artisan-type industries, which use essentially manual labor and little mechanization, began to be replaced by factories. Flour, biscuits, beverages, conserves, dairies, textiles, shoes, bricks, and other construction materials which were made by hand in little establishments were replaced. People began to travel much more and demand entertainment. The market for services grew at a pace one has seen only in advanced industrial countries."

Iran did not, however, leave industrial development entirely to IMDBI and the private sector. The government's Industrial Development and Renovation Organization sponsored thirty-seven important companies which make many products new to Iran: machine tools, modern oceangoing ships, power-transmission towers, insulators, and so on. One place where this industrial revolution is startlingly evident is the northwestern city of Tabriz, the setting seven hundred years ago of meetings of caravans from China and Europe. Though it dropped out of the world's attention in the thirty years since it was the site of the Soviet Union's attempt to bite off the surrounding province of Azerbaijan from Iran, Tabriz has grown in local fame as the engine-builder of Iran.

The prime mover for this new career is the fourteen-year-old Tabriz Machine Tool Plant, a large and lavish industrial complex designed to play mother to other factories. The plant can produce ten thousand tons a year of drills, pumps, lathes, milling machines, compressors, and presses, but it was built to be not so much a factory as a facility that would induce foreign firms to manufacture machinery in Iran. The plant could supply parts, training, design, foundry and forge services, and sophisticated machining, saving incoming industries from many start-up problems. Gould-Century of Chicago, for example, was in the mid 1970s making more than 200,000 electric motors, of up to 15 horsepower, a year, using foundry products from Tabriz Machine Tool, as well as graduates from its vo-tech school. Like other industries spun off by Tabriz Machine Tool, Gould inaugurated production in the mother firm's factories while building its own plant not far away.

Tabriz Machine Tool cost $70 million to build, $15 million of it in the form of a loan from the Czechoslovakian government, which also supplied licenses and technical advice. Czech-designed goods proved hard to market, and the plant had to spend money training the unskilled labor to be found in and around Tabriz, so production as late as 1974 ran at only 20 percent of capacity, and losses were—and are—heavy. Such are the bumps on the road to industrialization.

With the machine tool plant as a magnet, Tabriz came to house all of Iran's important engine-building factories. They included a Daimler-Benz venture that put together 12,000 diesels a year, mostly for the buses and trucks that Benz assembled in Teheran. Dorman Diesel, a joint venture with the British company, assembled stationary engines, much needed all over Iran for deep-well water pumping and electric power generation in remote places. British Leyland provided engines for its truck and bus assembly plant in Teheran. SKF of Sweden moved the Tabriz Industrial Zone into the business of manufacturing ball bearings.

A sort of sister to Tabriz Machine Tool (and like it, owned by the government's Industrial Development and Renovation Organization) is the Tabriz Tractor Factory. Its original collaborator, providing a loan and technology, was another Communist government, Rumania. This factory imported or assembled most of Iran's 33,000 tractors, but then Tabriz Tractor called in Canada's Massey-Ferguson to help increase production (Iran needs 200,000 tractors) and make more of the parts, including engines, in Tabriz.

Industrialization has pushed Tabriz's population to 599,000, making it Iran's fourth city (after Teheran, Isfahan, and Mashhad). Many of the immigrants are country men, drawn by good industrial wages, who leave their families on the farm. Several thousand are—or were until the revolution—foreigners: "guest workers" from the Philippines, technicians and managers from the United States, Britain, Germany, Sweden, Czechoslovakia, Rumania. But the influx cosmopolitanizes a city not quite ready to be cosmopolitan. At the Tabriz Club, a gymnasium of a room which doubles as the city's concert hall, the "best" families still gather at noon on Fridays to address one another in flowery language and consume large and solemn meals of sheeps' brains— an engagingly provincial scene. And on the streets women wear veils clutched so tightly sometimes as to reveal only a single eye. Thus Tabriz is a classic case of modernization straining tradition, and quite naturally it was one of the first cities to explode in the Islamic revolt.

Banking, apart from IMDBI, is another Iranian business that has progressed spectacularly because it started so low. How low is the point of a story that Kheradjou loves to tell, "one of those folk stories we all had to read as little boys.

"A small merchant going away had to deposit a hundred kilos of iron with the town's trustees; he was our merchant banker, you know. Upon his return he demanded the iron, and the trustee claimed that unbeknownst to him, a mouse had had a nest in his storehouse and had regrettably eaten all the iron. The merchant left in silence, but on the way out took with him the little boy of the trustee. The next day with an outcry he came to the trustee and claimed that he saw a vulture carry the boy away. 'How could a vulture pick up a big strong boy?' asked the trustee. 'If a mouse can eat a hundred kilos of iron, a vulture should be able to carry a ten-kilo boy,' said the merchant. He got his iron."

To the Koran, charging interest is immoral—an issue raised anew in 1979—and Iran had no banks at all as recently as 1889, when the British established the Imperial Bank of Persia. The first locally owned private bank was not founded until 1950. By 1975, thirty-five banks were doing business in Iran—such potent institutions as Bank Bazargani (the first private bank), Bank Sepah (the army bank), Bank Omran (the Shah's bank), and, on every street and in every village, Bank Melli. Twenty-five of them were straight commercial banks, including twelve with foreign partners, such as the ever-growing International Bank of Iran and Japan, a collaboration with the Bank of Tokyo. The other ten were specialized banks, like IMDBI or the Mortgage Bank. All told, the banks had eight thousand branches. Between 1963 and 1975, they managed to increase deposits from $643 million to $12.6 billion. In June 1979 the revolutionary government took control of the management of all banks.

In some respects banking remains disconcertingly backward, apparently because Iranians mistrust one another so much. "The system is too new to inspire confidence," a professor of business told me. The signatures of four bank officials are commonly required for cashing a check. At Bank Melli's main office I watched an unfortunate woman spend three quarters of an hour, while tellers spun their handcranked calculators, to cash a check for £1.85 drawn on an English bank. The jailing of debtors has been ended in Iran (though only in 1974), depriving banks of an effective means of collecting debts, so now when lending against real estate they insist on taking possession of the deed. Banks still largely shun consumer credit, computer accounting, certificates of deposit, trust accounts, branch-bank lending, and interbranch check cashing.

The institution that took on the task of nudging Iranian banking toward greater sophistication and social conscience is the Bank Markazi, the Central Bank of Iran. It was created, like Eve from Adam, out of the Bank Melli in 1960, when Bank Melli found that its burdens as a commercial bank and as a state bank had grown too heavy. The Central Bank took over government accounts and the issue of currency—a singularly glamorous obligation, since the main security for bank notes is the state collection of crown jewels.

The unit of currency that these gems support is the rial, which stayed close around seventy to the dollar for many years. After the revolution, its value sank as low as 115. In everyday parlance, Iranians often use the ancient unit of currency *toman,* which means ten rials.

Apart from chaos, discourtesy, mayhem, and occasional manslaughter, the most striking characteristic of automobile traffic in Iran is the uniformity of the cars. In any given vista, more than half of the vehicular population consists of four-door, four-cylinder compacts bearing a charioteer emblem and the odd trade name of Paykan, meaning "Arrow." Like amoebae under a microscope, bright-colored Paykans crawl, dart, squirm—and proliferate—in every street. Even most of the taxis are Paykans. The Paykan looks amazingly like the 1967 English Hillman Hunter, for the excellent reason that it is the licensed made-in-Iran copy of that car.

The maker of the Paykan is the Iran National Vehicle Manufacturing Company, and it got its start producing buses in 1964. Britain's Rootes Group, maker of Hillmans, then helped Iran National set up a car assembly line, and in 1967 the company turned out the first 6,654 Paykans. Since then Iran National, expanding desperately with IMDBI loans to keep up to the demand, has raised production to 130,000 a year. At first the car was merely assembled in Iran, but more and more parts are now manufactured in the country; an engine-making plant went into operation in 1974. The Paykan is now about 65 percent (by weight) native Iranian. Iran National's growing factories, together with its workers' town, dominate a long stretch of the highway just west of Teheran.

But Iran National has not had the field all to itself. Until the revolution zapped it, General Motors Iran assembled the Chevrolet Nova, the Buick Skylark, and the Cadillac Seville. Renault assembled its R-5 at 60,000 a year, and Mercedes-Benz, British Leyland, Volvo, and Mack all put together large trucks. The auto industry came to employ 10 percent of the Iranian labor force. The government nationalized all these companies, along with most of the rest of large-scale private industry, in the middle of 1979.

Who ever heard of the great industrial city of Ahvaz? Twelve years ago, certainly, no one could have thought of Ahvaz that way, for it was only a sleepy little place, the provincial capital, to be sure, but the manufacturer of nothing. But in 1967, working at first with imported steel plate, mills in Ahvaz began rolling pipe for the gas line then being built between Khuzistan and the U.S.S.R. The government, and private enterprise, added mills to make plate from billets, and the National Iranian Steel Industries Company inaugurated its remarkable gas-reduction mill to make sponge iron from ore imported from India. Together with the plants of the Ahvaz Pipe Manufacturing Company (an affiliate of the National Iranian Oil Company) and the Ahvaz Rolling and Pipe Company (which makes steel strips and small-diameter pipe as well as oil and gas pipelines), Ahvaz now has a large and integrated steel industry. The biggest project lately has been the manufacture of 800,000 tons of 48-, 52-, and 56-inch pipe for the now-canceled second trans-Iranian gas pipeline to the Soviet Union.

Further blessed with petrochemical supplies from nearby Abadan and Bandar Shahpur, as well as oil and gas from Khuzistan fields, Ahvaz now makes detergents, paints, drilling mud, ceiling fans, iron sheets, asbestos products, construction steel, sugar containers. Three big breweries produced most of Iran's beer until the revolution made that drink a no-no; another plant pasteurizes 150 tons of milk a day. The city's machine shops make parts for oil industry operations. A new English factory can manufacture anything from heat exchangers to pressure vessels, and a new silo stores 100,000 tons of wheat.

Yet with all its industry and its 329,000 people, Ahvaz has not quite grown into a cosmopolitan city. Palms in the squares and arcades to shade the sidewalks make Ahvaz seem a little like some drowsy town in Paraguay. On one street I saw a public typist, set up on the sidewalk to compose letters for illiterates. The downstream end of the Karun River, broad and muddy at this point, slices Ahvaz in two. In the third century, the Sassanians built a bridge here that lasted until its bricks went into the piers of the fine arched bridge of the Trans-Iranian Railway. As in Tabriz, the clash of the old and the new gave Ahvaz some of 1978's worst riots.

About a hundred miles downstream, the Karun flows into the Shatt-al-Arab, the estuary of the Tigris and the Euphrates. Just north of the confluence sits Khorramshahr, Iran's major port. Concrete quays line the bank of the Shatt-al-Arab for miles, with the ships of all the world, sometimes two abreast, moored against them. When I was there, Bulgarian trucks were loading crates labeled "Komatsu" and "Mitsubishi" for transport to interior Iran. Across the river is Iraq, seen here as palms and jujubes and a few one-story mud buildings, with people strolling on the bank. Even in times of tension between Iran and Iraq, the river people manage to get along, crossing in small boats without passports and speaking a mix of Persian and Arabic. Dhows with high stems and sterns ply the estuary, together with small naval vessels and tugs that can take barges up the Karun as far as Ahvaz.

The meanders of the river's mouths cut the green delta into many islands, and one of the larger of them is the site of Abadan (population 296,000), the refinery town built by the English around 1912. A bungalow city with green hedges and shade trees, Abadan looks, as Londoners always remark, like Hampstead Garden Suburb. With a shock one realizes that unlike all the rest of Iran, this is a city without walls, except for those surrounding the enormous refinery. The business of the city is blowing in the wind: the naphthous stink of petroleum refining. Big signs on streets near the refinery read NO SMOKING ON THIS ROAD. When not afflicted by the torrid heat of spring, summer, and fall, Abadan can become a trifle cold; I saw frost on a car one morning in January, and noticed a man who—in the thin-blooded way of tropical people—had dressed himself in a military greatcoat and a face-mask type of knitted helmet. As at Khorramshahr, in Abadan you can stand on the riverbank in front of the refinery and stare at Iraq, 200 yards away.

The idea of spreading the ownership of the means of production is one that wins at least token applause in all the capitalist nations. It seems to be a good answer to Marxist theory, and the stock market provides a mechanism for disseminating shares. Mutual funds, small-scale stockholding, investment of pension and union funds in stock— all these developments are interpreted as proofs that the owners of wealth want the rest of the people to have some of the profits. Even so, enlightened capitalists in the West would balk if the government forced them to share their wealth with others.

In 1975, the Shah decided that precisely this idea would earn him gratitude and support from the workers of Iran. He called the plan his Share Participation Program. Three hundred and twenty important manufacturing companies, predominantly owned by single families or similarly narrow groups, were forced to agree to sell 49 percent of their shares to their employees. If employees did not opt to buy all the shares, the stock had to be offered, first, to farmers, and then to the general public. "Family ownership is turning into public ownership," crowed former Central Bank head Hassan Ali Mehran.

In this Pahlavian version of the social contract, what Kheradjou called "a high-powered committee of ministers and representatives of the private sector" determined the value of a given company's stock on the basis of profits and prospects. To provide stock for their employees to buy, most company owners increased the stock issue, since they did not wish to part with their own shares, and welcomed the capital to be gained from selling the newly issued shares. Each employee could buy as much as $7,500 worth of stock, but most of them did not have that much cash, even if they used their profit-sharing bonuses, usually the equivalent of two or three months' pay, to buy stock. For workers with no cash, the government would lend as much as $600 at 4 percent for ten years, to use in buying stock. Dividends in Iran are customarily high and sometimes fabulous—your money back in one year. So dividends could in ten years ordinarily pay off the loan's capital and interest and leave a little profit to boot. A worker could sell his stock if he owned it free and clear—that is, after the loan was paid off.

Daily, when I was in Teheran, I read of companies that, biting the bullet, agreed to worker participation: Rey Spinning and Weaving, General Tyre and Rubber, Sepenta Industrial (pipes), Aladdin Iran (heaters), B. F. Goodrich, Melli Industrial Group, Kerman Cement, Pak Dairy, Marvdasht Sugar. One leading industrialist told me: "This will integrate the classes and head off the clashes." When he offered 20 percent of his firm's stock to workers, all of them bought some, and altogether they took the whole offering. "We're happy the workers took it because it stays in the company family. And Iranians take good care of whatever they regard as their own."

But the reality was quite different from this kind of euphoria. With Iranian cynicism, workers thought the plan some kind of trap. If the Shah had wanted to appeal to them, he could have freed their unions and called off his secret police, who swarmed through factories in search of "Communists." The Shah also lost the businessmen. To them, letting workers into ownership was just as revolutionary as land reform had been to landlords a decade earlier. They grumbled that the government underpriced stock to make it advantageous for workers to buy.

Despite official reassurances that their 51 percent of shares of stock preserved their power to manage, they feared that eventually the worker-owners would use their voting rights to elect representatives to the boards of directors.

My story of Iran's recent development in oil and industry sounds as though it were smooth and straightforward. But even apart from the great disruptions of 1978, the process has been ragged, halting, counterproductive, and afflicted with mortal growing pains. The country suffers appalling shortages—shortages of skilled labor, of water, of cement, of housing. Fate rains down disasters: a couple of years ago the French supplier of generators for Khuzistan's Reza Shah the Great Dam installed machines so defective that Teheran and the western half of Iran, counting heavily on this new source of power, suffered calamitous blackouts and factory closings. The black market price of a telephone hit $4,500 (but if you get one you can dial direct to Europe and the United States). SHORTCOMINGS IN HOSPITALS UNCOVERED, says one newspaper headline. CONSTRUCTION TIMETABLES WERE WRONG, says another.

Businessmen are depressed, enraged, baffled, and crabby. They fight foolishness and frustration, ignorance and incompetence, venality and red tape. They admit that Iran has advanced by comparison to its lowly beginnings, but they cry that it remains light-years from its goals. And Iran *is* an irrational place. A man who was angry at paying sixty rials a kilo for oranges in Teheran (so the story goes) drove seventy miles out of the capital to a warehouse in an orange-growing oasis, there to be told that the price was ninety rials a kilo. "Why higher than in Teheran?" he exploded. "Because Teheran is so far away," came the answer. (In point of fact, Iran lacks market towns, and much produce is taken to big cities to be graded and priced and sent back to where it came from.)

The main problems are bottlenecks—bottlenecks, ironically, of everything but money. The most painful bottleneck is the one that restricts the movement of goods. The most important and enduring is the lack of skilled labor and trained manpower. And these limitations are made worse by corruption, profiteering, and pollution. "Our oil revenue increased too fast to absorb and administer," one banker told me. "You can only eat as much as you can digest."

An abundance of jobs is an enviable problem, far less painful than the perennial unemployment in the United States. Nevertheless, Iran's manpower shortfall forms a serious obstacle to its growth. The Plan Organization says that Iran needs 560,000 skilled and semiskilled workers, 16,100 engineers, 22,600 doctors and nurses, 57,400 teachers, and

41,600 technicians. Though unskilled workers are what Iran has the most of, it still needs 10,000 more common laborers. The government has played with the idea of importing all the workers the country needs, and in practice has brought in thousands of Asians, including Vietnamese technicians, Pakistani truckdrivers, and Filipino airplane mechanics. One day at a big industrial plant in Teheran I glanced into the cab of a huge truck and noticed that the driver's features were Oriental. "Korean," the plant manager explained; in fact, there are three thousand Koreans in Iran, including many engineers and technicians.

> "You embarrass me, agha. I am discountenanced by your kindness."
> He quietly put the money in his drawer. "This was really not necessary.
> I am always at your service anyway."

This small scene from F. M. Esfandiary's novel *Identity Card* celebrates the ancient, courteous, and universal Iranian custom of "sweetening the mouth," of getting *pul-e cha'i* (tea money)—in plain words, of taking a bribe. In Iranian government and business, as many as twenty signatures are required to issue a check or put some order into effect. In theory, this prevents one crucial individual from demanding a payoff; in practice it often means that twenty individuals can open their desk drawers, stroll away for a moment, and return to discover that someone has thoughtfully deposited some bills within.

The periodic pileups at Iranian ports are partly the result of shady business. During a crackdown on profiteering, the government was likely to rule that merchants must not mark up goods more than 15 percent over the wholesale price as shown on the customs declaration. But customs declaration cost is often less than the actual cost, because merchants bribe shippers abroad to "underinvoice" (falsify the price) in order to reduce customs duties and cheat the government. Perceiving that a 15 percent markup will not bring a retail return even as large as the real wholesale price, merchants refuse to collect imports from docks, adding to the congestion.

The extortion of tea money takes many forms. "When you get a bill from a customs broker, it generally contains one item frankly labeled 'Bribe for inspector,'" an Englishman living in Tabriz told me. A businessman who proposed to open a drugstore in Shiraz reported that he had had to pay $100,000 "just to get to talk about a license." But not only government officials are guilty of bribe-taking. In business, as another Englishman explained it to me, "the boss has a bully-boy number-two man who collects money to get the boss's signature on a letter that somebody needs for a deal. The boss's bank account keeps growing, and he pretends he doesn't know why." Bribing does not necessarily get the promised results, however. Long ago, Vincent Sheean wrote of a conversation he had with a former Soviet ambassador to Teheran. The ambassador said that he had "come to the conclusion that Persia was 'fundamentally sound.' Asked to give the reasons for this view, he found an almost unanswerable one. 'They will take money from anyone,' he explained, 'from the British today and the Russians tomorrow, or from the French or the Germans or anybody else. But they will never do anything for the money. You may buy their country from them six times over, but you will never get it. Therefore I say that Persia can never go under. Persia is fundamentally sound.' "

Understating profits in order to dodge income taxes is commonplace. In facilitating the sale of stock to workers, the government priced shares partly in proportion to profits, so that a low declared profit resulted in a low value for shares. Hundreds of chagrined companies thereupon pleaded for a chance to declare their true high profits. In any case, "collecting taxes is hard because of the psychology that oil should pay for everything," an American expert, who was counseling the Iranian government, told me. "There's no beautiful Internal Revenue Service here." When oil revenue went up, tax rates went down. It may be hard for Americans or Europeans to imagine light and benevolent taxes, but Iran's Plan Organization says, with a straight face, that one of its goals is to "develop taxes into an important source of Government income" and use "taxation as an instrument to achieve balanced economic growth and fairer distribution of income." About one fourth of Iranians now earn enough to have to pay income taxes, compared to 2 percent a decade ago, and in 1979 taxes provided 24 percent of government income.

14

Farming the Desert

❊

Under the Shah, Iran turned from a net exporter of food to a net importer, and this fact, seeming to be stunningly irrational, helped powerfully to bring him down. In fact, it is something of a bum rap (as is the charge that his land reform was a sham). The truth is that Iran's agricultural output has grown, but its population and per-capita caloric intake have grown faster. Like industrialization, the development of farming in recent decades has been chaotic and ridden with mistakes—the chief one being to make the cities magnets for people who could have stayed on the farm. But the farm scene in Iran can't be painted all gray; it has to be painted in colors that make distinctions.

The scene is mostly dry dust and camel's-thorn. High humidity worsens summer temperatures as high as 131 degrees Fahrenheit. The population is only two million. But Khuzistan, the coastal plain (so uncharacteristic of plateau Iran) at the head of the Persian Gulf, is Iran's richest province—rich in oil and gas, rich in access to the sea, rich in new industry, and (most surprisingly, in consequence of modern development) rich in water and soil and agricultural produce. Aboil with change and development, this province symbolizes a main theme of Iran in recent times: fast economic growth in unlikely places.

Khuzistan, though only about as big as Arkansas, is something of a nation to itself—always has been. Here lived the Elamites, those shadowy people of unknown provenance who more than 4,500 years ago gave birth to a civilization that vied with Sumer. In Achaemenian and Sassanian times it was the land of the tribe called Khuz, whence its present name. Khuzistan was a walkover for the Moslem invaders, and when the rest of Iran Persianized Islam a couple of centuries later, Khuzistan remained mostly Arab in population and Arabic in language. Arab nationalism was strong in Khuzistan in the 1920s, and after Reza

Shah's abdication the Arab tribesmen there returned to their old dress and nomadic customs. The British, then dominant in what is now Iraq, played with the idea of annexing Khuzistan; later Egypt's Nasser claimed Khuzistan for the Arabs. The Shah's interest in developing Khuzistan came partly from his desire to bind it firmly to Iran. The province's new farms and industries draw Iranians from the plateau; now more than half the population is of Persian, Turkish, Kurdish, or Bakhtiari descent. A few years ago, the first Iranian-style teahouse opened in Ahvaz, Khuzistan's capital, and the schools now teach in Persian only.

The earliest power center in all Iran was Susa, the capital of Elam. The newest form of enterprise in Iran is agribusiness, symbolized by the vast sugar plantation founded by Hawaiian Agronomics International in Khuzistan. I found it instructive that ancient Susa (including the French-run archaeological dig there) is now surrounded by the plantation of this agribusiness. Khuzistan is a cradle and an engine: the earliest site of civilization in Iran, and powerful present-day producer of food and petroleum. The people of Isfahan say, smugly and all too often, that "half the world is Isfahan." A more accurate perspective of the Iranian universe might have it that "half the world is Khuzistan."

In 1956, having launched work on Iran's first significant power dam over the Qaraj River near Teheran, the banker Abol Hassan Ebtehaj, then in charge of the Iranian economy, began to ponder a much larger project in the mountains of northern Khuzistan. About that time, he happened to attend a World Bank meeting in Istanbul, and at the Hilton Hotel he ran into David Lilienthal, architect of the Tennessee Valley Authority. Ebtehaj forced Lilienthal to listen to an account of Iran's development plans, and invited him to Iran. Lilienthal, then chiefly occupied as a consultant in Colombia and Brazil on behalf of his own Development and Resources Corporation, was cool. "Many countries invite me but don't really want me," he told Ebtehaj. He agreed to go to Iran only if the Shah himself invited him.

Back in Teheran, Ebtehaj hurried to the palace. The Shah, about to leave for the airport, was waving away half a dozen petitioners, but to Ebtehaj he said, "Come with me to the airport." As the Shah drove the car, Ebtehaj proposed Lilienthal as consultant on the Khuzistan project. "Lilienthal? Excellent!" said the Shah. "No other person in the government then would have known who Lilienthal was," Ebtehaj remarked to me.

Lilienthal and his partner Gordon Clapp, another former TVA chairman of the board, arrived in early 1957 and right off attended a

briefing by U.S. aid officials, arranged by Ebtehaj. "The experts, to my horror, said that nothing could be done with Khuzistan," Ebtehaj recalls. "The place was too hot, they said. Lilienthal replied that the Imperial Valley in California got hot, too. They objected to the salinity in the soil and rivers. He said, 'There's salt everywhere.' I became convinced that the Khuzistan project was dead. But that afternoon at a cocktail party for Lilienthal, he told me, 'This is what all the experts said about TVA.' He said, 'Don't worry about what experts say.'"
Lilienthal went to the dramatic, box-walled canyon of the Dez River in northern Khuzistan, reachable then only by horse, and a week later sent Ebtehaj a telegram of enthusiastic approval. Among other evidence that impressed Lilienthal were the "Darius canals" on the northern Khuzistan plains—former irrigation ditches, built in actuality not by the emperor Darius but by the later Sassanian kings. Clearly visible from an airplane, they showed that the Iranians of about fifteen centuries ago had made this desert bloom.

Ebtehaj, as Eugene Black once remarked when he was chairman of the World Bank, was a "dedicated, enthusiastic man. He is a live wire. He is a difficult fellow. He makes a lot of enemies." Enthusiastically Ebtehaj persuaded Lilienthal and Clapp not only to consult on the Khuzistan project but to carry it out—"one of the gravest and most extensive and unusual responsibilities two Americans ever had in a country not their own," wrote Lilienthal later. Soon the two ex-TVA men selected a dam site and started the engineering. Ebtehaj appealed to the World Bank for a construction loan. The bank balked, ruling that its own engineers would have to validate the project. Turning into a difficult fellow, Ebtehaj somehow found $10 million to build an amazing tunnel road that spiraled inside solid rock from the bottom of the dam site to the otherwise inaccessible top—a prerequisite to construction. Perceiving that Ebtehaj had committed Iran to the Dez dam, the bank caved in and financed most of the ultimate cost of $68 million.

The resulting dam is, at 666 feet, one of the world's dozen highest and the fountain of Khuzistan's agricultural prosperity. Moreover, it proved the paradoxical utility of large dams in this land of few rivers and little rainfall. The less the supply of water, the more it must be conserved. Now fifteen large dams back up irrigation water in Iran, and most of them generate power as well. Only one regulates more water than the Dez dam, and it, too, is in Khuzistan: the great dam, completed in 1977 on the Karun River only a few miles from Masjid-e Sulaiman, site of the first oil discovery. Five more new dams are rising in other parts of the country. (But that difficult fellow Abol Hassan Ebtehaj had nothing to do with the newer dams. In 1961 he

made a speech in San Francisco that contained a little implicit criticism of the Shah, whereupon he was thrown in prison for seven months
on trumped-up charges that were later withdrawn. After that he stayed
out of government and until his retirement headed a large bank in
Teheran.)

Taking their cues from TVA, Lilienthal and Clapp provided not
only a dam but also a Khuzistan Water and Power Authority to distribute the dam's boons. Five hundred and twenty thousand megawatts
of electricity go out through high-tension lines just like the ones in
Tennessee, some to the national power grid and hence to cities like
Teheran, but most to the new industrial city of Ahvaz.

KWPA's more important job has been to channel Dez water to
farms, which involves building canals and leveling land. This task
went slowly, though it has dragged even worse in the case of other,
newer dams in Iran. But now broad, concrete-lined canals, some of
them following the routes of those built long ago by the Sassanians,
carry sparkling water to hundreds of miles of ditches, which spread
it over 209,000 acres of plains south of the old Sassanian city of Dezful
in northern Khuzistan. In the Zagros Mountains, which loom over the
plains, you can see the snow that will melt into more water to make
the desert productive.

The results of pouring water on the desert look miraculous. Riding
along one of the busiest highways in Iran, one sees pure green to the
horizons, broken only by the blue-green of the water in the canals.
One singular success is the Haft Tappeh Cane Sugar Industrial Company, started by KWPA, transferred to the Ministry of Agriculture and
Resources, and now sold off to private investors. This area, at a latitude
of 32 degrees, lies at the northernmost edge of the world's cane-growing
zone, but Haft Tappeh produces 60 tons of cane a year per acre, as
compared to the 30 tons a year of Louisiana plantations. Iranians love
sugar—drinking quantities of tea through a lump of sugar held between
the teeth is an important source of nutrition. Consumption runs around
850,000 tons a year, and Haft Tappeh by itself supplies 100,000 tons
of it, grossing $40 million—equal to more than half the cost of building
the dam that supplies the water. Haft Tappeh uses water in phenome-
nal quantities: 2,400 pounds of water for every pound of sugar that
comes out of its Dutch-built refinery, one of the most modern in the
world. The water goes mostly to leach from the land the salt left by
the growing cane; whenever Haft Tappeh puts new land into production, it must first make the area flat as a table and install clay
tiles deep in parallel trenches, in order to drain all this water away.

By providing *bagasse* (cane fiber) to the nearby Pars Paper Company plant, Haft Tappeh also supplies Iran with copybook paper, toilet
tissue, and corrugated box liners.

To see huge shimmering fields of sugar cane in the desert is amazing enough, and yet the conditions are such that this area can also grow sugar beets, usually a cold-climate crop, for a refinery in Dezful. Along with the sugar crops grow grains and vegetables and citrus fruits. You often see women in bright dresses harvesting endless fields of broad beans. Beside the watercourses, contorted jujube trees provide their plum-like fruit, as well as firewood and a leaf which, dried and soaked, is the key ingredient of the local shampoo.

But appearances can be deceiving, and the actual results from agribusiness in Khuzistan are mixed. Both the Haft Tappeh cane operation and the 40,000-acre sugar beet plantation run by Hawaiian Agronomics (a division of Honolulu's C. Brewer & Co., Ltd.) made profits until the revolution when Hawaiian Agronomics pulled out. "They make more sugar grow in Khuzistan than they do in Hawaii," banker Ebtehaj remarked to me. But several other companies scored flat failures. I saw hundreds of acres of cotton reduced by insects to bare stems, representing the fate of a company called H. N. Agro Industry of Iran and America. Iran California, backed by the Bank of America and Honolulu's Alexander & Baldwin, Inc., flopped and reverted to another of its investors, the Iranian government. A British entry, Iran Shellcott Company, had to back off and reorganize, returning much of its land to the government.

For an assessment of all this I visited Mehdi Samii, then head of the Agricultural Development Bank of Iran. "Agribusiness has not yet succeeded for many reasons, not one major factor," Samii told me. One difficulty was choosing crops. The possibilities were numerous— sugar, cotton, alfalfa, vegetables, citrus, grains—but it was anyone's guess which crops would best match the virgin soil (which lacks organic matter and minerals; both must be added) and the summer climate ("dry and O.K. for humans, but hard on plants," L. C. Cochrane, an American agronomist, told me). Another problem was scale. "We made the mistake of allotting too much land to some companies," says Samii, adding that "what works in a microplot experiment may not work in a macroplot." Foreign agronomists discovered some strange facts about the desert. "Weeds!" one of them exclaimed to me. "We said, 'Let's get rid of the weeds—they're too competitive.' Then we discovered that killing weeds killed trees. The weeds were drawing up moisture to the roots of the trees." A third obstacle was land-leveling: Khuzistan looks like a plain, but irrigation by flooding requires that many a small mound or rise be flattened—"more costly than anticipated," says Samii.

Most of agribusiness's land came from the bank, but as public land it had been used for grazing by villagers, who hated losing it. And as newly titled beneficiaries, they also resented being hassled to labor on corporate farms under foremen brought in from the Philippines or Korea. Cane cutting fell mostly to the poor Arabs. "If you've lived in self-sufficiency, you think any change is for the worse," Cochrane noted. But whether for better or worse, wage earning ($4.50 to $6 a day for shovel workers, $450 to $500 a month for welders or tractor drivers) brought change. Nowadays you see village men mounting motorbikes to ride off for fun in Dezful, which is their idea of a city. And some former subsistence farmers, perceiving and adopting the virtues of modern farming, have put their land into lettuce to make $5,000, $10,000, and in one case $40,000 a year.

Watering the desert in northern Khuzistan has changed the face of the land—and it may change the weather, too. One hears speculation that the planting, plus the evaporation that comes from pouring fifteen feet of water a year on the earth, will cool this whole area. If so, agribusiness will have accomplished on a grand scale what local farmers have been doing for centuries. Their walled and shaded orchards create a cool microclimate in which plants that would otherwise burn up prosper famously.

One of mankind's most astonishing inventions, unique to Iran, is the qanat, or underground irrigation canal. Thirty centuries or more ago, the Iranians discovered that water could often be found not far below the surface just where the mountains started to rise. Taken to flat land miles away, it could make the receptive desert soil bloom—it could "extend the sown over the sand," in somebody's felicitous phrase. But when they tried to move the water in ditches, it evaporated before it arrived.

The answer of these diligent and clever early farmers was to move the water in tunnels, dug by men. The technique was to sink wells a hundred feet or so apart along a line leading from the foot-of-the-mountain source to the fields that needed water. Then the excavators connected the bottoms of the wells with a continuous tunnel, exquisitely engineered to have a slight downward gradient from source to outlet. The wells served for the removal of the excavated earth, which the tunnelers raised in buckets and piled up in a ring concentric to the well mouth. After the last stretch of tunnel was punched through to the spring, cold clear water poured through the qanat, sometimes to be led onto the leveled fields, and sometimes to become the raison d'être of a cool, palmy oasis, growing dates and citrus fruits and melons, all green to its walled borders, where, in a ruler-edge transition, the tawny sands of the desert would begin again.

From an airplane, you can still see qanat well mouths, like rows of doughnuts, wherever good desert soil lies near a mountain. They delineate thousands upon thousands of miles of qanats, often crisscrossing, some ancient and caved in, as you can tell from the eroded dirt heaps and the filled-up wells, some freshly dug and pouring water at their lower ends. You reflect that for the Iranians, farming has mostly been more like mining, and that in these flat and sunny deserts millions of men have spent the better part of their lives underground.

The qanat is therefore more than an amazement: it is also a symbol of the colossal difficulties that have always confronted agriculture in Iran. The country's most intractable problem is that it cannot feed itself, even though two fifths of the working population are farmers. Though largely desert or steep mountains, Iran possesses 47 million acres (out of a total land area of 358 million acres) of potentially productive land. About a third of this land is cultivated (and about half of this third is irrigated); another third is pastures; the other third is fallow or unused. Two thirds of the cultivated land grows wheat or barley; the rest produces mostly rice, cotton, sugar beets, soybeans, tobacco, sunflowers, or fruits. Of the nation's 2.5 million farmers, 2.2 million work small plots (average size: 5.5 acres) at subsistence level or not much above it; only 320,000, working on mostly mechanized farms of 45 acres or more, are essentially in the business of growing food for others rather than for themselves. Farms produce only 15 percent of the gross national product, and per-capita income on farms is only $250 a year, compared to $2,220 for the country as a whole. The place where one finds poverty in Iran is on the farm.

Poor and unproductive though they may be, the bulk of the farmers are in one respect far better off then they were as recently as 1963. In that year the ownership of cultivable terrain in Iran was still just as feudal as it had been for centuries, three quarters of the land being held by landlords (mostly absentee) and the rest by the crown, the state, and religious endowments. Landlords counted their holdings in wholly owned villages, which provided housing for the serflike sharecroppers, protection for them from bandits, and an organizational unit for such communal work as digging qanats. Some landlords owned hundreds of the 67,000 villages; the Batmangelich clan boasted that its combined holdings were bigger than Switzerland. Each peasant farmed one or more tracts, defined as what one team of oxen could cultivate. The landlords bought and sold their villages—the central government confined itself to trying to collect taxes. The produce of farming was regarded as requiring five inputs: land, water, seed, oxen, and labor. The crop was accordingly shared five ways, and the landlord, always providing land and water, and usually seed and oxen, took from two to four fifths. The sharecropper's income ran about forty dollars a year, and he often had to submit his daughters to the landlord's *droit du seigneur.*

The tenure of land in Iran remained, as then-Minister of Agriculture Hassan Arsanjani put it, "a system from the Middle Ages." This system persisted for a built-in reason: the same landlords who benefited comprised 50 to 60 percent of the deputies of the Parliament, who had coerced their oppressed peasants into voting for them. Even in 1960 they had managed to abort land reform by passing a weak, self-serving law. "We are facing the reactionary front which has wasted fifty years of the parliamentary regime and has now confronted us with the choice of a 'red' or a 'white' revolution," said Arsanjani. "If the country remains in its present state, it will explode." In 1961, for reasons unrelated to land reform, the Shah dissolved this intransigent parliament, and while it was out of session decreed a real land reform, drafted by Arsanjani. The new law let each landlord select and keep one village, but compelled him to release all holdings beyond that to the peasants actually tilling the land. The government bought the released land at prices equal to ten times its annual revenue, and resold it to the peasants who were actually tilling it, allowing them to pay for it in fifteen annual installments.

The express purpose of land reform was to smash feudal landlords and emancipate their sharecroppers, and it worked. The proportion of land sown and cultivated by its owners rose from 26 percent in 1960 to 78 percent in 1972. The number of peasant farm owners tripled. "The peasant's horizon," says the land reform expert Ismail Ajami, "broadened into a growing identification with the nation and her affairs."

At first, landlords were furious. They neglected or even sabotaged qanats. They lost power. The succeeding parliament contained not landlords but farmers, land reform officials, and even civil servants. The Shah blamed the murderous riots of mid 1963, and the attempt against his life at the Marble Palace in 1965, on dupes financed by landlords. But the landlords began to soften when in the "second phase" of land reform the government gave them the option of renting their land to its cultivators, or joining the tillers in establishing farm corporations. The landlords also got first dibs at buying government-owned factories (built to get industrialization started in Iran) with the proceeds of the sale of their lands. "My father used to own three villages," says the scion of a former landholding family. "Now he owns three factories." I met a woman whose husband had lost his land in the reform, forcing them to sell their twenty-three-room house in Teheran and take jobs. It turned out to be the best break of their lives. He got a position teaching, something he had always yearned to do. She got a government job, and broke happily out of the overly sheltered life of the old-fashioned landed family.

In sum, the Shah's land reform, terminated in 1976, was no upset revolution, as in China. Indeed, the provision that lets them keep one village leaves many landlords still rich in land, particularly because they kept the best swatches. Yet the Shah successfully got much land into the hands of the men who work it, and he also achieved an ulterior objective, which was to break the political power of the rich landlords and strengthen himself. But land reform did nothing for about one fourth of the rural population, the paid farm hands, then and now poor and landless.

The reform was undoubtedly the vital sociopolitical first step toward greater agricultural output, but in the short run it has also been a hindrance. Greater output comes largely from farming on a scale big enough to let the farmers utilize machines. This means that newly titled small landholders have to throw in together in some larger organizational unit, and at least until lately they have mostly balked at doing so; to them that seemed like losing the land they had just gained. As a result, the government has felt obliged to leave the new proprietors to their own devices. Most of the governmental effort to raise agricultural production in the late 1960s and the first half of the 1970s went into agribusiness, such as those sugar plantations in Khuzistan; compared to agriculture, industrialization and militarization in Iran have received unfairly large shares of government investment.

As agriculture has stagnated, the nation's needs for food have grown at 8 to 10 percent a year; that is, in proportion to the growth of population multiplied by the higher per-capita consumption brought about by affluence. (The Iranians also waste lots of food, as anyone can discover if he is willing to peek into garbage cans. Good form at parties requires setting out far more food than the guests can possibly eat.) Once a net exporter of foodstuffs (chiefly specialties such as pepper, dates, cardamom, saffron, and ginger), Iran now must import 30 percent of what it eats—a percentage that rises every year. Though Iran raises a respectable 4.7 million tons of wheat a year, it must import a million tons more. It also imports meat (including mutton), chickens, rice, barley, citrus fruit, sugar, and 8,000 tons of eggs, all at a cost of about $1 billion. "It was a shock to me when we started buying American grapes," one farm expert told me, perhaps thinking of the Persian vineyards celebrated in the *Rubaiyat.* "Not to mention," he went on, "milk, cheese, butter, and apples."

Part of the problem is that a case can be made for the subsistence farmers and their traditional ways. It is true that with scythes they take days to cut as much grain as a combine can harvest in one pass. They thresh by tossing the grain in the air, leading one critic to wonder whether they do not expend as many calories in muscular energy as they gain in threshed grain. They may not even eat well. "These people are concerned about what they are going to eat not next week but *tonight,*" said L. C. Cochrane. Worse than that, subsistence farmers contribute little or nothing to feeding other Iranians.

Yet this humble and ancient kind of farming, symbiotic with the cruel land, succeeds well on its own terms. Behind the mud walls of the peasant's house there are compassion, security, roots. Women chop and gather brush to make fires for baking bread just as women did two thousand years ago. In big families, the young take care of the old. One woman told Cochrane that she had 117 cousins in the vicinity. Nomads in Khuzistan still move north to the cool mountains of Luristan province for the summer, the old people on horses, crates of chickens on the donkeys. Just before they return in the fall, the nomads plant a crop of winter wheat. While it grows untended, the people winter in black tents on the Khuzistan plains. When spring comes, they return to the mountains and harvest their grain.

One essential component of the subsistence farmer's life is the fat-tailed sheep. This slovenly animal looks nothing like the well-crimped Australian Merino or the snowball-shaped Rambouillet, but neither of these aristocrats would suit the Iranian sheepherder in the least. The secret is the tail—literally a hunk of fat weighing as much as thirty pounds. The fat tail is an asset in two ways. It stores nourishment so that the sheep can live for days without pasturage if necessary. And it displaces the fat in the mutton, making the meat less "sheepy" and more agreeable to the human palate. The fat-tail storage process suggests that the sheep has an efficient digestive system, and in fact it can live on about two thirds of what an American sheep eats. The fat-tailed sheep grows poor wool and not much of it, but the villagers manage anyway to make it into good carpets that supply them with cash. The sheep also provides milk; the women put some of it in a sheepskin pouch and punch it until it turns to butter.

Shepherds take turns grazing sheep; on a given day one villager gathers all his neighbors' animals, drives them to pasture, and returns them in the evening—no one seems to have any trouble telling which sheep is whose. The shepherds—many of them boys or girls—swathe their heads in colorful cotton cloth against the heat, and carry Biblical-looking crooks. Incidentally, villagers also raise a lot of camels, not for transport but for meat. Much meat used in commonplace stews or in ground form throughout Iran comes not from cattle but from camels.

Because subsistence farming preserves some admirable human values and harmonizes with harsh natural realities, many agricultural experts, pondering ways to increase farm productivity, advocate building on this base. Obviously, small farmers have got to begin growing more than just enough for their own needs. Obviously, these farmers should get the benefits of more water, power, fertilizer, credit, technical assistance, and mechanization, as well as schools, health care, market roads, and consolidation of remote villages. But their ancient wisdom and way of life may not necessarily have to be uprooted in the process. "Modern technology should be adjusted, tailored, and adapted to the agrarian structure in Iran," wrote Ismail Ajami, at the end of a 1975 study on "modernization of peasants." The village, contend its advocates, with missionary zeal, is an economic unit with an organic life of its own.

Working with all these factors—the immutability of the traditional farmer, the shortcomings of agribusiness, and the need for more food to reduce dependence on foreign sources—the Iranian government has tried various compromise forms of agricultural organization. By the terms of a law signed by the Shah in June 1975, small-scale farmers have lately been encouraged—with a zeal that amounts to coercion— to join twenty large "agricultural poles" that are supposed to supply big-scale efficiencies while letting farmers keep land titles and have a voice in determining crops. The law assumes that farmers are now ready to abdicate some of their independence for a promised sevenfold rise in cash income (even under landlords, tenants used to collaborate in working on one another's fields). By the terms of this plan, Iran's 67,000 villages were to merge into 30,000, each with enough population to justify clinics, piped water, schools, and access roads. In short, the agricultural pole is supposed to preserve the values of village life, but in bigger, better-serviced villages. Remaining self-employed landowners, rather than corporate hired hands, farmers are supposed to benefit from economies of scale, mechanization, technology, and low-interest bank loans.

Apart from the "poles," which were set up on Iran's most fertile land, farmers have in recent years been induced to join cooperatives; Iran has not only a Ministry of Agriculture and Resources but also a Ministry of Cooperatives and Rural Affairs. The nation's 2,800 co-ops get various government services, but their main function is to supply cheap credit through the Agricultural Cooperative Bank of Iran, jointly owned by the co-op unions and the government. Besides co-ops, a few thousand farmers have joined to form sixty-five farm corporations, each man relinquishing his title, recollectivizing the land, in return for shares in the company. These farmers get wages and share profits.

Finally, in spite of the failures, new agribusinesses have been started not only in Khuzistan but elsewhere, with lavish government incentives: low-cost leases, tax and customs exemptions, access roads, price supports, and assistance in feasibility studies, land leveling, irrigation, and drainage. A big agribusiness at Dasht-e Mogan is a joint venture of Iranians and Russians. Another, at Dasht-e Morghab, produces tomato sauce at the rate of eighteen tons an hour.

The various kinds of big-scale commercial farming—agribusinesses, corporations, "poles," and cooperatives—now control a quarter of Iran's irrigated land. But experts doubt that all the present efforts will make Iran self-sufficient. The use of fertilizer, even though the petrochemical industry can supply it, remains backward; Iran simply has not achieved a green revolution. Available water is, and probably always will be, a major constraint. "The most optimistic of us do not believe that even in 1990 we will be able to grow more than 80 percent of our food," banker Samii told me.

I could see, traveling around the country, that distinct regions present distinct successes or distinct problems. Azerbaijan, for example, one of the better-watered parts of Iran, with 13 inches of rainfall a year and an average elevation of 4,600 feet, is a breadbasket of grain and an abundant producer of grapes, almonds, and deciduous fruits. Many tractors roll across the land, but still most sowing, fertilizing, and harvesting are done by manual labor. Hired hands get six dollars a day plus board and room, and they are hard to find. Combining hamlets into New Villages has been going ahead fast, giving the farmers the benefits of banks, agricultural extension agents, good water, and even kindergartens for their children. Bone-jolting roads are being turned into smooth highways. With disposable income, many farmers are able at least once in their lives to fly to Mecca on the Moslem hajj.

By contrast, the farming area far to the east called Sistan is still suffering from troubles that began in the fourteenth century when the place was invaded by Tamerlane, the Tartar from Samarkand. In the course of his brutal devastation he was particularly fastidious about destroying Sistan's ability to grow food. In this area the westward-flowing Helmand River, greatest stream between the Tigris and the Indus, pours all its life-giving water into an emerald lake in the basin at the lower end of a large steppe called the Sistan Depression. This propitious place is one of Iran's cradles: mythology says that Rustam lived here, and Zoroaster used it as a refuge. Men started constructing caravanserais in Sistan fifty centuries ago; mounds representing their dissolved remains dot the landscape. I walked up, through shards of ancient pottery, to the top of one of them, Shahr-e Sokhta, where archaeological excavations have revealed charred roof beams and well-preserved straw mats. In Sistan the Achaemenians built a sacred edifice resembling the treasury in Persepolis, and the Sassanians built a dam on the Helmand that fed canals to irrigate the fertile delta land.

Tamerlane's name means Timur the Lame, and he got the wound that lamed him in a battle to subdue Sistan. From the silk brocade tent in which he habitually lived, this giant of a man, white-haired from birth, decreed Sistan's destruction, and saw to it while taking revenge that the dam was leveled and the ditches destroyed. Sistan never regained its ancient state of development, particularly the vast irrigation system, although in later centuries farmers around the lake managed to use the Helmand's waters sufficiently to grow grain and sugar and sustain 200,000 people. In the meantime, the Sistan Depression came under divided jurisdiction, the western two fifths, including the lake, going to Iran, the rest to Afghanistan. A dozen years ago, with American help, Afghanistan built a dam across the Helmand a few hundred miles upstream, diverting water to irrigate the land around it. Though not quite as bad a blow as Tamerlane's, the reduction in the flow of the Helmand wiped out farming in Iranian Sistan, and something like fifty thousand of its people fled to other parts of the country.

Under pressure from the Shah, Afghanistan agreed in 1974 to send more water down the Helmand, admitting that at least some of the water diverted by the dam was wastefully used to turn useless dry land into equally useless mire. (One of the ironies is that Afghanistan has been putting the Helmand's waters onto soil not nearly as fertile as the Sistan land that lost it.) The same year Iran started building a dam on the Helmand River near the Afghanistan border, intended to hold waters that Afghanistan spills over the top of its dam during the March–May flood season. With the new dam go canals that will deliver this water during the summer to the agricultural lands of Sistan. Six centuries after Tamerlane, the damage he did is finally being repaired. Already, using the water Afghanistan has started to send, and anticipating more when the dam is finished, Sistan is prospering, and some of its residents have returned, a move "facilitated" (as the governor of Sistan put it) or "forced" (as one Sistani told me) by the Shah.

I reached Sistan by Land Rover, the standard vehicle of the area, driving north up the washboard road that during World War II carried war matériel from India to the Soviet Union. Politically Sistan is part of the province of Sistan and Baluchistan, and I started from the provincial capital, Zahedan. During the first hours of the trip, while still in Baluchistan, I saw typically Baluchi mountains, some like slag heaps, some like saw teeth, pink and purple and sand color. Once or twice I went through a neat little oasis: palms, ponds, the inevitable gendarmerie station. At a point where the road comes within a mile or two of the Afghanistan border, a pickup truck jounced across the roadless desert from that direction, raising a plume of cinnamon dust. "Dope smugglers," the driver explained; trying to stop them is one of the functions of the gendarmes in this lonely outback.

With sand in our teeth and gravel hammering the fenders like machine-gun fire as the car chewed up the road at eighty kilometers an hour, we headed east from the main route. The land flattened. "This is Sistan," said the driver. We went through miles of low sand dunes, as dry, I thought, as Chile's Atacama desert, where not even microorganisms survive. But this country provides its own subtle kind of relief from monotony. Suddenly, in lightly vegetated land, we were among camels as far as the eye could see, each animal seemingly exercising territorial imperative over about forty acres. The camels eat *tagh,* the "miracle weed of the desert," whose seeds sprout after a single rain and whose taproots penetrate downward for as much as thirty feet to get moisture (at the same time stabilizing the sand). Sistan's camels are dromedaries—this area is too far south for the shaggy, double-humped Bactrians native to cold Central Asia. We passed the remains of a bus that had collided with a car, killing thirteen people. I insisted on stopping to look at a desert dwelling: three mud-brick rooms in a row, roofed by three mud-brick domes, all forming one side of a rectangular courtyard enclosed with mud walls a yard thick. Built into the outer angles of the courtyard were small outhouses: one a kitchen, the other a toilet. Farther on, at the Shileh "river," with not a trickle in it, I saw what appeared to be a lifeboat from an ocean liner. Like most deserts, this one gets a cloudburst every two or three years; the Shileh becomes a torrent five feet deep, and for a day or so cross-country bus passengers have to be ferried across the river.

The country changed again. We were near the Helmand delta, where the river moves in many channels to the lake, called Hamun. Signs of life: cows, goats, oxen plowing a wheat field, a new irrigation canal, a farmer hoeing, sheep, camels, a tractor, trees. The lake was lower than it used to be in winter before the Afghanistan dam was built; around its receded shore grew the kind of reed from which Sistanis make Titicaca-style boats, some big enough to carry a man and a horse.

Some Sistanis hope that more plentiful water, greening the land and ultimately growing some forests, will change the region's climate. In one respect, particularly, the climate could use some change. Summer brings the "wind of one hundred and twenty days," from the north or northwest, and dishes take on a coat of dust between one meal and the next. In the winter, blizzards blow; during March 1905, the wind speed reached eighty-seven miles an hour for sixteen days in a row. Despite the gales, though, Sistan when watered can grow two crops a year.

> Caviar comes from a virgin sturgeon,
> A virgin sturgeon's a very rare fish,
> Virgin sturgeon never need urgin',
> That's why caviar's a very rare dish.

Caviar (if I may be permitted to stray from farm-grown food to fish) comes from the Caspian Sea, and the whole south coast of the Caspian, the "caviar coast," is part of Iran. Climatically, the Caspian littoral and the Iranian plateau are diametrical opposites—it is as though Nicaragua's Mosquito Coast had somehow been welded to Wyoming. From the desiccated, *café au lait* plain around Teheran one climbs to the passes in the Elburz Mountains and then drops vertically downward for two miles to reach a sea, just sixty miles distant from the capital in a straight line, which is not at sea level but ninety feet below it. Gone are the high-plateau symbols that to the world mean Iran: blue-domed mosques, brick houses, deserts, winter wheat, camels. To replace them come resort hotels, thatch-roofed wooden houses with verandas, dense green forests, rice paddies, water buffalo. With the mountains standing like a wall, it has not been easy until recent decades for the people of the highland and the people of this unbefitting crescent of low country to communicate with one another. In some ways culture flowed to the coast across the sea more readily than over the mountains: Bandar Pahlavi, with lace curtains in the windows, hints of Russia; the latticework balconies bring to mind the Alps; the cypress-dotted landscapes suggest Tuscany. The vaulted Persian bazaar never made it over the mountains; on the coast people shop in open markets, amid ducks, geese, and sheep, to buy garlic and onions on strings. One poet called the Caspian "the sad green sea," but to Iranians bred on the plateau, this lush coast is swooningly exotic, delightfully distinct.

The Caspian is the world's largest lake, fed chiefly by the Volga and the Ural rivers in the Soviet Union, and by the not inconsiderable Sefid River in Iran. All this water and more—the lake drops about eight inches a year—evaporates to make clouds that blow south and drop forty to sixty inches of rain a year on the north faces of the Elburz Mountains. Strangely, this water cycle has not yet made the Caspian anywhere near as salty as the oceans, but it does give the Iranian coast the greenest scenery to be found in the whole Middle East. It also makes the air heavy, the vegetation dank, the sky often gray, and the atmosphere humid. Summers are fairly hot, but when fall comes the trees turn color, and once in a while in the winter there is some frost.

Starting from the barbed wire and control towers put up by the Russians at the border in the west, the Caspian coastal plain runs, 5 to 30 miles wide, for 394 miles to "Alexander's Wall," the Russian border point on the eastern shore. Actually built by the Sassanians, long after Alexander the Great, this wall, running 60 miles east across the steppe to the mountains, was supposed to defend Iran from the wild Turkomans; now, robbed of bricks, it is only a low embankment that ends three miles from the sea—a measure of how much the water has dropped. The coastal strip widens near each end, on the west for the extensive paddies that grow Iran's prized long-grained rice and on the east for a little Iranian pocket of The Steppes, the vast central Russian grasslands. In *Persia: An Archaeological Guide,* Sylvia Matheson calls this plain "one of the richest for prehistoric mounds in the Near East." Artifacts 119 centuries old have been found here. Now Turkomans with high cheekbones and slanted eyes live in felt *yurts* on this plain—a Central Asian scene. At the town of Gonbad-e Kavus there's a tower ten centuries old that must rank near the top among those Iranian architectural marvels the world at large hears so little of. Rather like a fluted candle with a snuffer on top, it stands 207 feet high, and has only one window, on the east near the top. This brick tower was the tomb of a local prince, and legend says that his glass coffin was not buried but suspended the equivalent of twenty stories up in the shaft, so that the rays of the rising sun would strike and illuminate the body through the window.

The hothouse summer nourishes tea, sugar cane, corn, cotton, olives, bananas, and citrus fruits. Where the Elburz Mountains rise grow maples, walnuts, and chestnuts; and to the east, in the government-run wildlife park, once a royal domain, the trees are oaks and sycamores. Just as seemingly out of place in desert Iran are the animals: teals and mallards; bears, wolves, and even some tigers; and high up in the range, ibex and mountain sheep. More than three million people, about a tenth of Iran's population, live on the coast, mostly farmers and fishermen. Only Rasht, with 187,000 people, amounts to a city. Bandar Pahlavi, the main commercial port, is also a resort, as are Chalus, Babolsar, Ramsar, and a dozen lesser towns, which also have hotels and sandy beaches. The ambience is not so much Miami Beach or Riviera as Atlantic City or North Sea. Three many-tunneled roads through the mountains, varying from mildly spectacular to wildly spectacular, connect Teheran to these watering places in three to five hours of driving (barring avalanches or accidents). The town of Sari makes silk of sufficient renown that it used to be exported to India, and gave its name to the flowing garment that the women there wear.

And about those virgin sturgeon: they prefer the southern end of the Caspian Sea because Soviet industry pollutes the northern end, so Iranians can fish them easily and produce enough caviar, or sturgeon roe, to fill their own needs and have three times as much left over to export. In fact, it is the Russians themselves who buy a good share of what the Iranians sell. I can scarcely conceive of such a thing as a ton of black fish eggs, all worth a nickel an egg: Iran's two big government-run plants at Bandar Pahlavi and Babolsar produce 220 tons every year, half the world's supply. Fishing by anyone but government operatives in the Caspian is prohibited. The roe comes from the beluga sturgeon, which can weigh a ton and live a hundred years, and from four other varieties.

Until 1952 the Russians dominated Caspian sturgeon fishing, which is why the adjective "Russian" seems to fall so easily in front of the noun "caviar." Russians ran the factories on the Iranian shore, until such colonialism finally became a little too unseemly. But the Soviet Union and Iran have begun to collaborate beautifully in the matter of sturgeon ecology, now that the price of roe is thirty dollars a pound. The two nations have set up five centers to breed fingerlings and release them at the rate of 66 million a year into the Caspian. The fingerlings take fourteen years to mature sufficiently to bear caviar, which constitutes 10 percent of the weight of a spawning fish. In the meanwhile, sturgeon kebab, made from big fish caught primarily for their roe, remains a passably good and indubitably plentiful dish on the Caspian coast.

15

Fire the Gun, But Not Loudly

❊

Oil and geopolitics make Iran perhaps the most strategically important small nation in the world. In recent decades, this has meant touchy relationships with—in approximate order of importance—(1) the United States, (2) the nations belonging to the Organization of Petroleum Exporting Countries, (3) the Arabs and the Israelis, and (4) the Soviet Union.

The first Americans in Iran were Presbyterian missionaries who in 1832 reached Rezaiyeh, near the Turkish border. They opened schools and hospitals, spread through the country, and won authentic respect and gratitude. Jordan Avenue in Teheran honors the most effective of the American educators, Samuel Jordan, who founded Alborz College and ran it from 1899 to 1940. A couple of American finance experts, W. Morgan Shuster (1911) and Arthur C. Millspaugh (1922–1927 and 1943–1945), conspicuously improved treasury and banking operations, and the American soldiers who served in Iran during World War II were welcomed as a counterweight to the British and the Russians, and admired for their gung-ho work on the railroads and highways.

But though American threats saved Azerbaijan from Soviet capture in 1946, the United States and Iran were not really thick with one another until, in 1953, President Eisenhower in effect rewarded Iran for deposing Mossadegh by vastly increasing Point IV economic aid. Iran ultimately got $455 million in grants and $596 million in loans, more than any other Middle Eastern country except Turkey. For the Shah, the price was to have to go along with the "pactomaniac" ambition of Secretary of State John Foster Dulles to quarantine the Soviet Union by encircling it with cold-warring opponents. In the Middle East, this impulse took the form of the Baghdad Pact of 1955, whose members

were Iran, Iraq, Turkey, Pakistan, and Great Britain (in those days
still the protector of the Persian Gulf). Not a decade freed from its
historic captivity by Britain and Russia, Iran found itself willy-nilly
a military front for the United States. For appearance' sake, Dulles
had kept the United States out of the Baghdad Pact, but when Baghdad
itself evaporated from the pact after the leftist Baath party toppled
the Iraqi monarchy in 1958, the United States jumped in openly by
signing bilateral mutual-defense agreements with Turkey, Iran, and
Pakistan. Under Article 2 of the treaty with Iran, the United States
agreed to land troops in Iran (if Iran so requested) to fight back any
Soviet invasion.

Then Dulles went on to demand authorization for the United States
to install missile bases in Iran, as it had in Turkey. Recalling the intensity of the cold war, the power of the Americans over Iran, and the
military logic of Iran as a missile-launching site, one is still astonished
that the United States never got bases in Iran. But although Iran had
been conquered over and over in history, it had never been colonized—
and to Iranians bases represented colonization. To accept them would
bring bloodshed and chaos. Besides, the Russians were frighteningly
enraged at this new American nuclear threat. Even while accepting
millions in American economic and military aid, Iran steadfastly refused the bases—and got away with it.

The Kennedy administration ushered in what Marvin Zonis calls
the "cooling of His Majesty's relations with the United States." President Kennedy's campaign speeches favoring "revolution" had upset
the Shah, who took it as support for his enemies. When the two met
in Washington, Kennedy—though he found the Shah "engaging"—tried
to persuade the monarch to buy fewer arms from the U.S. The USAID
mission to Iran closed in 1967, and the Shah's coronation that year
was in part a signal that Iran no longer needed foreign assistance.
"USAID helped Iran when no one else helped, and when we finished
we got out. It left Iranians liking us—to the extent that they like anybody," a slightly cynical American diplomat remarked to me in Teheran.

Then came Britain's 1968 withdrawal of its forces east of Suez,
and Richard Nixon's Guam doctrine, born of defeat in Vietnam, which
stated that the United States expected small menaced nations to take
a bigger share in defending themselves—and, not incidentally, U.S.
interests. Nixon compounded his error by instituting a policy of "giving
the Shah everything he wants" in the way of arms—leading Americans
in 1979 to ponder the folly of assigning Iran to responsibility for American security in a vital region.

But America needed Iranian oil and Iranian markets, so the Nixon,

Ford, and Carter administrations continued to paint the Shah as a strong and valuable friend. From this policy, so blindly dependent on the fate of one man, came the enormous flow of arms that ended up under the control of people hostile to the United States, as well as the ignominious flight of Americans who ultimately had to leave Iran.

During these years, it became an article of faith among Iranians that Americans owned the country. Actually, U.S. investment there was never high: a mere $217 million in forty-three enterprises. Iran did not want investment; Hassan Ali Mehran, governor of the Central Bank a few years ago, told me, "We are hard to bargain with. Partnerships have to be true partnerships. We admit very few foreign companies with equities of more than 50 percent." Instead the Americans in Iran were there to sell goods and to carry out service contracts.

The largest single business deal in history was a five-year agreement between the United States and Iran to trade $40 billion worth of goods. Under the now crippled deal, Americans sent entire hospitals, a gas-liquefaction plant, road-building machinery, telecommunication equipment, a $65 million housing complex, three quarters of a billion dollars' worth of food each year. Pregnant breeding cows were flown in from South Dakota. Consumer goods poured in; shopwindows displayed Helena Rubinstein cosmetics, Kenmore dishwashers, 3-in-One Oil, Vicks Vaporub.

Most of the sales, though, were to the military, and though Britain armed the navy (with fourteen Hovercraft vessels that can fly across the Persian Gulf in a couple of hours) and the army (with 644 Chieftain tanks that have 1,200-horsepower engines and the world's most advanced fire-control systems), the United States grabbed the rich air force market. The Imperial Iranian Air Force bought 140 F-4 Phantom jet fighters, with smart bombs, 100 F-5s, 79 F-14s, and 491 helicopters, a number of C-130 Hercules transports, six Boeing 747 transports, six Boeing KC-135 tankers, and one Boeing 747 tanker. Letting the Shah have F-14 Tomcats was the Pentagon's most serious error. This swing-wing U.S. Navy fighter, designed to knock down the best of the Soviet planes, the Mig-25 Foxbat, employs the Phoenix missile system. The F-14's secret manuals apparently were stolen during the revolution. The helicopters made Iran more advanced in this kind of gunship than most NATO countries, transporting the Iranian Sky Cavalry Brigade. As with sales, the biggest U.S. service contracts with Iran in the seventies were with the Iranian military: Grumman Aerospace Corporation's for the F-14 and Bell Helicopter International's for the choppers. Each company had two thousand technicians in Iran training Iranians.

The downfall of the United States in Iran came about because

American governments consistently believed in a *non sequitur:* the Shah would not and could not fall simply because it would be awful if he did. The prospect was so unthinkable that as late as August 1978, with rioting long since endemic, the Central Intelligence Agency said in a secret report that "Iran is not in a revolutionary or even prerevolutionary situation."

President Roosevelt freed Iran from British-Russian hegemony, President Truman forced the Soviets from Azerbaijan, President Eisenhower gave Iran $1 billion in aid, and President Nixon fostered the dangerously excessive arming of Iran. President Carter's contribution was to vacillate. Under pressure from Carter, who ran for election espousing human rights around the world, the Shah late in 1976 ordered his secret police to stop torturing prisoners. He freed hundreds of political prisoners; he turned the trials of at least some political dissenters into public proceedings in civil courts, and allowed the accused to pick their own lawyers; he let writers know that they could express themselves more freely, and they began to publish appeals for a rule of law. Logically these measures should have given the Shah's opponents hope. But logic does not reliably prevail in affairs of state. When a once dictatorial government begins to allow some measure of liberty, the beneficiaries ought logically to give thanks and peaceably wait for more; in practice, as de Tocqueville observed, oppressed people given a little freedom angrily demand to expand it at once.

When Carter went to Iran at the end of 1977, he burbled over his friendship with the Shah and forgot to reaffirm his attachment to human rights. To Iranians, this was a signal, a signal of letdown; the first bad riot broke out nine days later. At the end of the year the President was just as ambivalent. Asked if he thought the Shah could survive, he cut down the king by replying, "I don't know. I hope so." Soon a feature of the daily riots in Iran was the shout: "Death to Carter!" The next step in the history of U.S.-Iranian relations, which began with those long-ago Presbyterians, was to learn how to deal with the Khomeini revolution.

In no way was Iran more conspicuously active after 1970 than in forcing up the price of oil in the world. True, the Shah was not the inventor of the Organization of Petroleum Exporting Countries, nor the first to begin raising prices, but he ardently pressed for price rises, and eloquently argued the case for them—starting with his famous caustic demand to the rest of the world: "Why should I let you waste my oil?"

The OPEC cartel was founded in 1960 as a countervailing force against the seven sisters cartel of the world's major oil companies, who had proved in Mossadegh's time how effectively they could cooperate to boycott any oil-producing nation that got uppity. In its first years, OPEC merely negotiated production schedules with the oil cartel, since the organization lacked unity both between Iran and the Arab countries (then still at odds over Nasserism) and between the Middle East producers and such far-off OPEC members as Venezuela and Nigeria. In 1967, after the six-day war, the Arabs embargoed oil destined for the United States and West European allies of Israel, but Iran helped make up the loss, and OPEC's first try at putting up a common front failed. All this time the seven sisters purposely wanted to keep the price of crude low, in order to hold royalties down and to discourage the development of competitive oil fields, such as Alaska's; they made their profits by transporting, refining, and distributing oil. Three factors finally gave the producing nations' political cartel control over the oil companies' economic cartel. First, world market demand rose to equal supply, chiefly because the United States, running low at home, began to import Middle Eastern oil. Second, many independent oil companies, such as Getty and Occidental, began to compete with the sisters. Third, the producing nations, led by Iran and its National Iranian Oil Company, took over ownership of the crude in the ground, and much of the production equipment, through partial or total nationalization. Two days after Egypt attacked Israel in October 1973, the Arabs applied an oil embargo to Israel's friends in the West. This time Iran and the rest of OPEC's twelve nations held firm. The price of crude rose from $3.01 to $10.46 a barrel, and five years later to $13. As a result of these rises, writes the economist Fereidun Fesharaki, "largest-ever transfer of capital from one group of nations to others took place in 1974–75. The total OPEC receipts rose from $23 billion in 1973 to around $90 billion in 1974."

The world is still changing as a result of history's greatest jump in the price of a vital major commodity. No longer does the income to the treasuries of European nations, in the form of excise taxes on a given barrel of oil, exceed the income to the treasury of the nation that produced the barrel. As the most articulate theorist of high oil prices, the Shah chided the Americans: "You have not started to mine your coal mines; you are hesitant in developing your atomic resources; in solar energy not much is being done." But oil now costs enough to have made the Alaska pipeline worth building, and Britain and Norway are at last producing oil in the North Sea. More oil is going into petrochemicals for uses, such as fertilizer, that are probably more valid than burning, and in any case more valuable.

By mid 1979, the price of Iranian oil hit $23 a barrel, raising the value of the nation's reserves to $1.6 trillion. As far as I could tell, all Iranians agree on high-price oil. "The use of oil as an economic weapon is nothing new," said one. "The United States and all nations use their economic power. It's called statesmanship if used by strong nations, and blackmail if by weak." Fereidun Hoveyda, until the revolution Iran's representative at the United Nations, and a novelist as well, recalled that in 1969 the price of a barrel of oil was about equal to the price of a hamburger, a glass of orange juice, and a cup of coffee in any New York shop. "Is it an 'extortion' that we should be able to purchase now four or five hamburgers from a barrel of our diminishing resources?" he asks. Another Iranian pointed out to me that a barrel of Coca-Cola (the food-and-drink image seems to have a strange hold on the Iranians) would cost seven times as much as a barrel of oil.

When an Iranian student gets old enough to specialize in a second language, he rarely considers concentrating on Arabic. His mind leaps over his nation's neighbors to Europe and America, and he chooses English, French, or possibly German. The Arab nations symbolize strife, rivalry, racial difference, ancient conquest, and—with some famous exceptions—poverty. The Arabs are fellow Moslems, yes, but of a less developed theology; indeed, the whole Arab civilization seems not particularly attractive. Out of sheer wariness, there is an extensive diplomacy between the Iranians and the Arabs, and there are many governmental connections down to a fairly low level of bureaucracy. OPEC, too, ties Iran to some of the Arab nations. But cultural links are slender. Travel to the Arab countries is so light that not until 1977 did Iran Air start a direct flight between Teheran and Cairo, the two metropolises of the Middle East; and planes fly only twice a week between Teheran and next-door Baghdad. For Iranians, tourism in Arab countries consists almost wholly of religious pilgrimages to Mecca, in Saudi Arabia. Similarly, the flowing white robes of a visiting Arab are rarely to be seen in Iranian cities, and attract much curiosity. The white-skinned Iranians all too often speak disparagingly of "Bedouins," by which they mean to indicate the Negroid mixture in some Arabs in such nations as Egypt and Algeria. When in 1976 the seven Arab states around the Persian Gulf proposed to start something called the "Arabian Gulf News Agency," the Shah ordered his ambassadors in each of these nations to demand an explanation for this attempt to change the name of the gulf, and recalled the envoys to Teheran. "Do facts of history and geography change in this manner?" the Shah fumed. "Can Pakistan change the term 'Indian Ocean,' or add its own name to it?" Speaking to an Arab journalist, he said: "You must have a reason, and maybe there is the motive of enmity with us."

Before the six-day war of 1967, when Egypt's Nasser and the Shah of Iran were open enemies, the Shah allied himself with Israel on the principle, he explained, that "your enemy's enemy is your friend." Israel helped train the Iranian armed forces and secret police. Jews and Iranians have never been strangers to one another. For twenty centuries Iran has had a Jewish minority, by and large compatible with the majority. The founding of Israel attracted 47,000 Jewish immigrants from Iran, who now link the two countries through their connections with the 80,000 Jews left in Iran. Through all the Arab-Israeli wars, Iran was the main source of oil for the Israeli armed forces.

The dissolution of the Arab threat signaled by the death of Nasser brought the Shah back to neutral. Iran feared, as political scientists Ahmad Ghoreishi and Cyrus Elahi put it, that "if there is an overwhelming victory by the Israelis, 'radical' Arab leaders like [Libya's] Colonel Qaddafi may indeed increase in number throughout the Arab world." With Khomeini, Iran's strange-bedfellows relationship with Israel took the turn that might historically have been expected: political enmity. Iran announced that it would stop supplying oil to Israel, which meant that Israel lost its important export market in Iran.

Particularly intriguing are Iran's relations with Iraq, its sound-alike neighbor to the west. Iraq (whose name means "mudbank" in Arabic and bears no linguistic relationship to Iran, which means "Aryan") is a rainless desert that is nevertheless well watered by the Tigris and Euphrates, so that "if you tickle her soil it smiles a crop." It it half as big as Iran, with only a toe dipped in the Persian Gulf, and it is bounded by Kuwait, Saudi Arabia, Jordan, Syria, Turkey, and Iran. One of the birthplaces of civilization, Iraq has been identified, in turn, with Sumer, Akkad, Babylon, and Mesopotamia; its ancient notables include Hammurabi, Nebuchadnezzar, and Harun al-Rashid; its ancient cities include Ur, Nineveh, and Baghdad. It was ruled from Persia between 539 B.C. and A.D. 637; by Islamic caliphs until 1534; by Turkish Ottomans until 1914; by Britain until 1932; and by itself since then.

Iraq differs from Iran in race (Semitic), population (11 million, a third of Iran's), and geography (flat, sea-level desert and marsh). But like Iran, Iraq has oil (32 billion barrels of reserves), and having finished nationalizing it in 1975, aspires to use it for self-development. Huge new farms have been established beside the Euphrates, and with oil refining, petrochemicals, tractor manufacturing, cement mills, and textiles, Iraq will probably be the first industrial power in the Arab world.

As soon as it became an independent kingdom, Iraq fell into conflict with Iran. The issue was the estuary historically called Shatt-al-Arab, though labeled as the Arvand River on modern Iranian maps because the Shah took offense at the meaning of the old name, which is simply "Arab River." The 160-mile Shatt-al-Arab connects the confluence of the Tigris and the Euphrates to the head of the Persian Gulf, flowing through an ever enlarging swampy delta. The Iran-Iraq land border, coming from the north, reaches the Shatt-al-Arab about fifty miles upstream, and the river forms the border from there to the sea. The question has been: Which part of the river forms the border? Historically, Iraq successfully contended that the border was the east, or Iranian, bank of the river, which awards the navigable waters to Iraq. Ocean ships could thus reach Basra, Iraq's major port, sixty-five miles up the river, on all-Iraqi water. But by the same token, ships had to traverse Iraqi water to reach Iran's great oil refinery at Abadan, thirty miles upstream from the sea, or Khorramshahr, Iran's major port, six miles farther on. By international treaties, Iraq let all nations navigate the Shatt-al-Arab, but Iran always held that the east-bank border was unfair and onerous, and yearned to move the border to the center of the channel.

Another issue concerned the Kurds, one of the more important of the world's landless nations, who dominate the Iranian province of Kurdistan on the border of Iraq, and spread as far as Turkey, the Soviet Union, and even Syria. The land the Kurds claim most ardently is in Iraq, where they form nearly one fifth of the population. Supporting the Kurdish rebellion in Iraq was for a long time the Shah's most effective device for putting pressure on Iraq.

These frictions began to generate serious heat in 1958, when the leftist generals of the Iraqi army hanged two dozen royalists in the main square of Baghdad and created what the Shah of Iran deplored most, a republic. Their Baath (Renaissance) party established warm relations with the Soviet Union, which supplied copious weapons in hopes of access to the Persian Gulf. One commentator called Iraq "the elongated arm of Moscow." The United States broke diplomatic relations with Iraq in 1967 and has not resumed them yet. The Baathists became the personification of far-left Arab radicalism, spearheading the "rejection front" against Israel and championing the Palestine Liberation Organization.

In 1969 Iran challenged Iraq's dominion over the Shatt-al-Arab by sailing an Iranian-flag ship, escorted by naval vessels, up the river without paying right of passage to the Iraqi authorities. Iraq responded by expelling the Iranian ambassador. Both nations moved troops to the border, and they clashed occasionally all through the first half of the 1970s, to the accompaniment of a furious propaganda war. The great Kurdish leader Mustafa Barzani, a kind of Pancho Villa of western Asia, got encouragement, supplies, and even troops from the Shah to resume fighting. Nixon and Kissinger secretly forced the CIA (against its better judgment) to smuggle untraceable Chinese and Soviet arms for the Shah to pass on to the Kurds, to counterbalance the weapons Iraq was getting from the Soviet Union. Iraq began to suspect that the Shah might try to "liberate" that corner of the country, which includes the Kirkuk oil fields, and set up a friendly Kurdish government there.

In actuality, the Shah had no such intention, particularly as he observed the rise of Saddam Hussein in Iraq. This young man, still barely forty, became vice-president and gradually nudged President Ahmed Hassan al-Bakr out of the seat of real power during the early 1970s. Even as the Iranian radio called him a "Baathist butcher," Saddam Hussein was fretting at continuing the "military solution" of the Kurdish problem, because he had to knuckle under to the Russians to get arms. The Shah saw in Saddam the key to changing his western neighbor from an unnecessarily belligerent enemy to an unthreatening friend, in the process loosening the Soviet lock on Iraq. All the Shah had to do to get this gain was to call off his support for the Kurds. For his part, Saddam Hussein saw that these same dividends of peace merited a major concession by Iraq, and he agreed to draw the Iraq-Iran border right down the middle of the Shatt-al-Arab. These were the understandings that brought Saddam and the Shah into accord in 1975.

Mustafa Barzani died in 1979 in Alexandria, Virginia, his dream of the Kurdish homeland done for. The Shah was entirely conscious that he sacrificed the Kurds to get peace with Iraq. "We did not invent the Kurdish revolution. We found it a reality. The Kurdish revolution offered us a great opportunity and we took it. Did we really want to create a great Kurdish problem? No. We have a large Kurdish minority ourselves. We helped the Kurdish revolution against Baghdad, and when they stopped their hostile actions, we followed suit. Could we do anything else?"

Historically, Iran has always been perplexed about how defiantly, or how obsequiously, it should behave when confronting its overwhelmingly powerful neighbor to the north. Years ago, it is said, an Iranian official was asked, during a period of ticklish relations with the Russians, whether or not the Iranian military should fire a salute to honor a Soviet naval vessel visiting the Caspian Sea port of Bandar Pahlavi. After a moment's anguish, he replied: "Fire the gun, but not loudly."

With diplomatic tightrope-walking like that, augmented by luck, American aid, and Soviet blunders, Iran under the Shah achieved greater independence from the Russians than any other of the Soviet

Union's five non-Communist neighbors (Norway and Turkey rely on NATO; Finland and Afghanistan are semisatellites). During the first half of this century, Russian (and British) ambassadors wielded much power in Teheran, partly by "buying cabinet ministers like bags of wheat," as one American diplomat told me. The change may have come in 1953, when Soviet Ambassador Anatoly Laurentiev, sent to make trouble for the United States and the Shah during the Mossadegh crisis, met a mysterious end. Learning of Mossadegh's downfall, fearing punishment from Premier Georgi Malenkov, he first tried to flee to the American Embassy; stopped by his own guards, he then drank a cup of poisoned tea. The embassy doctor pumped his stomach, and he lived, but he utterly disappeared from public view.

The Russians at that point decided to reverse course, abandon their Iranian Communist colleagues, and make friends with Mohammed Reza Pahlavi. Visiting Moscow, the Shah and Queen Soraya became the first monarchs to stay at the Kremlin since czarist times. Malenkov and his successor, Nikita Khrushchev, sent friendly missions, praised the Shah's leadership, and managed to swallow Iran's adherence to the Baghdad Pact. When Iran in 1959 signed its mutual-defense treaty with the United States, the U.S.S.R. again turned hostile ("Iran has joined the ranks of the enemies of the Soviet Union"), and stayed so until 1962, when the Russian rupture with China forced the Soviet Union to seek out and cherish all potential friends. Then came real cooperation, such as the exchange of Iranian gas for the Russian-built steel mill at Isfahan, and collaboration in fighting pollution in the Caspian Sea. When a Russian pilot defected to Iran in 1976, the Shah coldly sent him back to certain execution, because the Soviet Union so obligingly returned Iranian guerrillas who fled across the border.

Iranians are blood brothers of the citizens of some of the Soviet republics. More Azerbaijanis live in the Azerbaijan Autonomous Republic than in the neighboring Iranian province of Azerbaijan. An Iranian government official who toured the Uzbekistan Republic told me that "the teahouses of Bukhara are just like the teahouses of Isfahan." Passenger trains operate between Teheran and Moscow once a week, taking four days and switching trucks at Jolfa to accommodate Russia's wide-gauge tracks; and lots of Iran's imports from Europe come via the Soviet rail system.

"Iranology is a big subject in the Soviet Union," I was told by Vladimir Fedorov, a Russian member of the United Nations mission in Teheran. "There are many institutes and hundreds of scholars. In the Russian language there is a critical edition of the poet Ferdowsi such as you simply cannot find in English. We published thirty-five thousand copies of our new Russian-Persian dictionary, and the bibliography

of works about Iran in Russian makes a book five centimeters thick."
When Crown Prince Reza toured Leningrad's Hermitage in 1976, he
learned that the museum possesses 800,000 items from Iran.

Beneath the bland collaboration of Iran and the U.S.S.R. during
the last decade of the Shah's reign, however, the tensions inevitable
when a small weak nation borders an immense powerful nation remained. After the Shah fell, the historic question resurfaced: Could
the Soviet Union be expected not to take advantage of turmoil in Iran?
From Peter the Great on, Russia has aspired to have a warm-water
port; Iran's Indian Ocean coastline would be an ideal site. More recently, the Soviet Union has been growing fearful that its oil reserves,
vast as they are, may not suffice for the future. If Iran drops into the
lap of the Russians, can they refuse to accept it? Can they refuse to
help it drop?

These questions bear interestingly on Iran's relations with China.
The "proximity and presence of the Soviet Union has put some restraints on Iran's attitude towards China," writes Jamshid Nabavi, a
professor of political science at the University of Teheran. "A third
country, from Russia's point of view, has to choose between real friendship and coexistence with one or the other of the two superpowers
of the Communist world. . . . In other words, history and geography
have chosen Iran's Communist partner." Iran recognized China in 1972
(and does not recognize Taiwan); but a close relationship was not in
the cards. Nevertheless, China took a benign view of Iran, regarding
it as "a country whose internal system and bourgeois ruling class are
fiercely engaged in a battle with international imperialism"—meaning
that Iran had successfully nationalized its oil industry. When the Shah
fell, China's Deputy Premier Deng Xiaoping lectured President Carter
for negligence in failing to support the king.

The British navy guarded the Persian Gulf for centuries, control-
ling Kuwait, Qatar, the little sheikdoms, and even Iran itself until Harold Wilson announced Britain's abdication of suzerainty east of Suez.
The Shah thereupon decided that Iran would be the major power guarding the gulf, and that is the main reason for his gigantic military build-
up. American strategists seemed pleased that the Shah was relieving
the U.S. of the burden of taking over from Britain (though it may also
be true that the Shah was preventing the U.S. from taking over). In
terms of the strategic importance of the gulf, and its geographical vulnerability, the need for defense seemed reasonable—"very legitimate,"
former Senator William Fulbright called it.

Three fourths of Europe's oil, four fifths of Japan's oil, and one
third of the oil that the United States imports—or, to put it another

way, all of Iran's production and a good share of the production of
Iraq, Kuwait, Saudi Arabia, Bahrain, Qatar, and the United Arab Emirates—flow out of the Persian Gulf. On an average day 200 tankers pass
through the mouth of the gulf, and they carry away 20 million barrels
of oil, worth about $400 million. To choke off this oil is to paralyze
the industrial West. For those who must defend this lifeline of nations,
it must seem that the devil himself had a hand in forming the gulf's
topography. Right at its mouth, the gulf narrows to the 170-mile-long
Strait of Hormoz, 80 miles wide at the most but only 21 miles wide
at the least. The north—Iranian—coast of the strait is a deep bay, into
which extends the slender, north-pointing Oman peninsula. The best
passage for deep-water tankers happens to lie just between two small
islands off the tip of the peninsula.

One or another of the currently quite stable members of the United
Arab Emirates occupy the west and east coasts of the Oman peninsula,
but by some accident of history the very tip of it is a detached territory
of the troubled sultanate of Muscat and Oman, the main body of which,
facing the Arabian Sea, forms the southeast coast of the Arabian peninsula. An Omani tribe called the Shuhi resides on the point that pro-
trudes into the Hormoz strait. The Shuhi are backward people who
carry tiny axes for weapons. But if some foreign power were to supply
a Shuhi with a rocket launcher, he could easily use it to hit a passing
tanker and set the ship and a large area of the sea on fire. Such a
blow would not, to be sure, close off the strait. It is too deep—180 to
300 feet—to be blocked by sunken ships, and wide enough to provide
alternative channels. But tanker owners would presumably refuse to
run the gauntlet, and the Shah was dead sure that he must never let
such an attack take place. To prove his insistence on security in this
area, the Shah in 1971 carried out his regime's only overt act of conquest: Iranian forces seized three tiny but strategic islands (Greater
and Lesser Tunb, and Abu Musa), all lying just west of the peninsula,
that had been claimed by one of the emirates after the British abandoned them.

The defense of the Persian Gulf and the hope that armed force
could keep Iran from being a pushover for the Russians were the reasons given for the Shah's huge military build-up in the 1970s. What
the armed forces seemed to be—in contrast to what they turned out
to be when Khomeini's revolutionaries took them on—was an impressive military machine. The strength in manpower was 319,500—81,000
in the air force, 220,000 in the army, 18,500 in the navy, with reserves
to a total of 700,000. Besides planes, tanks, and Hovercraft, the $20
billion that the Shah spent on arms provided these servicemen with
missiles, bases, and destroyers. Until the revolution put Americans to

flight, Rockwell International of Anaheim, California, which built the secret listening posts in Iran with which the CIA monitored Russian rocket testing, was constructing for Iran an advanced electronic communications-intelligence facility to intercept military and civilian communications throughout the Persian Gulf area.

All this was scandalously excessive in relation to danger, costly to Iran's social needs, wasteful to the economy, and wastefully carried out. To live in Iran under the Shah was to live in a country that seemed to be at war. Long olive-drab Soviet-built carriers hauled Chieftain tanks through the streets of the cities, while helicopters chopped through the air overhead. The tourist maps of Teheran showed vast green areas that might lead the innocent to suppose the capital is superbly equipped with parks, but most of them turned out to be army garrisons or ammunition dumps, behind high masonry walls or iron picket fences with signs that said, in English, PHOTO PROHIBITED. Inside, soldiers paced back and forth, rifles slung on their backs, bayonets fixed. In the cities of Iran, the sentry box was as common as the telephone booth. Convoy trucks went by, full of soldiers, and a certain proportion of people in any crowd were uniformed men; one learned to recognize the red hats and white-laced paratroop boots of the Imperial Guard, and the black berets of the paratroops. The annual armed forces march-past, staged in mid-December on Azerbaijan Liberation Day, was a little like May Day in Red Square. The Shah floated down out of the air in a helicopter, mounted a horse, and led off the parade as far as the imperial reviewing stand. There he sat, in a gilded armchair, for hours, rising to salute each regimental flag. In front of him passed tanks, self-propelled artillery pieces, missile launchers, frogmen in wetsuits, units of the motorized infantry, elite troops of the Imperial Special Forces, goose-stepping policemen, and what a French journalist called "an indigestion of rifles." The blat of helicopter gunships and the brass of military bands filled the air. Except on television, the public did not see this show. For the Shah's security, it took place on an isolated stretch of the freeway leading westward from Teheran.

The military's share of the government's expenditures in recent years has been around $5 billion. As a share of gross national product, the Iranian military got 18 percent, compared to 8 percent for the U.S. military. A sizable part of Iran's true military expenses, moreover, such as base construction, was concealed as public works and handled by the Plan Organization.

The huge scale of Iran's military build-up cost not only money but also extraordinary distrust, friction, confusion, and corruption. For one thing, the Shah felt that he had to protect himself against overthrow by one or more of his own officers. He made a point of personally keeping an eye on his generals, with frequent face-to-face conferences. And he studied the dossier of every officer above the rank of major who was proposed for promotion, before allowing the advance.

In the dossiers the Shah searched for motivation and enthusiasm as well as loyalty among his officers, but good men were hard to find, particularly in the lower ranks. Iranian culture works against the development of fighting men. Officers often dislike to spend time with their troops; they allow friendship to interfere with mutual constructive criticism; and they suffer from what one observer calls "a strong national strain of cynicism. The saying 'Leave me out, I'm on the sidelines' is very common." Higher officers, empowered to make contracts, frequently and disloyally succumb to bribery. While I was in Iran, the Shah had to depose Rear Admiral Ramzi Abbas Atai, the commander of the Imperial Iranian Navy. Atai was convicted of taking money from firms that had business with the navy, but the Shah must have been equally furious at the comical way he learned of the admiral's transgressions. As I heard it from an American adviser to the Iranian navy, a leading Teheran jeweler one day showed Empress Farah a rare and costly gem, thinking that she might like to buy it. She declined—but after a couple of months asked to see it again. The jeweler told her in embarrassment that he had sold it to Admiral Atai. The Shah, observing that such an expensive jewel was beyond the means of an honest admiral, started an investigation that ended with five years of prison and a fine of $4 million for the officer. One of Atai's subordinates committed suicide. The same American adviser told me sourly that the walls of a navy building on Kharg island had been put up so poorly that they displayed a slant visible to the eye, but none of the naval officers balked because they were ripping off bribes from the contractor, the subcontractor, and the subsubcontractor.

Big multinational corporations sprayed payoffs around Iran, as they did elsewhere, to sell weapons to the armed forces. Northrop Corporation, without confessing any specific crimes, rebated $2 million to the Iranian government in atonement for ethically questionable payments to third parties who supposedly helped the company get orders for F-5 jet fighters. Northrop paid Kermit Roosevelt (the CIA agent who helped save the Shah in 1953) as much as $75,000 a year to open doors in Iran. Northrop also paid $705,000 to one of the Shah's nephews, Shahram Pahlavi, for "services" to the company at a time when it was getting a contract to help build a telecommunications network in Iran. In 1978, the Shah finally barred members of his family from business deals in which they stood to benefit.

The concept of a rebate (like Northrop's) stemmed from Iran's official position that any bribes or payoffs that a foreign company might be foolish enough to make should come from its profits, and not be tacked onto the government's bill. For a company to admit paying bribes, the Iranian government said with a straight face, was to admit overcharging; the effect was to make bribe-givers pay twice. Grumman Corporation, which promised $28 million (and actually delivered $6 million) in "commissions" to shady go-betweens to get its contract to build F-14s for Iran, got caught in such a crossfire, and had to compensate Iran with $24 million in spare parts.

In the end, what looked impressive was not. Put to the test of crushing the Iranian people (which Iranians all along understood was a more important function of the military than defense from foreign attack), the Shah's armed power collapsed in days. Conscripted soldiers could see no sense in shooting their "brothers" on orders from their aloof officers. The divisions among officers created by the Shah's suspicions of them worked against formulating a strategy for handling revolt. Corruption took its toll on professionalism. The rout was so complete that even when the military agreed to serve the new revolutionary government, it had almost nothing to offer.

16

The Iranian Revolution

❧

His formula was humble: "The king handles the destiny of Iran—I deal with the price of bread." By such a clear and candid understanding of his relationship to his monarch, Prime Minister Amir Abbas Hoveyda stayed in office twelve years, far outlasting any of his predecessors in the years since 1906, when the modern version of this office was created. Resigning in 1977, he became minister of court—the next to last minister of court, as it turned out, in the age-old Iranian monarchy. He transmitted the letter, described on the first page of this book, that touched off the Khomeini revolution. But though he was central in the kind of governance that brought the Shah down, Hoveyda, far from a fool, was a civilized and complicated man.

One dark solsticial evening several years ago, he received me for a glass of Scotch and water in his study in the prime minister's residence. The place was a mess. Books, mostly in French and English, lay on every horizontal surface, and climbed the walls in stacks like bricks. On the coffee table there was scarcely room for his Dunhill Royal Yacht Mixture—he smoked pipes ceaselessly. Four all-bands transistor radios surrounded him, variously tuned to London, Cairo, Paris, and Teheran, so that he could get the news from all over by merely flipping the switch. A statue of Buddha sat on a shelf in this small circular room, and a crystal chandelier sent down an enveloping light. Hoveyda, who was fifty-six years old at that time, sat slumped and comfortable in a black leather Eames chair, a short, bald man, a bit thick in the middle, with slender fingers, a wide smile, and disconcertingly somber and observant eyes.

Hoveyda was the son of a diplomat, and until he was grown he rarely saw Iran; were it not for his mother, he might not even have learned Persian. While he was a boy, his father was posted to Syria, Palestine, Egypt, Saudi Arabia, even Yemen, and as a consequence

Hoveyda spoke perfect Arabic. He attended secondary school at the Lycée Français in Beirut, and got his higher education at the Université Libre in Brussels (M.A., political science) and the Sorbonne (Ph.D., history). Caught in Paris by the German invasion, the Hoveydas got back to Iran in 1942 through Germany, Yugoslavia, Bulgaria, and Turkey. He served as an artillery officer in the Iranian army until the end of the war, when he took a foreign service job repatriating Iranians from what was by then his best-loved city, Paris.

"Materially, life in Paris just after the war was difficult, but intellectually it was pure gold," recalled Francophile Hoveyda. His friends were people like Jean Paul Sartre, Simone de Beauvoir, and Georges Bidault, as well as Yves Montand and Juliette Greco. He continued his studies, "but I never studied what I didn't like. I'd skip four months and go to Florence." He learned to speak French "luminously," in the word of one of his deputies. He also learned fluent English and passable German.

For a dozen years, Hoveyda filled various posts in the foreign service, including a period with the United Nations High Commissioner for Refugees between 1952 and 1956. In 1959 the foreign ministry loaned Hoveyda to the National Iranian Oil Company, which brought him to the attention of Hassan Ali Mansur, an aristocratic politician who had created a "progressive" school of thought about applying education and technique to government. This thinking appealed to the Shah, who made Mansur prime minister in 1964. One of Mansur's ideas was that the cabinet should be a team, rather than a set of scrapping rivals, and he picked Hoveyda to be minister of finance. When a religious madman assassinated Mansur the next year, the Shah raised Hoveyda to the prime ministry.

Hoveyda seemed quick-minded and open—and shrewd and wary as well. "He is cultured, literate, knows the basis of Western culture, the Bible, European history," said one associate. He also adored machines and gadgets: calculators, electric shavers, cameras, and the computer terminal that he kept at his fingertips while prime minister. Digital clocks, too—but, he claimed, "I do not accept the time dimension." Day-and-night work was his obsession, and he said it was the cause of his 1971 divorce from his wife after a marriage of only four years. She could not stand to be left out of his life so much, but she remained his friend, and every morning sent him the orchid that was always to be seen in his buttonhole.

After my evening with Hoveyda, I walked away from his study slowly, for I wanted to take in the valuable Qajar-period portraits of last-century shahs and the modern Iranian abstractions (Hoveyda had an eye for pictures) hanging in the blue-carpeted upper hall of his residence. While I dawdled, Hoveyda reappeared from his study. "Want to see a prime minister's bedroom?" he asked genially. This chamber gave off the same hall, and we looked in. It was a large room with attractive blue wallpaper, but more cluttered even than the study. On the floor were five attaché cases that Hoveyda planned to go through before retiring, a tape player, and an Exercycle—"just a joke; I promised the doctor I'd try to lose weight." One half of the bed was reserved for His Excellency; the other half was strewn with French newspapers, books, a telephone, a dictating machine, and a notebook for small-hours big thoughts. The bench at the foot of the bed was piled three feet high with books; Hoveyda must have been the world's best-read politician.

The last time I saw the visage of Amir Abbas Hoveyda, he was not face to face with me, but rather pictured on the front page of the *New York Times* in early April 1979. The picture, made a few weeks before, showed a greatly changed man. The face wore a gaunt, much-aged, and frightened look. The news was that he had undergone a three-day trial that ended, after a night session, at 6 A.M. The revolutionary court, after a couple of minutes of discussion, convicted him of "sowing corruption on earth." At 6:15, Hoveyda was dead, his body riddled by bullets from a firing squad.

In contrast to his faithful servant Hoveyda, the Shah of Iran escaped with his life, though not with much dignity. Unwelcome almost everywhere, he managed short stays in Morocco and the Bahamas, then settled in Cuernavaca, Mexico, thanks to heavy pressure on the Mexican government from the Shah's friends Henry Kissinger and David Rockefeller. The Shah lived under intense guard, for Iran's top revolutionary court had put out a contract on him: a reward of $131,000 to anyone who would assassinate the former king. "I do not fear being assassinated," said the Shah. "I believe in Providence."

How sweeping the Iranian revolution was! Iran under the Shah was on the way to becoming a kind of Asian Germany, strong in steel, machine tools, mining, petrochemicals, natural gas, hydroelectric and nuclear power, agribusiness. The Iranians had to have color television and literacy and Kleenex and plentiful cars and direct-distance dialing and subways and cornflakes and bullet trains and orthodontics and F-14s. Under Khomeini Iran has become a fanatic Islamic republic, deriving its law from the Koran and its government from religious leaders. Crime is punished with the lash or the firing squad, on the principle of an eye for an eye. In speeches, Khomeini was drawn again and again to the concept—perhaps metaphorical, perhaps real—of "cutting off hands."

In dozens of ways Iran turned topsy-turvy. The Shah's vaunted armed services, which the Western world respected as policemen of the Persian Gulf, turned out to be patsies for any revolutionary bold enough to stick a carnation in a soldier's rifle muzzle, while at the same time mullahs took to carrying the Kalashnikov automatic rifle so favored by Middle Eastern terrorists. The Imperial Iranian Air Force, rated most loyal of the Shah's services, led the way in surrendering to the bearded holy man, and the crack Imperial Guard, copied after Cyrus the Great's Ten Thousand Immortals, joined other tens of thousands of soldiers who turned out to welcome Khomeini when he came back to Iran. Generals depicted in late 1978 as potential men on horseback to save Iran were summarily executed early in 1979. The revolutionaries attacked and captured supposedly impregnable military bases, and turned the weapons stored there into arms for their own ragtag militias.

The Iranian student abroad, so commonplace as to have become virtually a class of society in Europe and the United States, is replaced by a more devout, home-educated youth. The Shah had imported Western-style social security (which turned out to invite some of his regime's worst corruption); the Ayatollah proposes redistribution of wealth and free electricity and bus rides for the poor. The Shah in 1975 created a Ministry of State for Women's Affairs, headed by a thoroughly modern Iranian woman who had graduated from the University of Colorado; Khomeini dismayed Iran's sizable women's liberation movement by loosing fanatics who called women in Western dress "whores." By force, diplomacy, and education, the Shah had reduced Iran's once obstreperous tribes and minorities to submission; with the revolution, the Kurds, the Turkomans, and the Baluchis (all Sunni in religion) renewed their hopes of creating ethnic nations, and some people in Azerbaijan—as well as some people in Moscow—looked again at the concept that Iranian and Soviet Azerbaijan ultimately belong in the same Soviet Socialist Republic.

Had Iran exchanged a bad regime for a worse one? The great majority of Iranians thought not. Yet in Ayatollah Khomeini's perpetual scowl one might detect ominous portents. Displaying bitter vengefulness, he turned an astonishingly bloodless and already won revolution into a carnival of kangaroo-court executions—six hundred by mid 1979—for vaguely defined crimes. Displaying an undue obsession with sex, he thundered that unveiled women were "naked." Mixed swimming in pools was banned, and women were required to wear clothes and chadors while bathing. All forms of entertainment came under question; television turned into a wasteland of exhortatory speeches and patriotic songs. Iran was to be a no-fun country. Totally convinced that only he was right, the Ayatollah scoffed at cultures other than Islam: "There's nothing in the West." Khomeini came to power partly on his fabulous demonstration of his ability to say "no." Could the adversary mentality successfully run a country in desperate need of positive decisions?

The answer would seem to be no. By mid 1979, Khomeini had acquired as enemies government technocrats, unemployed working people, army officers, and journalists. He had started a small war with the Sunni Kurds, who strove to make the province of Kurdistan autonomous in accordance with their 2,000-year-old goal of independence; and he did battle with the Sunni Arabs of Khuzistan. Two well-armed guerrilla militia, the Marxist Fedayeen and the leftist Mujahadeen, turned against him. Denouncing political parties, he lost the support of his important fellow ayatollah, Shariatmadari, who had formed a Moslem People's Republican Party. The words that came to be associated with Khomeini were blood, chaos, violence, spleen, absurdity, incompetence, dictatorship, censorship, execution, war, and—for perpetually benighted Iran—a hopeless future.

Abroad, the Iranian revolution was deeply upsetting—at least to the West. In the worst case, it could trigger World War III, by leading to a desperate energy shortage in the West. Depending on the degree to which the U.S.S.R. can influence Iran, and with it the Persian Gulf oil producers, the Russians might destroy the U.S.–European military alliance by throttling Europe's oil. Short of that, the U.S.S.R. might be able to position itself as a military power on the Indian Ocean coast of Iran. The loss of CIA listening posts in Iran, which monitored Soviet missile performance, lowered American ability to verify Soviet compliance with the proposed strategic arms limitation treaty, and thus made its ratification vulnerable to attacks by Senate hawks.

And more Americans and Europeans were forced to cut and run from Iran in mass evacuations, never an act that heightens a nation's prestige. Secrets of American weaponry were lost to hostile Iranians and probably to the Russians, an upshot not given enough consideration when Nixon decided to bet the American chips on the Shah. John Foster Dulles's Central Treaty Organization, linking Turkey, Iran, and Pakistan, gasped and died. Iran, which had become one of the United States's largest foreign customers, cut back its purchases sharply.

For months Iran's oil exports stopped, forcing the United States to prepare for rationing of gasoline. The consortium of foreign oil companies that marketed much of Iran's oil under the Shah, which had its ancestors in the British company that found oil in Iran in 1908, awaited dissolution.

For Israel, the Iranian revolution was almost unrelievedly bad news. Losing the source of half of Israel's oil imports was only the beginning. It was the arrival of the Palestine Liberation Organization's Yasir Arafat in Teheran, as Ayatollah Khomeini's first foreign visitor, that measured the depth of Khomeini's opposition to "Zionism" and his alliance to Arab Moslems in the "holy war." An immediate effect was to let Iraq, one of Israel's more fanatic enemies, cease worrying about danger from Iran and focus its military strength westward. Paradoxically, the Iranian revolution set Arabs to worrying, too. Agreed on anti-Zionism, the mostly Sunni Arabs are suspicious of the attraction of Shiah and the dour charisma of its salient figure, Khomeini. In Iraq, Sunni political leaders must take into account a population more than half Shiite. In turmoil-ridden Lebanon, the largest religious group is Shiite, and in Syria President Hafez al-Assad is a member of a reclusive Shiite sect ruling a Sunni majority.

In early 1978, as the first rumbles of the year of revolution began to be heard, perhaps the only person who might have predicted the rise to power of Ayatollah Khomeini would have been the Ayatollah himself. Certainly I did not foresee such a drastic revolution; I did not correctly estimate the strength of Islam and the moral force of one relentlessly uncompromising old man. But in studying Iran, I had uncovered factors that would have made me, if I were an Iranian, want to overthrow the Shah.

The first of these is that monarchy, despite the sheer institutional weight of it in Iran, is an anachronism, eventually doomed everywhere. Everyone, including Iranians, knows that governments exist in which the electorate, not some bloodline king, ultimately makes the decisions. Put simply, freedom is generally preferred to dictatorship. The Shah was on the wrong side of that argument.

One corollary to this is that monarchy, or dictatorship, cannot prevail without repression, which damages the dignity not only of specific victims but also of those forced to stand by and tolerate it. No nation needs a SAVAK. The adulation and lies of a censored press are abhorrent. Another corollary is that ordinary people can see the folly of inordinately excessive military expenditures and support the common-sense proposition that the money wasted could improve their own lives. Beyond that, the people of Iran yearned for authentic justice, so much so that Islamic canon law began to seem not like a romantic revival but like a viable "natural" law.

The most ironic factor in the fall of the Shah was the discovery, perhaps first driven home to Americans by the failure of Lyndon Johnson's war on poverty, that the application of money to a problem doesn't automatically solve it. Iran's annual oil income jumped in 1973 from

$4 billion to $20 billion, and it paid for much industrialization, wise and unwise, and for many imports, sensible and foolish. But it inevitably brought with it inflation and a train of other problems. In 1975, Hoveyda tried to attack inflation by organizing student goon squads to arrest "profiteering" businessmen and try them in kangaroo courts. Thousands of small merchants and shopkeepers—and some big shots as well—were jailed, fined, or banished to remote towns—a classic example of the monarchic mentality of curing problems by force. This exercise of power, though probably well meant and justified by the facts, cost the Shah his last support among the bazaaris and among more prominent businessmen, too. But when the government gave up this predoomed kind of price control, inflation leaped to 30 percent a year. The resulting wage jumps attracted hundreds of thousands of farm laborers to cities, with the double effect of creating miserable slums—not common before then but tinder for rebellion—and cutting agricultural production. Neither the Shah nor Hoveyda found enough time to make farm output rise, and as a higher population with higher appetites demanded more food, Iran, once self-sufficient, had to import it.

These imports, together with military arms and the machinery needed for industrialization, overloaded seaports and forced ships to wait in the Persian Gulf as much as 150 days. Though lavishly funded, the government's economic Plan Organization failed in its essential job of making the government spend efficiently. One group of planners designed a highway across a valley that another group planned to flood with the reservoir back of a dam.

Factories got built, but most of them produced at costs too high to let Iran export their output competitively, as the Shah had hoped to do when Iran's oil runs out, in about twenty years. That date now looms as a major crisis. The Hudson Institute, an American think tank, warns that "Iran, in the final decade of this century, could prove to be no more than a half-completed industrial edifice."

Oil wealth caused banks to spring up in scores, with thousands of branches. Again, a double effect: bazaaris were further enraged at losing much of their traditional moneylending business, and mullahs were offended by the growth of an industry that goes against the Koran's ban on lending for interest. When the mobs ran wild in 1978, they left four hundred banks burned out in Teheran alone.

Finally, and most dramatically, the Shah fell because of the Hidden Imam. No one believes (yet) that Ayatollah Khomeini *is* the authentic twelfth imam, lost since the year 874, even though many Iranians now address him with the honorific "Imam." But Khomeini represents a deep current of belief in Shiite Islam, a current that was to many, including the Shah, hidden during the materialistic 1960s and 1970s. In particular Khomeini stood for Islam's belief that temporal leaders like the Shah were illegal under the Koran. When Khomeini's preachings finally began to be heard, he turned out to have a following of millions who found, inside themselves, that his beliefs were theirs. And so they rose up in a mass revolution the like of which the world has rarely seen.

Acknowledgments

My gratitude goes to my wife, Deborah, who took part in the reporting and research for this book; to Cass Canfield, who suggested the topic; to Corona Machemer, who edited the book; and to James Bill, whose writings were singularly useful. I am also profoundly grateful to the hundreds of Iranians whom I interviewed, from the Shah on down, but I feel that with Iran in tumult and its future unpredictable, no useful purpose would be served in naming them.

Bibliography

❋

Amuzegar, Jahangir. *Iran: An Economic Profile.* Washington: The Middle East Institute, 1977.

Amuzegar, Jahangir, and M. Ali Fekrat. *Iran: Economic Development Under Dualistic Conditions.* Chicago: University of Chicago Press, 1971.

Arberry, A. J. *Hafiz.* Malta: St. Paul's Press Ltd., 1974.

Armajani, Yahya. *Iran.* Englewood Cliffs, N.J.: Prentice-Hall, 1972.

Avery, Peter. *Modern Iran.* New York: Praeger, 1965.

Baraheni, Reza. *The Crowned Cannibals.* New York: Vintage Books, 1977.

Bateson, Mary Catherine. *At Home in Iran.* Teheran: St. Paul's Church, 1974.

Bayne, E. A. *Four Ways of Politics.* New York: American Universities Field Staff, 1965.

———. *Persian Kingship in Transition.* New York: American Universities Field Staff, 1968.

Bill, James Alban. *The Politics of Iran.* Columbus, Ohio: Charles E. Merrill Publishing Co., 1972.

Binder, Leonard. *Iran: Political Development in a Changing Society.* Berkeley: University of California Press, 1962.

Cottam, Richard W. *Nationalism in Iran.* Pittsburgh: University of Pittsburgh Press, 1964.

Davar, Firoze Cowasji. *Iran and India Through the Ages.* London: Asia Publishing House, 1962.

Echo of Iran. *Iran Almanac and Book of Facts.* Teheran: Echo of Iran, 1975.

Esfandiary, F. M. *Identity Card.* New York: Grove Press, 1966.

Esfandiari, Soraya. *Soraya.* Garden City, N.Y.: Doubleday, 1964.

Farhat, Hormoz. *The Traditional Art Music of Iran*. Teheran: High Council of Culture and Art, 1973.

Frye, Richard N. *Persia*. London: George Allen and Unwin Ltd., 1968.

Frye, Richard N., and Lewis V. Thomas. *The United States and Turkey and Iran*. Cambridge, Mass.: Harvard University Press, 1951.

Ghirshman, R. *Iran*. Baltimore: Penguin Books, 1954.

Ghirshman, Roman, with Vladimir Minorsky and Ramesh Sanghvi. *Persia the Immortal Kingdom*. London: Orient Commerce Establishment, 1971.

Graham, Robert. *The Illusion of Power*. London: Croom Helm, 1978.

Hawker, C. L. *Simple Colloquial Persian*. London: Longmans, 1961.

Hedayat, Sadegh. *The Blind Owl*. New York: Grove Press, 1969.

Hicks, Jim. *The Persians*. New York: Time-Life Books, 1975.

Hobson, Sarah. *Through Persia in Disguise*. London: John Murray, 1973.

Hoyt, Edwin P. *The Shah: The Glittering Story of Iran*. New York: Paul S. Eriksson, Inc., 1976.

Hureau, Jean. *Iran Today*. Paris: Editions B. Artaud, 1972.

Islami, Nassrollah. *Persian Cookery*. (N.p.; n.d.).

Kayhan Research Associates. *Iran Yearbook*. Teheran: Kayhan Group of Newspapers, 1977.

———. *Iran's 5th Plan*. Teheran: Kayhan Group of Newspapers, 1974.

Laing, Margaret. *The Shah*. London: Sidgwick & Jackson, 1977.

Lilienthal, David E. *The Journals of David E. Lilienthal*, vols. 4 and 5. New York: Harper & Row, 1969 and 1971.

Mace, John. *Modern Persian*. London: St. Paul's House, 1975.

Marlowe, John. *Iran: A Short Political Guide*. New York: Praeger, 1963.

Matheson, Sylvia A. *Persia: An Archaeological Guide*. London: Faber & Faber, 1972.

Ministry of Foreign Affairs. *Iran*. Teheran: Information Ministry Press, 1974.

Morier, James. *The Adventures of Hajji Baba of Ispahan*. London: J. M. Dent (n.d.).

Morris, James. *Persia*. New York: Universe Books, 1970.

National Iranian Oil Company. *Petroleum Industry in Iran*. Teheran (n.d.).

Nicholson, Reynold A. *Rumi: Poet and Mystic*. London: George Allen and Unwin Ltd., 1973.

Overseas Liaison Committee. *An Analysis of US-Iranian Cooperation in Higher Education*. Washington: American Council on Education, 1976.

Pahlavi, Mohammad Reza. *Mission for My Country*. London: Hutchinson, 1960.

———. *The White Revolution.* Teheran: Kayhan Press (n.d.).

Perkins, Justin. *A Residence of Eight Years in Persia Among the Nestorian Christians; with Notices of the Muhammedans.* Andover, Mass.: 1843.

Pope, Arthur Upham, and Phyllis Ackerman, eds. *A Survey of Persian Art.* 14 vols. Teheran: Manafzadeh Group (n.d.).

Rivlin, Benjamin, and Joseph S. Szyliowicz, eds. *The Contemporary Middle East: Tradition and Innovation.* New York: Random House, 1965.

Roosevelt, Kermit. *Arabs, Oil and History.* New York: Harper & Brothers, 1947.

Ross, James, trans. *Sadi's Gulistan.* Shiraz: Marefat (n.d.).

Rypka, Jan. *History of Iranian Literature.* Holland: D. Reidel, 1968.

Sanghvi, Ramesh. *The Shah of Iran.* New York: Stein & Day, 1968.

Shahbazi, A. Shapur. *The Irano-Lycian Monuments.* Teheran: Institute of Achaemenid Research, 1975.

Silvert, Kalman H., ed. *The Social Reality of Scientific Myth.* New York: American Universities Field Staff, 1968.

Solberg, Carl. *Oil Power.* New York: Mason/Charter, 1976.

Stevens, Roger. *The Land of the Great Sophy.* London: Methuen & Co., Ltd., 1962.

Vachha, P. B. *Firdousi and the Shahnama.* Bombay: New Book Company, Ltd., 1950.

Van Donzel, E., with B. Lewis and Ch. Pellat, eds. *Encyclopedia of Islam.* Leiden: E. J. Brill, 1973.

Villiers, Gérard. *L'irrésistible Ascension de Mohammad Reza Shah d'Iran.* Paris: Plon, 1975.

Wilber, Donald N. *Iran Past and Present.* Princeton, N.J.: Princeton University Press, 1975.

———. *Persepolis.* London: Cassell & Company, 1969.

———. *Riza Shah Pahlavi.* Hicksville, N.Y.: Exposition Press, 1975.

Zonis, Ella. *Classical Persian Music.* Cambridge, Mass.: Harvard University Press, 1973.

Zonis, Marvin. *The Political Elite of Iran.* Princeton, N.J.: Princeton University Press, 1971.

Afterword

The events of the year that followed the first publication of this book (which went to press in October 1979) shaped a drama that was bizarre and gripping in its details and yet easily predictable in its motivations. What gripped the world's attention was the seizure of American hostages, the attempt by the United States military to rescue them, the death of the Shah in exile, and the war between Iraq and Iran. What could have been predicted was that a nation given to revenge and martyrdom, as Iran is, would invite such a sea of troubles.

In the balance as struck by many in the West, Iran seemed once again to have shown its penchant for its own doom, so often demonstrated in its long history. The hostage kidnapping was a cheap and cowardly extortion. Iran tempted Iraq to the attack by its heedless weakening of its armed forces and its economy. Iran's abandonment of its position as a world oil power seemed incomprehensible. Opening itself to the possibility of Russian attack seemed insane. And how could any nation survive in a modern world without such Western institutions as separation of church and state, or an efficient and productive economy?

All these were valid views. But in the balance of events as struck by most Iranians, the picture was precisely the opposite. By seizing the hostages Iran had exacted just vengeance for the United States' long support for the Shah. The nation's indifference to the weakness of its economy and its loss of oil sales showed that it had cast off rat-race worldliness and materialism. Iran could bask in the admiration that millions of third-worlders gave to the uncompromising Ayatollah Khomeini.

And these views too were valid. Says University of Chicago historian William H. McNeill: "The real truth, as we've been seeing from our troubles in Iran, is that there are no self-evident truths that apply to everybody—in the West and in the Middle East. What is right in the West

is often not at all right in the world of Islam." Iranians may desire
Western wealth and power, as symbolized by the Shah, but they want
to live by the laws of Islam, as symbolized by the Ayatollah. To Iranians,
the age-old institutions that are described in a good part of this book are
precious. Their religion, their culture—poetry, music, architecture,
customs, cuisine—and their values, even martyrdom and revenge, must
be preserved, and if the cost is the trouble encountered after the revolution, so be it.

On Sunday morning, November 4, 1979, a mob of young Iranian
militants (precisely who they were remained unknown to the world's
diplomats, journalists, and intelligence agencies a year later) stormed
the United States embassy compound in Teheran and seized what after
some thinning out became the famous 52 American hostages. The militants' goal was to extract from the United States the return of the Shah,
who had thirteen days before journeyed from exile in Mexico to get
treatment in a New York hospital. In succeeding days, television
imprinted on American minds traumatic images: blindfolded hostages,
American flags burned and trampled upon, the impassioned faces of
thousands of chanting Iranians.

President Carter faced a moral and political dilemma. Submitting
to blackmail is dangerous for both persons and nations. Still, saving the
Shah's skin ranked low in many Americans' priorities when weighed off
against their simple desire to have the hostages back. Carter floun-
dered. While arranging to deport the Shah to Panama, he tried to
negotiate for the hostages by sending emissaries, by appealing to the
United Nations and the World Court, by freezing $8 billion in Iranian
assets in the United States, and—in secret—by commissioning a military rescue force.

On April 25, 1980, the commandos struck, landing on a remote
airstrip in the central Iranian desert. A few hours later, after a helicopter and a C-130 transport collided on the ground to start a fire that
killed eight servicemen, the rescuers withdrew in humiliation. A panel
of generals and admirals later blamed insufficient rehearsal of the
mission and its failure to foresee bad weather—a dust cloud that dis-
abled two helicopters. (Even if the mission had freed the hostages, the
Iranians could have seized new hostages from among several hundred
Americans who still lived in Iran.)

A month and a half after the seizure of the hostages, the Soviet
Union invaded Iran's northeasterly neighbor, Afghanistan. The Iranian
revolution provided the Russians with three possibly decisive reasons
for this invasion. First, the Iranian revolutionaries openly favored
exporting their Islamic fanaticism, which in Afghanistan set Moslem

believers against the Soviet puppet government. Second, Iran's turmoil raised Russian hopes for acquiring a warm-water port on the Indian Ocean, possibly the Iranian naval base of Chah Bahar, only 300 miles from Afghanistan's southern border. Finally, the revolution greatly weakened Iran's ability to deter the Russians (as it might have under the Shah), and annihilated any possibility that the United States might aid Iran in such an effort.

The seizure of the hostages may have been a well-planned plot or a simple act of fanaticism; in either case the consequences went far beyond anything the militants could have dreamed, and mostly in the direction of war. Even before the invasion of Afghanistan, the United States moved a Navy carrier force into the Arabian Sea, and later the Americans acquired access to sea and air ports in Oman, Somalia, and Kenya. The U.S.S.R. strengthened its fleet in the area. SALT II, the strategic arms limitation treaty between the United States and the Soviet Union, went on ice, and died with the election of Ronald Reagan, a critic of American softness in dealing with Iran.

The whole concept of world democracy suffered, both from Iran's demonstration that a small nation could get away with grabbing and holding diplomats and from its scorn for United Nations mediation. The World Court, having proved itself impotent in dealing with Iranian terrorism, returned to its comfortable world of boundary disputes and the like.

For Iran, the saddest consequence of its own debilitating fanaticism was the attack by Iraq that began on September 23, 1980. Pressured by the Shah, Iraq's strongman President Saddam Hussein in 1975 agreed to divide with Iran navigation rights on the Shatt-al-Arab river between the two countries (*see pages* 275 *and* 276). With the Iranian revolution, Hussein saw a chance not only to get back all of the river, but also possibly to seize some of the oil-rich, Arab-claimed province of Khuzistan and simultaneously to make himself the new policeman of the Persian Gulf. For a pretext, Hussein cited Ayatollah Khomeini's attempts to recruit to his side the more than half of the Iraqi population that is Shiite.

Dictators seldom end their lives surrounded by peace, praise, and gratitude. In his case, Mohammad Reza Pahlavi met an end seemingly devised to extract from him the last drop of humiliation and bitterness. Not cured in New York, the Shah, after his expulsion from the United States, suffered both bodily from lymphatic cancer and mentally from the ignominy of exile on a torrid Panamanian island. He distrusted Panama's ability to protect him, and on March 23, 1980, flew to Egypt to take advantage of a permanent invitation from his friend President

Anwar Sadat, a republican who had always had a quixotic attachment to the Persian language and the Persian royal House. Sadat put up the Shah in Kubbeh Palace, a house in the Cairo suburbs that once belonged to King Farouk. The Shah must have remembered the pang he felt when that fellow king lost his throne in the 1950s. And he must have known, before he died on July 27 from a collapse of his circulatory system, that he would be buried, as he was, in the mausoleum of Cairo's Rifai Mosque, where his own father was for a while interred after his dethronement and peripatetic exile.

If the Shah took note of these parallels, he may also have reflected that in one corner of his mind he had always feared a tragic end. In Persepolis in 1971, he had invited the world's leaders to a lavish celebration to mark the 2,500th anniversary of the coronation of Cyrus the Great. In his speech at this high point of his reign, the Shah chose to quote a quatrain from Omar Khayyam. His choice, somber and prophetic (and an echo of the quatrain that begins this book), was this:

> The worldly hope men set their hearts upon
> Turns ashes—or it prospers; and anon
>   Like snow upon the desert's dusty face,
> Lighting a little hour or two—is gone.

Index

Aalam, Hossein, 190
Abadan, 4, 221, 226, 246
Abadan Tech, 194–195
Abbas, Shah the Great (Safavid), 34–35, 37, 38, 39, 159
Abdorreza Pahlavi, 78, 195
Abu Ali Sina. *See* Avicenna
Abu Ali Sina Technical University, 194
Abu Bakr, 140, 152
Achaemenes (Achaemenian), 14–15
Achaemenian dynasty: 14–22, 150, 152, 200, 251, 262–263
  art and architecture, 10, 11, 17–22, 25
Ackerman, Phyllis, 210
Adult Education, National Center for, 182, 185–186
Afghanistan and Iran, 39, 40, 263
Aga Khan IV, 141
Agha Mohammed (Qajar), 39
Agricultural Cooperative Bank of Iran, 261
Agricultural Development Bank, 239
agriculture, 234–235, 251–265
  agribusiness, 252, 254, 255–256, 259, 261–262
  ancient beginnings of, 11, 17
  cooperative farming, 261
  crops, 254–255, 266
  land reform, 72, 145, 251, 257–259
  productivity, 259, 289
  subsistence farming, 257, 259–261
Agriculture and Resources, Ministry of, 254, 261
Ahmad (Qajar), 40, 43
Ahmed Pahlavi, 78
Ahriman. *See* Angra Mainu
Ahura Mazda, 18, 149, 150, 151
Ahvaz, 223, 226, 234, 245–246
Ahvaz Pipe Manufacturing Company, 245

Ahvaz Rolling and Pipe Company, 245
Ajami, Ismail, 261
Ala, Hossein, 52
Alam, Amir Assadollah, 69
Alexander & Baldwin, Inc., 255
Alexander the Great, 20, 21–22, 26, 201
Ali, Husayn. *See* Bahaullah
Ali, Imam, 111, 140, 141, 144–145, 157
Ali Reza Pahlavi, 77
Allah, 30, 141, 207
Allen, George, 54
Alp Arslan (Seljuk), 32
American Wives of Iranian Husbands, 124
American Women's Club of Iran, The, 131
Amnesty International, 135
Amuzegar, Jamshid, 3, 5, 26, 97
Anaconda Company, 238
Anahita, 149, 150–151
Anglo-Iranian Oil Company, 56, 222, 223. *See also* British Petroleum Company
Anglo-Persian Oil Company, 42, 221. *See also* Anglo-Iranian Oil Company
Angra Mainu, 18
Annenberg, Walter, 9
Anti-Opium and Alcohol Society, 179
Arab Conquest, 30–31, 151, 200, 251
Arabian Nights Entertainments, The. See *Thousand and One Nights, The*
Arafat, Yasir, 288
Arberry, A. J., 202
Archaeological Museum (Teheran), 13, 34
archaeology, 11–13, 27. *See also* Persepolis
architecture
  ancient, 10, 11, 17–22, 29
  Islamic, 35–38, 158–161
  modern, 108, 113–114, 211–212
Ardalan, Nadir, 195
Ardeshir (Sassanian), 28

Armajani, Yahya, 60–61, 151, 222
Arnold, Matthew, 201
Arsanjani, Hassan, 72, 257–258
Artaxeres I (Achaemenian), 21
Arvand River. *See* Shatt-al-Arab estuary
Aryamehr Steel Mill, 232–234
Aryamehr University of Technology, 194, 197
Aryans, 10, 13–14, 27, 49, 88
ash anar (soup), 166
Ashraf Pahlavi, 41, 48, 50, 77–78, 117
Ashura (day of mourning), 6, 7
Aslanian, Emanual Melik, 210
Assassins (Shiite sect), 32–33, 141, 180
Assyrians. *See* Christianity: Nestorians
Atai, Ramzi Abbas, 281
Atatürk, Kemal, 43
Avery, Peter, 39
Avesta, 29, 150
Avicenna, 31, 194, 207
Azarabadegan University, 193
Azerbaijan, 27, 40, 49, 50, 262, 277, 286
Azhari, Gholam Reza, 5, 6

Bab, the, 163, 164
badji (servant), 131
Badpa, Parviz "Killer," 171
Baghdad Pact, 268–269
Bahai, 163–164
Bahaullah, 163–164
Bahman-Beigui, Mohammed, 188–190
Bahrain and Iran, 66–67
Bakhtiar, Shahpur, 8
Bakhtiar, Teymour, 133–135
Bakr, Ahmed Hassan al-, 276
Banisadr, Abdul Hassan, 129, 145
banking and finance, 110–111, 178, 215–216, 239–241, 243–244, 261, 289
Bank Markazi. *See* Central Bank
Bank Melli, 236, 243, 244
Bank Omran, 83–84, 243
Baraheni, Reza, 136
Barzani, Mustafa, 275–276
bast (taking refuge), 40
Bateson, Mary Catherine, 131
Bayne, E. A., 40, 65
bazaari (merchant), 110, 111, 148, 289
bazaars, 109–111
Behesht Zahra cemetery, 156–157
Bell Helicopter company, 131
Bill, James, 72, 128, 137
Birds in Winter, 213
Biruni, 32
Black, Eugene, 236, 253
Blind Owl, The, 125
Borujerdi, Ayatollah, 142, 145
British East India Company, 179

British Museum (London), 13, 17
British Petroleum company, 223, 225. *See also* seven sisters cartel
Browne, Edward, 164, 204
Brown, George, 66
Buddhism, 152
Bushehr, Mehdi, 78
business and industry, 109–110
    profiteering, 249–250, 281–282
    shareholding, 73, 246–248
Byron, Robert, 36, 38

calendars, 6, 44, 176–178
Cambyses, 15
camels, 264
Canada and Iran, 242
caravanserai (inn), vii, 27, 32, 262
carpets. *See* rugs, Persian
Carter, Jimmy, 269–270, 271, 278
Caspian Sea, 88, 265–267
caviar industry, 265–267
C. Brewer & Co., Ltd. *See* Hawaiian Agronomics International
Central Bank, 8, 81, 244. *See also* Bank Melli
Central Intelligence Agency, 58–60, 61, 66, 134, 138, 271, 276
Central Treaty Organization, 269, 287
chador (body veil), 117–120, 127, 148
characteristics, personal, 26, 30, 33, 88–100, 186
    ancestors, 88
    bribes and lies, 92–94, 250, 281–282
    daily customs, 174–176
    ethos, 89–90, 96–99
    hospitality, 99–100
    individualism, 91
    physiognomy, 125
chelo (steamed rice), 165–166
China and Iran, 28, 29, 278
Christianity, 28, 151, 152, 153, 154
    Armenians, 15, 111, 126–127, 162
    Nestorians, 127, 162
Chronique de la Répression 1963–1975, 136
Church, Frank, 223
Churchill, Winston, 100, 204, 221
Clapp, Gordon, 252–253, 254
Classical Persian Music, 208
climate, 12, 88, 103–105, 251, 255, 256, 262, 264–265
Cochrane, L. C., 255, 256, 260
Comaneci, Nadia, 172
Compagnie Française des Petroles, 223. *See also* seven sisters cartel
constitution, 40, 53, 67–68, 78, 145
Coon, Carlton, 11
Cooperatives and Rural Affairs, Ministry of, 261

Cottam, Joseph, 58, 61
Croesus, King, 15
crown jewels, 81–82, 244
Culture and Arts, Ministry of, 191, 210, 213
currency, 70, 244
Curzon, Lord, 81, 221
Cyrus I (Achaemenian), 15
Cyrus II, the Great (Achaemenian), 10, 15,
    67, 71, 162, 177
Czechoslovakia and Iran, 242

Daily Express (London), 57
Daniel, the Prophet, 17
D'Arcy, William, 221, 222
Darius I (Achaemenian), 16–21, 25, 93, 150
Darius II (Achaemenian), 21
Darius III (Achaemenian), 21–22, 25
Dashti, Ali, 201
dastmal-e-zofaf (defloration handker-
    chief), 120
Davar, Firoze Cowasji, 30, 200
Dekhoda Dictionary, 202
Delougaz, Pinhas, P., 12
Demavend College, 195
Demavend, Mount, 103
demography, 63, 101, 124, 127–128
Deng Xiaoping, 278
dervishes, 153
Development and Rural Cooperative Bank.
    See Bank Omran
Dez dam, 253–254
dolmehs (appetizers), 166
doogh (yogurt drink), 169
dress, 170
drinking, 168–169
driving, 100, 114–116
drug abuse, 178–180
Druses (Shiite sect), 141
Dulles, Allen, 58
Dulles, John Foster, 233, 268–269

Ebtehaj, Abol Hassan, 236–237, 252, 253
Ecbatana, 14, 17, 18, 22
Economic Affairs and Finance, Ministry of,
    92
economy, 234–238, 288–289
    GNP, 220, 235, 257, 280
    labor force, 245, 248–249, 255–256
    planning and development, 236–238, 259,
        289
    taxes, 250
education, 70, 73, 133, 137, 181–198, 216, 237
    American assistance, 193, 194, 195, 197
    English as a second language, 191, 195,
        203
    illiteracy, 181–186
    Iranians abroad, 197–198, 286

education *(cont'd)*
    primary and secondary schools, 186–188
    private schools, 190–191
    quality, 190, 192, 195–197
    television, 206–207
    tribal schools, 126, 188–189
    universities, 186, 191–197
    vocational schools, 189–190
Education, Ministry of, 182, 183, 186
Egypt and Iran, 48, 252, 273–274
Eisenhower, Dwight, 58, 223, 268, 271
Elahi, Cyrus, 274
Elam, 12, 13, 14. *See also* Susa
Elburz Mountains, 87, 103, 105
Emani, Seyyid Hassan, 145
Ente Nazionale Idrocarburi (ENI), 224
Esfandiari, Soraya, 54–55, 59, 61, 81, 277
Esfandiary, F. M., 119, 249
Eshragi, Sahrab, 128
Esther, Queen, 162
Etelaat (newpaper), 3
Exxon company, 222, 223, 226. *See also*
    seven sisters cartel

fakir (mendicant), 153
Family Protection Act, 124
Farabi, Abu Nasr, 207
Farabi University, 194
Farahnaz Pahlavi, 5, 77
Farah Pahlavi, 5, 6, 9, 67, 70, 74–77, 80, 161,
    187, 194, 211–212, 213, 281
Farah Pahlavi University, 194
Farhat, Hormoz, 130, 208, 209
farmandehi (leadership command), 67
Farmanfarmaian family, 122
Farschian, Mahmud, 212–213
farsi (Persian language), 204. *See also*
    language
Faryar, A., 183, 184, 185
Fatemeh Pahlavi, 78
Fatemi, Huseyn, 119
Fath Ali Shah (Qajar), 39, 81
Fatima (Shiite saint), 142–143
Fattahipour, S., 185
Fawzia Pahlavi, 47–48
Fedorov, Vladimir, 277
Fekrat, Ali, 236
Ferdowsi, 22, 23, 32, 140, 185, 200–201, 277
Ferdowsi University, 193, 197
FitzGerald, Edward, 199, 201
food, 165–169
Ford, Gerald, 269–270
Foreign Residents Advisory Bureau, 132
forestry, 73
Fortune magazine, 71, 234
Forughi, Mohammed Ali, 50
France and Iran, 43, 47, 194

French Archaeological Mission, 12
Fuad, King, 48
Frye, Richard N., 38, 61, 71, 153

Gandiliss, Georges, 194
General Motors Iran, 245
Genghis Khan (Mongol), 26, 33, 158
geography, 11, 87–88, 263–264, 265–266
George, James, 18
Georgetown University, 197
Germany and Iran, 42, 49, 50, 194
ghazal (lyrical sonnet), 202
Ghermezian, Nader, 216
Ghiassi, Teymour, 171
Ghirshman, Roman, 11, 12, 13, 14, 27, 29,
    70
Gholam Pahlavi, 78
Ghoreishi, Ahmad, 274
Gilan, University of, 194
Goethe, Johann Wolfgang von, 202
Golestan Palace, 62, 82, 109
government and politics, 51, 52, 56–62, 67–
    69, 91. *See also* constitution and Par-
    liament
Gowhar Shad, 159, 160
Graham, Robert, 84
Great Britain and Iran, 40, 42–43, 49, 50,
    51, 56, 57, 179, 220–222, 243, 244, 252,
    278
Great Book of Music, The, 207
Great Civilization, 66
Greece and Iran, 21–22, 26–27
Grigorian, Marcos, 212
Gromyko, Andrei, 52
Grove's Dictionary, 130
Grumman Aerospace Corporation, 7, 282
Gulbenkian, Calouste Sarkis, 222
Gulf Oil company, 223. *See also* seven sis-
    ters cartel

Hafez, 33, 201, 207
Hafez, 202
Haft Tappeh Cane Sugar Industrial Com-
    pany, 254, 255
hajj (pilgrimage), 89–90, 111
Hajji (title), 90
Hajji Baba of Ispahan, The Adventures of,
    93–94
Hamadan. *See* Ecbatana
Hamid Pahlavi, 5, 9, 78
Hammurabi, 13, 17
Harvard Business School, 195
Harvard University, 194
Hashshashin (hashish eaters), 32. *See also*
    Assassins
Hawaiian Agronomics International, 252,
    255

Hazrat Ali. *See* Ali, Imam
Hedayat, Sadegh, 125
heech (nothing), 212
Hemmasi, Mohammed, 127
Hendi, Ruhollah. *See* Khomeini, Ayatollah
    Ruhollah
Hermitage Museum (Leningrad), 278
Herodotus, 15–16, 96
Herzfeld, Ernst, 44
Hicks, Jim, 17–18
Hidden Imam, 139, 140, 141, 144, 145–146,
    147, 152, 164, 289–290
Hitler, Adolf, 49, 50, 51
H. N. Agro Industry of Iran and America,
    255
holidays, 4, 6, 7, 157, 163, 176–177, 224, 280
    Friday, 177–178
    Now Ruz (New Year's), 18, 20, 23, 145,
        176, 178
Homayun, Dariush, 3
Homo erectus, 11
Hoover, Herbert, Jr., 223
Hormoz, Strait of, 279
Hoveyda, Amir Abbas, 3, 5, 164, 283–285
Hoveyda, Fereidun, 273
Hoving, Thomas, 211
Hua Guofeng, 64
Hudson Institute, 289
Hulagu (Mongol), 33
Husain, Imam, 60, 140–141, 148, 157
Hussein, Saddam, 276

Identity Card, 119, 249
Imam Jomeh. *See* Emani, Seyyid Hassan
Imam Mahdi. *See* Hidden Imam
imam, meanings of, 141, 145
imamzadeh (shrine of imam), 229
Imperial Bank of Persia, 40, 243
Imperial Court, Ministry of the, 68–69, 130,
    206
Imperial Guard, 286
Imperial Iranian Air Force, 286
Industrial Development and Renovation
    Organization, 241, 242
industrialization, vii–viii, 216, 232, 240, 289
    automobiles, 244–245
    engines and tools, 241–242
    mining, 238–239
    paper, 254
    shortcomings of, 248–249
    steel, 232–234, 245
Industrial Mining and Development Bank
    of Iran, 83, 239–241, 244
Information and Tourism, Ministry of, 3,
    205, 206
Iran, 60–61
Iran California company, 255

Iran Center for Management Studies, 195
Iranian Jurists, Association of, 6
Iranian Language, Academy of, 203
Iranian Writers Association, 6
Iran National Vehicle Manufacturing
    Company, 244
Iran (official name), 44, 274
Iran Oil Journal, 205
Iran Pan American Oil Company, 230
Iran Past and Present, 32
Iran Shellcott Company, 255
Iran: A Short Political Guide, 92
Iraq and Iran, 274–276, 288
Isfahan, 32, 35–38, 74
    mosques and minarets, 35–37
    streets and bridges, 35, 38
Islam, meaning of, 154
Islamic law, 145, 146, 153, 157, 181, 288
Islamic Marxists, 146–147
Islamic revolution, 3–9, 162, 239, 243, 245
    significance of, 285–290
Ismail (Safavid), 34
Ismail, Imam, 141
Israel and Iran, 273–274, 287–288
Italy and Iran, 224
ivan (recessed portal), 28, 35, 36, 37

Jafar, Imam, 141, 157–158
Jafari, Shabin, 59–60, 172
Jamshid, 23
Japan and Iran, 228
Jesus Christ, 148
Johns, Frank, 178
Jordan, Samuel, 268
jube (water channel), 106
Judaism, 15, 37, 111, 126–127, 154, 274
Julian, Emperor, 28
Jundi Shahpur University, 193–194

Karim Khan Zand, 39
Kashani, Ayatollah Abolqasem, 56, 58, 59
Kavir (Salt) Desert, 87–88
Kayhan International, 92
kebab, 166, 169
Kennedy, John F., 134, 269
Kent State University, 197
Kerbela, 140, 157, 211
Kerman, University of, 194
Kerr, Clark, 192
Khan, Abbas Ali, 41
Kharazmi, Mohammed al-, 204
khareji (outsider), 131
Kharg Chemical Company, 229–230
Kharg island, 228–231
Kheradjou, Abol Gasem, 239, 240, 241, 243,
    247

Khomeini, Ayatollah Ruhollah, 57, 90, 124,
    156, 288, 289–290
    as religious reformer, 84, 120, 168, 197,
        206, 207, 285, 286–287
    as revolutionary, 3, 5, 6–7, 8, 111, 142, 286
Khorasan, 27
khoresht (sauce), 166, 167
Khorramshahr, 49, 246
Khosrow (Sassanian), 30
Khuzistan, development of, 251–256
Khuzistan Water and Power Authority, 254
Kia, Sadegh, 200, 203
Kissinger, Henry, 285
Konya, 153
Koran, teachings of, 30, 43, 44, 93, 118, 123,
    141, 144, 147, 154, 156, 160, 168, 181,
    202, 212, 214, 243
Kurds. *See* tribes: Kurds

La-ila-ha Il-lah-lah (There is no god but Al-
    lah), 7, 154
Lamberg-Karlovsky, Carl, 12
Land of the Great Sophy, The, 25
language, 17, 88, 90, 91, 181, 199–207
    Arabic alphabet and numerals, 31, 200,
        203, 204
    Aramaic, 26–27, 200
    dialects, 203
    Indo-European origin, 199–200
    Middle Persian, 43–44, 200, 203
    New Persian, 200, 203
    Old Persian, 200, 203
    poetry, influence on, 200–202
    transliteration, 203
Laurentiev, Anatoly, 277
Leila Pahlavi, 5, 77
leprosy, 77
Le Rosey Institute, 46–47
Levy, Reuben, 24
Lilienthal, David, 252–253, 254
Lincoln University, 197
Literacy Corps, 182–183
Louvre museum, 13
Luristan Bronzes, 13
Lut (Sand) Desert, 87–88

McCarthy, Joseph R., 60
McCloy, John, 236
madressah (Moslem school), 181
Magi (Zoroastrian priest), 150, 151, 152
Mahdavi, Shirin, 132
Mahmud (Afghan), 39
Mahmud Pahlavi, 78
Mahmud (Turk), 32
Malenkov, Georgi, 277
Mamun, Caliph, 158
Manes, 29, 152

Manicheanism, 29, 152
Mansur, Hassan Ali, 284
Marble Palace (Teheran), 62, 76, 80
Marlowe, Christopher, 19
Marlowe, John, 92
marriage customs, 120, 123–124
Marshall Plan, 222
masachuseti (technocrats), 238
Mashayekhi, M., 185
Mashhad, 158–162
   Shrine of Imam Reza, 145, 158–161
Masjid-e-Sulaiman, 14
Massachusetts Institute of Technology, 197, 238
Massoudi, Farhad, 97
Matheson, Sylvia, 266
Mattei, Enrico, 224
Mecca, 35, 37, 89–90, 155, 156, 159, 273
Mehrabad airport, 9
Mehran, Hassan Ali, 247, 270
mektab (Moslem school), 181
Metropolitan Museum (New York), 13, 28–29
Michigan State University, 207
Milanian, Hormoz, 203–204
Millspaugh, Arthur C., 268
military forces and defense, 181, 237, 278–282, 286
   American arms sales, 270
   manpower, 7, 279
   secret police, 132–138
Mithraism, 151
Mithras, 151
Mobil Oil company, 222, 223. *See also* seven sisters cartel
modern art, 210–213
Modern Iran, 39
modernization, vii, 43–46, 96, 123, 139, 220, 243. *See also* Westernization
Mohammed, the Prophet, 30, 73, 89, 118, 140, 141, 143, 148, 176, 215
Mohammed Reza Shah Pahlavi, 41, 46, 54–55, 76, 78, 121, 164, 171–172, 203, 285
   characteristics, personal, 63–64, 65
   as foreign policy maker, 224, 269, 271, 272, 276
   last year in power, 3–9
   as modernizer, 72–74, 182–183, 185, 187, 236, 252, 258–259, 286
   as monarch, vii, 50–54, 61–62, 64–72, 90, 277
   as Moslem, 144–145, 161
   as politician, 56–61, 133, 134, 135, 142
   wealth, personal, 82
Moharram, 6, 157, 176
Mohassess, Ardeshir, 213
Molk, Kamal-ol-, 212

Molk, Nizam-al-, 32, 33, 36
monarchy, institution of, vii, 10, 26, 65–68, 69–71, 81, 288. *See also* Peacock Throne
   subjecthood in, 128–130
Mongol dynasty, 33, 36, 210
Montazeri, Ayatollah Hussain Ali
Morier, James, 93–94
Mossadegh, Mohammed, 47, 50, 55–61, 82–83, 206, 223, 268
Mossaheb, Shamsol Moluk, 117
Motamedi, Ghassem, 198
muezzin, 145
mullahs, 128, 143–144, 181
   ayatollahs, 3, 141, 148, 162
   mujtahids, 141, 143–144, 146, 148
   opposition of, 5, 43, 44, 56, 58, 59, 118, 120, 139, 145, 148–149, 158, 198
Museum of Contemporary Art (Teheran), 211–212
music, 207–210
   groupings, 207, 208
   instruments, 207, 208, 209
   poetry, influence on, 207, 208
Muzaffar as-Din (Qajar), 40

Nabavi, Jamshid, 278
Nadir Shah, 39, 81, 159, 211
Najef, 3, 6, 142
Naqsh-i-Rustam tomb, 21, 25
Naraghi, Ehsan, 74, 97–99, 201
Nasir al-Din (Qajar), 39, 40, 42
Nasr, Seyyid Hossein, 75, 154
Nassiri, Mohammed, 172
Nassiri, Nematollah, 4, 5, 59, 60, 132
National Consultative Assembly. *See* Parliament
National Front party, 5–6, 8, 56, 57, 58, 135
Nationalism in Iran, 58
National Iranian Gas Company, 226
National Iranian Oil Company, 8, 83, 194–195, 220, 223, 224, 225, 226, 230, 245, 272
National Iranian Radio and Television, 206–207
National Iranian Steel Company, 234
National Iranian Steel Industries Corporation, 234, 245
National Petrochemical Company of Iran, 228
National Police, 135. *See also* SAVAK
National University, 192
Neanderthal Man, 11
Nebuchadnezzar, King, 37
Negarestan Museum of Eighteenth and Nineteenth Century Iranian Art (Teheran), 211

Nemazee, Husang, 171
newspapers, 4, 75, 129, 205–206
New York Times, 285
Niavaran Palace (Teheran), 9, 79–81
Nietzsche, Friedrich Wilhelm, 150
Nixon, Richard, 269–270, 271
Nizami, 201
Northrop Corporation, 281
nuclear energy, 239

Ohrmazd. *See* Ahura Mazda
oil industry, 5, 7, 8, 57, 58, 88, 219–231, 234–
    235, 278, 287
    discovery and development, 14, 40, 220–
        226, 271–273
    gas resources, 220, 226–227
    OPEC regulation, 271–273
    petrochemical technology, 227–228
    production, 5, 8, 219, 220, 224, 225
    revenue, 219, 220, 227–228, 235, 238, 288–
        289
    tankers, 228–230, 278–279
Oil Service Company of Iran, 224–225
Omar, Caliph, 30, 140
Omar Khayyam, vii, 32, 199, 201
Omayyad dynasty, 140, 141
OPEC (Organization of Petroleum Export-
    ing Countries), 8, 271–273
Ottoman Empire, 34, 40
Overseas Consultants, Incorporated, 236
Owens, James K., 195

Pahlavi dynasty, vii, 10, 43–44, 71, 145
Pahlavi family, 74–79. *See also* Ahmed, Ali
    Reza, Ashraf, Farah, Farahnaz, Fate-
    meh, Fawzia, Gholam, Hamid, Leila,
    Mahmud, Mohammed Reza, Reza
    Cyrus, Shams, and Taj-ol-Moluk Pah-
    lavi
Pahlavi Foundation, 83–84
Pahlavi. *See* language, Middle Persian
Pahlavi University. *See* Shiraz, University
    of
Pahlev, Surena, 151–152
Pakravan, Hassan, 134
Palau Islands, 225
paludeh (fruity ice cream), 167
Parliament, 43, 45, 53, 61, 67–68, 133–134,
    145–146
Parsees, 151. *See also* Zoroastrianism
Parthian dynasty, 27–28, 150
Pasargadae, 10–11, 15
Paykan (automobile), 116, 244–245
Peacock Throne, 39, 81
Pennsylvania, University of, 193, 197
Perron, Ernest, 47

Persepolis, 15, 17–22, 93, 150
    Apadana of, 19–20
Persia, 38
Persia: An Archaeological Guide, 266
Persia the Immortal Kingdom, 70
Persian Cossacks, 41, 43
Persian Gulf, 9, 63, 273, 278–280
Persia and the Persian Question, 81
Persian Revolution, The, 164
Persia. *See* Iran (official name)
Pesaran, M. H., 235
Peters, Wesley, 195
petroleum industry. *See* oil industry
Philip, Hoffman, 108–109
Pishevari, Jafar, 52
pistachio, 168
Plan and Budget Organization, 236–238, 289
Plutarch, 22
Point IV program, 236, 268
Political Elite of Iran, The, 79
Politics of Iran, The, 128, 137
Polo, Marco, 33, 200
Pope, Arthur Upham, 210
population. *See* demography
proverbs, Persian, 26, 71, 91, 92–93, 97, 120
pul-e cha'i (tea money), 249

Qajar dynasty, 39–40, 42–43, 78, 109, 159–
    160, 163, 181
    art, 211
qanat (underground canal), 106, 109, 175,
    256–257
Qelitchkhani, Parvis, 173
Qom, 3–4, 142–143, 157

radio. *See* National Iranian Radio and Tele-
    vision
Radji, Parvis, 132–133
Ramadan. *See* Ramazan, 157
Ramazan, 157, 168, 176
Rashid, Caliph Harun-al, 158
Rastakhiz party, 91
Razi, 31
Razmara, Ali, 52, 56–57
Red Lion and Sun, The, 128, 156
Reindeer, 4
Reza Cyrus Pahlavi, 5, 76–77, 278
Reza, Imam, 141, 143, 158, 160
Reza Shah Pahlavi, 41, 42, 54, 58, 71, 78,
    161, 179, 222
    as abdicator, 48–50
    as father, 46
    as modernizer, 43–46, 101, 108, 109, 117,
        118, 170, 181–182
    as usurper, 43
rial, 70, 244
Rockefeller, David, 285

Rockwell International company, 280
Rogers, William P., 83
Rome and Iran, 27–28, 151–152
Roosevelt, Franklin D., 50–51, 100, 222, 271
Roosevelt, Kermit, 58, 59, 223, 281
Rose Garden, 201
Ross, Albion, 57, 58
Royal Dutch-Shell company, 223. *See also* seven sisters cartel
Rubaiyat of Omar Khayyam, vii, 199, 201, 210–211
Rudaki, 31, 107–108, 200
Rudaki Hall (Teheran), 108
rugs, Persian, 170, 213–216, 234–235
Rumania and Iran, 242
Rumi, 152–153, 201, 207
Rustam, 24–25, 262
Ruz Now (New Day), 185

Saadi, 33, 69, 94, 201, 207
Sabet, Habib, 71–72
Sadek-Kouros, Hind, 11
Safavid dynasty, 33–39, 154, 179, 210
  architecture, 35–38
SAGA company (Norway), 225
Saleh, Jahanshah, 180
Samii, Mehdi, 255, 262
Sanjabi, Karim, 5–6, 7
Sar Cheshmeh Copper Mining Company, 238
Sassan (Sassanian), 28
Sassanian dynasty, 28–30, 150, 152, 193, 200, 251, 253
  art and architecture, 28–29, 245–246
Saudia Arabia and Iran, 273
SAVAK (secret police), 4, 132–138, 139, 162
Schwartzkopf, Norman, 51, 58
Science and Higher Education, Ministry of, 186
Scott, Sir Walter, 88–89
Seleucid dynasty, 26–27
Seleucus (Seleucid), 26
Seljuk dynasty, 32–33, 36, 153
seven sisters cartel, 223, 224, 225, 271–272
Seyyid (descendant of Mohammed), 89
Shah Abbas the Great (Safavid), 34, 35, 37–39
Shahanshah (king of kings), 44, 64, 67
Shahbanou (consort), 74
Shahbazi, Shapur, 129
Shah Mohammed Reza Pahlavi. *See* Mohammed Reza Shah Pahlavi
Shahnama (Epic of the Kings), 22–25, 32, 140, 172, 201, 210–211
Shahnaz Pahlavi, 76
Shahpur I (Sassanian), 28
Shahpur II (Sassanian), 28

Shahram Pahlavi, 281
Shah Rukh, 159
Shams Pahlavi, 8–9, 48, 54, 78, 117
Share Participation Program, 247–248
Shariat, See Islamic law
Shariati, Ali, 147
Shariatmadari, Sayed Ghassem, 3, 5, 142, 147–148, 149, 287
Sharif-Emami, Jafar, 5
Shatt-al-Arab estuary, 246, 274–275, 276
Sheean, Vincent, 249–250
sheep, 12, 101, 260
sherbet, 167
Sherley, Sir Anthony, 38
Shiah Islam, 3, 31, 34, 44, 88, 139–149, 208, 210, 288, 289–290
  Hidden Imam, 139–141, 144–146, 147
  religious practices, 4, 6, 7, 118, 127, 154–158, 168
  Shrine of the Eighth Imam, 158–162
Shiat Ali. *See* Ali, Imam
Shiraz, University of, 193, 197, 210
Shoso-in, 29
Shuster, W. Morgan, 268
Simon, William, 66
sigeh (temporary marriage), 123
Sistan, 262
Siyalk, 11, 13
social classes, 128
Sohravardi, 75
Soraya. *See* Esfandiari, Soraya
Sotheby Parke Bernet, 215
Soul of Goodness in Things Evil, The, 201
Southern California, University of, 207
Soviet Union and Iran, 39–40, 41–42, 51, 57
  and Azerbaijan, 49–50, 51–52, 277
  cooperation between, 226–227, 232–233, 267, 276–278
  and the Persian Gulf, 278, 287
sports, 91, 170–174
Stalin, Joseph V., 51, 52, 78
Standard Oil of California company, 222, 223, 225. *See also* seven sisters cartel
Standard Oil Company, 221
Stanford University, 207
Stevens, Sir Roger, 25, 37
Sufism, 152–154, 201, 207
Sunni Islam, 31, 32, 34, 88, 126, 140, 154, 210, 286, 288
Survey of Persian Art, A, 210
Susa, 12, 13, 18, 19–20, 22, 252
Sykes, Christopher, 52

Tabatabaie, Seyyid al-Din Zia, 43
Tabriz, 4, 33, 241–243
Tabriz Machine Tool Plant, 241–242
Tabriz Tractor Factory, 242

Taheri, Amir, 99
Taj-ol-Moluk Pahlavi, 5, 8–9, 48, 117
Takht-e-Jamshid (Throne of Jamshid), 22.
    See also Persepolis
Tamerlane (Mongol), 158, 201, 262, 263
Tanavoli, Parviz, 212
Tapeh Yahya, 12
taqiyah (dissimulation), 93, 94
Tavus (Peacock), 81
taxation, 250
taxis. See driving
Teheran, 5, 6, 39, 69–70, 110–116, 162–163
    climate, 103–105
    construction, 112–114
    map of, 107
    museums, 13, 34, 211–212
    parks and palaces, 76, 77, 108, 109
    pollution, 105–106
    stores and streets, 75, 101–103, 106–109,
        111–112, 215
    transportation, 103, 116
Teheran, University of, 44, 53, 191–193, 197
Tehrana, 100
Tehran. See Teheran
television. See National Iranian Radio and
    Television
Texaco company, 222, 223. See also seven
    sisters cartel
Thousand and One Nights, The, 158, 200,
    210
Thus Spake Zarathustra, 150
Time magazine, 55
Tocqueville, Alexis de, 271
toman, 244
Towhidi, M., 227–228
trade, 110, 227, 231, 234
Trans-Iranian Railway, 45, 49, 50
tribes, 54, 124, 125–127, 182–183, 186, 188–
    189, 203
    Bakhtiaris, 40, 54, 126, 221
    Baluchis, 154, 182–183, 189, 214, 286
    Khuz, 251
    Khuzistan Arabs, 126, 154, 189, 251–252,
        260, 287
    Kurds, 40, 126, 154, 214, 275–276, 286, 287
    Lurs, 42, 126, 189, 214
    Qashqais, 40, 51, 126, 188–189, 214
    Turkomans, 40, 154, 173, 214, 266, 286
Tripartite Alliance, 51
Truman, Harry, 52, 56, 271
Tudeh party, 51, 52, 59
Turkey and Iran, 32, 34, 40, 42

United Nations and Iran, 52, 57
United States Embassy, 108–109
United States and Iran, 7, 56, 62, 130–132,
    224, 268–271, 287

United States and Iran (cont'd)
    educational assistance, 193, 194, 195, 197,
        207
    investment and trade, 225, 270
    military assistance, 50–52, 58–60, 269, 270

Valerian, Emperor, 28
Valian, Abdol Azim, 161, 162
Valle, Pietro della, 20
vaqfs (church estates), 161
Vaughan, Leo, 94, 99
Vaziri, Ali Naqi, 210

water, need for, 73, 88, 253–254, 256–257,
    262, 263, 264, 265
Westernization, 96–99, 167, 169–170, 171,
    175, 177, 206, 210, 219, 231. See also
    modernization
White Revolution, 72–74, 77, 134
Wilber, Donald, 32, 60
Wilson, Arnold, 221
Wilson, Harold, 278
Wise Men. See Magi
women, status of, 29–30, 44, 78, 117–124, 194,
    286
    and the family, 121–124
    and illiteracy, 184, 188, 189
    and sexism, 120–121
    and the veil, 117–120
Women's Affairs, Ministry of State for, 286
Women's Organization of Iran, 184
World Bank, 58, 240, 253
World Full of Nightingales, A, 94
World Literacy, National Committee for,
    182, 183–185
World War I, 42
World War II, 48–51, 222, 268

Xerxes I (Sassanian), 19, 21, 162

Yazdegerd (Sassanian), 30
Yogi, Maharishi Mahesh, 163

Zagros Mountains, 87
Zahedi, Ardeshir, 7, 58, 76
Zahedi, Fazlollah, 58–59, 60, 61
Zamani, M. H. Saheb-ol-, 120, 123, 124, 202
Zarathustra. See Zoroaster
Zarathustrianism. See Zoroastrianism
Zayandeh River, 37, 38
Zenderoudi, Hossein, 212
Ziai, Mahmud, 33, 89, 90, 92, 94, 100
Zonis, Ella, 208, 209
Zonis, Marvin, 79, 269
Zoroaster, 140, 149, 150, 200, 262
Zoroastrianism, 18, 23, 29, 30, 139–140, 149–
    152, 153, 221
zurkhaneh (house of strength), 172

Catalog

If you are interested in a list of fine Paperback
books, covering a wide range of subjects
and interests, send your name and address,
requesting your free catalog, to:

McGraw-Hill Paperbacks
1221 Avenue of Americas
New York, N.Y. 10020